Diploma in
Pre-school Practice

2nd edition

Penny Tassoni

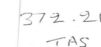

Heinemann Educational Publishers
Halley Court, Jordan Hill, Oxford OX2 8EJ
Part of Harcourt Education

Heinemann is the registered trademark of Harcourt Education Limited

First published 2006

11 10 09 08 07 06
10 9 8 7 6 5 4 3 2 1

British Library Cataloguing in Publication Data is available from the British Library on request.

10-digit ISBN: 0 435 40210 2
13-digit ISBN: 978 0 435 40210 5

Edited by Caroline Low, Virgo Editorial

Designed by GD Associates

Typeset and illustrated by 𝕋 Tek-Art, Croydon, Surrey

Original illustrations © Harcourt Education Limited, 2006

Cover design by Jonathan Williams

Printed by Scotprint Ltd.

Cover photo © Sally and Richard Greenhill

Picture research by Chrissie Martin

Contents

Acknowledgements   v
About the author   v
Foreword   vi
Introduction   vii

Core Units

Unit 1: Understanding and promoting the development of pre-school children   1

The nature and patterns of children's development   2
The environmental, social and genetic factors which influence children's development 88
Using observation and assessment to promote pre-school children's development   94
The effect of relationships on children's development   111
Using reflective practice to understand and promote pre-school children's
development   121

Unit 2: Providing learning communities for pre-school children and their families 127

The potential outcomes of parents' participation in the provision for their
pre-school children's care and education   128
Appropriate curriculum frameworks for children between 0–5 years of age   138
Providing experiences that promote all areas of children's learning and
development   154
Promoting the well-being and progress of individual pre-school children   179
Ways to ensure that all parents have the opportunity to benefit from the
learning community provided by their children's pre-school   182
Using an understanding of reflective practice to examine the effectiveness of
own practice in providing learning communities for pre-school children and
their families   187

Unit 3: Making the pre-school setting a supportive and safe environment   195

Providing an inclusive and anti-discriminatory environment in a pre-school
setting   196
Providing a healthy, safe, secure and stimulating environment that promotes
pre-school children's learning and development   209
Providing for pre-school children's physical needs in ways that promote their
well-being   238
Providing an environment that promotes pre-school children's emotional
security   264
How to implement policies and procedures in a pre-school setting to protect
young children from abuse   268
The role of good working relationships in making the pre-school setting a
supportive and safe environment   285
The effectiveness of own practice in making the pre-school setting a supportive
and safe environment   289

Optional Units

Unit 1: Working to support parents with literacy, numeracy and language needs in a pre-school setting　295

Why engaging in support for parents with literacy, numeracy and language needs is an important activity for pre-school settings　296

How to make available to parents opportunities to develop their literacy, numeracy and language skills　303

How to enable parents to access support to develop their literacy, numeracy and language skills　307

Reviewing the activities undertaken by the pre-school setting to enable parents to develop their literacy, numeracy and language skills　319

Unit 2: Working with children with disabilities and special educational needs, and their families, in a pre-school setting　325

The importance of making the pre-school setting inclusive for children with disabilities and special educational needs　326

How to promote the care and education of children with disabilities and special educational needs in a pre-school setting　335

How the pre-school setting can work in partnership with the parents of children with disabilities and special educational needs　357

How the pre-school setting can work in partnership with other agencies to promote the care and education of children with disabilities and special educational needs　361

Unit 3: Working in a parent-managed pre-school setting　369

Ways in which pre-schools might be managed by parents　370

The contribution of the parent management committee to the community development role of the pre-school setting　371

The role and responsibilities of the parent management committee of a pre-school setting　375

Ensuring effective communication between the parent management committee and the staff of a pre-school setting　384

The responsibilities of the parent management committee and the staff of a pre-school setting for creating and implementing policies and procedures for the setting　387

The role of the parent management committee and the staff of a pre-school setting in ensuring that the setting has the resources to implement the setting's plans, policies and procedures　390

Glossary　397

Index　401

Acknowledgements

Every effort has been made to contact copyright holders of material reproduced in this book. Any omissions will be rectified in subsequent printings if notice is given to the publishers.

Photo acknowledgements

Brand X Pictures: 369; Creatas: 42; Corbis: 244; Eyewire: 127, 295; Getty Images/Iconica: 159; Getty Images/PhotoDisc: 22 (right), 24 (top), 55, 128; Harcourt Education Ltd/Malcolm Harris: 84; Harcourt Education Ltd/Tudor Photography: 18 (both), 20 (right), 22 (left), 24 (bottom), 28, 325; Masterfile/Rick Gomez: 169; Photos.com: 195

All other images by Harcourt Education Ltd / Jules Selmes.

Author acknowledgements

As with many writing projects, this book has required a team approach. Thanks must go to the Heinemann team, especially Beth Howard for her support, and to my mother, Jennifer Enderby, whose eye for detail in looking at the proofs was invaluable. I would also like to thank Barbara Thompson, Pat Townshend and Annie Simpson at the Pre-school Learning Alliance for their help and advice during the writing process. I would also like to thank Unni Jakobsen and her team for welcoming me to the St. George's Pre-school, Lewisham and for her permission to reproduce some of the pre-school's paperwork. I would also like to thank Judith Stevens, Penny Cartwright and Katy Elsom of the LEARN team at Lewisham for their support and also permission to reproduce the Lewisham *Early Years Profile*. Finally, I must again thank the Tassoni Team for their continued support and time.

About the author

Penny Tassoni is an education consultant, author and trainer. She specialises in the whole spectrum of early learning and play. Penny has also worked in a variety of roles for CACHE, the awarding body in childcare, education and playwork, including that of lead examiner for the Diploma in Pre-school Practice. She currently works as a reviser for the CACHE awards, and contributes to CACHE's professional development and tutor days. Penny has written over twenty books, including the popular *Planning Play and the Early Years,* and is a regular contributor to *Practical Pre-school* and *Nursery World.*

Foreword

The Pre-school Learning Alliance (PLA) has been pleased to work with Heinemann to produce this comprehensive book to support students on the CACHE Level 3 Diploma in Pre-school Practice. The qualification was reaccredited in April 2006 to meet the revised National Occupational Standards in Children's Care, Learning and Development and this book reflects the changes made.

This thoroughly revised and updated edition provides information, case studies based on real situations, and pointers to think about when working with children in sessional and full day care settings. A wide range of topics is covered, including understanding and promoting the development of pre-school children and providing learning communities for pre-school children and their families. These topics reflect the strong ethos that the Alliance places on the potential of early years workers to play a key role in the provision of learning opportunities for children, their families and the wider community.

Whether you are an experienced childcare practitioner keen to ensure your knowledge is up to date with current early years practice or looking to ensure you have the management level skills to lead settings effectively, I am confident that this book will meet your needs in an interesting and engaging way.

Steve Alexander
Chief Executive Officer
Pre-school Learning Alliance

Introduction

Welcome to your Diploma in Pre-school Practice course. Working with young children is a demanding but hugely rewarding career. The Diploma in Pre-school Practice aims to prepare you for this role as enthusiastic, well-trained and well-informed staff are now recognised as playing a vital component in children's and their families' participation in the pre-school.

A major feature of working in the early years sector at the moment is the need to remain up to date and be adaptable, as there have been considerable changes to the way in which we work with children over the past few years, with further developments still likely to come.

The Diploma in Pre-school Practice is a respected Level 3 qualification and will give you the underpinning skills, knowledge and confidence to steer you through these exciting times.

Course structure

During your course, you will study the three core units and one of the optional units.

Core Unit 1   Understanding and promoting the development of pre-school children
Core Unit 2   Providing learning communities for pre-school children and their families
Core Unit 3   Making the pre-school setting a supportive and safe environment
Optional Unit 1 Working to support parents with literacy, numeracy and language needs in a pre-school setting
Optional Unit 2 Working with children with disabilities and special educational needs, and their families, in a pre-school setting
Optional Unit 3 Working in a parent-managed pre-school setting

Assessment

In order to gain certification, you will need to complete an assignment for each of the units that you study. These assignments are set by the awarding body (CACHE) and can be found in your candidate handbook. Assignments are marked using grading criteria that you will be given. A good tip when completing assignments is to read the grading criteria very carefully and to double check that you have met them before handing in your work.

Core Unit 3 is currently assessed externally – this means that it is marked by an external examiner. The remaining assignments will be marked and moderated within your centre.

About this book

This book has been written specifically to help you with your Diploma in Pre-school Practice. It provides information in a clear and accessible way and will support the teaching that is being provided by your tutors. The book has been written to match the Diploma in Pre-school Practice syllabus and is therefore a good tool to aid your study of the units and the completion of the assignments.

Features of this book

The units in the book follow the headings of the syllabus closely. The different features of the book are described below. These specific features will not only help you develop your understanding of the relevant issues within pre-school settings, but will also add interesting topical information to give you a holistic understanding of childcare.

 Good practice Practical suggestions for promoting good practice in a pre-school setting.

 Applying theory to your practice Activities and theoretical learning tasks which help you relate the theory to your own experience.

 Frequently asked questions Short topics or questions encouraging you to think about the current issues raised in the text.

 Case studies Case studies of real (or simulated) childcare-related issues. These are aimed at enabling you to explore key issues, broaden your understanding and see the theory in practice.

 Thinking and research Activities giving you topics to think about, check out and research.

 Test yourself Questions at the end of each unit which help test the knowledge you have gained as you worked through the unit.

 Preparation for assignment Tasks that are designed to help you prepare for the end of unit assignment.

Key features A list summarising the key topics, key definitions and key features of important theories covered in that section.

Glossary Throughout the text are words highlighted in colour. These are key words that you will be expected to know and understand through your course. The meaning of these words can be found in the glossary (pages 397–400).

Good luck with your course!

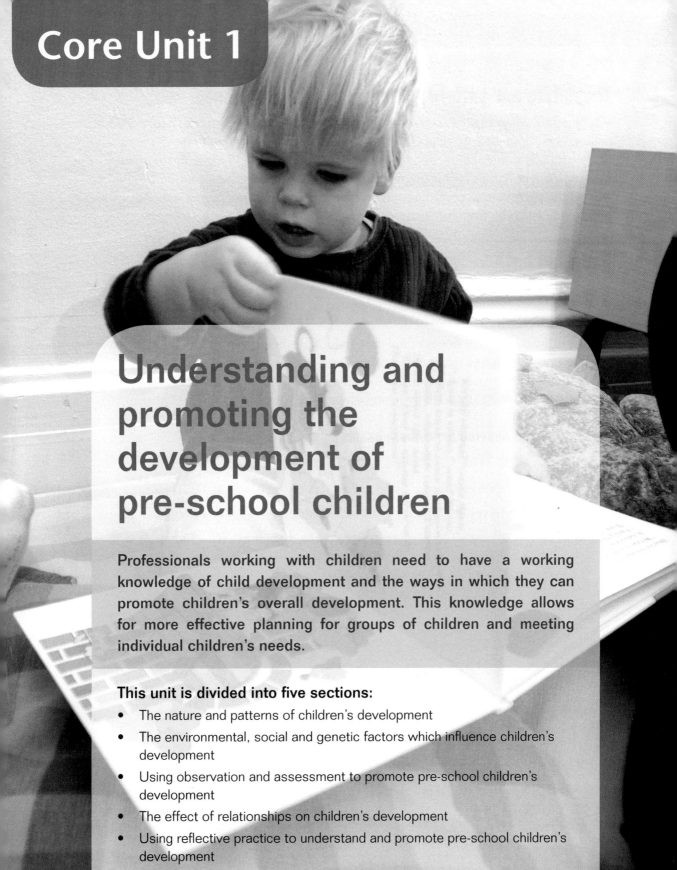

Understanding and promoting the development of pre-school children

Professionals working with children need to have a working knowledge of child development and the ways in which they can promote children's overall development. This knowledge allows for more effective planning for groups of children and meeting individual children's needs.

This unit is divided into five sections:

- The nature and patterns of children's development
- The environmental, social and genetic factors which influence children's development
- Using observation and assessment to promote pre-school children's development
- The effect of relationships on children's development
- Using reflective practice to understand and promote pre-school children's development

The nature and patterns of children's development

Watching the ways in which children grow and develop is a rewarding experience for professionals and parents alike. This section begins by looking at the usual patterns of development of children aged 0–16 years before focusing in more detail at the development of babies and younger children. Understanding the 'journey' of children from 0–16 years is now considered to be essential so that you can see not only where children have come from but also the road ahead for them.

Babies at birth

Most babies are born around the 40th week of pregnancy. Babies who are born more than three weeks early are described as premature. Premature babies are likely to need a little more time to reach the same levels of development as a baby who is born at around 40 weeks. Many people think that babies are helpless but they are born with the ability to do quite a few things: they can recognise their mother's voice and smell; they are able to cry to let everyone know when they need help; they are also actively learning about their new world through their senses, particularly touch, taste and hearing.

What you might observe in newborn babies

Reflexes

Babies are born with many reflexes, which are actions that they perform without thinking. Many reflexes are linked to survival. Examples of reflexes include:

- *Swallowing and sucking reflexes.* These ensure that babies can feed and swallow milk.
- *Rooting reflex.* Babies will move their head to look for a nipple or teat if their cheek or mouth is touched. This helps babies to find milk.

Startle reflex.

Walking and standing reflex.

- *Grasp reflex.* Babies will automatically put their fingers around an object that has touched the palm of their hand.
- *Startle reflex.* When babies hear a sudden sound or see a sudden bright light, they will react by moving their arms outwards and clenching their fists.
- *Walking and standing reflex.* When babies are held upright with their feet on a firm surface, they usually make stepping movements.
- *Falling reflex.* This is known as the Moro reflex. Babies will stretch out their arms suddenly and then clasp them inwards in any situations in which they feel that they are falling.

Close contact between mother and baby, especially when feeding

Babies and their primary carers, usually their mother, begin to develop a close bond from very early on. Babies sometimes stare at their mother, and mothers are very aware of their baby.

What newborn babies need:

- a calm and relaxed environment
- plenty of cuddles, talk and eye contact
- gentle handling and bathing
- opportunities to get to know their primary carers, usually their mother
- frequent feeds of milk
- time to sleep.

Babies at one month

In just one month, babies have changed already. They may appear less curled up and more relaxed and have usually started to settle into a pattern. They sleep a lot of the time, but will gradually start to spend longer periods awake. They cry to communicate their needs and their parents may be starting to understand the different types of cries. Babies are also learning about their parents or carers: they may stop crying when they hear their soothing voices; they also try hard to focus on the face of whoever is holding them – they can focus at a distance of 20–25 cm (8–10 inches).

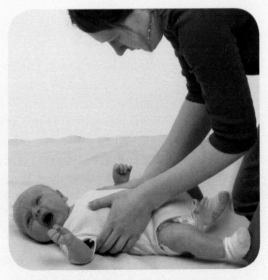

Babies stop crying as they are picked up but start crying when they are put down.

3

What you might observe in babies at one month

- Babies stop crying because they hear a familiar voice.
- Babies stop crying as they are picked up but start crying when they are put down.
- Babies start to relax at bath time or when their nappies are changed.
- Fleeting smiles when asleep (smiles of contentment begin from five or six weeks).
- Babies coo when contented (from around five or six weeks).

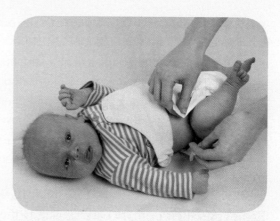

Babies start to relax at bath time or when their nappy is changed.

What babies of one month need:

- plenty of cuddles and physical contact
- opportunities to sleep
- frequent feeds of milk, both day and night
- eye contact, smiles and gentle handling
- opportunities to lie flat and kick without a nappy
- their head supported when they are picked up or being carried
- safe physical care, including nappy changing and skin care.

Babies at three months

Babies at three months have grown in height and weight. They have grown out of their early clothes and have changed in many ways. Some babies have learnt the difference between day and night and are able to sleep through the night. They are likely to cry less and most parents are getting better at knowing what their cries mean. They are also starting to sleep a little less and are more alert. They may smile quite often and show that they know the sound of their parents' voices and movements. Babies' bodies are also developing. They are able to lift their head up and look about when they are put on their tummy.

What you might observe in babies at three months

- Babies smile back when they see a smiling face.
- Excitement when it is time to be fed.
- Interest in playing with fingers.

Interest in playing with fingers.

Babies start to notice mobiles.

- Enjoyment of bath time.
- Babies lift and turn their head.
- Babies start to notice mobiles and other objects around them.

What babies at three months need:

- opportunities to be cuddled and to watch others
- rattles to hold and mobiles to look at
- their head supported when they are carried
- regular milk feeds
- gentle handling
- safe physical care, including nappy changing and skin care.

Babies at six months

Babies at six months have learnt many skills. They are very alert and turn their head to see what is happening. They enjoy playing and show it by smiling and squealing with delight. They can now reach out and grab a toy and move it from one hand to another. They are able to focus in on an object and explore it if it seems interesting. Babies also start to show that they understand a little of what is being said to them, and they try to communicate. They usually enjoy their food and are beginning to try to feed themselves by grabbing a spoon (this can be quite messy). Many babies will also be getting their first teeth, which can be painful for them.

Babies at six months are also getting stronger. They can sit up with support in a high chair and are able to roll over from their back to their front. They can push themselves up with their hands if they lie on their front and can hold this position for a little while. They also sometimes look as if they are parachuting as they lift both their hands and feet up in the air and balance on their front. These movements help them to get ready for crawling later on.

Babies at six months have usually settled into a routine and will have periods in the day when they nap and others when they are keen to play and to be held.

What you might observe in babies at six months

- Smiles of delight when they are playing with their primary carers.
- Enjoyment when simple games such as pat-a-cake are repeated.
- Arms lifting up to show a carer that they want to be picked up.
- Curiosity and looking to see what is happening around them.
- Toys and objects being explored in the mouth as well as with fingers.
- Babbling, laughing and squealing.
- Different cries according to whether the baby is tired, bored or hungry.

Pushing up using their hands.

Toys and objects being explored in the mouth as well as with fingers.

What babies at six months need:

- plenty of physical contact, talk and eye contact
- times when they can lie on their stomach and back
- opportunities to play simple games and look at books with adults
- chances to explore toys and objects

Continued ▶

- time to sleep
- a range of foods that are soft and have been mashed, as well as milk feeds
- good, safe physical care, including nappy changing, bathing and skin care
- a safe environment so that they cannot fall, swallow small objects or hurt themselves.

Babies at nine months

Babies' physical development is now very noticeable. Many babies will be crawling or finding other ways of being mobile. They are also able to sit up without any support. These new movements mean that babies can explore more. They also spend a lot of time sitting and playing. When they are mobile they can move quite fast, and this is a period in which adults need to think carefully about safety. As well as large movements, babies are also picking up objects, handling them and becoming more skilled at touching things. Objects still get popped into the mouth and so, again, adults need to be very aware of what is around.

Babies' language is also coming along. Babbling has become more tuneful and longer strings of sounds are put together. Babies are also learning what some key words mean. They may start to get excited when they hear words such as 'drink' or 'dinner'. Babies are also starting to show who they enjoy being with. From around eight months, they start to cry when they are left with a stranger and actively try to be with their parents or main carers.

Babies are also likely to have made a cognitive leap in their development. This is sometimes referred to as object permanence. At around eight or nine months most babies will understand that objects and people do not disappear but continue to exist when they are out of sight. This is an important breakthrough and is one explanation of why babies at around this time begin to protest when their familiar carer leaves the room. You can test object permanence by playing with a toy with the baby and then hiding it while the baby watches. Younger babies will carry on playing with something else, while babies at around nine months will 'find' the hidden toy.

What you might observe in babies of nine months

- Trying to stay near their parent or carer.
- Protest when a parent or carer leaves the room.
- Tuneful strings of babbling.
- Using fingers to feed.
- Exploring objects using hands and mouth.
- Passing objects from one hand to another.

Crawling or rolling.

Passing objects from one hand to another.

- Reaching over to pick up an object.
- Crawling or rolling.
- Sitting up without any support.
- Looking for objects that adults 'hide'.

What babies at nine months need:

- the same carer if they are not being looked after by their parents
- physical contact and cuddles
- finger rhymes and songs
- a range of toys such as push-and-pulls, stacking beakers and balls
- opportunities to play simple games with an adult, including peek-a-boo
- a diet rich in nutrients, including milk feeds
- opportunities to feed themselves
- good, safe physical care, including nappy changing, bathing and skin care
- a safe environment so that they cannot fall, swallow small objects or hurt themselves
- good adult supervision as they play.

Babies at one year

The first birthday of a child is for many families a special event and a cause for celebration. This in part dates back to times when not all babies survived their first year. Babies have developed considerably over their first year and are now mobile and may be on the verge of walking. They may try to stand up by holding onto furniture and some babies are already walking by holding onto things. Good adult supervision is essential. Babies are now able to crawl very quickly and have eyesight that is just as developed as that of adults. This means that if they spot something that they want, they will quickly make a move to get it.

As well as gaining mobility, babies are also becoming skilled at using their hands. Objects are touched, moved and organised. They enjoy putting things into containers and taking them out again, or dropping things and looking to see what happens to them. A strong feature of their play is the way in which they enjoy doing something over and over again. They may keep taking their hat off or pulling off their socks.

At one year, babies are able to sit up and feed themselves using their fingers. Most also know what they do and do not like. Food that they enjoy is eaten, while other foods may be thrown on the floor.

Babies also know who are their parents and main carers. They cry when they are left with someone they do not know and smile when they recognise their parents. They are also keen to stay near their parents and carers, and will stop playing to see what they are doing.

Babies are able to understand more of what is happening around them. They not only notice what other people are doing but also understand more and more of what is being said. Long strings of babbling are still the way in which babies try to communicate, but

Repetitive play as they enjoy doing something over and over again.

Feed themselves with their fingers.

hidden in the babbling are the beginnings of first words. These are usually noticed by parents and carers from around 13 months.

What you might observe in babies of one year

- Standing up and holding onto furniture.
- Waving bye-bye.
- Fingers pointing at objects to draw an adult's attention to them.
- Tuneful babbling that sounds like talking.
- Small objects being picked up and handled.
- Repetitive play as they enjoy doing something over and over again.
- Recognising the routines of the day (e.g. becoming excited when they hear the bath water running or have a bib put on).
- Able to feed themselves with their fingers.

What babies at one year need:

- Babies at one year need much the same things as at nine months (see the list on page 8).

Children at 18 months

The word 'toddler' is used for children who have begun to walk. It is a delightful term, as toddlers do walk with a side-to-side movement. At 18 months children have literally begun to find their feet. They start to move quickly and enjoy the freedom that this gives them. They are also keen to play with adults and are often fascinated by other children. They notice what older brothers and sisters are doing as well as children of their own age.

Around this age toddlers start to want some independence. They have learnt that they are separate from their parents and start to become their own person. They cry and protest if they want something and do not get it. They can be quite persistent and this can be a cause of accidents. A child who wants to hold a cup of tea will, for example, notice where it has been put and may try to climb up to reach it.

Children's language skills are still developing. Most children will be able to use several words and will understand a lot of what adults are saying. This does not mean, however, that they can understand the need to share, to wait and be co-operative. Many parents say that at this age their children start to develop a mind of their own.

Toddlers can be quite restless and change moods quickly. This can be tiring for parents and carers. Toddlers also become distressed when they are left with unfamiliar people, and need a recognisable adult if they are not with their parents or carers.

Signs of temper and frustration.

Enjoyment of pop-up and posting toys.

What you might observe in children of 18 months

- Walking up and downstairs with adult help.
- Less babbling and more recognisable words.
- Signs of temper and frustration.
- Eagerness for independence (e.g. trying to feed themselves with a spoon).
- Enjoyment of pop-up and posting toys.
- Sitting and pushing off with legs on sit-and-ride toys.
- Determination to try things by themselves.
- Interest in other children.
- Awareness of where their parents are and what they are doing.

What children of 18 months need:

- good adult supervision as they play
- safety equipment such as reins, harnesses and safety gates
- physical contact and cuddles
- finger rhymes and songs
- a range of toys, including toy telephones, sit-and-rides and simple puzzles
- opportunities to climb and space for physical play such as rolling or kicking a ball
- opportunities to feed themselves

Continued ▶

- safe physical care, including nappy changing, bathing and skin care
- a safe environment so they cannot fall, swallow small objects or hurt themselves.

Children at two years

By two years old, children are very much showing their individuality. They know what they want to do, touch and hold. They can now move confidently and enjoy walking and being able to pick up things and play with them. They like to do things for themselves and are keen to do more and get frustrated when they are not able to. This is sometimes because adults realise that what they want is dangerous and at other times because their skill does not match what they want to do. Their frustration can lead to temper tantrums and emotional outbursts. This is often a way of communicating how they are feeling and is why this period is sometimes known as the 'terrible twos'.

While toddlers do get frustrated and angry, they are also emotional in other ways. They smile, laugh and squeal with enjoyment. They notice other children and enjoy being near them, even though they may not actively play together. Favourite games are played over and over again. Toddlers are also starting to enjoy pretend play. They may take an empty cup and pretend to drink from it or give a teddy a hug. Two-year-olds are often starting to chat aloud and to point out objects and name them.

Some two-year-olds are starting to be ready to move out of nappies (although some children are not physically ready until they are three years old).

What you might observe in children of two years

- Enjoyment of singing and dancing to music.
- Pointing to pictures of familiar objects and naming them.

Enjoyment of singing and dancing to music.

Running.

- Anger and frustration if they cannot do what they want to do.
- Delight and happiness when they are enjoying something.
- Keen to show things to adults.
- Playing on sit-and-ride toys.
- Running and climbing.
- Playing with building bricks and doing simple jigsaw puzzles.

What children of two years need:

- good supervision and safety equipment
- time to explore and play with safe objects
- opportunities for physical play, such as slides, swings and balls
- toys that encourage role-play, such as teddies, pushchairs and dressing-up clothes
- time for cuddles and sharing of books, songs and rhymes
- a good range of toys that build different skills
- adults who can support and play alongside them
- adults who can anticipate their needs and potential frustrations.

Children at two and a half years

Children at two and a half years are still keen to be independent. They may find it hard to wait and to understand why they cannot always have what they see or do want they want. Their language is really starting to develop. Some are putting two words together to express their ideas and others are even starting to use sentences. Good supervision is still needed, as children's developing physical skills combined with their determination can mean that they go to extremes to get hold of an object. Moving chairs to climb up or standing on tables to reach up high is fairly common.

Children are also starting to play more with other children of their own age, although some of their time will be spent simply playing alongside others. Pretend play and play with small-world toys is now popular, as are tricycles, slides and climbing frames. They are still keen to have plenty of adult attention and will enjoy snuggling up for a cuddle as well as spending time helping an adult.

Separating from parents remains difficult unless children really know who they will be with. This is often the period in which toilet training starts in earnest and, if children are ready, they can be out of nappies within a few days.

Turning pages in a book.

Playing alongside other children.

What you might observe in children aged two and a half years

- Pretend play with farm animals, teddies or in the home corner.
- Playing alongside other children and copying their actions.
- Two-word compounds such as 'daddy-gone' or 'drink-no'.
- Temper tantrums if they are frustrated.
- Pedalling a tricycle or pushing it along with their feet.
- Turning pages in books and pointing out objects.

What children of two and a half years need:

- a balanced diet with sufficient calories for increased energy
- a relaxed approach to toilet training
- time to choose activities and to play with others
- opportunities to explore materials such as sand, water and dough
- familiar carers if children are not with their parents
- opportunities to develop independent skills such as pouring out drinks
- a range of toys and equipment, including outdoor play, small-world toys and home corner, as well as sand, dough and paint
- adults who play alongside children and play simple games
- nursery rhymes, songs and sharing books
- excellent supervision and safety equipment.

Children at three years

Most children at three years of age are making a huge developmental leap. This is linked to their use of language: suddenly, instead of showing that they are not happy, they can say so, and temper tantrums start to decrease. Children begin to understand more about what is happening and to understand the needs of others. From this point onwards most children are able to play with other children, and the sharing of toys and equipment becomes less difficult. Other children start to become important in their lives. In consequence they may look forward to going to pre-school or nursery each day. Children feel easier being separated from their parents, as they can now understand that their parents will return; they are more able to talk to the staff looking after them.

Interest in other children and some co-operative play.

What you might observe in children aged three years

- Able to use the toilet.
- Enjoy dressing up and playing with small-world toys.
- Keen to help and copy adults.
- Interest in other children and some co-operative play.
- Able to walk up and down stairs on alternate feet.
- Interested in mark-making, painting and books.
- Enjoyment of sand and water play.
- Speech that is easily understood.

Playing with small-world toys.

What children of three years need:

- opportunities to play with other children, under supervision
- adults who encourage independence but who also play with and cuddle children

Continued ▶

- opportunities to explore new play materials, objects and equipment
- time to play repetitively with materials of their own choosing
- a wide range of different play activities and equipment
- time to play outside as well as inside
- opportunities to look at books, to draw and to paint
- adults who act as good role models, since children copy their behaviour
- praise and acknowledgement from adults
- a safe environment that encourages them to be independent.

Children at four years

By four years old, most children have made huge steps forward in their development. They will be fairly fluent in their speech and should be easily understandable to adults who do not know them. There will still be the odd grammatical mistake and interesting pronunciation of a word, but by and large they will have mastered the spoken language. Most children's behaviour will be co-operative but this is dependent on their getting plenty of praise and recognition from adults.

Most four-year-olds also enjoy being with other children and will be starting to plan their play and have definite ideas of what they want to do. They are also learning to be independent. They can generally dress and feed themselves, and can organise their play if they are given the opportunity. They enjoy being with responsive adults, especially when they are being given responsibility and encouragement.

Most children will be attending some pre-school provision, such as a playgroup, nursery or crèche. This is important for them as they generally enjoy the company of other children and are beginning to develop friendships. They will also be learning – often without realising it, as activities will be planned for them. Depending on where they live, many children during this year will be starting school. For some children, this is a difficult transition, as they have to adapt to being part of a much larger group.

What you might observe in children at four years

- Children are settled into the routine of the setting and are able to separate from their parents easily (if they have been in the setting for a while).
- Co-operative play between children along with the odd squabble and argument.
- Children responding well to adult praise and recognition.
- Children seeking out particular playmates.
- Children asking questions and enjoying talking.
- Speech and pretend play that model adult life.
- Children riding on tricycles, climbing and enjoying simple ball games.
- Drawings that have meaning for the child and are recognisable.

Singing nursery rhymes.

Pretend play that models adult life.

- Skilful use of the hands to do activities such as threading, pouring and using scissors.
- Concentration when an activity has caught their interest.
- Enjoyment of singing and knowledge of some nursery rhymes.

What children of four years need:

- opportunities to play with other children
- sensitive adult help and direction where appropriate
- opportunities to explore new play materials, objects and equipment
- time to relax and enjoy favourite activities
- a wide range of different play activities and equipment
- time to play outside as well as inside
- opportunities to look at books, to draw and to paint
- practical activities that help children learn about numbers and their environment
- adults who act as good role models, since children copy their behaviour
- time when adults listen and chat to children
- praise and acknowledgement from adults
- a safe environment that encourages them to be independent.

Children at 5–6 years

In these years, changes in physical development are much less rapid. Instead, children gain in confidence and co-ordination. This is true also for other skills, such as their spoken language and ability to socialise. A good example of this is the way that, at around this time, children begin to enjoy hearing and making jokes.

At around five years old, most children have begun in formal education. This can be a difficult transition period for some children, especially if they are not interested in learning to read and write. For children who are ready, learning to read and write can prove exciting and they may enjoy the intellectual challenge of a classroom. As well as school, some children will also be doing activities such as swimming, dance or music. The ways in which children play are also starting to change: children of this age are keen to work out the rules of different situations and enjoy playing games with rules.

Friends are also important to children of this age. Many children will start to have established friendships and preferences. Staying for tea or even overnight is quite common and helps children to learn about other families, although of course children still rely on their parents to meet many of their emotional needs.

What you might observe in children aged 5–6 years

- Enjoyment of jokes.
- Beginning to decode some familiar words.
- Keen to understand and use rules.
- Some friendship preferences.
- Ability to kick and control a ball.
- More legible handwriting and increased fine manipulative movements.

Enjoyment of jokes.

Increased fine manipulative movements.

What children aged 5–6 years need:

- adults who encourage independence and are sensitive to children's needs
- opportunities to listen to stories and to share books
- a balanced diet and sufficient sleep
- adults who are able to supervise and support play
- activities outside school
- boundaries that children can understand.

Children at 7–9 years

Children's development in this period is more gradual than before. Children continue to grow in height but the main changes are in the way they think and reason. This can be seen in the way they play: their games and play become more organised, and they invent as well as follow rules. The way in which children think and reason also shows itself as they start to be able to solve simple problems and enjoy practical situations in which they have to work things out for themselves. Most children are also co-operative and enjoy being given responsibility. They respond well when adults give clear explanations for rules and when their behaviour is acknowledged and praised.

In these years, reading and writing become easier, although there will be variations in the speed at which children become competent and confident in this respect. Children also become more physically skilled. This results in them being able to do things more quickly, confidently and accurately. Doing up a coat, for example, is now an easy task, as is cutting out with scissors or drawing a simple picture. Friendships are becoming increasingly important. Many children will have groups of close friends and some will have 'best friends'. The lack or temporary absence of a friend starts to become an issue. Children may want to attend a club only if they know a friend is also likely to be there.

As most children are at school, life in the classroom and playground is a major influence on them. This is also a period in which children start to compare themselves with others. In some ways this is part of the thinking process, as they carry on working out what they are like. They may notice which children are the fastest runners, best readers or quickest at finishing tasks. This can start to affect their confidence and even enthusiasm.

What you might observe in children aged 7–9 years

- Clear differences in the play activities that interest boys and girls.
- Co-operative play.
- Stable friendships.
- Verbal arguments, persuasion and negotiation.

Turn-taking.

Reading a book silently to themselves.

- Telling jokes and enjoying chatting.
- Play that involves turn-taking.
- Enjoyment of playing and making up games with rules.
- An understanding of rules and consequences.
- Children who tell others the rules and are keen to point out when rules have been broken.
- Skilful, precise and confident hand movements.
- Reading books silently.
- Writing short stories, with less adult help required.
- Painting, drawing and making models independently.
- Enjoyment of stories, imaginative play and small-world play.

What children aged 7–9 years need:

- opportunities to play with other children
- toys and equipment that stimulate children's development
- time to organise own play and games
- adults who can support but not interfere in children's play
- praise and acknowledgement that makes children feel special and nurtured
- support and encouragement during tasks children find difficult
- chances to be independent, e.g. staying at a friend's house overnight
- sensitive adults who can spend time listening to children.

Children at 9–11 years

In some ways this period in most children's lives can be summed up as the 'calm before the storm'. Most children are fairly confident and have mastered many skills, and they will often have decided what they are good at. They can now read, write, draw and use some logic. They are often skilled communicators and enjoy having friends. This is a time when many children feel quite settled, although from the age of 9 years onwards the first signs of impending puberty will show in girls. Breasts are likely to 'bud', and at around 10 or 11 years girls will begin to grow rapidly in height too. Some girls may even start menstruating before the age of 11 years, particularly where their weight to height ratio is high.

Detailed and representational pictures, which children enjoy drawing.

What you might observe in children aged 9–11 years

- Detailed and representational pictures, which children enjoy drawing.
- Stories and writing that show imagination as well as being legible and reasonably grammatical.
- Problem solving (e.g. how to play co-operatively, use materials fairly).
- Enthusiasm when given areas of responsibility.
- Greater co-ordination and speed when carrying out both fine and large movements.
- Stable friendships (usually same sex).
- Awareness of consequences of behaviour and increased thoughtfulness.

Greater co-ordination and speed when carrying out both fine and large movements.

What children aged 9–11 years need:

- opportunities to try new activities and experiences and to develop new ideas
- time to be with friends
- opportunities to develop problem-solving and organisational skills
- praise and encouragement from adults
- adults who look for ways of encouraging independence

Continued ▶

- a range of toys and equipment that will stimulate children, including books, drawing materials and construction toys
- opportunities to make dens and hide-outs, and engage in physical play
- information about puberty.

Young people at 11–13 years

This period in children's lives marks the start of their growing independence. While parents remain important, children begin to show signs of wanting to grow up. They may, for example, now ask to walk home or get buses home by themselves. Some children also begin to question rules at home and may try to push the boundaries. Young people's relationships with others of the same age become increasingly important. This can put a lot of pressure on children as their friends may have very different ideas to their parents. This period also sees other pressures on children. They are likely to be changing to another school for the next stage in their education. Quite often the new school will be larger and the curriculum more formal. They may have a series of teachers during the day, rather than just one or two.

This period also marks physical changes for young people as their bodies begin to prepare for adulthood. Girls' puberty usually begins at around 11 years, while for boys, puberty may not start until they are 13 or 14 years old. The physical changes can cause embarrassment and anxiety and so create further pressure. Girls who feel that they are developing too quickly or not quickly enough can lose self-esteem.

What you might observe in young people aged 11–13 years

- Enjoyment when with their friends.
- Growth and changes to their body.
- Growing awareness of the roles of boys and girls.
- More confidence around the home and in familiar situations.
- Arguments with parents as young people start to become independent.

Enjoyment when with friends.

Anxiety about coping with the pressures of school.

- Times when young people enjoy 'childish' activities (e.g. sitting on a swing, watching cartoons, playing games).
- Anxiety about coping with the pressures of school.

What young people aged 11–13 years need:

- opportunities to take control and be given responsibility

- clear boundaries that they can see the sense of and have helped to negotiate

- adults who can listen carefully and are sensitive to young people's needs

- praise and encouragement to support self-esteem

- support in coping with the transition to new educational settings

- understanding adults who can listen and help young people to cope with peer pressure and puberty

- opportunities to relax and to take exercise

- a balanced diet with sufficient protein and iron for growth

- time in which to enjoy being a child again, rather than a young person.

Young people aged 13–16 years

In this period young people move closer to adulthood. Physically, by around the age of 15 or 16 years, girls will have finished becoming women. For most boys, puberty will start around 14 years and is likely to take around three years to complete.

Pressure in school is likely to increase as most young people are preparing for examinations and may be starting to think about their future. During these years, some young people will begin to 'drop out' of education. They may show avoidance behaviours such as truanting, messing around in classes and bullying.

At around 16 years, young people will need to decide whether to leave education and find a job. Some will have developed skills that are equal to those of adults, for example, the ability to use computers or to draw.

Being with friends is likely to be more important than being with family. Young people who do not have a group of friends are likely to feel that they are missing out and may become anxious. Some may experience bullying if they are not part of a group. This can have a huge effect on their self-esteem and in extreme cases can result in suicide attempts, to draw attention to their unhappiness. For perpetrators, outcomes are not good either, as they may learn that this is a way of gaining respect from others.

This is a time when young people are also trying to explore their own identity. They may have tastes in music, clothes and activities that are different to those of their parents. This may cause clashes as young people try to develop their own personality and space. They may test the boundaries at home and even at school. As the transition to adulthood is not complete, young people will also at times revert to 'childlike' comments, activities and games.

While for some young people this period can be one of anxiety and conflict, for others it can be an enjoyable period as they spend time with friends and are able to dream a little about the future.

What you might observe in young people aged 13–16 years

- Confidence and enjoyment when with friends.
- Thoughts and ideas that are different to those of their parents.
- Uncertainty about how to talk to unfamiliar adults.
- High level of skills (e.g. using a computer).
- Enjoyment of 'childlike' activities.
- The need to experiment with identity and responsibility, e.g. through haircuts, piercings, untidy bedrooms and clothing.
- Examples of behaviour linked to high self-esteem, e.g. wanting to be responsible, caring for others, interested.
- Examples of behaviour linked to low self-esteem, e.g. smoking, misuse of substances, early promiscuity and really untidy bedrooms.

Young people's thoughts and ideas can be different to those of their parents.

Examples of behaviour linked to low self-esteem.

What young people aged 13–16 years need:

- adults who listen and are non-judgemental
- adults who are aware of the difficulties that young people may face, such as bullying and peer pressure
- opportunities to discuss boundaries
- opportunities to take control and become independent
- time to relax and enjoy being with friends
- information about drugs, alcohol, sex and sexuality
- a balanced diet and opportunities to find out about healthy eating
- opportunities to take exercise
- information about careers and educational opportunities.

Development between 0 and 5 years: the crucial years

The first five years of a child's life are considered the most crucial in terms of development. In these five years, a huge amount of learning takes place. Children develop physical skills, language and socialisation skills, attitudes towards learning, and feelings of independence and confidence. In this way, each child begins to develop his or her own unique personality.

Many studies show that children who have been deprived of stimulating and caring environments in these early years are left with a permanent delay in some aspects of their development. In areas of development such as language and emotional development, some psychologists therefore talk about a 'critical' or 'sensitive' period in which development needs to take place.

Development is measured in different areas

Whilst every child is very much an individual, it is also helpful to understand that development usually follows a set sequence or pattern. Babies, for example, babble before they produce actual words and walk before they run. These sequences of development have been well documented over the years and this information can help you to work out the stage of development that a child has reached. The overall development of children is usually divided and measured in five different areas, as the spider diagram below shows.

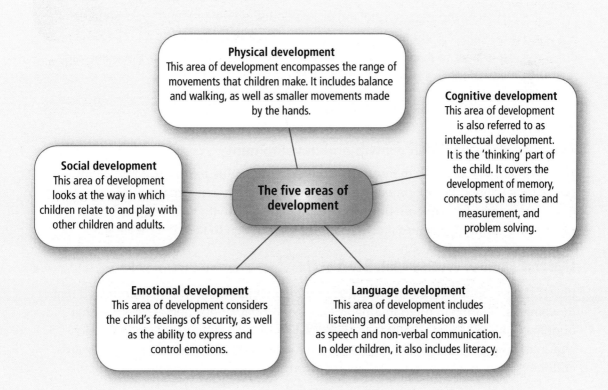

Physical development
This area of development encompasses the range of movements that children make. It includes balance and walking, as well as smaller movements made by the hands.

Cognitive development
This area of development is also referred to as intellectual development. It is the 'thinking' part of the child. It covers the development of memory, concepts such as time and measurement, and problem solving.

Social development
This area of development looks at the way in which children relate to and play with other children and adults.

The five areas of development

Emotional development
This area of development considers the child's feelings of security, as well as the ability to express and control emotions.

Language development
This area of development includes listening and comprehension as well as speech and non-verbal communication. In older children, it also includes literacy.

How development is measured: norms, expectations and milestones

To measure children's development, professionals look at the skills that children have acquired in different areas, including language, physical development and social development. These skills are sometimes referred to as milestones and are usually linked very broadly to children's ages. The age band given is always an 'average' age. You should note here that 'average' is a balance, thus some children will inevitably show some skills earlier while others develop later. An example of a milestone for a baby is smiling: most babies are smiling at six weeks, but some will do so earlier than this and others start smiling later.

The charts on pages 31–4, 35–7, 39 and 40 state the development that children are expected to show by different ages. These charts show 'normative' or 'expected' development. While these charts can be helpful, they should be seen as a guide only. They give a picture of most children's development rather than the individual child's.

Key points in measuring development

- Development usually follows a set pattern or sequence.
- 'Normative' and 'expected' development are terms used to suggest what the majority of children are experiencing at any given age.
- Charts showing 'normative' or 'expected' development should be seen as approximate guides only.
- It is best to avoid labelling children as 'ahead' or 'behind' – there are wide variations in the rate at which children acquire skills.

The difference between growth and development

The term 'growth' refers to the way in which cells subdivide to, for example, allow bones to lengthen. 'Development' refers to the skills that a child masters. Many aspects of children's development are firmly intertwined with growth; for example, babies cannot walk until their bones are long and strong enough to take their weight.

Expected physical development, 0 to 5 years

Physical development concerns the way in which children control their body and make movements. Bearing in mind that babies are not mobile at first and are born with a bundle of reflexes, it is incredible to think that by the age of six or seven years most children have acquired all the physical movements needed for adulthood. Afterwards, children simply become more skilled and stronger at these movements.

Applying theory to your practice

Walking is a key milestone in a baby's development. Ask five parents at what age their child began to walk.

1 Compare the ages to the milestone for walking on page 32. What differences are there?

2 Why is it important to use normative development charts as a guide only?

Types of physical movements

The movements that children make are often divided into groups.

Fine motor

This broad term covers small movements that are generally made using the hands. It includes:

Fine motor movements help children to control their hands.

- *Fine manipulative skills:* these movements require the fingers and thumbs to carry out co-ordinated small tasks, for example, threading beads onto a string. Quite often, these movements also require hand–eye co-ordination.
- *Fine motor skills:* these movements involve the wrist and hand, for example, unscrewing a lid from a jar.

Gross motor

This is another broad term, which covers large movements. It includes:

- *Gross motor skills:* these are movements that are made using the whole limb, for example, kicking a ball or moving the arm to throw a beanbag.
- *Locomotive skills:* these are movements that enable mobility. For babies, this may mean rolling, crawling or bottom shuffling; for older children it means walking, running and skipping.

Co-ordination

In order to achieve many physical skills, a blend of movements is required in the right order. The maturation of the central nervous system plays a key role in helping children to become co-ordinated (see below). Children gradually become more co-ordinated as they practise particular movements and skills, and learn to use their hands, feet and eyes together.

- *Hand–eye co-ordination:* many activities require hands and eyes to work together. This is what is meant by hand–eye co-ordination. To pour a drink, for example, the brain needs to take information from the eyes and use it to inform the hands to make certain movements.
- *Foot–eye co-ordination:* in addition to hand–eye co-ordination, children also have to learn to guide their feet. Climbing stairs and kicking a ball requires this type of co-ordination.
- *Balance:* balance is a complicated skill, although one that many people take for granted. Most children rely on visual input for balance, and the ability to balance develops with age. Balance is required for children to carry out any task in which their weight shifts from one foot to another, such as walking, hopping and climbing.

Kicking a ball requires foot–eye co-ordination.

Physical development is essential to children's overall development

Physical development is an essential ingredient in children's overall development as it allows them to explore and thus learn about the world around them. The development of physical skills also helps children to become increasingly independent, for example, as they learn to feed and dress themselves. This independence helps them to become confident.

Key principles of physical development

The three key principles of physical development were first outlined by Arnold Gessell, an American paediatrician (see below).

1   *Development follows a definite sequence*
    As you watch children growing and developing, you can observe a pattern emerging by which certain movements have to be in place before others can develop. For example, children have to be able to walk before they can skip (see also page 30).

2   *Development begins with the control of head movements and proceeds downwards*
    Babies gain control of the head and top of the spine before other parts of the body. This is thought to be a survival mechanism as it is important for babies to turn their head to feed.

3 *Development begins with uncontrolled gross motor movements before becoming precise and refined*

At first, a young baby's arm and leg movements are uncontrolled. However, some control is quickly gained, first of the arms and then of the wrist and hands. By six months, most babies are able to take an offered toy with reasonable ease. As an adult, you may have had a similar learning experience if you have learnt to use a computer with a mouse. Most people struggle at first to use a mouse and keep the cursor visible on the screen; gradually, more refined movements are learnt, which allow the cursor to be positioned more accurately.

Arnold Gessell – a key theorist

Arnold Gessell (1880–1961) is known for his work on children's physical development. Through his observations of babies and young children he developed a theory of physical development that has served as the basis for subsequent research. Gessell suggested that the maturation of the central nervous system underpinned development (see below), with stimulation not necessarily having a significant role. However, this view did lead to some paediatricians adopting a 'laissez-faire' attitude towards children with disabilities, which has subsequently been challenged.

Applying theory to your practice

Look at a three-year-old trying to put on a coat. How smoothly and quickly can this task be managed? Follow this observation by looking at a five-year-old or even an adult. Can you see the differences between the speed and smoothness of movements?

The links between the central nervous system and physical development

Children's physical development is underpinned by the central nervous system, which comprises the brain and the spinal cord. The central nervous system is responsible for collecting, interpreting and sending out information to all parts of the body. This information is continually collected through the body's senses of taste, touch, smell, sight and sound. It is then transformed into electrical pulses that are carried by the

The brain takes in information through the senses and then interprets it. This enables you to recognise someone very quickly.

nerves up through the spinal cord and into the brain. From the information that is received, the brain then responds and sends out instructions to muscles, glands and organs, again using the network of nerves. The whole process is surprisingly fast, which means that the body can quickly take action against possible danger – for example, withdrawing from something that is very hot. The speed at which information flows through the body means that many movements feel 'automatic'.

In babies and young children, the central nervous system has to mature. Babies are initially reliant on the many survival reflexes with which they are born, and the central nervous system has to learn how to interpret and control these responses. This is a gradual process, which is why a baby's movements are at first so uncoordinated. The need for the central nervous system to mature is one reason why different children walk, talk and move out of nappies at different rates.

Stages and sequences of physical development

Understanding the sequence of children's physical development is useful: it will allow you to match activities to the age groups of the different children with which you work. The charts of normative development on pages 31–4 show the milestones or skills that most children have developed by different ages. It is, however, essential to remember that such charts can act only as a guide – when planning it is also important to remember the needs of individual children.

Physical development during the first year

Age	Developmental pattern
Newborn	A newborn baby has many developmental reflexes that are designed to help him or her survive, for example, being able to cry and suck. These gradually disappear as the baby gains voluntary control of his or her body. *Rooting reflex* – moves mouth to look for food if face is touched. *Startle reflex* – throws out hands and legs as if trying to catch something if hears a sudden sound. *Grasp reflex* – fingers automatically tighten around anything put in the palm of the hand. Grasp is so tight that baby can be lifted up. *Crawling reflex* – when placed on front, knees are tucked up underneath. This is because of being curled up in the womb.
6 weeks	Starting to have more periods of alertness. Looks at carer; stares at bright lights. Is soothed by carer's voice. Follows objects and faces at close range. Arm and leg movements are jerky.
3 months	Smiles and coos. Kicks legs strongly and moves arms. Movements are less jerky, although still not co-ordinated. Can find hands and bring them to the mouth. Looks at and plays with fingers. Is alert and looks around. Can lift and turn head from side to side when lying on front. Can hold a rattle for a short time although cannot co-ordinate arms to bring it to mouth.
6 months	Smiles, laughs and makes sounds. Follows adults' movements. Grasps objects. Beginning to roll over. Pulls up legs with hands when on back. May put foot in mouth. Sits up with support, although some babies are starting to sit up for short periods without support. Pushes head, neck and chest off floor when on front.
9 months	Sits up well without support. Can reach out for toys from sitting. May be crawling or shuffling on bottom. Uses fingers and thumb to pick up objects. Can bang objects together. Babbles and starts to understand words such as 'bye-bye' and 'no'.

Stages and sequences of physical development from 1–7 years

Age	Fine motor development	Gross motor development	The carer's role	Toys and equipment
12 months	• Picks up objects with thumb and forefinger • Picks up and holds toys such as rattles • Points to objects • Holds cup with help • Puts small objects in a container	• Mobile – either crawling, rolling or shuffling (some may be walking) • Sits up unsupported for long periods • Walks with assistance • Tries to crawl up stairs	To support this stage of development, carers need to supervise carefully and give plenty of praise and encouragement. You need to spend time playing alongside the child, e.g. making a tower of bricks for the child to knock down or putting a cuddly toy in the child's truck for him or her to push along.	• Stacking beakers • Large balls • Push-and-pull toys • Bricks
15 months	• Holds and drinks from cup using two hands • Builds tower of two blocks • Makes marks with crayons • Tries to turn pages in books	• Crawls down stairs feet first • Walks independently • Seats self in small chair	Carers need to supervise children of this age very carefully as they are keen to explore and may start to climb. Children enjoy discovering new toys especially if they make sounds. You can help children by showing them how to use toys and by playing alongside them. Children of this age can often follow simple instructions; for example, a child may collect his or her hat and put it on. These early self-help skills need to be encouraged and praised so that children gain in confidence.	• Picture books • Bricks • Shape sorters • Toys that make music • Large crayons
18 months	• Strings four large beads • Turns door knobs and handles • Pulls off shoes	• Bends down from waist to pick up toys • Squats down to look at toys • Rolls and throws a ball • Walks down stairs with adult help	The main role of the adult is to allow children the time and space to play. Children are likely to spend more time playing alone and may play quite repetitively, e.g. putting objects into and out of boxes. As children gain in self-help skills, such	• Prams • Rocking horses or chairs • Threading toys • Bricks • Toys to ride on

Continued ▶

Age	Fine motor development	Gross motor development	The carer's role	Toys and equipment
18 months contd.		• Pushes and pulls toys whilst walking	as taking off shoes and coats, they need to be praised and allowed time to complete the task.	
2 years	• Uses a spoon to feed him or herself • Zips and unzips large zippers • Places five rings on a stick • Draws circles and dots • Builds a tower of five to six bricks • Begins to use a preferred hand	• Kicks a ball that is not moving • Climbs on furniture • Puts together and pulls apart snap-together toys • Walks up and down stairs confidently	Children of this age are enjoying exploring their environment and are beginning to have favourite toys and activities. Going to play parks and using swings and rocking equipment are a particular treat. Children's self-help skills are developing although there may be times when the child becomes frustrated; for example, an arm of a coat may be twisted and the child cannot get his or her hand through. Praise and encouragement needs to be offered and you need to look at ways of making children feel independent.	• Rides and sits on toys • Push-and-pull toys • Shape sorters • Bricks, crayons • Dough • Picture books
3 years	• Turns pages in a book one by one • Holds crayon and can draw a face • Uses a spoon without spilling • Washes and dries hands without help • Puts on and takes off coat	• Walks and runs forwards • Walks on tiptoes • Throws large ball • Kicks ball forward • Jumps from low steps • Pedals and steers a tricycle	Children of this age are starting to enjoy playing together and take pleasure in new challenges. Adults need to provide stimulating activities (for example, painting and cooking) which allow children to develop their fine motor movements, as well as opportunities to engage in pretend play.	• Large outdoor apparatus • Puzzles • Paints and crayons • Dough • Sand and water • Tricycles • Prams • Dressing-up clothes
4 years	• Buttons and unbuttons own clothing • Cuts out simple shapes • Draws a person with head, trunk	• Walks on a line • Aims and throws ball • Bounces and catches large ball • Runs, changing direction	Children at this age are gaining in confidence and are able to become more independent. You can encourage them to wipe up spills, pour drinks and tidy away; this will help prepare them for school.	• Balls • Climbing frames • Slides • Materials for creative activities • Crayons • Glue

Continued ▶

Age	Fine motor development	Gross motor development	The carer's role	Toys and equipment
4 years contd.	and legs • Puts together 12-piece jigsaw puzzle	• Hops on one foot • Pedals and steers a tricycle confidently	prepare them for school. Most children of this age enjoy being busy and playing co-operatively.	• Scissors • Puzzles • Construction toys • Books
5 years	• Forms letters; writes own name • Draws recognisable pictures of trees, houses, people and animals • Colours in pictures neatly • Dresses and undresses easily • Completes 20-piece jigsaw puzzle • Cuts out shapes using scissors quite accurately • Draws around a template	• Skips with a rope • Runs quickly and is able to avoid obstacles • Is able to use a variety of large equipment, e.g. swings, slides • Throws large ball to partner and catches it • Hits ball with bat or stick	Children are starting to enjoy playing games with rules, for example, snakes and ladders, chase, etc. You can help them by introducing new games into their play, such as hide and seek, as well as encouraging children to invent their own games. Adult support and encouragement is needed as there may be times when arguments break out. You should also be encouraging children to be as independent as possible, e.g. folding their clothes when changing and hanging up their coats.	• Hoops • Balls • Roller skates • Bicycles with stabilisers • Large equipment • Creative materials, e.g. paints, crayons, card and paper • Construction toys • Board games
6–7 years	• Is able to sew simple stitches • Cuts out shapes accurately and neatly • Handwriting is evenly spaced and may be joined • Drawings are detailed and representative • Makes a simple sandwich • Ties and unties shoelaces	• Rides a bicycle without stabilisers • Runs • Chases and dodges others • Hops, skips and jumps confidently • Kicks a ball with direction • Balances on a beam or wall	Children of this age are independent and able to do many day-to-day tasks, e.g. tidying away, laying the table. They are gaining in confidence and enjoy trying out new activities, e.g. making models, origami, cooking. They are starting to have preferences and their own hobbies; for example, some children will be learning to swim whilst others may go to karate or dance lessons. By 8 years, some children may need to be encouraged to join in some types of physical activities. This is often due to self-consciousness; they feel that they are not as good as other children.	• Bicycles • Skateboards • Roller skates • Balls • Bats and rackets • Kits, e.g. modelling kits, origami • Jigsaw puzzles • Board games

Expected patterns of social and emotional development, 0 to 5 years

These two areas of development are often written about together because a child's social development is linked to his or her emotional development. A good example of this is friendship: a child who is very aggressive and cannot control his or her anger may find it hard to sustain friendships. As with all areas of development, children gradually develop the skills and understanding required. In addition, these areas of development are thought to be linked, especially to children's direct experiences.

What is social development?

Human beings are understood to have an underlying need to be with others. Indeed, most people have a lot of social contact – they generally live, socialise and work with other people. Children have to learn how to be with others. Social development is thus particularly about the ability to form and sustain relationships, which includes the ability to adapt behaviour in ways that are acceptable to others.

What is emotional development?

Emotional development is a very complex area. It includes the development of the personality and values as well as the feelings a person has about him or herself. Children's emotional development affects their underlying ability to build relationships and to socialise.

Emotional development includes:

- the development of self-awareness and confidence
- being self-reliant and independent
- being able to leave a main carer
- controlling emotions such as anger
- expressing emotions such as joy, anger and sadness
- understanding and empathising with others
- moral development.

Stages and sequences of emotional and social development

Age	Description of development
From birth to 1 year	Important social skills are learnt in the baby's first year. Babies learn some of the skills of socialisation. They learn that making eye contact, smiling and laughing can keep their carer's attention. The first year is also critical in terms of emotional development. Babies need to develop a strong bond – or attachment – with their carers. In some ways, developing this bond may be instinctive as, at birth, babies are able to recognise the smell of their mother and are quickly soothed when they hear her voice. Babies who have a strong bond or attachment with their primary carer at the end of their first year will be more comfortable when they socialise with others. *Continued* ▶

Age	Description of development	
From birth to 1 year	1 month	Watches primary carer's face.
	3 months	Smiles and coos.
		Enjoys being handled and cuddled.
	6 months	Laughs and enjoys being played with.
	8 months	Fears strangers.
	9 months	Plays peek-a-boo.
		Discriminates between strangers and familiar adults.
	12 months	Is affectionate towards family and primary carers.
		Plays simple games such as pat-a-cake.
1–2 years	During this year, children learn more social skills. They are able to play with their primary carers and are comfortable with other familiar adults. They start to explore their environment but need the reassurance that their primary carer is nearby. At the end of this year, children often start to notice other children and become able to play alongside them. In terms of emotional development, children are very dependent on their primary carer. They will protest and cry if their primary carer leaves them and it is important that they are left with someone who is familiar to them. Although they are still dependent on their primary carer, they are starting to realise that they are individuals. They recognise and begin to use their own name. The end of this year also makes a change in many children as they become increasingly aware of what they want. They begin to show anger and frustration if they cannot get their needs individually met.	
	15 months	Begins to explore environment if familiar adult is close by.
		Begins to use words to communicate with.
		Has a stronger feeling of being an individual.
	18 months	Language is increasing.
		Points to objects to show familiar adults.
		Explores environment and shows independence but still needs familiar adults.
		Shows strong emotions, e.g. anger, fear and joy.
	2 years	Plays near other children – parallel play.
		Begins to talk when playing – pretend play.
		Imitates adults' emotions.
		Shows strong emotions, e.g. anger, fear and joy.
2–3 years	This is an important year in a child's life although it is not often an easy one for carers – hence the expression 'terrible twos'! Children in the first part of this stage are keenly aware of what they want to do, although they become easily frustrated because their own physical and language skills are not developed enough to meet these desires. They also find it difficult to understand why they cannot have what they see because they lack the concept of ownership or objects being unsafe. Frustration is often vented through temper tantrums or inconsolable crying. These tantrums and strong feelings lessen as children gradually develop more language and physical skills. Carers working with this age group need to be very sensitive and organised so that children are not in a position where they can become frustrated. Children often need their comforters with them during this year to help them feel more secure, especially as many children will also be having their first experience of being separated from their primary carers on entering pre-school settings. This is an important step as children need to learn to socialise without the back-up of their primary carers. The first experiences of separation need to be carefully handled and children entering pre-school settings will need a lot of reassurance from early years workers.	

Continued ▶

Age	Description of development
2–3 years	There is also a wide variation in the way that children progress over the year, so it is best to avoid categorising these steps. During this year most children will: • move out of nappies • have a strong sense of their identity, including their gender and age • be happy to leave their primary carer for short periods • start taking an interest in other children, e.g. telling primary carer if baby is crying • start to wait for their needs to be met.
3–4 years	This is a more settled year for children. Most of them are happy to leave their primary carers and socialise with other children and adults. The first real friendships start to develop, with children seeking out particular friends. Social skills, e.g. turn-taking, sharing and concern for others, are shown. Emotionally, children still need reassurance from their immediate carers but are more independent and may play by themselves for longer periods. They still feel strong emotions, and quarrels and temper tantrums are still apparent at times. Many children will still be reliant on their comforters,, especially when they are unwell or unsure of a situation. During this year most children will: • be affectionate towards family, friends and carers • want to help and please primary carer and other familiar adults • imitate in play actions they have seen, e.g. putting teddy to bed, feeding dolls • share playthings • play with other children – mostly pretend play • show concern for other children, e.g. rub back of crying baby.

Socialisation – a process beginning with the main carer

Babies first learn about other people by being with a main carer. For most children, the main carer will be the child's mother or father; for other children, it will be another family member, a foster parent or an adoptive parent.

The role of the main carer in the child's life appears to be quite critical. The main carer and baby often form a close tie or bond. The process by which this happens is referred to as 'attachment'. It was initially thought that a baby forms only one close attachment: to the person providing him or her with the most time and care. However, it is now recognised that a baby can form equally strong attachments to other people who play a significant role in his or her life.

Developing relationships outside of the family

A strong attachment to at least one key person remains essential to the child's early life and social development. From this secure base, babies and toddlers are ready to explore and learn about other people. They do this at first by watching the reactions of the main carer to other people. A toddler, for example, will often peep out from behind the main carer's legs to watch the dialogue between the 'stranger' and the main carer. Learning in this way is called 'social referencing'. By about three years of age, children begin to feel more comfortable with people who are not family or familiar to them, but for short periods only. They gradually understand that they can leave their 'secure base' and come back to it.

Qualities of different relationships

Recent work by Willard Hartup (published in 1989) suggests that children's relationships can be defined as either vertical relationships or horizontal relationships:

*   Children's relationships with parents, teachers and adults are vertical because they are not equal – adults have greater experience, skills and knowledge than children do.
*   Children's relationships with each other are horizontal because they are at a roughly equal stage of development.

Both types of relationship are essential to a child's overall emotional and social development. In vertical relationships, children gain skills and learn about social behaviour; in horizontal relationships, children have the opportunity to practise their social skills.

vertical relationships

horizontal relationships

Vertical and horizontal relationships.

Thinking and research

Whilst children of a similar age are playing, listen to their conversation and watch their behaviour. How do the children talk and behave with each other?

Continued ▶

Follow this by watching one of the same children playing alongside an adult. Does the child notice what the adult is doing and is the adult helping the child gain the skills of socialisation?

1   Do you think that adults' relationships with children are always 'vertical' as suggested above?

2   To what extent do you think that the age of the child affects the way in which adults interact and socialise with him or her?

Social stages of play

As part of the socialisation process, children learn to play with other children of a similar age. Playing with other children is an important part of a child's social development – it appears that it allows the child to practise his or her social skills.

The socialisation process begins with the baby learning to play and respond to adults and carers. Gradually, he or she begins to take an interest in other children, although the child will watch them initially rather than engage in play.

The sequence by which children are able to engage in play with others was first noted by Mildred Parten in the 1930s. Her social stages of play are widely recognised, although

Social stages of play

Age	Stage	Features	Examples
0–2 years	Solitary activity	The child engages in play and is uninterested in children of a similar age.	Mai and George are just over one year old. They rarely make eye contact and play by themselves. They each attract their carer's attention when they want company.
2–4 years	Parallel activity Associative play	The child is happy to play with the same materials as another child. Little communication and eye contact takes place between them.	The child begins to be more aware of other children and may copy their play. Josh and Niamh are both playing with cars. They are two and a half years old. They each have their own game and move out of each other's way. Aran sees that Gracie has a ball. He gets a ball from the basket too. Aran sees that Gracie is kicking the ball. He kicks his too and laughs.
4–7 years	Co-operative activity	The child plays and engages with other children. He or she is able to take turns and, when older, negotiate roles and ideas.	Jamal is four years old. He is waiting for his friend, Tom, to return from washing his hands so that they can start a game. They talk about what they are doing and take turns.

it is now thought that babies are generally more aware of others and that many three-year-olds engage in a type of co-operative activity (called associative play). In addition, it is worth noting that older children who are capable of playing co-operatively may sometimes choose to play by themselves.

The development of friendships

As children get older, friendships play an increasingly important role in their lives. By the time they reach their teenage years, children's relationships with their friends are as important as those with their families. Learning about friendships and having particular preferences begins quite early in childhood, as the table below shows.

Stages of social interaction

Age	Features	Examples
0–2 years	Children notice other people, including adults and older children, and are fascinated by other babies. By the age of two years, toddlers play side by side.	Ritchie is 12 months old. He crawls over to look at a baby who is in a carrycot. He peers in and wants to touch the baby's eyes.
2–4 years	By the age of three years, most children show a friendship preference for particular children with whom they play regularly. They play with children of the same or a different gender, and the activity appears to be more important than who is there.	Jasmine is four years old. She looks round the room to see if she can find her friend, Ragav. She likes playing in the home corner with him.
4–7 years	From this age, many children show stable friendships, although they will play with other children. Friendships tend to be with those of the same gender.	Charlene, Helen and Jodie skip together during play time.
8–11 years	Friendships are generally based on what the children enjoy doing together. They are usually with children of the same gender. There is some evidence to suggest that boys' friendships are group-based and more relaxed, with girls having closer but fewer friendships.	Tom goes out to play with some of his friends. They all enjoy sport and often get together with a couple of boys from a neighbouring school. Manjeet has two close friends. They all go to drama and netball clubs after school.

Frequently asked questions

Forming friendships

  One of the parents is worried that his child does not have a 'best friend'. The child is four years old.

Continued ▶

> **A** Whilst some children quickly pair up with other children, it is not unusual for children of four years to have a 'carousel' of friends. Play interests seem to determine, to a large extent, who children spend their time with. Take time to look at the child and check whether he is socialising and playing with other children. Look to see where he spends his time and see if there are patterns to his play. If the child seems otherwise happy and does interact with other children, reassure the parent.

The importance of self-reliance and self-help skills

Most people take for granted the ways in which they are able to do many different things for themselves and take the initiative. For children, the development of self-reliance is essential to their budding self-confidence and ability to take responsibility for their actions. Skills such as being able to dress and pour a drink, or learning to cope with choice, encourage the child to become more self-reliant. For adults working with children, this means thinking about the ways in which children can be helped to do things for themselves – for example, asking a young child to fetch his or her coat rather than getting it for him or her.

Self-help skills include:

- getting dressed
- choosing activities
- tidying away toys
- pouring drinks
- laying out tables ready for snack time
- carrying trays
- preparing simple foods, for example, peeling a banana or cutting a kiwi fruit.

Expected intellectual development, 0 to 5 years

Cognitive development is a complex area that is the source of much scientific interest. It generally concerns the way in which people organise their thinking, and people's ability to make sense of the world and what is happening to them. Problem solving, prediction and noticing patterns are examples of skills related to cognitive development. While children are learning to organise their thoughts and are discovering about the world, their thinking and logic appear quite different from that of adults. This section focuses on the expected cognitive development in children up to five years of age, and considers some of the components involved in processing information.

Taking in information – perception

A good starting point when looking at cognitive development is perception. A person's thoughts are governed by the information that the brain receives from the five senses.

The brain creates a perception using information from the senses, such as sight and smell.

From this information – what a person hears, sees, tastes, smells and touches – the brain creates a perception of the situation. This is a process of translating the different information from the senses into a more accurate representation. For example, the information that the eyes send to the brain is a two-dimensional upside-down image; the brain learns from other senses, particularly touch, that this is not an accurate representation and creates a better one (a three-dimensional image). This translation process happens amazingly quickly, so most people think that what they 'see' is simply the information from their eyes.

The rabbit/duck test

The rabbit/duck test shows how the brain translates the images that the eyes receive into meaningful representations. If you look at the image, you can see either a rabbit or a duck. While it is possible to see both, you will not be able to see both at the same time.

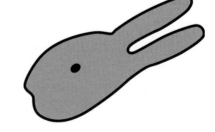

The rabbit/duck test.

Attention and concentration

Attention and concentration are closely linked skills. When you notice something and focus your attention on it, you take in information more deliberately. In order to be able to notice something, the brain must be aroused by the information that it receives through the senses. Levels of arousal can fluctuate, for example, some people can sleep through storms.

Concentration is the ability to sustain attention. In order to concentrate, children's brains have to learn to filter out information that is not relevant. This is not an easy process since the brain is constantly receiving information, for example, sounds from other children, feelings of hunger, the sight of people moving. The ability to focus and sustain interest develops with age, so while a toddler is easily distracted from an activity when shown another toy, an older child will be less distracted.

It is worth remembering, however, that for both adults and children, concentration is easier to sustain when the activity is enjoyable and stimulates the senses. Thus, concentration spans are variable and dependent on the activity. A three-year-old may be able to spend 20 minutes playing in the sand but find it hard to sit still at other times.

Applying theory to your practice

1 Which of these activities consistently hold children's interest for long periods in your setting?

- Sand play
- Dough
- Water
- Story time
- Outdoor play
- Snack time

2 In what ways do these activities stimulate the senses?

3 In what situations do you find it hard to concentrate?

Attention Deficit/Hyperactivity Disorder (ADHD)

Children with ADHD find it hard to concentrate and settle on one activity. Their attention span is limited and they are often easily distracted. There are many theories as to why this may occur, but it would appear that for some children their brains are not sufficiently aroused to sustain attention. For other children the opposite appears to be the case: the brain receives too much information, which the child is unable to filter out sufficiently. Treatment for ADHD is variable but drug treatments to either stimulate or dampen arousal systems are generally used.

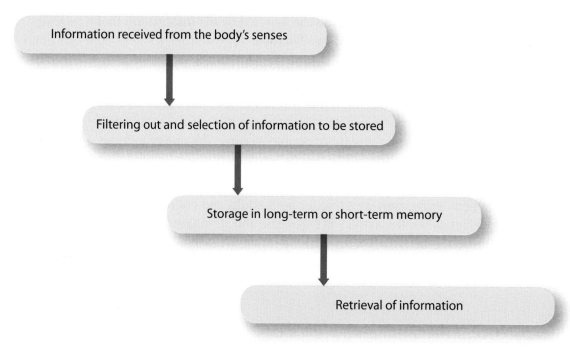

Memory flow chart.

Memory

The role of the memory is to store information. If you could not store information you would forget everything that you learnt. As well as storing information, you also need to be able to retrieve it – this is what happens when you remember. Psychologists looking at memory believe that information is stored in different ways. It would seem that young children do not process information and store it in the same way as adults do. This may be one reason why adults cannot remember early childhood, although babies definitely have a memory of people, foods and smells.

In addition to storing information, you need to know what information is stored and make connections between stored and new information. For example, if someone says that they have food poisoning, you might make a connection between that person and a TV programme you saw about food poisoning. Making new connections and being able to locate your knowledge in this way is referred to as a metacognitive skill. The absence of this skill in older children and adults is thought to cause learning difficulties.

The role of language in cognitive development

The development of language appears to be extremely important in supporting cognitive development. As well as using language for communication, language is used to organise thinking. Many people know that they can hear 'inner speech' and this allows them to organise themselves or 'self-direct'. In young children, self-direction shows itself from around two or three years of age, although speech is not internalised. A young child often appears to be doing a running commentary on his or her activities, even while alone. It appears that while older children and adults can think inside their heads, young children need to vocalise their thoughts. This accounts for children's often unexpected remarks and questions, and why children appear to switch off if they cannot talk.

Learning concepts

Many of the concepts that children need to learn are those adults take for granted. Some concepts, such as time, are very abstract as you cannot physically see them. Children learn some concepts by playing with materials and exploring their world; others are learnt by adults focusing the child's attention on them.

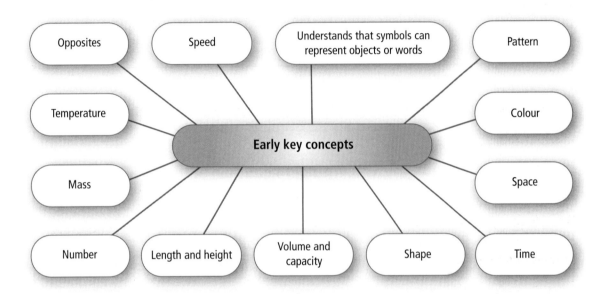

Opposites · Speed · Understands that symbols can represent objects or words · Pattern · Temperature · **Early key concepts** · Colour · Mass · Space · Number · Length and height · Volume and capacity · Shape · Time

Stages and sequences of cognitive development

It is quite difficult to outline stages of cognitive development in young children because it is dependent on the stimulation and experiences they receive. For example, a child who has not heard or been shown the names of different colours may not have acquired these concepts. The table on page 46 therefore shows probable sequences and stages of cognitive development; as with other normative charts, it should be used only as a guide.

Expected language and communication development, 0 to 5 years

Being able to communicate is an important skill that most people take for granted. Language has many purposes: it helps people to communicate with others and is understood to play an important role in processing information and organising thought. While most people think of language as just speech, it is important to remember that language is also about listening, reading and writing, and includes sign languages such as British Sign Language.

Probable sequence of tasks in children aged 0–6 years

Age	Features
0–1 years	• Looks for an object that has been removed. • Places an object in a container when asked. • Finds an object that has been seen and then hidden.
1–2 years	• Takes out objects one by one from container. • Points to parts of the body. • Scribbles. • Points to a named picture.
2–3 years	• Completes a three-piece puzzle. • Copies a circle. • Matches textures. • Is able to point to little and big, e.g. 'Which is the big teddy?' • Matches three colours. • Stacks beakers in order.
3–4 years	• Tells if an object is light or heavy. • Is able to repeat a simple story. • Matches one to one, e.g. putting a cup with each saucer. • Points to long and short objects. • Is able to sort out simple objects. • Knows primary colours. • Names three shapes. • Counts ten objects with support.
4–5 years	• Picks up a number of objects, e.g. 'Find me four cubes.' • Names five textures. • Names times of the day associated with activities, e.g. bedtime, dinner time. • Names eight colours. • Matches symbols (letters and numbers). • Is able to decide which object is the heavier. • Places objects beside, behind and next to. • Counts by rote up to twenty.
5–6 years	• Counts accurately up to twenty items. • Prints own name. • Arranges objects in order of size. • Names days of week in order. • Tells month and day of birthday. • Sight reads ten or more words. • Predicts what happens next. • Points to half and whole objects, e.g. half a cake. • Counts up to 100 by rote.

What is language?

Linguists who study language development and the nature of language have concluded that all languages, regardless of where they are used, share certain features. It is particularly interesting that all languages have 'rules', which linguists refer to as grammar. Children have to learn these rules, which include the actual sounds that are used in speech.

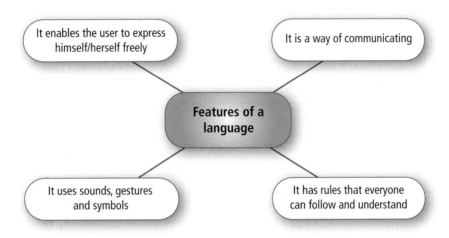

It enables the user to express himself/herself freely

It is a way of communicating

Features of a language

It uses sounds, gestures and symbols

It has rules that everyone can follow and understand

The number of sounds that are needed in any language varies. In English, children need to master 40 sounds or *phones*, in order to pronounce words. It is thought that the babbling stage that all babies go through reflects their need to sort and rehearse these sounds, while toddlers and pre-school children learn how to put sentences together. Amazingly, babies and children appear to go through this process without needing to be 'taught'.

Thinking and research

Learning to read using a phonic system requires that children learn to link the sounds in language to shapes in words. At the time of writing, a system known as synthetic phonics is to be used as the prime way in which children are to be taught to read. Find out more about phonics by visiting www.literacytrust.org.uk and www.dfes.gov.uk.

The development of language in children

As with many areas of development, children appear to follow a set pattern when learning language. In addition, there seems to be a critical period in which children need to be 'switched on' to language. This begins from birth, with babies in their first year tuning into their home language and learning how to gain attention and read other people's expressions. This first year of language development is very important and is known as the pre-linguistic phase.

Pre-linguistic stage of language development

Stage	Age	Features	Comments
Cooing	6 weeks	Cooing.	Babies making cooing sounds to show pleasure. These early sounds are different to sounds made later on, mainly because the mouth is still developing.
Babbling (phonemic expansion)	6–9 months	Babies blend vowels and consonants together to make tuneful sounds, for example, 'ba', 'ma', 'da'.	Babbling has been described as learning the tune before the words. The baby seems to be practising sounds. Babies increase the number of sounds or phonemes; this is sometimes called phonemic expansion. All babies, even deaf babies, produce a wide range of sounds during this period.
Babbling (phonemic contraction)	9–10 months	Babies babble but the range of sounds is limited.	The range of sounds or phonemes that babies produce becomes more limited and reflects the phonemes used in the language that they hear. In theory, at this stage it would be possible to distinguish between babies who are in different language environments. At 10 months of age, babies can understand 17 or more words.

Comprehension, or receptive language, appears before expressive language. At the end of their first year, babies are likely to understand as many as 20 words. The baby will speak his or her first words later, with many parents recognising their child's first words at around 13 or 14 months.

The chart on page 49 shows the 'linguistic' phase of language development from around 12 months of age onwards. As with other areas of development, it is essential to remember that the speed at which children learn and pass through milestones can vary enormously – this chart can be a general guide only. It is, however, useful to note that most children can be understood by people who are not their parents or carers

Stages of linguistic development

Stage	Age	Linguistic stage	Examples
First words	12 months	First words are often present alongside babbling, although parents and carers may not realise this. Babies use gestures such as pointing to attract their parents'/carers' attention. Receptive language is strong – most babies understand about 20 words and can interpret facial gestures.	Harry points his finger to a cat that he sees. Sari waves when she hears the words 'bye bye'.
Holophrases	12–18 months	Receptive language is developing very quickly. At 13 months, most toddlers understand about 50 words. Toddlers use single words or 'holophrases'. By 15 months, most toddlers will speak about 10 words.	Anya goes to fetch her coat when her mum says that they are going to the park. Mark says 'dink' when he sees his beaker.
Two word utterances – telegraphese	18–24 months	Once toddlers can speak several words, they begin to combine them to make mini-sentences. Vocabulary increases as children learn around 10 to 30 words a month. By two years, many children can speak about 200 words.	Simon says 'bye cat' when a cat gets up and leaves the room.
Language explosion	2–3 years	Vocabulary increases dramatically. Sentence length begins to increase. Plurals, negatives and questions are used.	Kate says, 'Park to see fishes. No cats in park. Fishes in park.'
Virtuous errors	3–4 years	Speech is intelligible to adults who are unfamiliar with the child. The child is beginning to use longer and more complex sentences. Children begin to use grammar, for example, plurals and past tenses, but may make virtuous errors. Speech patterns and expressions are copied from adults.	Damien says, 'We wented to my grans and we saw lots of sheeps.'
Fluency	4–8 years	Language is fairly fluent by four years of age. Children enjoy talking and using language to entertain, explain and argue. From five years onwards, children begin to enjoy jokes and be interested in print. By six to seven years, children have mastered very basic reading and writing skills.	Rayan asks George if he knows what time it is when an elephant sits on a fence. George says he doesn't know. Rayan replies, 'Time to get a new fence.' They both laugh.

by the time they are three years old. Children whose speech is still very unclear or not developed at this age may need additional support.

The emergence of first words

At around 13 or 14 months, many parents report that their toddler is beginning to use his or her first words, although the child will continue to babble. These words may not be pronounced correctly but they have meaning for the child and the adult. Many of children's first words are usually nouns, for example, 'cat', 'drink', 'mummy', although words such as 'come', 'go', and 'no' are often also present. Furthermore, children generally use the same word for several meanings, for example, 'dink' may stand for all foods and drinks as well as spoons and items used for feeding. To vary the meaning of the word, children also use gestures such as pointing and change the tone of their voice. These one-word meanings are referred to as 'holophrases'.

Telegraphese

Once toddlers have begun to use single words, the next step is to begin combining words. Mini sentences are created by combining two words, for example, 'daddy–gone' or 'cat–more'. This stage of speech is referred to as 'telegraphese' because the non-essential words have been missed out (in a manner similar to old-style telegrams). It is thought that the child is able to choose the key words that will have meaning in a sentence because these are the ones that have been stressed by adults in their speech to the child.

Language explosion

From around two years of age, children suddenly begin to learn and use more and more words. Where previously words had emerged relatively slowly, children now acquire several new words each week. After a few months, it becomes hard to track how many words a child has acquired because he or she has learnt so many. It would appear that once a child has 'clicked' about words, he or she steadily acquires and uses them in increasing numbers.

Virtuous errors

When learning language, all children make grammatical mistakes. One example is that they may add '-ed' onto the end of every verb, saying things such as 'I swimmed'. These mistakes are actually logical ones that arise from the child's attempt to apply the rules of grammar. Roger Brown (1926–98), a linguist, refers to such mistakes as 'virtuous errors': they show that the child has developed some understanding of grammar. Grammatical mistakes gradually decrease, although they will be found in most children's speech until they are six or seven years old.

Can all children develop language?

While it is generally accepted that humans have an inbuilt ability to learn language (see also page 47), not all children are able to learn spoken language. For some children their cognitive development means that they cannot process and think in symbols.

scissors (to cut)   drink (cup)   ball

Some common Makaton signs.

Since spoken language is based on symbols, this prevents them from mastering it. For example, when the word 'cat' is said, a cat does not necessarily appear – the word stands for the actual animal. Children who find it hard to process symbols are therefore often taught Makaton signs or a picture-based system of communicating. These help children because visual symbols or pictures are closely related to the action or object.

Makaton and other visual-based systems of communicating are useful because children can understand the link between the words that are being used and their meaning. The decision to use visual systems of communication with children is normally taken on the advice of speech therapists and in conjunction with parents. For some children this is a short-term measure as, once they learn how language works, they are able to use and increasingly understand speech. Note that Makaton is not a complete language and is used as an aid to communication.

Children who learn more than one language

While most people speak one language only, many children speak a different language at home from the language they use in the setting. Where a child speaks two languages, he or she is referred to as bilingual. A child who can speak more than one language is referred to as multilingual. The development of the second, and in some cases third, language depends on two key factors:

- the age at which the child is exposed to the language
- the length of time that the child is exposed to the language.

Children who learn another language as a baby

Children who are exposed to more than one language as babies or toddlers usually make similar progress to other children, although they may be slightly later in saying their first few words. The slight delay in producing first words is thought to be caused by the baby needing more time to 'tune in' to two different sound systems. The advice given to parents and carers who are hoping that their child will learn more than one language is that the child should learn to associate a language with a person, for example, the mother always speaks in Greek; the father speaks in English. This helps the baby to 'tune in' and learn the grammatical rules of each language. Speakers jumping from one language to another can be a primary cause of delayed or confused speech in bilingual children.

Children who learn another language in the pre-school

Some children enter the pre-school setting with little or no English. For these children, extra support is required to help them acquire the new language. The process of learning a new language as a young child remains similar to that of a baby learning its first language, although the process is faster. Children begin by 'tuning in' to the sounds being used. Receptive language quickly develops, with children developing an understanding of certain key words. Once they have some receptive language, single words emerge followed by short sentences. The speed at which children learn the new language depends on the quality of the adult support and the emotional environment of the setting.

Good practice

Helping children who are learning the language of the setting

- Find out about how much language the child has already learnt.

- Make sure that the child is allocated a key person to help him or her settle in.

- Provide plenty of one-to-one support for the child with the key person, to help him or her 'tune in' to the sounds of the language and learn some key words.

- Do not force a child to speak – words will appear only when the child is ready.

- Repeat key words and use gestures so that the child knows what you are referring to.

- Simplify sentences as you would with a baby or toddler.

- To help the child learn some first words, use books with simple pictures of objects and activities.

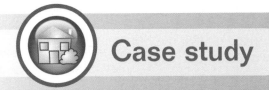

Case study

Rayan speaks Turkish at home and has very little English. He goes to the Busy Bee pre-school three times a week. Rayan's key person, Becky, has built up a good relationship with him and his parents. Together they have agreed that Rayan will need to settle in gradually. When Becky works with Rayan, she makes sure that he can understand her by using facial gestures and repetition, and by pointing to objects. She tries to stress the key words in any sentence and repeats them. She has also made Rayan a simple picture book. Together they look at the book when the other children are having their story. Rayan points to the pictures of the sand pit, water tray and other objects that he recognises. Becky repeats the names of the objects. Becky also organises games of picture lotto that Rayan and other children play together. In the first few weeks, Rayan needed to stay close to Becky, but he is now keen to play with the other children. He is beginning to point to things and say single words.

1   Why do young children need to be offered emotional support when joining a setting?

2   Give two reasons why Rayan needs to spend time with his key person.

3   Why are facial expressions and gestures important in helping a child to learn a language?

The holistic nature of development

Whilst it is helpful in terms of looking at normative development or milestones to consider separate aspects of children's development, it is essential to remember that development is a package. The term 'holistic' is often used in this context as a way of describing the importance of looking at the 'whole' child. This is essential because aspects of development are closely interconnected. A child who enjoys doing jigsaw puzzles is likely also to have good fine motor movements, whilst a child who is very sociable is likely to develop good communication and language skills.

As well as aspects of development being interconnected, some skills that you might assess for a particular aspect of development are actually interdependent. A good example of this is whether a child can write his or her name. To do this skill, which might be a milestone for literacy, requires that a child has fine motor movement, hand–eye co-ordination, a cognitive ability to remember abstract symbols as well as the confidence to attempt the task! Remembering the interconnected nature of development is, therefore, essential when assessing children and particularly important when you are trying to understand how best to help an individual child.

Effects of developmental delay

Whilst children's development follows a pattern, the speed of their developmental journey can be quite individual. Most children stay within sight of 'expected development' or age-related milestones, yet others may show much slower progress in one or more areas. Identifying and meeting the needs of these children as soon as possible is now given priority. This is because developmental delay in one or more areas can affect a child's overall progress. This goes back to development being a holistic process. A child whose language is delayed may find it hard to control his or her behaviour and so may find it harder to make friends. Thus a language delay has the potential to impact on social and emotional development. In the same way, a child who has difficulty with fine motor skills might avoid any activities where these skills are needed and so may miss out on some learning.

The extent to which developmental delay affects children varies enormously. It is dependant on the underlying cause of the delay, be this temporary or permanent, the support that a child is given and also how quickly the delay is identified. Early identification is often seen as the key to helping children and is one of the reasons why pre-school settings appoint a member of staff as a SENCO (see Optional Unit 2).

Emotional development

For many children, developmental delay is most likely to have some effect on their emotional development. This is because children's self-concept is still developing and they are learning about themselves. Sadly, some children come to the conclusion that because they are 'different' this means that they are not 'good' or 'clever'. If they have some physical delay, they may also become dependent on adults to help them with tasks and so lack confidence to use their own initiative. It is therefore essential that adults look at ways of boosting all children's self-esteem through praise and also by giving children choices and opportunities to 'shine'.

Behaviour

Developmental delay can also have an effect on children's behaviour. Common behaviours that are linked to delay include frustration and aggression, as well as withdrawal and lack of communication. The link between developmental delay and behaviour means that it is always worth considering whether unusual or unwanted behaviours are actually of deeper significance. A child who cannot hear instructions may appear not to be co-operative, whilst a child who is finding it hard to manipulate a puzzle may become frustrated and throw it to the ground.

The contribution of brain research to understanding children's development

The study of child development is likely to change shape over the course of the next few decades. An exciting development in medical technology has allowed scientists to study the functioning of the brain. Magnetic Resonance Imaging (MRI) has allowed scientists, for the first time, to look at which parts of the brain are used during certain tasks. This branch of medical science is known as neuroscience; it is particularly exciting since it provides insight into how the brain grows and develops during a person's lifetime. Whilst neuroscientists are keen to point out that their study of how the brain works is in its very early stages, there are already some findings that are affecting practice in pre-school settings.

Stimulation

Stimulation to new sensations, ideas and experiences seems to be vital for healthy brain development

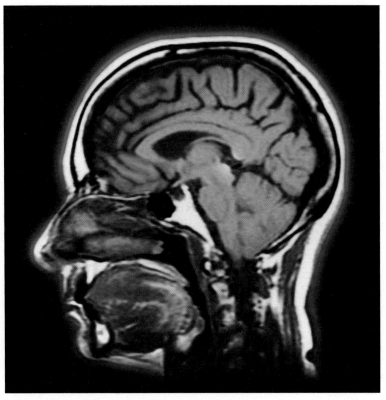

Brain scans can tell us which parts of the brain are active.

in babies and young children. Babies are born with 100 million neurons which could be compared to lightbulbs. For the brain to work effectively, these neurons need to light up simultaneously and to do this they need to connect up; the term 'neural connections' is used to describe the way in which they may do this. Neural connections are sparse at birth but new connections are made at amazing speed during a child's early years. Neural connections can be seen when children's brains are scanned. Babies and toddlers who have not been stimulated have fewer and less complex neural connections. Where neurons are not able to connect with others or where connections are not used, a natural pruning process takes place. This means that stimulation by talking and playing with babies and children is now seen as being essential. Interestingly, adults can increase their neural connections throughout their life by taking on new tasks, experiences and learning. Failure to do this means that pruning occurs and further depletes the connections!

Theoretical perspectives of child development

Theories of child development often shape practice in the early years setting. They can provide insight into the way children learn, and explain specific behaviours and responses. Having a good understanding of child development theories and perspectives is therefore useful when working with children and their parents.

Perspectives within child development

The academic subject whose focus is the way in which children develop is developmental psychology. Psychology is a relatively new social science that looks at what is going on in human bodies and minds. As people and children have different life experiences and are generally not born or raised in laboratory conditions, it can be very hard for psychologists to prove their theories beyond doubt. This means that when considering psychological theories, you will see that there are often several approaches to, for example, the way in which people learn.

Nature or nurture?

This is an ongoing debate in developmental psychology. The nature or nurture question centres on the extent to which behaviour, intelligence and personality are the result of life experience or reflect inherited and instinctive characteristics. In the early days of psychology, people tended to hold very fixed positions with regard to this debate. Today, however, most psychologists accept that both are likely to be influential, although theories generally fall into either camp.

Is this an inherited or a learnt trait?

Psychological perspectives of emotional and social development

One of the keystones in children's emotional and social development is the development of relationships with others. This means that it is useful to have an understanding of the way in which children learn to make relationships.

Attachment theories

Attachment theories consider the way in which babies and parents or carers interact and develop special relationships or bonds. They also assess the consequences for babies and children when separation takes place, and when bonds are not developed sufficiently with parents and carers.

Key terms used when looking at attachment:

- *Attachment/bond* – these terms indicate a close tie or special relationship between the carer, usually a parent, and the child.
- *Separation* – a temporary or permanent absence of the parent or carer.
- *Separation anxiety* – distress that is shown by the child when separation takes place.

Continued ▶

- *Deprivation* – the permanent absence of the parent once a bond has been established.
- *Privation* – this term refers to situations in which the child has not been able to form an attachment because no adult or carer was present.

Cupboard love theories of attachment

The relationship between child and carer was originally thought to be one of 'cupboard love'. The idea was that the baby cared for the person whom they learnt to associate with feeding them. This theory was discredited by many experiments, including one known often as Harlow's monkeys (see below).

Harlow's monkeys

In 1959, two researchers – Harry Harlow and Robert Zimmerman – carried out an experiment to determine if there was more to attachment than food. Two artificial monkeys were placed in a cage. One was made from wire and the other was made from cloth. Baby monkeys were put into the cage. Half the baby monkeys were fed by the 'wire mother'; the other half were fed by the 'cloth mother'. The researchers found that all the monkeys spent time clinging to and using the 'cloth mother', even those who had not been fed by her. This experiment showed that food alone is not the source of attachment.

Bowlby's theory of attachment

In the 1950s, a psychiatrist called John Bowlby was commissioned to look at the effects on children of being raised in orphanages. This was important work as many children after the Second World War were orphaned. Bowlby's report and later book had a great impact and succeeded in changing attitudes and practice. His theory of attachment has since been criticised and expanded on but it is still considered to be a landmark in child development theory.

- *The importance of a principal attachment*
  Bowlby concluded that babies need to form one principal attachment. He suggested in his early work that this would be with the mother; however, he later conceded that it could be with the father or another carer. Bowlby found that where a principal attachment was not formed, there were serious implications for the child. The child would sustain long-term psychological damage that would affect subsequent relationships.

- *The critical period*
  Bowlby suggested a timeframe in which the principal attachment should be made. He thought that babies need to form this attachment by 12 months of age, and that any separation from the principal carer during the child's first four years of life would have serious consequences for the child.

- *Quality of attachment*
  Bowlby also looked at the quality of the principal attachment, although subsequent research has studied this in greater depth. Bowlby felt that parenting is more than just feeding and caring for the physical needs of the child; the child also needs support and care.

- *Patterns of distress*
  Bowlby noted that babies and young children show a definite pattern of behaviour when they are separated from their principal carer. This pattern is known as separation anxiety. Children move from one stage of separation anxiety to another (see flow diagram on next page). Bowlby concluded that if a child is left in the final stage of separation anxiety for long periods, he or she could suffer severe emotional disturbance.

- *Stranger danger*
  Most babies and toddlers are very wary of strangers, typically from around eight months to three years of age. If held by another person or left alone with a stranger, children will automatically return closer to their carer and will cry. Bowlby felt that attachment behaviours such as 'stranger danger' are instinctive. He suggested that fear of strangers is probably a protective device designed to prevent young children from straying into danger by leaving their principal carer.

Protest
A stage where the child shows distress – cries loudly, screams and may even show physical protest by kicking and throwing him or herself on the floor.
Children do not want to be comforted and want only to be reunited with the principal carer.

Despair
In this stage, the child appears to be calmer, even accepting of the principal carer's absence. The child may accept comfort from others, but his or her body language shows withdrawal and depression. He or she does not want to join in with others, and may cry quietly or show comfort behaviours, such as sucking his or her thumb or rocking.

Detachment
This stage is reached when the separation continues. The child appears to have come to terms with the separation, but has actually 'cut off' the relationship. If reunited with the carer, the child may ignore and show no signs of wanting a relationship with the carer.

Stages of separation anxiety.

Criticisms of Bowlby's work and subsequent research

Bowlby's theory of attachment is widely acknowledged to have 'set the scene' for explaining the importance and consequences of children having a secure emotional base. However, his work has been criticised by many developmental psychologists, while further research has expanded on his understanding of children's early relationships.

- *Quality of care*
  One criticism of Bowlby's work is that he failed to account for the quality of care provided. Subsequent research (for example, by the scientists James and Joyce Robertson in 1971) has suggested that where care is sympathetic to the child and surrogate attachments can be made, the effects of short-term separation are reduced.

- *Babies and children can make more than one attachment*
  Bowlby's early work has also been criticised for failing to explore whether babies and young children can make more than one strong attachment. Bowlby emphasised the role of the mother, and this led to some mothers being pressurised into staying at home rather than seeking employment. Later work suggested that babies and toddlers make a similarly strong attachment to those fathers who are involved with them.

- *The strength of attachments*
  Bowlby's early work did not concentrate on the quality and strength of attachments; this area was expanded further by the researcher Mary Ainsworth (from work published between 1971 and 1978). Ainsworth noted that the quality of a baby's

attachments affected his or her behaviour during separation. Children who are securely attached are more able to explore their environment, using their principal carer as a 'safe base'. Ainsworth suggested that a secure attachment is established as a result of the principal carer's sensitive and caring behaviour towards the child. Her research suggested three categories of attachment, as shown in the table below; the majority of children show type B attachments.

Ainsworth's categories of attachment

Category	Behaviours
Type A: Anxious Avoidant	The baby appears to be indifferent to its mother or principal carer, showing little or no distress during separation. The baby is easily comforted by others and ignores the mother or principal carer on their return.
Type B: Securely Attached	The baby is distressed when the mother or principal carer leaves and seeks immediate reassurance from the mother/ principal carer when they reappear. The baby then calms down and can resume play. Other adults can comfort the baby during separation, but there are marked differences in how the baby responds to the stranger and the mother/principal carer.
Type C: Anxious Resistant	The baby is clingy and difficult when the mother/principal carer is present. He or she has difficulty using the mother/principal carer as a safe base (unlike types A and B). The baby becomes very distressed when the mother/principal carer leaves and continues to show distress when they return. The baby alternates between clinginess and resistance to the mother/ principal carer; other adults cannot provide comfort.

Implications of attachment theories: settling in

For pre-schools, there are several implications of attachment theories. Firstly, it is important to recognise that many children even at three years of age are still likely to be affected by the 'stranger danger' instinct. Their distress when left in the company of people they do not know is genuine, and ideally you should be looking for ways of preventing this from occurring. This means providing a settling-in process that allows the child to form an attachment to a member of staff before being separated from his or her parents. This is the idea behind a key person system. Once the child has settled in, he or she should go on to develop several attachments, both with his or her peers and other members of staff.

Frequently asked questions

Attachment theory in practice

Q **Can leaving babies and young children in pre-schools or nurseries damage them?**

A There has been quite a lot of research into the effects of childcare on young children. The conclusions depend very much on the quality of nurture provided and whether a key person system is in place so that babies and young children have continuity and a person to whom they can make a substitute attachment. High quality childcare can be enriching for babies and children, although it is important that parents are still valued and act as first educators.

Loss and grief

Sadly, there are times when a child's main attachments are no longer available to him or her, possibly because of bereavement or separation of parents. In such instances, children will grieve. There are several theories of grief, but it is generally accepted that there is a grieving process through which both children and adults go. The phases of this process, however, are not automatic and clear-cut. This means that a child who one day appears to be coping well may on another day be particularly distressed. It is also important to be aware that there is no definite timescale to grief, so children may need continued support over several months and even years.

Phases of grief

1 *Disbelief and shock*: this is the initial stage of grief in which the truth of the situation is hard to bear.
2 *Developing awareness*: an acute stage of grief in which the realisation sets in that the person is gone. The implications are often hard to bear and strong feelings emerge, including guilt, anger and depression.
3 *Resolution*: the final stage of grief in which the person begins to come to terms with what has happened and re-establish a pattern to life.

While the grieving process can be seen to have three distinct phases, some grief theorists focus on the components of grief. R. Ramsay and W. de Groot outline nine components of grief (from work published in 1977) and their associated behaviours (see table on next page). The way in which children experience these components is widely variable.

Ramsay and de Groot's components of grief

Component	Features and feelings	Ways to support the child
Shock	Numbness, disbelief, apathy, disinterest.	Wherever possible, try to lessen the shock by preparing children ahead of time.
Disorganisation	Inability to cope; difficulty in thinking and organising; panic and anxiety.	Reassure the child. Make sure that he or she has plenty of time and support; keep to familiar routines and surroundings; provide close physical comfort.
Denial	Searching for the missing person; believing that there has been a mistake; refusing to accept that the person has gone.	Support the child but avoid false promises, especially in situations where parents have separated. Tell older children that this is part of the grieving process.
Depression	Yearning, pining; despair; intense sorrow; feelings of powerlessness.	Physically comfort the child. Be ready for the child to need objects and photos of the missing person, etc.
Guilt	Thinking that he or she is in some way responsible; assessing the ways in which he or she has acted.	Reassure the child that the loss or separation has not occurred because of him or her.
Anxiety	Can show itself in many ways: some children become concerned that the remaining people around them may also go.	Provide plenty of reassurance and understanding. Do not trivialise the child's concerns. Provide familiar routines and make sure that any changes are explained carefully to the child.
Aggression	Outbursts of anger against family and friends; anger and acts of aggression that may not have a particular cause.	Be understanding but maintain boundaries. Avoid punishment, confrontation or negative comments. Be ready to provide physical comfort. Activities such as role-play may help the child to express hidden anger.
Resolution and reintegration	Beginning to accept the situation; feelings of grief are less frequent, although they continue to emerge.	Be ready to allow the child to set the pace, but encourage him or her to join in with activities. Be supportive when, from time to time, grief reappears; for example, an event may cause the feelings of yearning and pining to return.

Personality development

The term 'personality' is generally used to describe the differences in how people relate to others. There are several theories of personality development, which can be categorised into three major approaches:

- biological, or trait, theories
- behaviourist theories
- psychoanalytical theories.

Biological, or trait, theories

Biological and personality trait theories are based on the idea that there is a genetic or biological component to personality. These theories reflect the nature element of the nature versus nurture debate (see page 56). They primarily look at how a child or adult behaves in certain situations or with other people. There are several variations of these theories but most suggest that a child is in some way partly pre-programmed to respond in certain ways, and that the child's responses will, in turn, affect the way that others respond to him or her. For example, some babies are born with an easygoing temperament that encourages parents and other people to respond in a relaxed manner.

Trait theories suggest that personality can be measured in some way. This has given rise to the common practice of carrying out psychometric tests by employers.

Behaviourist theories

Behaviourist theories suggest that the child learns and develops his or her personality in response to others. There are two strands to this approach:

- Firstly, children repeat behaviours and responses such as smiling because they are encouraged to do so by the adults around them. A mother, for example, may make more eye contact and smile back at a smiling baby; the baby thus learns to smile frequently.
- A second strand to the behaviourist approach is that babies and children subconsciously copy reactions that they have seen in adults. A child who often sees aggressive faces or is physically disciplined will repeat both these expressions and behaviour.

(For details of operant conditioning and social learning theory, see pages 76–8.)

Psychoanalytical theories

Psychoanalytical theories view personality as the result of what is happening inside the mind. The two most famous theorists linked with this approach are Sigmund Freud (1856–1939) and Erik Erikson (1902–94). While there are considerable differences in their theories, they share the belief that personality is shaped during childhood and reflects the way in which basic inner conflicts have been resolved. Both theories suggest that these conflicts and resolutions occur at different times in childhood.

> ### Sigmund Freud – the father of psychoanalysis
>
> Freud's work is considered revolutionary and has had a huge impact both on attitudes to parenting and the treatment of people with emotional problems. Freud was the first theorist to recognise that some of people's actions and speech, and facets of their personality, are not always deliberate and conscious. He suggested that people have a conscious and unconscious mind, and that the unconscious mind guides a person in ways that he or she does not realise. Freud's work led him to believe that childhood is fundamentally linked to personality and behaviour.

Components of the unconscious mind

Freud suggested that the unconscious mind consists of three main components. While the id is present at birth, the ego and the superego develop during childhood.

- *Id* – this part of the mind is purely interested in obtaining pleasure and having its needs met. It therefore represents the selfish part of our make-up. Freud suggested that the id was the only part of the unconscious to be present at birth.

- *Ego* – Freud suggested that the ego starts to develop in babies after a few months. It is the 'planning' component of the mind. While the ego thinks about consequences, it does so only to satisfy the id's desires and is therefore focused on its own rather than other people's needs. The ego is therefore amoral. For example, a child sees a biscuit; the id wants it and the ego thinks about how best to get it. If the biscuit is snatched, an adult may confiscate it; therefore asking for a biscuit politely may be the best means of obtaining it.

- *Superego* – later on in childhood, the ego learns to take into account the needs of the superego. This is the moral part of the unconscious mind and is subdivided into two parts: the conscience and the ego ideal. The conscience threatens the ego with guilt if it meets the id's desires in an amoral way, while the ego ideal rewards the ego if it acts properly.

Unconscious conflict

Freud argued that once all the component parts of the mind have developed, the ego is caught between the demands of the id and the potential punishment/rewards of the superego. The result is that the ego is trapped in a situation of great tension or anxiety, called unconscious conflict. Freud suggested that unconscious conflict causes people to have dreams, show neurotic symptoms and behave in certain ways.

Psychosexual stages

Freud also described how the personality develops during different stages of childhood. He suggested that both adults and children are driven by the biological instinct to procreate. This drive he called libido, or life force. Such ideas sexualised behaviour and were very shocking to Victorian society.

Freud argued that the libido develops through several distinct stages in childhood. Each stage is characterised by the ways in which the child gains pleasure from a different part of his or her body. The child's personality develops in line with this progression,

Freud's five stages of personality development

Age	Stage	Area of pleasure	Features of stage	Effects on personality and behaviour if *fixation* occurs
0–1 years	Oral	Mouth	Babies are gaining pleasure from feeding and sucking. They will also be weaned during this stage.	Behaviour linked to pleasures gained in the mouth, e.g. overeating, smoking, thumb sucking. Also naivety – 'Swallows anything they are told.'
2–3 years	Anal	Anus	Children are learning to control bowel movements. They learn that adults praise them when they master toilet training or can be angry with them if they do not.	Freud argued that if children were toilet trained too early and were too controlled, they would develop 'controlling' habits, e.g. extreme tidiness, meanness, stubbornness; if children did not have enough encouragement to become toilet trained, they would become over-generous, gushing in personality.
4–5 years	Phallic	Genitals	Children are exploring their bodies and are noticing their genitals. They are also learning about their gender. Freud felt that girls needed to adopt the gender role of their mother, while boys had to separate from their mother and follow the gender role of their father (see also the Oedipus complex).	Vanity, recklessness
6–12 years	Latent	None	Freud felt that this was a resting period for children in terms of their emotional development.	None
13–18 years	Genital	Genitals	Children are developing into mature adults. If they have passed successfully through the other stages, they will be able to make strong relationships with the other sex.	

depending on how the child adjusts to each stage. Interestingly, Freud's psychosexual stages link closely to the biological maturation of young children's bodies.

Children who have not satisfactorily passed through a psychosexual stage are likely to have part of their libido stuck or 'fixated' at that point. This in turn affects the development of the child's later personality and behaviours. Freud suggested that fixation occurs either because the child has not received enough pleasure, or because he or she has remained for too long in a particular stage. The reactions of the parents to the child are also seen to have an important influence.

The Oedipus complex

As part of the phallic stage, Freud suggested that boys have to deal with the 'Oedipus complex'. In the Greek tragedy by Sophocles, *Oedipus Rex*, Oedipus kills his father before falling in love with and marrying his mother. Freud suggested that this story mirrored a hidden reality – around 4–5 years of age, boys really do fall in love with their mother and become deeply jealous of their father. Freud argued that boys are therefore in competition with their father for their mother's love. However, they are also frightened that he will castrate them. This leaves the boy with an inner conflict: should he carry on loving his mother and risk his father's anger?

To resolve the Oedipus conflict, Freud suggested that boys attempt to befriend their fathers by copying their behaviour. While this part of Freud's theory has come under intense criticism, it is interesting to note that many boys do indeed hold onto their penises and begin to play in quite sex-stereotypical ways at this age.

Criticisms of Freud's work

Freud's work is seen as being revolutionary because he provided an explanation for dreams, phobias and conditions that appeared to have no medical cause. His work, however, has been widely criticised because his research consisted of subjective interviews and notes rather than comprehensive research. His work also involved adults rather than children, and he focused particularly on men rather than women.

Erikson's theory of personality development

Erik Erikson provides another key theory of personality development. He was originally a student of Freud, so his work was heavily influenced by Freud's theories. However, while Erikson agreed that childhood was crucial to personality development, he also suggested that aspects of personality continue to develop during adulthood. He suggested that, at key life stages, people are presented with different hurdles or 'dilemmas'. The way in which the individual copes with these dilemmas affects his or her ongoing personality development. For example, there comes a point when young adults have to decide whether they wish to settle down with a partner or whether they want to maintain their independence. Erikson's theory is outlined in the table on pages 67–8.

Erikson's stages of personality development

Age	Dilemma	Stage	Effects on personality
0–1 years	Basic trust versus mistrust	Babies have to decide whether the world and the people around them are safe and friendly or hostile.	If babies do not have their needs met, they may decide their world is a hostile one. This can mean they find it harder to form relationships later.
2–3 years	Autonomy versus shame and doubt	Children are learning to explore their environment and develop some control over their bodies and bowel movements. They may try to do things for the first time, e.g. dressing.	If children are not given encouragement to explore or are made to feel guilty about toilet accidents, they may feel doubt about themselves. This can mean they will be less independent when older.
4–5 years	Initiative versus guilt	Children are increasingly able to plan and carry out activities. They also need to learn about their gender role – similar to Freud's phallic stage.	Children need to feel they are independent, although they also need to learn what the boundaries of their behaviour are. Too much control may result in fearful, dependent children, whereas a very permissive attitude may leave children without any guilt or conscience.
6–12 years	Industry versus inferiority	In these years, children are comparing themselves to other children.	Children who experience failure and notice that they are not as competent in some areas as their peers, may lose confidence and feel inferior. Children in this stage who meet only with success may become over-confident and lack humility and empathy.
13–18 years	Identity versus confusion	Adolescents need to consider their identity – sexual identity and also what they wish to become in the future.	Ideally, at the end of this stage, adolescents have a firm idea of who they are and what they want to do with their life. If they have not worked through this stage, they may 'drift'.
19–25 years	Intimacy versus isolation	This age group may be considering whether to live alone or find a partner to settle down with.	Adults must decide whether to form a couple or stay single. If this conflict is not resolved, they may find themselves unable to commit to a relationship. *Continued ▶*

Age	Dilemma	Stage	Effects on personality
26–40 years	Generativity versus stagnation	Adults in this stage are often having their own children or are making progress in their careers.	In this stage, adults are trying to make an impact on the future. Most people have children or try hard in their careers. If adults feel they have not left their mark on life, they may feel bitter and resentful.
41 plus years	Ego integrity versus despair	Adults in this stage are thinking more about their mortality.	In this stage, adults are trying to come to terms with themselves and the way they have lived. They may feel satisfied and accepting of themselves or they may feel depressed and bitter.

Theoretical perspectives of intellectual development

There are several theories of how children learn. Understanding how these theories work can be very helpful when thinking about how best to plan for children's learning.

Learning theories can be broadly divided into three major approaches:

- Constructivist
- Behaviourist
- Social learning.

Constructivist approaches to learning

Constructivist approaches to learning consider children to be active learners and thinkers. There are three theorists in particular whose work has been very influential in terms of early years practice. Their work has been explored and developed further by others.

Jean Piaget (1896–1980)

Piaget's interest in children's thinking and logic began while he was working on intelligence tests. Piaget was fascinated by the way in which children regularly gave similar but wrong answers to some questions. He eventually concluded that children's logic is different from that of adults and began to explore why. Using his own children as a basis, Piaget wrote detailed observations about their development. He finally concluded that children 'construct' their ideas based on experience; this is why the term 'constructivist approach' is used in relation to his theory. Piaget used the term 'schema' to mean a child's conclusions or thoughts. Piaget felt that children's schemas would change as new pieces of information became known.

Assimilation

Child constructs a schema based on what he or she knows.

The lady at the nursery stays there because I always see her there.

Equilibrium

The schema remains the same whilst the child's experiences seem to confirm his or her ideas.

Every day, the lady at the nursery is waiting for me in the room.

Disequilibrium

The child has information that seems to cast doubt on his or her schema or idea. Things do not add up any more!

I am in a shop, but I can see the lady from the nursery.

What is she doing here?

Accommodation

Child adapts his or her thinking and constructs a new schema incorporating this new information.

The lady at the nursery doesn't stay there all the time.

The process by which children's schemas form and change.

Stages of development

As well as trying to understand how children's thinking develops, Piaget looked at the different stages of children's development. Piaget believed that children's thinking processes are linked to their biological development – the process by which structures develop within the brain. (Recent work on brain development now shows that children's brains do actually grow and develop from birth onwards.) Piaget concluded that these different stages of development are influential in children's thinking.

Piaget grouped children's cognitive development into four broad stages. He identified each stage by ages, although he did suggest that not all children would reach the final stage; the table on the next page outlines these stages. Note that subsequent work has suggested that Piaget may have underestimated children's development.

Piaget's four stages of cognitive development in children

Stage	Age	Features
Sensori-motor	0–2 years	Children develop physical schemas as they gain control of their movements. At around 8 to 9 months of age, babies begin to understand that objects continue to exist even if they cannot see them. This is known as object permanence and may explain why most babies begin to protest when their carer leaves the room.
Pre-operational	2–7 years	Children begin to use symbols to stand for things, for example, a piece of dough represents a cake. Language is also a way of using symbols. Children also show egocentrism – believing that everyone sees the same things or has the same thoughts as them. Piaget felt that children in this stage were easily tricked by appearances (see, for example, his experiments on conservation below).
Concrete operations	7–11 years	Piaget felt that this stage marks a significant change in children's logic: they are less easily deceived by appearances and can apply rules and strategies to their thinking. The term 'concrete' is used because Piaget felt that children were helped in their thinking when they could do and see things in practical ways, for example, physically counting out items.
Formal operations	11–15 years	In this stage, children are able to think entirely in the abstract, for example, they can multiply numbers in their head or read maps without having to turn the page.

Conservation

One of Piaget's tests to identify a key stage in children's development centres on the child's ability to 'conserve'. Conservation means understanding that certain things do not change in quantity or quality, even though their appearance does change. The classic conservation test involved taking a few buttons and placing them in a line. The adult then changed the position of the buttons by increasing the space between them.

Piaget suggested that young children find it difficult to conserve because they are easily taken in by appearances. This explains why

Piaget's classic conservation test using buttons.

children reach different conclusions from adults. For example, a three-year-old may think that a man wearing a women's dress has become a woman, or that a volume of water has changed simply because it has been poured into a different sized container.

How Piaget's work has affected early years practice

Piaget's work has had a huge influence on early years practice. Before his work was recognised, children's education was generally about getting them to remember knowledge; children were seen as passive rather than active learners. Piaget's work stresses the importance of encouraging children to learn from their direct experiences. This is sometimes referred to as active learning. Piaget's work has also been developed further by others. The educational psychologist Chris Athey has produced notable work looking at how children play and has produced a play theory based on schemas (published in 1991).

Criticisms of Piaget's work – Donaldson

While Piaget's work is hugely influential and highly regarded, his findings have subsequently been reviewed and criticised. Margaret Donaldson, an educational psychologist, challenged his work and considered other studies which repeated his experiments in different ways. Her book published in 1978 entitled *Children's Minds* was highly regarded. In the book she argued that children found it hard to complete the tasks of 'conservation' and 'decentration' (the ability to imagine what something is like from another perspective) because they were not meaningful and contextual. She cited examples of other studies which had made the tasks more child-friendly and had produced different results. A 'teddy' rather than an adult changing the position of the objects used in the conservation tests changed children's responses. Margaret Donaldson's work has been influential. She has shown how important it is for activities to build on children's knowledge, experiences and interests.

Vygotsky's theory of cognitive development

Lev Vygotsky (1896–1934) was a developmental psychologist whose work was influential in Russia in the 1920s and 1930s, but unknown in western Europe. His theory of children's cognitive development is similar to Piaget's; however, Vygotsky believed that children's learning takes place through the process of socialisation. He therefore placed great emphasis on the role of adults and other children in a child's learning. Because of the social aspect of Vygotsky's learning theory, it is often referred to as a social constructivist theory.

Vygotsky's view was that children are born to be sociable, and that by being with their parents and friends they acquire skills and concepts. He believed that learning is first done socially but that the child is able to subsequently internalise his or her learning. Language, which Vygotsky saw as fundamental to learning, is one example of the internalisation of learning. Speech is at first used to communicate socially with others, but then gradually the child learns that he or she can use speech to direct him or herself;

eventually this is done as an 'inner voice'. For Vygotsky, this explains why children often go through a stage of talking aloud, seemingly to no one in particular.

The role of the adult

For Vygotsky, those people surrounding the child play an important role in his or her learning. He saw the child as an 'apprentice' who learns by being helped and challenged by others. Vygotsky used the term Zone of Proximal Development (ZPD) to describe the relationship between a child's possible learning and his or her current abilities. The example below shows how a child's actual abilities and skills can be developed further through contact with others.

How Vygotsky's work has influenced early years practice

Vygotsky's strongest influence on early years practice has been in making practitioners aware of the importance of their role in developing children's thinking. Piaget did not stress the role of the adult, which led to a feeling among practitioners that if they provided a stimulating environment, children would learn for themselves.

Current abilities
Terri is five years old. She has quite good fine manipulative skills and wants to do the zip up on her new coat.

Learning through socialisation
*Terri's mum spends a few minutes showing her how to make the zip work.
Terri has a go herself and is encouraged by her mum.*

Development of skills and concepts
*Over a few days, Terri becomes increasingly skilled at doing her coat up.
She no longer requires her mum to help her. She has now learnt about how to do zips up.
Her skills and knowledge have been developed during this process.*

Developing skills through contact with others.

Preparation for assignment

Reflecting on the role of the adult in understanding and promoting development

Vygotsky and Bruner (see below) both saw responsive adults as being important in children's learning.

Try out the following observation:

1   Observe the way in which a child is playing.

2   Consider what skills the child has already acquired.

3   Think of a way of joining in the child's play and extending these skills.

4   Consider how you might be able to tell if your support has helped the child to learn.

Bruner's modes of learning

Jerome Bruner (1915–present) built on the work of both Vygotsky and Piaget. Bruner agreed with Piaget's view that children are essentially active in their learning and ready to explore their world. He also felt that some biological processes explain why children's logic develops in stages.

The importance of language in learning

In terms of Vygotsky's approach to learning, Bruner suggested that adults should adapt the ways in which they work with children to meet the child's immediate needs. The term 'scaffold learning' or 'scaffolding' is often used to describe the support an adult provides in a child's learning. This term was first used by David Wood and his co-workers (1976) but neatly sums up Bruner's approach to helping children learn. Bruner emphasised the way in which an adult may help a child to use language, for example, by asking questions that allow the child to solve a particular problem.

Modes of learning

While Piaget considered learning in terms of stages of cognitive development, Bruner considered learning according to the ways in which information is represented or stored.

- *Enactive mode*
  People often learn a skill by repeating physical movements, for example, learning to tie their shoelaces. Bruner suggested that this is the first cognitive skill that babies are

Bruner's modes of learning

Mode	Age	Description and use
Enactive	0–1 years	Learning and thought takes place because of physical movements.
Iconic	1–7 years	Thoughts are developed as mental images.
Symbolic	7 plus years	Symbols are used to help thinking, for example, language.

able to use. Bruner's enactive mode mirrors Piaget's sensori-motor stage, in which children are learning to control their bodies (see page 70).

- *Iconic mode*

    An icon is something that is visual. Bruner suggested that the iconic mode involves a person making a mental picture of things that he or she has experienced. You may, for example, shut your eyes and imagine the room. Bruner's iconic stage relates to Piaget's pre-operational stage during which children concentrate more on appearances; this is what confuses children during Piaget's conservation test (see pages 70–1).

- *Symbolic mode*

    Like Piaget, Bruner believed that, at around seven years of age, children's thinking changes dramatically. Bruner linked this change to the child's ability to use symbols and thus the use of language. In symbolic mode, thinking occurs without needing to have direct experience. For example, you may listen to the news on the radio and retain this information, even though you have not directly witnessed the events mentioned.

Bruner's work and memory

Bruner's work shows significant parallels to information processing theories. These highlight the way in which memory influences the ability to process information. In symbolic mode, people use language as a tool to trigger information stored in the memory. For example, the words 'Treaty of Rome' may help you to remember about that period of history, even though you were not present at the signing of the Treaty of Rome!

How Bruner's work has influenced early years practice

Bruner expanded on Vygotsky's work by showing how adults can stimulate children's thinking. Bruner's emphasis on the importance of language has also been influential. Bruner felt that the development of language is central to the child's ability to move from the iconic to the symbolic mode. This has meant that, for example, in the Foundation Stage curriculum, there is considerable emphasis on the importance of language.

Behaviourist approaches to learning

Behaviourist theories of learning consider the ways in which people learn by responding to events and other people. This approach is quite different from the other two theories of learning. Central to this approach is the notion that children and adults are in some ways recipients of learning, and that learning is particularly tied to what people experience and what happens to them. There are two separate theories within the behaviourist approach: classical and operant conditioning.

Classical conditioning

The key name associated with this theory is Ivan Pavlov (1849–1936). Pavlov was working as a physiologist looking at the digestive systems of dogs when he noticed that, at feeding time, the dogs would begin to salivate even though no food was present. Pavlov thought that this was because the dogs had learnt to associate certain noises with food, and thus would salivate just upon hearing the noises. He decided to investigate this effect further by carrying out a series of experiments. In one of his most famous experiments, Pavlov found that dogs that normally would not salivate if they heard a bell could be 'conditioned' to do so. By presenting the food and the bell together, the dogs learnt to associate the sound of the bell with the presence of food. After a short time, hearing the bell alone would make the dogs salivate.

Classical conditioning and children

This theory of learning is not seen as having widespread use with children. It does, however, explain some phobias and reactions that children may have acquired – that is, learning by association. You should also remember that a child's first visits and early separations from his or her parents must be happy, otherwise a child will associate coming into a setting with being unhappy.

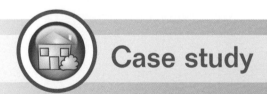 **Case study**

Jonathan's parents take him each week to the park. One day, while he is on the slide, he hears some very loud bangs. Some workers nearby are demolishing a wall. He cries. The next time he is in the park, he refuses to go near the slide.

1 Explain why Jonathan dislikes the slide.

2 Why will it be important to reassure Jonathan and to let him see gradually that the slide is harmless?

Operant conditioning

Put at its simplest, operant conditioning suggests that people learn and are influenced by the results of what they do. For example, if you try something and like it, you are more likely to do it again.

Thorndike's Law of Effect

The original idea of operant conditioning was put forward by Edward Thorndike (1874–1949), although he did not use the term operant conditioning. Thorndike showed through his experiments that the results of behaviour affected future behaviour. He called this 'The Law of Effect'. In his famous experiment, Thorndike put cats into boxes from which they could release themselves if they pressed a lever. He placed fish outside the boxes, which was visible to the cats. Gradually, the cats became faster at getting out of the boxes to get the fish.

Skinner's reinforcers

B.F. (Burrhus Frederick) Skinner (1904–90) built on Thorndike's theory in the 1950s and shaped it into the widely recognised 'Operant Conditioning Theory'. While Skinner partly accepted the work of Pavlov, he suggested that humans and animals were actually more involved in their learning and that they drew conclusions as a result of the consequences of their actions. He called the consequences 'reinforcers'. He suggested that there are three types of reinforcers:

- *Positive reinforcers*: these meet a need or desire, for example, gaining a sticker, winning a prize or enjoying an activity. Skinner suggested that positive reinforcers are the best and most effective type of reinforcers.
- *Negative reinforcers*: these result in repeat behaviour in order to prevent something from happening. For example, you learn to wear an apron because otherwise your clothes are spoiled.
- *Punishers:* these are strong shocks that are designed to prevent you from repeating an action, for example, learning to not touch a hot iron again. Punishers were seen by Skinner as being the least effective way of working with people.

Effective positive reinforcers

In early years settings, a variety of positive reinforcers are often used with children. These include stickers, praise and smiles as well as small rewards such as being the first to choose something. Food can be a strong positive reinforcer but it should not be used as there is a danger that unhealthy attitudes towards food will develop.

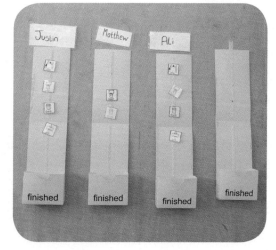

Positive reinforcers are often used with children in early years settings.

Attention and recognition as positive reinforcers

Many early years practitioners find that children will often repeat activities and behaviours if they receive some kind of attention or recognition. A child who is praised is more likely to do something again. Unfortunately, an adult's attention is such a powerful positive reinforcer that it can also lead to children showing unwanted behaviour in order to get an adult's attention. Thus, in some cases, ignoring a child's unwanted behaviour may be the best strategy, and then spending more time with the child once he or she is showing appropriate behaviour.

Operant conditioning and children

Operant conditioning is a powerful means through which children learn. It is used particularly in shaping children's behaviour. In terms of early years practice, it might help you to remember the following:

- activities need to be enjoyable as this will encourage children to repeat them
- children find attention a positive reinforcer and learn how to do things to gain adults' attention; this may include behaviour that is inappropriate.

Differences between classical and operant conditioning

The key difference between classical and operant conditioning is timing.

- Classical conditioning takes place when two things are presented at the same time and are thus associated together.
- Operant conditioning stresses that learning occurs after an action or behaviour.

Criticisms of the behaviourist approach to learning

Whilst most psychologists would agree that some of people's learning takes place in the way that Skinner describes, the behaviourist approach fails to account for why children's logic and conclusions about the world can be so different from those of adults. It is also a passive model of learning that relies heavily on adult input.

Social learning theory

Social learning theory, though simple, has widespread implications. At its heart is the idea that children learn by imitating the actions, gestures and words of others. The key theorist linked to this theory is Albert Bandura (1925–present). He showed through a range of experiments that children would remember and act out what they had seen.

Good practice

Social learning theory and children

This theory has strong implications for your practice with young children.

- *Behaviour*
  Social learning theory indicates that any behaviour you wish children to adopt should be modelled by you; for example, if you want children to share, they must see you being able to share. Equally, you need to be careful that children do not learn about inappropriate behaviour from you. An adult who shouts and whose tone of voice is aggressive is likely to find that children will learn this type of behaviour.

- *Working with children*
  Social learning theory also reveals that children often learn how to do things by being alongside and involved with role models. In some ways, this is the traditional way in which children learnt. Practitioners may, for example, sit with a group of children and play with dough; children will notice how the adult is handling the dough and be likely to copy.

The Bobo doll experiment

The most famous of Bandura's experiments is often referred to as the Bobo doll experiment. In this experiment, three groups of children saw a film in which an adult attacked a large inflatable doll (the Bobo doll). There were different endings to the film including:

- the adult being told off by another adult.
- the adult being rewarded with sweets and lemonade.

After watching the film, the children were put in a room with a range of toys including the Bobo doll. The children who had seen the aggression go either unpunished or praised were considerably more aggressive towards the doll. The experiment also showed that if the children were asked to be aggressive towards the doll, all of them could repeat the adult's actions they had witnessed.

Frequently asked questions

Social learning theory in practice

Q **Should children be told to say sorry?**

A This can be a hot topic amongst staff. Children can say sorry if they understand and know what they are saying sorry for. It is important that this is done when children are genuinely regretting their action. The danger of making it a blanket approach is that some children gain a lot of extra attention from the adult at the point at which they are showing inappropriate behaviour; this extra time and attention can sometimes act as a reward. In other cases, children can learn that by saying 'sorry' they can do anything to anybody! Encouraging children to help the other child or make the other child feel better in some way is often a better and low key approach.

Theoretical perspectives on language development

You have already looked at the way in which children develop language (pages 48–53). There are several different theories relating to language development that are useful to consider.

The behaviourist approach to language development

The behaviourist approach considers that the environment in which the child is brought up is critical to language development. Skinner, whose learning theory we considered on pages 76–7, suggested that language develops through positive reinforcement. He suggested that when a baby makes a sound, the parent is likely to respond. This in turn prompts the baby to continue to make sounds. Skinner used this process to explain why babies who at first make the same type of sounds regardless of their home language, will eventually learn which sounds to use. He suggests that parents will respond more to sounds that they recognise, for example, when a baby says 'dada' or 'mama', the parent is likely to smile more and pay greater attention to the baby.

There are many difficulties with the behaviourist approach to language development. Firstly, it fails to explain why children make 'mistakes' when they first speak. If the child is only learning to repeat language that he or she hears, then why do all children make similar mistakes? Secondly, this theory does not adequately explain why children's first sounds and words tend to be similar.

Nativist approaches

Nativist approaches to language development consider that people's ability to learn language is, in some ways, instinctive. A key nativist theory is that proposed by Noam Chomsky (1928–present). Chomsky suggested that a cognitive structure enables language acquisition; he called it the Language Acquisition Device. Chomsky argued that there must be some type of cognitive structure to enable humans to work out the rules or grammar of language, however complex they are. This theory explains why all babies make the same babbling sounds regardless of where they are born. It also explains why children all over the world seem to learn language in a similar way. Chomsky's view is widely recognised, but the role of adults in helping children to speak is still considered a major influence.

Is there a critical period in which language must be learnt?

It has been suggested that if children are not exposed to language in the first ten years of life, they will never develop the ability to speak. This idea points to a 'critical period' for language development. There is some evidence for and against this idea.

* Teenagers and adults who have been brain damaged as a result of an accident find it harder to regain language they have lost, whereas younger children with similar injuries find it much easier. This would support the idea of a critical period.

* Children who have suffered severe deprivation have still managed to acquire some language. One of the most famous examples of this is the case of Genie. Genie was 13 years old when, in 1957, she was rescued from an upbringing characterised by extreme deprivation. She had spent her childhood in appalling conditions: she was punished for making any sounds and was strapped and bound. When she was found, Genie could understand only a few words and essentially had no speech. Although she made progress in learning to speak, Genie struggled with the rules of language. The case of Genie casts doubt on the idea of a 'critical period' for language development, as Genie was able to develop some speech.

The constructivist approach to language development

The constructivist approach to language development centres on the use of language in helping children to think rather than on how language is learnt. Piaget, Bruner and Vygotsky all agreed that language and thought are linked, although Piaget differed in his views because he saw language as a tool. He believed that thinking required people to develop language to assist in their thinking.

In contrast, Vygotsky and Bruner both suggested that language organises and drives people's thought process (see also page 82 on language and cognitive development). Both suggested that the role of adults was crucial and that through social interaction, a child's thinking and language could develop. This approach is sometimes referred to as a 'social interactionist approach'.

Applying theory to your practice

Do you ever find yourself talking aloud? For example, 'Right, I have done that. Now I need to get out those...' Does talking aloud in this way help you to organise yourself?

Links between behaviour and development

Children's development can shape their actions and reactions. It is important to be able to understand the links between behaviour and development, as this allows you to consider how best to meet a child's needs. (See also pages 87–8 for strategies to help children learn about social behaviour.)

Understanding the term 'behaviour'

An important starting point is to consider the term 'behaviour'; it can be used in more than one way.

- In common speech, 'behaviour' often refers to socially acceptable or unacceptable behaviour. Expressions such as 'just look at that child's behaviour' are usually negative and quite judgemental.
- Psychologists use the term 'behaviour' to refer to the responses that people show, i.e. their actions and reactions. This way of using the term is neutral and often more helpful when considering children's needs.

Children's responses are affected by their development

The way in which children act is heavily influenced by their stage of development. Babies in the first few weeks cry because it is their only way of gaining attention. From around six weeks, crying usually decreases as parents become more skilled at understanding their babies' needs. The baby also learns to smile, coo and laugh.

Because of the link between development and behavioural responses, early years practitioners need a good understanding of each area of development and how it is reflected through a child's behaviour. The charts below show some of the behaviours that can easily be misunderstood, but that are directly linked to the child's stage of development.

Physical development

Physical development is about gaining control of movements. This allows the child greater independence. As well as learning to use and control movements, children also learn about their bodily needs.

Physical development

Behaviour reflecting the needs of the child	Link to development
A young child may prefer to stand rather than sit during activities.	The child can see what he or she is doing more clearly. Standing over an activity may also increase the amount of strength that the child can apply, for example, when rolling out dough.
A child declares that he or she is too tired to walk any more.	Young children are not aware of their body's needs and so do not realise that they are getting tired until the body sends out 'exhausted' messages. Children cannot pace themselves in the same way as adults.
A child runs instead of walks.	Young children enjoy the ability to move and running makes them feel good. An awareness of safety develops only later.

Cognitive and language development

Children's ability to digest and make sense of information is directly linked to their cognitive development. Language acquisition is also linked to cognitive development; thus significant changes to the way in which children think and act occur as they learn to use language effectively.

Cognitive and language development

Behaviour reflecting the needs of the child	Link to development
The child may flit from one activity to another.	A child's attention and concentration span develops with age and is directly linked to the way in which he or she processes information. Sensory activities usually help young children to concentrate for longer periods.
The child may fiddle when he or she is meant to be listening.	A child's ability to sit still and process the spoken word is limited until language is completely mastered. The child will respond best to active situations in which he or she can absorb information through a variety of senses. Children fiddle in order to meet their sensory needs.
The child may forget what he or she has been told to do.	Children are better at processing information visually rather than through words. Children may also find it hard to apply information to a different situation.
The child may show impulsive behaviour such as snatching.	Young children find it hard to think through the consequences of their behaviour. A child's understanding of the effects of his or her behaviour on others will develop much later.
The child may have a tantrum or outburst.	Tantrums and unexpected outbursts are usually linked to frustration and difficulties in expression. Once children can use language effectively and understand what is happening, these outbursts tend to diminish.

Emotional and social development

At the core of the child's emotional and social development is the need to feel settled and secure. Whether this need is met depends on the child's ability to form relationships with others. In addition, communication is essential to developing relationships. Children usually become more skilled at developing relationships with others when they have acquired some skill in language.

Emotional and social development

Behaviour reflecting the needs of the child	Link to development
A child protests when his or her carer leaves, or becomes very clingy to one member of staff.	Separation anxiety is powerful in young children and is marked by strong emotions. In order to cope with these feelings, the young child needs to form a close attachment to adults in the setting. The more settled and attached a child becomes, the more able he or she is to become independent.
A child takes things from another child.	Young children do not necessarily understand the notion of 'possession' and are quite impulsive. As a child's cognitive understanding and language develops, he or she is able to understand the concept of possession.
A child does not take turns.	Turn taking and co-operation is a skill that gradually emerges from around three years of age. It is linked to children's language development and their experiences of socialising with other children.
A child does not make friends.	While babies can be aware of other babies, many children do not play with other children of the same age until their language and communication skills are quite developed. Thus many children under three years old will not automatically play with other children.

Case study

Amanda is two and a half years old. She has started at her local pre-school. At the start of each session, she tries to stay near the play leader and follows her around the hall. She does not appear to be interested in joining in with other children, and will often just stand and watch.

1 Explain how Amanda's actions are based upon her stage of development.

2 Why is it important for staff to understand her needs?

3 Give one suggestion as to how Amanda's needs might be met.

The role of play in promoting development

Traditionally, play was seen as a trivial pastime in which babies and children indulged. The understanding of play is now more sophisticated: play is generally recognised as being essential to a child's growth and development. This understanding of play is the reason why the Early Years Foundation Stage and other early years curricula emphasise the importance of providing play environments and activities that encourage children to learn through play (see also Core Unit 2).

Examples of how play promotes development

In some ways, it could be argued that all play activities promote development. This is because any activity that engages children's thinking and physical activity will be beneficial. There are, however, some activities that work well with children across the age range to promote development, and as such are always worth providing. This is because they are sensory and provide children with open-ended challenges.

Water play

Water play is enjoyed by babies, toddlers and children of all ages. Water play encourages physical development but also develops concepts of capacity, space and measures.

Play that involves thinking can be very beneficial.

Paint and mark making

Mark making can begin as early as 15 months. The feel of making marks with crayons, paints, chalks and charcoals is enormously powerful. Children develop fine motor control, learn to express themselves and communicate through their marks.

Making dens and houses

Small spaces have enormous appeal for children of all ages. Tents made from sheets or curtains draped across structures provide children with an opportunity for role-play. As children's social skills develop, den making can become a co-operative exercise.

Cooking

Not only is cooking a good life skill, but children of all ages benefit by learning about measuring, making choices and also mastering tools. For cooking to be truly beneficial it is important to choose recipes that allow children to do plenty of things for themselves.

Equipment and materials that promote children's development

The charts below give some indication of the types of materials and equipment that can promote different areas of a child's development. While the charts indicate some broad age bands, remember that you will always need to consider the needs of the individual child.

Equipment and materials that promote children's physical development

Age	Examples of equipment and materials	The role of adults
1–2 years	**Gross motor**: sit-and-ride toys, brick trolleys, large cushioned bricks and shapes, swings, rockers **Fine manipulative**: pop-up toys, stacking beakers, large crayons, bricks, cuddly toys	Children are likely to learn how to walk at this time, and will be unstable at first. Close supervision is therefore essential as children are likely to bump into objects and fall over. Children's fine manipulative skills are still developing and a child may continue to use his or her mouth to explore new items. Close supervision of what a child places in his or her mouth is essential. Adults can help children to learn how to use toys by playing alongside them.
2–3 years	**Gross motor**: soft balls, sit-and-ride toys, tricycles, push-and-pull toys, small climbing frames, rockers **Fine manipulative**: simple jigsaws, pop-up toys, duplo, toys cars and trains, dough, sand, paint, tea sets	Children need to have enough space in which to run and explore their environment. They will need careful supervision and encouragement. Children often know what they want to achieve but may not quite have the physical skills to achieve it. Adults should look for signs of frustration and provide support where appropriate. *Continued* ▶

Age	Examples of equipment and materials	The role of adults
3–4 years	**Gross motor**: balls of different sizes, bean bags, obstacle courses, tricycles, pushchairs, climbing frames, slides **Fine manipulative**: dough, sand, scissors, floor puzzles, dressing-up clothes, cooking activities, construction toys	A child's sense of balance and general control is increasing. This means that many children are ready for new challenges, for example, walking on small walls or trying out an obstacle course. Children's fine manipulative skills are developing, which means that they require increasing opportunities to be independent and make choices.
4–5 years	**Gross motor**: bicycles with stabilisers, roller skates, stilts, tricycles, wheelbarrows, pushchairs, see-saws, balls, hoops, play tunnels **Fine manipulative**: junk modelling materials, paint, small construction kits, jigsaws, dough, water and sand, collage materials, board games	Children are beginning to enjoy co-operative games and may copy each other's behaviour. Supervision is still important but should be unobtrusive. Children's fine manipulative skills are fairly developed and they enjoy setting themselves challenges, for example, making a house out of a box or building a bridge for a train. Aim to offer support and help, rather than direct these activities.

Equipment and materials that promote children's cognitive and language development

Age	Examples of equipment and materials	The role of adults
1–2 years	Toy telephone, pop-up toys, lift-up jigsaw puzzles, picture books, items for heuristic play such as corks, wooden hoops, baskets, metal containers, plastic bottles	Adults need to acknowledge children's communication by smiling, talking to them and engaging them in simple rhymes. Children should be encouraged to explore their environment and to enjoy seeing the effect they have on materials. Heuristic play helps children to learn many concepts by playing with everyday materials.
2–3 years	Jigsaw puzzles, construction bricks, picture books, pop-up books, water and sand play	Adults need to listen carefully to children and act as their 'language partner'. Adults should not correct mistakes in pronunciation or grammar but recast the sentence using the same words. Books, nursery rhymes and songs also help children's language development. Children need time to explore and will enjoy making simple structures, either by themselves or with a little support. Adults need to be careful not to intervene too quickly as children will want to learn by trial and error. *Continued* ▶

Age	Examples of equipment and materials	The role of adults
3–4 years	Tape recorders, picture books, role-play, dressing-up clothes, floor puzzles, construction bricks and toys, interlinking train sets, objects to sort, magnifying glasses	Children's language should be increasingly fluent and recognisable. Adults need to model vocabulary in context, so that children can eventually add it to their repertoire of words and expressions. Adults should also share stories with individual children and small groups. Opportunities to make marks and 'pretend' writing should be built into play sessions. Adults should seek out interesting objects for children to touch and feel, so that they can explore the properties of materials.
4–5 years	Memory games, activities where children can set their own challenges, a large range of books and stories, feely bags, junk modelling, board games which encourage counting and symbol recognition	Adults need to look for ways of developing children's vocabulary so that they can express their ideas and feelings. Adults should provide games and activities that encourage children to do some simple problem solving. Adults must be aware that very directed activities will not give children scope to explore their own ideas.

Equipment and materials that promote children's social and emotional development

Age	Examples of equipment and materials	The role of adults
1–2 years	Toys that are familiar to children; rockers, see-saws and swings, which give children a physical sense of being rocked	Adults need to recognise a child's need for routine and security. A child will need to form a strong relationship to one or more members of staff. Children should also be allowed free access to comforters, as this helps them to feel secure.
2–3 years	Cuddly toys, pushchairs, tea sets and other props for role-play, so that children can act out their feelings	Children can get very frustrated; this may show itself as tantrums or tears. Adults need to look for ways of giving children choices and opportunities to be independent. Adults will need to be patient and think ahead to prevent situations from arising in which the child becomes upset.
3–4 years	Dressing-up clothes and small-world toys, such as farm sets and play people; materials such as sand, water, dough and paint	Adults should continue to look for ways of helping children to feel independent. This may mean encouraging children to, for example, tidy up, pour out drinks or prepare snacks. Malleable materials can help children to play out their feelings. Adults should also model descriptive words for feelings, for example, 'upset', 'angry', 'jealous', so that children can learn gradually to talk about how they feel. *Continued ▶*

Age	Examples of equipment and materials	The role of adults
4–5 years	Stories and books to help children talk about how they are feeling; dressing-up clothes and props; simple games and activities in which children can play together, for example, cooking, playing cards	Adults need to encourage children to understand their feelings and learn how to describe and manage them. Friendships between children are beginning to emerge. Adults can help children to play together by creating situations that foster teamwork.

The environmental, social and genetic factors which influence children's development

You have seen in earlier sections that development is a process. There are many factors that can influence this process, so it is useful to have some understanding of them. This section looks at the major influences that can affect a child's development.

Avoiding making assumptions

While few people would dispute that children's development is influenced by a variety of factors, it is actually very difficult to assess the extent to which an individual child's progress and development is being affected by any one factor. This is a complex area of study and whilst it is important to be aware of factors that affect children, it is essential not to fall into the trap of making assumptions about children. This can lead to children's needs not being fully met. A good example of this is the way in which it might be easy to assume that a child whose family are refugees is quiet because of the trauma of leaving his or her native country, whereas the child might be quiet because of a hearing loss.

Environmental and social factors

The place in which a child grows up can influence his or her development in a multitude of ways.

Housing

On a basic level, children need to live somewhere that provides warmth and shelter, and is clean and well ventilated. Sadly, these basic requirements cannot always be met because poor housing and poverty go hand in hand. Research suggests that poor housing can affect children's physical development because repeated infections stunt a child's growth. Higher levels of colds, lung infections and asthma are associated with poor housing. Poorly designed housing is also likely to result in more accidents as stairwells, balconies and kitchens may not be child-friendly. Overcrowding and lack of internal space can also make a difference to children's ability to play safely.

Access to safe outdoor environments

Children need fresh air and large-scale physical activity. This promotes good bone development, lung capacity and muscle strength. Vigorous outdoor activity also helps children to develop independence and confidence through learning to balance, jump and run. While some children are lucky enough to have a garden or access to a nearby park, other children are not as fortunate. They may be unable to take outdoor exercise frequently. Children who do not have access to a safe outdoor environment may be less physically skilful than other children and may feel less confident in large spaces.

Pollution

Ideally, all children need to breathe in clean air. The effects of pollution on children's health are only just being discovered. It is now thought that the increase in childhood asthma may be related to levels of air pollution.

Outdoor activity helps a child develop.

Safe environments

All children need to be kept safe, although they also need opportunities to explore their environment. This balance is quite hard to achieve, but most parents are aware of potential dangers and are able to provide adequate supervision and equipment to keep children safe. In some instances, children may be exposed to environments that are inherently dangerous. Where accidents occur, children's development may be affected; for example, a head injury can cause cognitive delay.

Access to pre-school education

Pre-school education can have a major influence on children's lives. The EPPE project which is carrying out ongoing research into the effectiveness of pre-school education has already reported that children who have had some pre-school education show increased capabilities in the first three years of formal schooling. Attending pre-school gives children increased opportunities for play and socialisation. Quality interactions between staff and children can also extend children's thinking and language skills. The importance of pre-school education means that children do not have access to provision locally might be disadvantaged.

Cultural factors

Each family lives in slightly different cultural circumstances, with different approaches to parenting. It is very hard to quantify the influence that culture has on individual children, which includes exposure to music, arts, language and food. Thus, some children will learn more than one language while others will listen to music traditional to their culture. The way in which culture affects a child's overall development is therefore virtually impossible to identify as, even within a culture, families have their own traditions and individual differences.

Culture can also play a part in attitudes towards parenting and education. You can sometimes see this in the pre-school as the parents' cultural background can influence their attitudes towards play. Some parents can see play as a fruitless activity and they may believe that children need to learn by being formally taught.

In the same way, parents may have strong beliefs about gender roles. Activities that are messy may not be deemed appropriate for girls whilst some parents may be concerned if their son is dressing up in girls' clothes. Where parents have these feelings, it is important that you are able to find ways of resolving the differences. It can be helpful to show parents the curriculum plans and the learning intentions for activities, and to encourage them to come into the pre-school and see the learning for themselves.

Case study

Zeynep's parents believe that children should be taught formally. They keep asking if the pre-school can give her homework so that she can learn her letters and numbers. They are happy for her to play but do not see that she is learning. They also prefer that she does not play outdoors with boys as they feel that this type of play is not desirable for girls.

1 Why is it important for Zeynep to spend time in playing?

2 Explain how you might work with the parents to reassure them and resolve this situation.

3 Why is it important to talk with parents about their expectations of education and play?

Family values and beliefs

Attitudes and beliefs change from family to family, and from generation to generation. This can contribute to the development of children in often very subtle ways, most notably in terms of social behaviour. Codes of social behaviour are partially learnt at home. For example, while some families eat around the table, others prefer to eat while watching television; some children have a very specific bedtime routine, others do not.

It is important to remember that the 'ideal' family does not exist and that, as children get older, they learn to adapt their social behaviour to suit the situation.

As well as social behaviour, families play a major part in stimulating children and helping them to learn particular skills. A child whose family enjoys board games may learn to roll dice at an early age, while a child whose family goes swimming every day may quickly learn to swim. Children also learn attitudes towards learning from their parents. If they see their parents interested and keen to gain new skills and knowledge, this is likely to rub off on them. This is one of the reasons why pre-schools see themselves as learning communities.

It is also important to recognise that some families will have strong beliefs that influence the care and upbringing of their children. These beliefs might be religious, social or moral ones. Such beliefs are important as they help the child develop a feeling of identity and this is linked to children's emotional development.

Genetic influences

Scientists are increasingly finding out about they ways in which genetic make-up affects human development. It has been understood for several years that genetics plays a major part in physical development and growth. Genes are responsible for children's height and other physical characteristics, such as eye colour and hair type. In addition, scientists are learning about the ways in which an individual's genetic make-up may predispose him or her to certain types of disease and illness. Asthma, for example, is thought to have some sort of genetic component.

While there is a clear genetic influence on physical development, there remains fierce debate as to the extent to which personality and particular aptitudes and skills are genetically influenced. This reflects the nature versus nurture debate (see page 56). Many scientists are reaching the conclusion that while genetic make-up predisposes people towards certain qualities, environmental triggers also play a role. For example, a child may be genetically predisposed to play music but also needs to be encouraged to sing or play an instrument.

How much of this child's personality will be influenced by inherited genes?

Chromosomal disorders

As well as inherited influences on development, some children have chromosomal disorders that affect their development. Many chromosomal disorders have no inherited component and are a chance occurrence – a result of nature's lottery. Normally, 23 chromosomes from the mother are combined with 23 chromosomes from the father.

In some cases, chromosomes are damaged or missing, or a new variation occurs. Changes to the usual chromosomal pattern can result in children's development being affected, for example, the ability to process information or to learn to communicate. The extent to which a chromosomal disorder will affect a child can vary enormously; thus two children with the same disorder may show different developmental progress.

Economic factors

The financial situation of a child's family can have some impact on his or her overall development. A child growing up in poverty is statistically more likely to have accidents, poorer health and leave school with a lower level of qualifications. It is for these reasons that organisations such as the Child Action Poverty Group campaign for an end to child poverty.

The reasons behind the statistics are quite complex, but a low income essentially means that a child has less access to those factors that contribute favourably towards the achievement of his or her potential, such as access to safe environments, good housing, diet and nutrition. Poverty also puts many emotional pressures on parents and these should not be underestimated. In a society that values material goods, living in poverty can undermine a person's self-confidence, which in turn affects the person's relationship and parenting skills.

Case study

Mario has recently come to this country with his family as asylum seekers after a solider shot his brother, who died as a result. The family has been housed in a one-bedroom flat and are living on a tiny weekly income. The children are aged three and four years and have few toys, outings or chances to play.

Consider the effects that living in cramped accommodation has on a child's physical development.

1 How might attending pre-school help children who live in poverty?

2 Why might a supportive pre-school benefit the whole family?

As with all influences on development, it is important to remember not to 'stereotype' a child who may come from a low-income family. Some parents are able to provide favourable conditions for their children despite their financial situation.

Nutrition and diet

The human body is a complex balance of chemicals and water. Food therefore plays an essential role, providing the body with the chemicals required to sustain health and well-being. Ideally, good nutrition should begin before conception and into pregnancy, as it is now known that the mother's and even the father's diet can have some effect on development. For example, it is thought that the mother taking folic acid supplements during the three months before conception and the first few weeks of pregnancy can prevent spina bifida (a disorder where the vertebrae in the spinal column do not form/ close properly).

In terms of a child's development, a balanced nutritious diet helps the child to fight off infection and provides his or her body with the nutrients or chemicals necessary for growth. A balanced diet will also provide children with sufficient calories, or energy.

In this country, very few children are under-nourished (receive insufficient food). However, a surprising number are malnourished, which means they fail to receive the appropriate balance of nutrients. Ironically, while some children are overweight or even obese, they are not necessarily getting the right nutrients.

Potential effects of obesity

The number of young children who are either overweight or obese has risen in the past few years. This is a worrying trend: in addition to not getting the nutrients they need, the extra weight may prevent the children from taking part in physical activity. This in turn can affect children's co-ordination as well as their ability to play alongside other children. The effects of children being overweight are still be researched, but it is already known that this can affect their social and emotional development. Children may develop low self-esteem as a result of disliking their body. They are also more likely to become victims of teasing and bullying as well as discrimination. The need to help children eat a healthy diet means that most pre-schools now provide fruit and vegetables as snacks as well as information and advice for parents.

Thinking and research

Using the Internet, find out the current levels of childhood obesity. You might find the website www.britishheartfoundation.org.uk useful.

1 What are the current trends in childhood obesity?

2 What effects does obesity have on children's later health?

3 Suggest one way in which the pre-school might have a role to play in preventing childhood obesity.

Lifestyle

It is worth remembering that the 'ideal' family does not exist, but that there exists a range of family structures. The nuclear family consisting of married parents and their children is no longer the 'norm', despite the way in which the media portrays families. In addition, contrary to popular myth, the majority of single parents are not teenagers but older parents, some of whom are widows and widowers.

Politicians and public figures often give the impression that one style of family structure is better than another style. Statistics to provide evidence in support of these ideas can be very misleading. A good example is that of single parents. While it may be true that children from single-parent families do less well academically, many people believe that the cause of this is not the family structure but the economic circumstances of the parent, or the conflict caused within the family by the breakdown of the parents' relationship.

In addition to family structure, lifestyle also includes whether or not parents work, how they use their disposable income and the way in which they socialise. Assessing the effects of lifestyle on children is very difficult with the exception of abusive situations where children are undoubtedly adversely affected. The key is probably to look at the support that a child gains from within the family. Children who feel secure are likely to thrive, regardless of the circumstances in which they live.

Using observation and assessment to promote pre-school children's development

As a professional working with children, you need to find out about their strengths and interests as well as their development. This information allows you to plan activities that will help children to benefit from the pre-school; it also helps you to identify children who need extra support. This section looks at the reasons why you observe children and the range of observation methods that are used to identify children's progress.

The National Standards, which are used to inspect pre-school settings before registration is awarded, emphasise the role of observations and record-keeping. This means that you will need to show that you plan and record activities based on observations of children.

Methods of assessing development

The words 'observations' and 'assessment' are often used together. It is helpful to understand the differences between them.

- An observation is a record that is kept while children are being watched. It is a tool for assessing children. The key advantage is that it provides you with your own picture of the child.
- Assessment is the process by which you consider children's growth, development and progress. You may compare a child's progress in relation to expected development for his or her age or to previous assessment on the child. Assessments are based on observations.

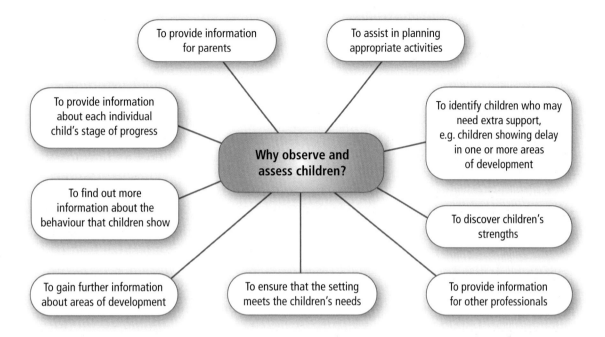

To provide information for parents

To assist in planning appropriate activities

To provide information about each individual child's stage of progress

Why observe and assess children?

To identify children who may need extra support, e.g. children showing delay in one or more areas of development

To find out more information about the behaviour that children show

To discover children's strengths

To gain further information about areas of development

To ensure that the setting meets the children's needs

To provide information for other professionals

Why observe and assess children?

There are many reasons why it is important to observe children. Firstly, it is the key way in which you can plan for children's progress and development. By observing children you can find out about their patterns of development and their individual interests. This means that you can plan more effectively to take account of their needs and, just as importantly, their strengths.

Observation and assessment can also help you to check that the provision in the setting is right for the child. You may see that a child finds it hard to play alongside other children, and from this realise that the child needs more adult support. Observations can also help you to notice whether a child is making progress or has particular strengths or difficulties. In this way, you can identify those children who need additional support (see also Optional Unit 2).

As well as helping you to be aware of children's development, observations encourage you to talk to parents and share particular highlights or concerns with them. This feedback is particularly vital where children attend extended sessions, as parents will need to know what their child's day has been like.

In addition, observations can provide information for other professionals when concerns about a child's development or behaviour have been expressed. Pooling information from both the child's parents and pre-school setting will help professionals to get a more rounded picture of the child's needs.

The role of observation and assessment in building a profile of individual children

All children are different and unique. This means that pre-schools keep individual records for each child. The aim of these records is to build a profile of the child based on observations, assessments, pictures and photographs, as well as information that parents might want to share. The aim of a profile should be to help you understand the needs, interests and strengths of each child. Profiles should be used to plan effectively for individuals and groups of children. They are also used to share information with others; for example, a child who is about to attend full-time school. Profiles should be contributed to by parents and shared with them. This is important as parents are able to bring a different perspective on their child as they see the child in a range of different situations. It is good practice for the child's key person to be responsible for building and maintaining the profile.

Building a profile and using it to further children's development is a process

The way in which individual pre-schools build a profile on children can vary, but it is worth seeing it as a process. The process involves collecting information from several sources, analysing it and then using it to plan for a child's development. It is important that a system is designed that is manageable, to prevent situations where records are not maintained. It is also important that the system supports and involves parents and finally, that it provides opportunities for assessment of the child.

The use of summative and formative assessment

Information gathered about the child has to be analysed. This is often an ongoing process where you might just add information about a child's progress or show that a child can now complete a skill or task. This type of ongoing assessment is known as formative assessment; it looks at the child in context with that child's progress. At other times information might be reviewed and a summative assessment produced. This is an assessment based on the overall picture of the child at that point in time – it is in effect a summary. Summative assessments usually show how the child's development links to what might be expected of children of a similar age. This can be useful as it provides a focus for adults and parents. Summative assessments might be used when a child leaves a setting, at fixed points in a year or if another professional needs information about a child.

Naturalistic observations

Naturalistic observations are ones that 'catch' children whilst they are engaged in an activity and are not structured. This means that an observer may simply

Naturalistic observations require you to watch children whilst engaged in an activity.

observe a child to see what he or she is doing rather than create a situation or use a pre-structured sheet. There is a growing trend to use naturalistic observations as they are convenient and not time intensive. Naturalistic observations have the potential to provide plenty of information across the developmental areas. The most common method of carrying out a naturalistic observation is to use a method called narrative or written record.

Narrative or written records

This type of observation method is known by several names, including free description, narrative and written records. The method itself is quite simple: the observer records what he or she sees. It is a popular method because it allows the observer to produce a 'picture' of a child's activity.

Using this method

The narrative records method is simple to use. You will need to decide what aspects of a child's development, play or responses you wish to focus on. This decision is essential because this is an open method of recording; without an aim, you are likely to find it hard to know what to record.

Make a note of the time that you begin the observation. Note down what the child is doing at the start of the record and who else, including other children, is present. Write down what you see as you see it, including the actions and responses of others towards the child. This should mean that you write in the present tense, almost like a sports commentator. Each time you stop or pause, you should note down the time. Most observers carry out this observation as non-participants so that they can be more objective. It can be hard to monitor and write down your own responses.

Advantages and disadvantages of narrative or written records

Advantages	Disadvantages
• Narrative records are an open method of recording. This means that you should have a large pool of information from which to draw. • This method provides a fuller and more detailed picture of the child. • This method does not require any special equipment or prepared sheets, so it can be carried out quite spontaneously.	• Narrative records are a subjective method of recording. Since it is impossible to 'catch' everything, the observer will continuously be making choices about what to focus on. • This is a tiring method of recording, so the observer will need to stop from time to time.

Key points when using narrative or written records

- Record only what you see, not what you suspect the child is thinking.
- Make your notes as detailed as possible.
- Note down body language and facial expressions.
- Try to 'catch' speech as well as movements.

Snapshot observations

Some pre-schools find it helpful to carry out snapshot observations on children. Snapshots are brief notes and have been adapted from the written records technique. They are extremely popular in pre-schools and nurseries. Using post-it notes you jot down what the child is doing. As the name implies, snapshot observations are extremely brief; during a session you might observe several children doing different things. It is important that the snapshots are collated and that a system is developed to ensure that all areas of the curriculum

14/11/05   14.55 pm

Ayse
Turns head when she hears a voice outside focuses and then smiles when she sees Charlie

Example of a snapshot observation carried out on Ayse, aged four months.

or developmental areas are assessed. It is also useful to put the child's name on the top of the post-it note when you are hoping to carry out snapshots about several children. It is also important to put the time and date of the snapshot.

Sociograms

Sociograms are a way of identifying children's friendship preferences and the reciprocity of those friendships. They are not a perfect tool, especially with children under four years old as most children choose their playmates according to the play activity rather than a friendship loyalty. There are different approaches to constructing a sociogram. The method described below is used as a starting point and as a way of listening to children about who they like to play with. Sociograms are not strictly an observation method as they rely on what children tell or show us rather than direct observation.

Using this method

The simplest way of using this method is to ask children when they are alone, who they most enjoy playing with or alternatively show them photographs of other children in the group. You then need to write down their responses. (You might also be interested in finding out what they like doing with this child, such as playing outdoors, as this can help you build up a picture of whether children are choosing playmates on the basis of shared play interests.)

Once you have talked to each of the children in the group, you can see whether there are any children who are not named by others, and also which children seem to name each other. Note that whilst you might find that some children are named more frequently than others, you cannot assume that children who are rarely or not named do not have friends or are not popular. The next step is to observe individual children and see the quality of their social interactions. This can be done using a variety of methods, such as target child or event sampling.

Example sociogram

Name of child	Who they named as play partners	Comments
Mustaf	Stephen, Ellie, Tommy	Quick to find Stephen's photo
Stephen	Mustaf, Simon, Tommy	Talked about role play and being outdoors
Jacob	Amy	Seemed to have difficulty in picking out any photos

Advantages and disadvantages of sociograms

Advantages	Disadvantages
This method can identify children who may need support with social skills.	There are many variables as children may not remember about friends who are absent or they may give a name based on who they last played with. This is a recording method that should be used as a starting point.

Time sampling

Time sampling is a useful method of recording because it allows the observer to look at a child for longer periods. This method can also be adapted to focus the observer on particular areas of development.

Using this method

A time sample records a child's activity at regular points during the observation, for example, every five minutes over an hour or every ten minutes over a session. You will need to begin by preparing a sheet.

At its simplest, time samples are just the times followed by a short narrative about what the child is doing. At the allotted time, you simply write down what the child is doing. You can adopt the 'running commentary' style used in free descriptions (see above). However, as the idea behind this method is literally to 'sample' what the child is doing, you should keep your observations brief so that they provide a 'snapshot'.

Advantages and disadvantages of time sampling

Advantages	Disadvantages
• Time sampling is a simple method that provides an easier way of noting down what a child does over a long period than, for example, free description. • It has the potential to build up a picture of a child's activity during a day or session method • The method can be used to gain information about several developmental or curriculum areas.	• The simplest type of sampling can be very subjective. • There is a danger that interesting activity falls outside of the 'time slot'.

Using a more structured sheet

Time samples can be made more focused by adding columns that record specific behaviours, for example, speech, activity and social grouping. This type of time sampling has the advantage of focusing the observer on specific behaviours, which is likely to make the observation more objective.

Longitudinal observations

Sometimes it is helpful to build a picture of a child over time to see the rate of developmental progress which the child is making. It can also help to see whether strategies and support provided for that child have been effective. When observations are completed regularly over a number of weeks, the term longitudinal is used. Ideally, alongside a regular pattern of observations, a range of observation methods should also be used. Longitudinal observations are good for noticing changes in patterns of behaviour or progress in development.

Event samples

An event sample is a really useful observation method. Traditionally used to look at children's unwanted behaviour, the method can however be used much more widely to help you learn more about a child.

Using the method

This is not a 'traditional' observation as recording takes place only when a child shows a particular behaviour – the 'event'. Thus, if you want to look at how often and in what circumstances a child talks to an adult, for example, you will record only when this happens. This method is therefore used to look in detail at a child's specific activity or behaviour.

Begin by identifying what information you need to collect to find out more about the 'event'. You may wish to record the time when the event occurs, whom the child is with, and where it happens, as well as other information specific to the aim of the observation. Next, prepare a sheet on which to collect the information. For each type of information to be recorded, add a column on the sheet. It can also be useful to add a comments column, because you may wish to record additional information. An example event sample sheet is shown below.

An event sample sheet

Date	Time	Type of interaction	With whom?	Where?	Comments
23/11/05	10.05–10.07am	Child-initiated	Naseer	Sand tray	Playing side by side.

Advantages and disadvantages of event samples

Advantages	Disadvantages
• Event samples are a useful way of doing some 'detective work' about a particular aspect of a child's behaviour or activity. • This method assesses the frequency with which the chosen 'event' occurs; it can therefore be used over time to see whether strategies or support for that child have been effective.	• This method may require the assistance of other people as you may not have seen the 'event' yourself. In this way the observation's validity and objectivity are called into question. • Event samples do not work well if the prepared sheet has not been thought through carefully.

Voice recording, photographs and filming

As well as traditional paper-based methods of observing children, you can also use different media. Voice recording, digital photographs and filming children can all be useful in gaining information about the child. They can also help you to 'see' things that you might otherwise miss whilst trying to write. These methods must only be used with specific parental permission and you should also be ensuring that they can be kept confidential and properly stored.

Voice recording using Dictaphones or MP3 players is very useful in order to assess children's speech. By comparing previous recordings, you can see whether children's speech has become more complex or more intelligible. In the same way, filming children can reveal whether their physical movements are showing greater co-ordination and skill. These methods are often liked by parents as they provide a lovely record of their child at pre-school and parents can be presented with them when the child leaves.

Checklists and tick charts

Checklists and tick charts are very simple to use. A sheet is prepared with a list of statements. The observer needs to read carefully through the tasks or skills and note whether a child is able to do them; a tick or remark is recorded on the prepared sheet accordingly. The observation can be done unobtrusively, by simply watching the child and hoping that he or she will show the skills to be recorded, or as a participant, by asking the child to do the required tasks.

Designing checklists and tick charts

Many settings have commercially prepared checklists and tick charts, which are often based on developmental milestones. It is possible to design your own checklist or tick chart, but you will need to think carefully about what information you wish to collect. Designing your own checklist or tick chart has many advantages, as you can add more detail.

When to use this method

Checklists work well when the wording is accurate and focused. This tends to mean that they are suited to consider aspects of children's development, for example, 'Can count three buttons without touching them' or 'Turns head in response to sound'. This method can establish a baseline which means that you can carry out a follow-up at a later date and look out for progress.

Using this method

This method needs a little preparation. It is important to have the checklist sheet in front of you and to read it first. This way you will be able to focus on observing the child rather than on the sheet. It is also important to decide whether you will need to ask the child to complete tasks or whether the context in which you observe the child will

Advantages and disadvantages of tick charts and checklists

Advantages	Disadvantages
• Checklists and tick charts are simple to use. • They can provide an ongoing assessment. • They are useful for assessing development and concepts.	• Overuse of tick charts and checklists can produce children's records that are ineffective. • The design of some tick charts and checklists can be poor.

provide evidence of the skills. It is important also to remain as objective as possible, especially if the checklist statements are open ended; for example, 'can cut with scissors' is a generalised statement but probably means that the child has sufficient proficiency to cut evenly and follow a line rather than just snipping.

Factors to consider when making observations

There are many factors that need considering when carrying out and also analysing observations.

Consulting with children in appropriate ways

The focus on empowering children means that it is now good practice to involve children in their care and education. This includes observations. Involving children may mean talking to them about what you are doing whilst you are observing them, showing photographs or playing back soundtracks to them. It also means respecting children so that if they tell or show you that they do not want to be watched as they play or take part in an activity, you stop. Consulting with children may also be asking children for their feedback about what they enjoy doing. With the very young child, you might take in a teddy and ask the child what Teddy would most enjoy doing. You can also give children cameras and ask them to take photographs of their favourite activities, equipment and friends. This information can be helpful in getting a child's perspective.

Working in partnership with parents

You know that working closely with parents and valuing their role as first educators is important in the pre-school. In terms of observations, this means sharing what you have

Working closely with parents and valuing their role as first educators is important in the pre-school.

observed and your thoughts with parents. This is an essential part of working effectively. As parents will have given permission to carry out observations in the first instance (see below) and observers will, wherever possible, have developed a day-to-day relationship with them, sharing observations should not be difficult. It is also good practice to find out information about children's responses at home and in other situations where parents are with their child. This is because children do show different skills and reactions when they are in the home setting. Where there are concerns about a child's development, it is important to pool information with parents.

Key points to remember when talking to parents

- Explain the limitations of the observation method.
- Focus on the child's strengths as well as development areas.
- Be honest and straightforward about what you have seen.
- Ask for parents' views.
- Talk through ways in which the child might be helped.

Gaining permission

Years ago, parents had few rights in relation to what was written about their children. Fortunately, this situation has now changed, reflecting the trend that parents should be seen as equal partners in the care and education of their children. It is now accepted practice for parents to give permission before observations are carried out on their child. Information gained from these observations should be shared with parents, so that a proper exchange of information and views can take place.

The law regarding information that is held about people has also changed. The Data Protection Act (1998) at first applied to personal information that was held on a computer only. This Act has subsequently been amended so that anyone can ask to see any type of written personal information, including handwritten notes. This means that parents have a legal right to look at and, if necessary, challenge what has been written about their child.

Confidentiality

As well as checking that parents are happy for their child to be observed, it is important to understand that any records or information about individual children is confidential. Breaching this confidentiality is a breach of trust, which is treated as a disciplinary matter in many settings. Thus, records of observations should be stored securely and shared only with those who should have access to them. Parents' permission should always be asked before any information is passed on to people outside the setting, for example, speech and language therapists.

Key points to remember when observing children

- Check that parents are happy for their child to be observed.
- Share information about what you have observed with parents.
- Make sure that the recorded information, and the way in which it is written, is accurate.
- Store records and information securely.
- Do not share information other than with those who should have access to it.

Limitations

A good starting point is to remember that observations and assessments have serious limitations. You must never assume that you 'know' the child based solely on a few observations. Children will show different skills and attitudes in a range of situations. Observing a child in only one situation will fail to provide a rounded picture of that child.

Comparison of methods of observing children

Method	Uses	Individual	Group	Advantages	Disadvantages
Written/ narrative record	All areas of development	Yes	No	No prepared sheet is required; a flexible method.	Difficult to maintain recording; may miss information; potentially subjective.
Time sample	All areas of development; understanding interests	Yes	Yes	Useful for observing an individual or small group of children over an extended time.	Interesting responses or behaviour may fall outside of the time slot.
Checklist	Skills and concepts	Yes	Yes	Simple method of ongoing assessment.	Overuse and poor design can produce records that are ineffective.
Event sample	Specific behaviours and responses	Yes	No	Useful for monitoring specific aspects of a child's behaviour or responses.	Recording sheet has to be well designed; other staff may not notice and fill in sheet.

Continued ▶

Method	Uses	Individual	Group	Advantages	Disadvantages
Sociogram	Development of friendships	No	Yes	Useful to identify children who are not settled within the group.	Is not reliable with children under four years; many factors may affect the outcome, e.g. if a particular child has been absent for a while.
Sound recording	Language	Yes	No	Can be replayed which makes analysing language easier.	Sound quality can be poor; other children may also be recorded at the same time.
Filming	All areas of development	Yes	Yes	Helps bring observations to life; parents enjoy having a record of their children.	Other children whose parents have refused permission may stray into shot; can be an intrusive method for children and other staff.
Photographic	All areas of development	Yes	Yes	Helps bring observations to life; parents enjoy seeing photos.	Other children whose parents have refused permission may stray into shot; does not show what has happened before or afterwards.

Validity and reliability

Several factors may influence both the type of observations that are carried out and the way in which this is done. It is important to understand these factors as they can affect the validity and objectivity of the observation.

Participative versus non-participative

It is important to understand that a person's performance changes when the person knows that he or she is being observed. In some cases, being watched can improve and enhance performance; in others, it may adversely affect performance. Children, too, react differently when they are being observed. Thus, methods in which the observer asks the child to do something or interacts with the child may produce slightly different information from other methods in which the adult is unobtrusive or non-participative.

In terms of observation methods, there are advantages to the adult being present with the child. The adult can clarify what the child is trying to do, or ask the child to do a particular task in which he or she may not otherwise choose to engage.

Open versus closed data

Observing children is not quite as easy as it may seem at first glance, since there is potentially much to watch. Because it is impossible to note everything down about a child, the observer will have to be selective. This means that two people watching the same child at the same time may note down very different things.

Some observation methods are designed to make the observer more objective by providing closed data; a checklist is a good example of a closed data method. These methods focus the observer on specific things that a child does; for example, noting whether a child can build a tower of three bricks. The observer is not required to note down any additional information, for example, how the child is doing the task or whether he or she is enjoying it.

Open data methods allow more freedom for the observer to note down what he or she believes to be relevant. This has the advantage of providing a larger pool of information. However, the disadvantage of open data methods is that they are likely to be more subjective.

Preparation for assignment

Using observation methods

- Choose a child to observe.
- Use three different observation methods.
- For each method, write about its effectiveness.

Methods for assessing development

Carrying out observations, collecting children's work and gaining information from parents forms the backbone of developing a profile for individual children, but it is essential that time is taken to do some analysis. Analysing a child's progress may help you to determine whether a child may need additional support. It will also help you to plan more effectively and base your planning on children's interests. It is therefore useful to both write some notes at the time an observation is carried out or other information is inserted into a child's records, but also to periodically carry out some summative assessment.

Analysing specific observations

It is always worth making a few notes about a recording as soon as possible afterwards, when it is fresh in your mind – a week later, the impetus will have been to some extent lost. Below is a list of questions that might act as triggers when analysing an observation.

Questions when analysing observations

- What did you specifically notice about the child?
- How has the child changed or progressed since your last recording?
- Were there any new skills or development of skills that you noticed?
- What was the child interested in?
- How sociable was the child?
- Did the child seem aware of other children or adults?
- Was the child engaged by the activity?
- Did the child seem relaxed and positive?
- What have you learnt about the child from this recording?
- What positive information will the child's parents enjoy hearing about?
- Are there any aspects of the child's development that give concern and need sharing with parents? (See also the section on identifying developmental delay on pages 110–11 and Optional Unit 2.)

Assessing using early years curriculum frameworks

The current frameworks in England for early years encourage adults in the pre-school to look at children's development. The curriculum in England breaks into steps the skills and attitudes that children need in order to progress towards the Early Learning Goals. This is helpful as you can look at children's progress not just in the context of the developmental areas but also in terms of curricula areas. By identifying a child's current development, you can plan using the guidance and the ideas within it, to provide further activities for children. In addition, many early years services have produced their own 'profiles' for pre-schools and nurseries to use in support of the curricula. It may therefore be useful to look at what is available in your local area.

Assessing children's development against milestones

A good starting point when analysing observations is to look at children's normative development or milestones. This is particularly useful when developmental delay has been suspected. It also provides a context in which to think about the needs of the child.

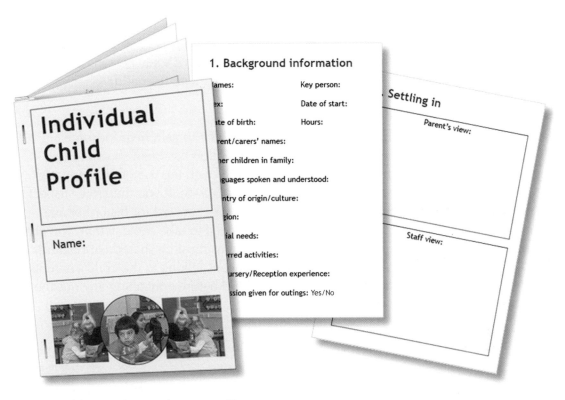

1. Background information

Names: Key person:

ex: Date of start:

te of birth: Hours:

rent/carers' names:

er children in family:

guages spoken and understood:

ntry of origin/culture:

gion:

ial needs:

rred activities:

ursery/Reception experience:

ssion given for outings: Yes/No

Settling in

Parent's view:

Staff view:

A section of the Lewisham Early Years profile.

However, it is important to remember that charts of normative development are a guide only and that children's development can show variations.

Considering children's developmental needs

Observations and the information they provide can help you to focus on the support and challenges that children need. Identifying developmental needs is about thinking of activities, support and equipment that will be of benefit to the child. A good approach when thinking about how best to meet these needs is to work out what the next steps will be in the child's development. For example, a child who is able to complete a small jigsaw puzzle may enjoy the challenge of something more complex; a baby who can bang his or her beaker up and down in the highchair may enjoy banging together a spoon and a lid.

Thinking about children's developmental needs allows you to check that activities are suitable or are adapted to meet the needs of individual children. This is very important because across a group of children of the same age, there will be variations in each child's developmental needs.

Recording children's next steps

It is helpful as part of this process if some formal recording of children's progress, interests and possible next steps are recorded. This can help with planning but also provides a baseline for future reference. Some settings do this by regularly 'reviewing' children's profiles and producing a summative assessment. This is contributed to by parents and is shared with them. This can be done by the child's key person but it should be shared with members of the adult team who also work with the child.

Identifying developmental delay

Analysing children's progress is an essential way in which to gain help for some children who have developmental delay. Early intervention has been shown to be very effective, even where this is provided in-house through the use of differentiated activities or Individual Learning Plans (see also pages 145–6). If you therefore suspect that a child's development is very different from what is expected for his or her age, even where there has been some progress, you will need to take some action. The SEN Code of Practice 2001 states clearly that these concerns must be shared with parents as you are working in partnership with them. This means talking to the child's parents about your observations and your analysis of the child before contacting any outside professionals.

Case study

Stacey's key person, Kerry, had noticed that her speech was not particularly clear given her age. She talked to Stacey's mum about this and it was agreed that together they would keep an eye on it. Stacey's mum also said that at home she tended to be quite frustrated and her behaviour was not always easy to cope with.

Kerry looked at Stacey's profile and, by using targeting, added to it some observations around speech and language. Kerry and Stacey's mum decided that whilst there was some progress, Stacey would benefit from getting some further support. Stacey's mum decided to go and see the health visitor. The health visitor referred Stacey for a hearing test. The hearing test showed that Stacey was not fully hearing and that this was affecting her speech. Stacey was given a hearing aid and this made a significant difference. Her behaviour changed and overall she seemed much happier. Her speech also improved and this meant that she talked more and found it easier to play with other children.

1 Why is it important to share information with parents?

2 How can early identification benefit children and their families?

3 Explain the role of profiles in supporting children with developmental delay.

Talking to a child's parents about developmental delay requires tact and awareness, and it can be helpful to agree with the parents that further observations are undertaken. It is always easier where there are strong partnerships with parents so that there is a level of mutual trust and support. It is also worth thinking about the time and place where you might talk to parents about your concerns. Where parents also believe that a child is showing signs of developmental delay, they may wish to consult their health visitor or GP, who will then refer the child to the appropriate services (see also pages 362–4). Sometimes outside referral will not be necessary and together with parents, you may decide to help the child by providing an individualised programme or additional support in some areas.

Reflecting on practice

Finally, in addition to thinking about the information gained directly about the child, it is important to consider your own and your setting's practice. It is a good idea, especially when considering a child's concentration, distraction levels or communication, to think about whether the activities and layout of the setting have an influence on the child. Reviewing several children's profiles may also lead to a pre-school becoming aware of its own strengths and weaknesses in its provision. You may find, for example, that children are making excellent progress in early mark making and name recognition, but are less interested in early number. This may indicate that further training and development is required in this area of the curriculum. In the same way, you may notice that whilst babies and toddlers are making good progress with their speech, few children choose to take a book to an adult. This might mean that adults in the setting need to take more opportunities to get out simple picture books and look at the pictures with babies.

The effect of relationships on children's development

Children do not learn and grow in a vacuum. People around them, including siblings and other children, all have an input or effect on their development. This section looks at the way in which relationships and communication can benefit children.

The importance of providing choice and decision-making opportunities

It is increasingly recognised that children benefit from being empowered. Empowerment means looking for ways of helping children to take responsibility and ownership over their life. The idea is that through becoming self-reliant and learning competence, children will develop a strong self-esteem. The concept of empowering children is reflected in the early years curriculum as well as in Every Child Matters (see next page).

In terms of working with young children, empowerment means involving children in decisions and providing opportunities for choice. The key for adults is to assess children's stage of development and to make sure that opportunities are given for children to take some control. A ten-month-old baby, for example, might want to try to feed himself and so the adult will look for an extra spoon, whilst a group of four-year-olds might be asked by the adult in the pre-school about their play interests and be encouraged to get out the equipment and toys that they need by themselves.

In order for children to learn about making choices and decisions, it is important that choices and decisions are meaningful for them. Offering choices between sizes of paper may not be a real choice if children did not want to sit and do the art activity in the first place! It is also important to respect children's choices so comments such as: 'You don't really want that one, do you?' should be kept to a minimum. This might mean that sometimes children make 'mistakes', but even here it is worth remembering that this is how children learn. A child may, for example, insist that he or she would like to use glue rather than sticky tape to hold a model together. Whilst you may explain the disadvantages, allowing the child to experiment and discover this for him or herself is useful and safe learning.

The early years curriculum stresses the importance for children having opportunities for child-initiated activities, sometimes referred to as 'free play'. This is a key way in which children can take responsibility and make decisions, and forms a major part of pre-school provision. It is also important to help children learn to take responsibility. This might mean that you encourage children to help themselves to the toys and equipment that they need, but gently remind them that they will need to put them back later on.

Every Child Matters: Change for Children

Every Child Matters is a programme designed to improve children's lives. The programme was a direct result of the Laming Inquiry (2003) which followed the death of Victoria Climbié. The programme places better outcomes for children firmly at the centre of all policies and approaches involving children's services. These outcomes are:

- be healthy
- stay safe
- enjoy and achieve through learning
- make a positive contribution to society
- achieve economic well-being.

The programme has been embedded into legislation via the Children Act 2004. A major guiding principle of Every Child Matters is to empower children so that they go onto make healthy and safe choices; this includes being able to take up opportunities. The outcomes of Every Child Matters are forming the backbone of inspections in England.

Thinking and research

Using the website www.everychildmatters.gov.uk, think about how helping children to be responsible for choices and decision making links to the aims of Every Child Matters.

Good practice

Ways in which the pre-school may encourage children to make decisions

The pre-school is an excellent environment for children to experience decision-making and choice. Below is a list of ways in which adults in the pre-school might encourage choice, responsibility and decision-making:

- use treasure basket and heuristic play for babies and toddlers so that they can learn to explore freely (see page 165)
- provide opportunities for child-initiated 'free play' so that children choose their own play interests and take responsibility
- provide opportunities for children to make their own snacks and drinks
- look for ways of providing a selection of materials, e.g. collage, junk modelling
- ask children to set their own boundaries on games
- encourage children to ask questions about what is happening.

Helping children to make relationships with adults and other children

Children need support in order to make relationships with adults and other children. In the pre-school you can help children make relationships in many ways. The starting point is probably to ensure that during the settling-in process, a child's relationship with his or her key person is strong. This means that the key person needs to:

- take time to learn about the child
- show genuine interest in the child and his or her family
- be responsive to the child.

In some ways the importance of this first relationship in the pre-school cannot be overemphasised. Children who are comfortable with their key person are more likely to feel emotionally secure enough to build relationships with others.

Once a child has settled in, a key person should look for ways of helping a child join with other children and of helping him or her to become used to other adults in the setting. This can be done by informally 'introducing' the child to others. You might, for example, suggest that you find some others for a game or show another member of staff what you are doing.

You can also help children by 'thinking aloud' so that children learn about how your actions might affect others. You may, for example, say: 'Jack looks a little sad. Perhaps that is because he is looking for someone to play with. Let's go and see him.'

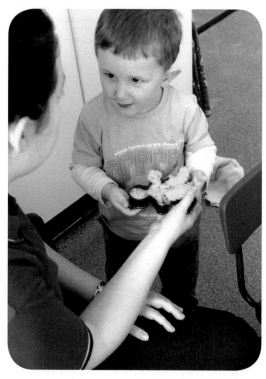

A child's relationship with his or her key person is critical to the child's emotional development.

Development of relationships is linked to stage of development

Making relationships with other children that are mutually supportive is also heavily dependent on a child's stage of development. Whilst you might encourage children to be interested in others, you need to understand that most children do not develop friendships and find it easy to be co-operative until they are around three years old: this age seems to be a turning point for most children because this is when they seem to be 'cracking' language. They are also finding turn-taking a little easier and are less impulsive.

Providing opportunities for pair and small groups

One way in which you can help children to develop relationships is by looking for opportunities for children to play together or to join in an activity. Asking two children at a time to help prepare snacks or to be involved in a game can help children get to know each other. The adult can act as a conduit and provide sufficient structure so that the very young child can cope.

You can also help children by acting as role models. Children benefit by seeing how adults wait their turn, listen and also ask before taking things. It is also useful if adults can explain why they are doing things; for example, 'I think that I am going to get a drink. I will just see if anyone else wants one.' By showing children your thought processes in this way, children can learn how to build and maintain relationships.

Good practice

Encouraging babies and toddlers to take turns

Some games help babies and toddlers learn to take turns. Putting out your hand and saying 'thank you' can encourage a baby to put a toy in it. The game here is to give the object back to the baby so that he or she learns that it is returned. Quickly, this movement can become a game in itself, which may be repeated again and again. Taking turns in this way helps the very young children learn about the reciprocity of relationships at a very practical level.

Communicating with children

One of the skills required of adults in the pre-school is to communicate effectively with children. Good communication not only helps children to build relationships, it also helps them to benefit from activities and routines.

Using everyday opportunities

In your planning you may identify particular activities that promote children's language, yet it is useful to see everyday routines and all activities as having the potential to build children's language. Helping children to acquire language and the skills of communication is essential as they are tools which aid children to control their behaviour, process information and also make relationships. Everyday opportunities include greeting children in the morning, setting out snacks and drinks, tidying up and even accompanying children on trips to the toilet!

How to communicate with babies

One of the key roles of an adult is to interact and communicate with a baby. This is essential because in a baby's first year of life he or she will learn the skills of language and begin to break its code. Adults must therefore spend time talking, responding and playing with babies. However, it is important to understand that babies do not learn language in a vacuum: they pick up words and skills because of the emotional relationship they have with their carer.

Linguists looking at the ways in which adults engage with babies have found that adults naturally use a different pattern of speech with babies. This has been dubbed 'parentese'. When parentese is used, adults actually help babies to break the language code – this is because facial expressions become more exaggerated, emphasis is placed on the key words in sentences, and key words are repeated. Interestingly, the adult's voice also changes: intonation is stronger and pitch is higher. It is much easier to 'switch' into parentese when you are holding a baby. When you are in close contact in this way, the baby can see your face more easily and this helps him or her to gain emotional security and learn language skills.

Older babies will try practising the language code before they have completely cracked it. They will start to put pauses in their babbling and raise their voices as though waiting for a response. These early attempts at speech have been called 'learning the tune before the words'. It is vital that you acknowledge babies' early attempts at communication with a smile and a comment. This helps babies learn that conversation is a two-way process in which they play a vital role.

As well as using parentese, babies need you to point out and name objects that are relevant to them, for example, saying, 'Look there. There's your HAT. It's a big HAT for a little boy, isn't it?' By showing the baby the object that you are talking about and stressing the word slightly, he or she can begin to work out what the word means. Later, at around nine months of age, babies begin to point things out. You will also find that when babies speak their first words, these usually relate to things that they can see rather than abstract words. However, an exception to this rule is often the word 'no'!

How to communicate with toddlers

Toddlers need adults to acknowledge their desire to communicate. In children's second and third years, speech is not yet fluent although children will be keen to use words and two-word sentences, as well as point out objects. It is essential to respond positively to the toddlers' urgent desire to communicate. Toddlers need you to firstly recast what they have said: this is to check that you have understood their meaning and also to elaborate. For example, a child might say to you 'drink-gone-now' and you might acknowledge and elaborate by saying, 'Yes, it looks like you have finished your drink now. Has it all gone?'

Through elaboration, toddlers' speech improves and they begin to move towards full sentences. Outwardly correcting pronunciation or the way a child is trying to communicate with you must be avoided as research shows that if children are frequently 'corrected' the number of utterances they make reduces. It is also essential to make eye contact with children and also to get down to their level. At other times, you need to use a running commentary style of talking which invites children into the conversation. 'I am just going to put these over on this table. Yes, you can help as well. Do you like the blue ones, me too!'

How to communicate with children aged three to five years

In the early stages of language development it is important for adults to do plenty of the talking. In the next phase the roles need to be reversed over time so that the adult spends more of his or her time listening and asking interested questions. Thus the style of interaction is a little different, with children being empowered. You may, for example, find that children want to show you things that they have found or made, and they will want you to show interest and more importantly to listen to them as they talk. It is important that questions are not used as a form of 'testing' the child as this can actually prevent children from talking to you.

In this stage of language development, children are very receptive to new vocabulary and so the old adage 'don't talk down to children' is poignant. It is important to use a wide vocabulary yourself but to use it in a contextual way. For children who have more than one language, it will be important to assess their level of the setting's language and if necessary to take time with individual or small groups of children to promote interaction. It is also important not to assume that children understand everything, so checking for meaning is important.

How to stimulate children's interest in the world around them

Adults can help children by drawing their attention to things around them. This is essential as a way of promoting children's language and also helping them to process information. Indoors you can provide interesting objects for children to touch, explore and examine such as clockwork toys, buttons or old photos. You can also draw children's attention to what happens when water is poured from a height or when a tower of bricks is built beyond a certain height. Talking to children, asking questions and stimulating them is almost a mindset as it can take place virtually anywhere, anytime.

Using opportunities offered by babies' physical care routines

Formal activities for babies are not always necessary and it is important not to neglect the possible learning that can take place during everyday routines. The physical needs of a baby are important because they keep the baby healthy, but the one-to-one moment can also provide opportunities for adults to engage with him or her. It is therefore essential that sufficient time is taken during everyday care routines and that, wherever possible, the baby's key person carries them out. Counting, singing rhymes and drawing a baby's attention to parts of their body or the environment are the type of learning opportunities that come from the physical care routines.

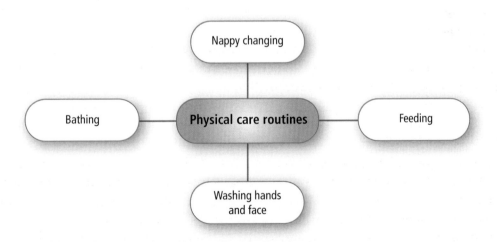

Responding to children's behaviour

A good starting point when thinking about how to promote behaviour is to remember why it is useful. Social behaviours are like codes or passwords. Behaviour that is very different from that expected by others can result in a person becoming marginalised or isolated. Children also need to learn the different codes that are used in a variety of situations; for example, the code for behaving at home is different to that for a library.

In pre-schools, children need to learn what is socially acceptable behaviour. This includes gradually learning to take your turn, to share and play co-operatively, and to be responsible for equipment and toys.

Helping children to learn socially acceptable behaviour

One of the ways in which you can help children to understand what is 'wanted' behaviour is to give clear messages about what is expected of them. In order to do this, it is important that staff working in the pre-school understand, agree and implement the behaviour policy. This avoids situations where staff give mixed messages. It is also helpful for children to be clearly told what is expected of them in new or unfamiliar situations. Very young children will also need reminders even in familiar situations. This is best done at the start of sessions and activities rather than afterwards. Expectations should be positive rather than negative, for example, 'you will need to walk' rather than 'don't run'.

Ways of helping children to understand expectations

Children need to learn about socially acceptable behaviour and so you need children to understand your expectations. As with other areas of practice, you need to be aware of the stage of development of the child. Long explanations may be too difficult for very young children, so communication will need to be brief and to the point. An effective way of helping children to understand what is expected of them is to demonstrate what is required, for example, by pointing out another child who is waiting for his or her turn, or by indicating where toys are put away after play.

Reminding children of expectations

While adults are often good at transferring and using information from one situation to another, young children may find this difficult. A child may know that he or she must wait his or her turn before going on a slide, but may push past another child to get to a tricycle. Thus, some children will need gentle reminders or prompts. For the adult, this means thinking ahead and predicting possible difficulties that children may encounter.

Good practice

Communicating expectations

- Tell children what they need to do.
- Use visual methods, for example, to show the child what he or she needs to do.

Continued ▶

- Be concise in your language.

For example:

Adult: Of course you can get out the jigsaw puzzle. Remember to put it back in its place when you have finished. Can you show me where it goes?

Child: It goes there. (*Child points*)

Adult: That's right. We put the jigsaw back just there. (*Adult taps the shelf*) That means that we can find it quickly if we need it out again.

Understanding the importance of role models

You have seen that social learning theory (see pages 77–8) draws attention to how children learn from watching and copying the behaviour of others. Adults will therefore need to show the behaviour that they wish children to imitate. This means, for example, asking children if you can join in their play so that they learn how to do this for themselves.

Good practice

Being a good role model

- Make sure that you listen to children – this will encourage them to listen to others.
- Show children how to take turns.
- Make sure that your tone of voice and overall actions are gentle and calm.
- Help children learn from your actions how to manage emotions.

Providing feedback

It is helpful for children to be given feedback about their behaviour. Feedback may mean praising or acknowledging a behaviour that a child has shown. For the child to be able to repeat the wanted behaviour, he or she will need to know what it is that he or she has done. This means using phrases such as, 'You waited for your turn. That's fantastic because it meant that Jade didn't get hurt.' These acknowledgements are more effective than comments such as 'good girl' or 'good boy', which do not teach the child about his or her behaviour.

Children should also be given feedback about behaviour that is not appropriate. Feedback works best when it is immediate. A simple 'look' can be enough for some children to desist from some activities, followed by a smile and recognition when the child shows more appropriate behaviour. In other instances, an adult will need to talk to a child. It is best if children are given clear messages about what they should be doing, as there is always a danger that children will learn that adult attention can be gained by displaying inappropriate behaviours.

Good practice

Providing feedback

- Make sure that children understand which element of their behaviour is not appropriate.

- Focus on giving information to children about what they should be doing instead.

- Avoid lengthy explanations in situations where you suspect that children are attention seeking.

- Praise and encourage children as they begin to show more appropriate behaviour.

Using humour and non-confrontational strategies

It is useful if children learn how to create a positive atmosphere. Using a sense of humour can therefore be an invaluable strategy. It avoids possible confrontation and helps children to change direction without them hearing any negative messages. Puppets can also be used to help children show wanted behaviour as they can distract toddlers and also give older children motivation for doing tasks such as tidying away. One pre-school, for example, has a 'tidy away parrot' that comes out and watches the children.

How parent partnerships can provide children with a positive model for relationships

Babies and children seem to be primed to learn from the reactions of their parents and other adults. A young baby, for example, reacts differently on seeing photographs of people smiling as opposed to people frowning. In the same way, if a toddler falls down and is shaken rather than hurt, the decision as to whether to cry is dependent on the reaction of the adult: if the adult looks relaxed and says 'Oops a daisy!' the child may not cry, but if the adult appears very anxious there is a greater likelihood of tears. This process is sometimes called social referencing. The way in which you work in partnership with parents can therefore have a significant influence on children. From watching the relationship between parents and adults in the pre-school, children can gain a positive model. They may notice the way in which you greet each other, listen and respond, and also work as a team. This process is a subtle one but nonetheless important.

Applying theory to your practice

Observe a child whose parent has come into the pre-school and is talking to an adult. Watch how many times the child looks up to monitor the responses of the two adults.

Repeat this observation again, but observe a child of a different age.

Using reflective practice to understand and promote pre-school children's development

The term 'reflective practice' is increasingly used as a way of improving services to children and their families. Reflective practice is like taking a mirror to what you and your pre-school are doing and considering how effective it is. This process is of huge benefit not only to children and their families but also for you personally. As a result of reflecting on your practice, you might decide to adapt a routine, activity or even approach towards an individual child. Reflecting on your practice might also result in you attending further training or doing additional reading.

The importance between theory and practice for reflective practice

In this section on child development, you have looked at the patterns of children's development as well as theories of development. The skill of working with children is to be able to link those theories with your practice.

Using reflection to reinforce understanding of children's development

One of the advantages of being a mature student with experience of working with children or having one's own children is that the theories of child development can feel more meaningful. Child development out of the context of working with and observing children can seem bland, but you can reinforce your understanding of children's development by observing children, reflecting on past experiences and then relating these thoughts to what you now know. A baby who repeatedly drops a spoon on the ground and is keen to turn it into a game is suddenly acting out Piaget's theory

Reflective questions about settling in children

You have looked at the theories of separation and also attachment. This is an excellent example of how you might check that you are connecting theory to practice. Below is a list of the type of questions that you might ask yourself in order to reflect.

- How does the settling-in procedure reflect the need for children to develop an attachment?

- How do you respond and work with individual children to maintain and develop an attachment?

- Are children showing through their responses signs of separation anxiety?

- How might you work to lessen their anxiety?

Are children showing through their responses signs of separation anxiety?

of object permanence and Skinner's theory of positive reinforcement. Reflecting back between your practice, theories of child development and children's responses should give indications of how you can work effectively with children. This in turn makes your professional work with children both interesting and challenging.

Linking knowledge of child development to own practice

Not only do you need a good understanding of child development, it is essential that you consider it when you are working with children. Activities need to be developmentally appropriate in the same way that your responses to children's behaviours need to reflect their stage of development. Below are some examples of questions that might be used to help you reflect on certain areas of practice with children. In order to reflect effectively, observations and assessments of children's responses, play and products are essential. Watching children as they play, sit or even leave their parent can tell you about the child's needs but also give you clues about how well you are providing for him or her.

Reflective questions about children's behaviour

The link between behaviour and development is as you have seen very strong. There are also theories of how children learn behaviour that can help you to promote their behaviour. Below are examples of questions that might help you to reflect on your practice.

- What types of behaviour is the child showing?
- Are these typical behaviours for this child's stage of development?
- In what type of situations is the child likely to show unwanted behaviour?
- How do you work to avoid these situations from occurring?
- How do you encourage the child to take responsibility for his or her own behaviour?
- Is the child showing unwanted behaviour in response to being frustrated or anxious?
- How do you react to situations when the child shows unwanted behaviour?
- Does this reaction make a long-term difference to the child's behaviour?
- What type of positive reinforcements is the child offered in response to wanted behaviour?
- What alternatives have you tried using?
- Are there any issues that are affecting the child's behaviour; for example, boredom, need for attention, lack of understanding, language development?
- How are you addressing these issues?

Reflecting on own practice

Reflecting on one's own practice requires a level of objectivity but also means being prepared to be honest and positive. Watching children's responses can sometimes provide information about how your practice is meeting their needs, but other sources of information are useful too. You can, for example, ask a colleague to observe you as you work, or invite a Pre-School Learning Alliance tutor or development worker for feedback. It is also useful to observe others at work and to consider how you might learn from their approaches. For example, a colleague may be extremely skilled at working with a child and gain positive responses; observing how your colleague manages to achieve this and then integrating what you have seen into your own approach might change the child's responses.

Reflecting on activities

Planning activities for individual and groups of children and carrying them out is a major part of day-to-day work for most staff in pre-school settings. Below is a list of questions that might be helpful in reflecting on an activity whilst you are working with children.

Reflective questions about children's activities

- How did this activity link to the children's stages of development?
- Did most children appear to be engaged and interested in the activity?
- Can you identify the ingredients that helped the children to be interested, i.e. the activity was sensory and the children were active?
- Were children encouraged to take control and be active during the activity?
- How much input from you was needed?
- Why was this input needed?
- How did you encourage children to be active in their play and learning?
- What did the children learn from the activity?
- Was this learning planned or spontaneous?
- How could this learning be reinforced or built upon?
- What did individual children gain from the activity?
- What was your role in helping children to learn?
- What types of resources were used?
- Were there sufficient resources?
- Which resources attracted children's attention?
- What further resources could have been used?
- What were the limitations of this activity?
- How could these limitations be addressed?

Test yourself

1 Explain what children gain from making their own decisions and having some responsibility.

2 Why is it important for observation and assessment of children to take place?

3 Why is it essential for a range of methods to be used when assessing children?

4 How can play help children's holistic development?

5 List three factors that might influence the validity of an observation.

Further references and reading

Bee, Helen (1999) *The Developing Child*, 10th ed. (Pearson)

Meggitt, Carolyn (2000) *Child Development: An Illustrated Guide*, 2nd ed. (Heinemann)

Pre-school Learning Alliance (2005) *Child in Focus* (A084) (Pre-school Learning Alliance publications)

Riddall-Leech, Sheila (2005) *How to Observe Children* (Heinemann)

Core Unit 2

Providing learning communities for pre-school children and their families

Children's learning and development is closely linked to the support and stimulation they receive from adults, especially their parents.

This unit is divided into six sections:

- The potential outcomes of parents' participation in the provision for their pre-school children's care and education
- Appropriate curriculum frameworks for children between 0–5 years of age
- Providing experiences that promote all areas of children's learning and development
- Promoting the well-being and progress of individual pre-school children
- Ways to ensure that all parents have the opportunity to benefit from the learning community provided by their children's pre-school
- Using an understanding of reflective practice to examine the effectiveness of own practice in providing learning communities for pre-school children and their families

The potential outcomes of parents' participation in the provision for their pre-school children's care and education

Recognising parents as the educators of their children

The importance of recognising parents

A good starting point when looking at the importance of parent participation in pre-schools is to be aware that they are children's earliest and enduring educators. From day one of a child's life, his or her parents have been instinctively teaching and thus helping the child. Parents are likely to have helped their children learn to feed and to tune into the sounds of language, and will have taught them basic communication techniques such as smiling and nodding. Parents also provide children with basic emotional security. They may rock them as babies, wipe their noses but also smile at them and show their concern and love. Children are hugely influenced by their parents' care and love. The attachment that parents have with their children also means they pass on their underlying values, culture and religion. Parents also pass on their passions for hobbies such as reading, sport and music.

Children are hugely influenced by their parents' care and love.

The role of parents is thus a heady and complex potion and one that the pre-school takes seriously and recognises as important. The aim of the pre-school in relation to parents is therefore to work alongside them and to complement and support their role. The aim is to see the pre-school as a centre of learning for children and their families rather than just for children alone. This approach has great benefits for children and parents alike, as you will explore below.

What it means to recognise parents

Recognising parents means making sure that they feel a part of the pre-school and part of their child's education. It means taking time to get to know parents as individuals, finding ways to support them and also to learn from them. Recognising parents also means understanding that parents have an enduring relationship with their children that is central to the children's well-being and achievement. Pre-schools are welcoming places in the local community where parents feel that they have a stake and are listened to.

Supporting parents by making the pre-school a centre of learning for children and adults

By involving and working with parents, the pre-school can strengthen its role as educators. Whilst many parents do not see themselves as 'teachers', they are often acutely interested in their children's well-being and development. By encouraging parents to be involved in the play activities that the pre-school provides and sharing with parents the rationale for these activities, the pre-school can enable parents to build on them at home. Thus a child may be introduced to an activity in the pre-school which is then developed at home by his or her parents. A favourite book discovered at pre-school may be shared at home or a parent might point out how a pelican crossing works in response to a discussion in the pre-school about crossing the road.

The direct involvement of parents within the pre-school also has lasting benefits. Parents who have been actively involved in the pre-school gain confidence, skills and knowledge that help them support their children during their formal schooling. Parents may go onto play an active part in primary and secondary schools by, for example, becoming governors or helping out in classrooms. This is especially important for those parents who may be new to the education system of this country or whose own experience of education was an unhappy one.

How family expectations can influence children's learning and development and parents' participation in their children's pre-school

Several studies have shown how family expectations shape children's learning and development: parents that value education are more likely to have children who fulfil their academic potential. This translates into practical things that parents might do in order to promote their children's development. Parents who understand the importance of reading may spend some time each day sharing books or take their child to the library for a story session. In the same way, parents who understand the importance of play in learning might sit and play with their children. Parents who have high expectations for their children's learning and development are also quite active in finding out about early education and so are often keen for their children to attend pre-school. Interestingly, such parents are also likely to have positive attitudes towards education and may also have benefited from their own education. This can create a cycle whereby children whose parents have benefited from education have more opportunities than those children whose parents did not.

The link between parents' educational background and achievement of children is well researched and it is now a priority of the government to ensure that all children regardless of family background and achievement gain from their education (see the material on Every Child Matters on page 112). The pre-school with its open access, non-judgemental support for parents can play a significant role in helping children gain a footing on the educational ladder. In the long term, this should mean that increasing numbers of children are able to fulfil their potential and that the virtuous circle of positive attitudes and later achievement can be extended to include all children.

As well as the impact on children's learning and development, family expectations have the potential to affect whether parents become involved in the pre-school. Parents who have not benefited from their education often feel that organised community activities are not open or designed for them. They are the group of people who are least likely to attend public meetings, join committees or become magistrates. Reasons for this are complex but often link to strong feelings of 'not belonging' or believing that their voice is not valued. The pre-school can change this by:

*   making sure that it is welcoming to all parents
*   offering parents a wide range of opportunities to be involved in the activities through which it is run and managed
*   helping parents to feel that they have a stake in society.

Respecting diverse family structures and child-rearing practices

Today it is important to recognise that there are many family structures in which children might live. Being aware of the range of family structures is useful. It helps you to ensure that your communications and activities will not exclude any families or make any parent or child feel that he or she does not belong. By being aware and showing respect for diverse family structures you can help all children and their families feel accepted and welcomed. A good starting point is to understand the range of potential structures.

There are many different types of family structure present in the UK and the traditional picture of a family composed of two parents with two children is no longer representative, as the inset box below shows.

Types of family structure

*   *Nuclear family* – two parents (male and female) and their children living alone. This is a family structure that was particularly prevalent in the last century as mobility increased.
*   *Lone-parent family* – one parent living with children alone. This can sometimes be through the death of a partner as well as due to a breakdown in a relationship.
*   *Extended family* – aunts, uncles, cousins and grandparents. Members of the extended family may live close by each other or in the same house. This was a familiar family structure across the UK when mobility was restricted; it is still popular in many cultures.
*   *Reconstituted family* – families where parents and their children from previous relationships live together.

Thinking and research

Changing social trends

The following facts about current family structures are taken from 2005 Social Trends:

- The proportion of children living in lone-parent families in the UK more than tripled between 1972 and spring 2004, to 24 per cent.

- The proportion of people living in the traditional family household of a couple with dependent children has fallen from one half to two fifths.

Find out three more facts about social trends by visiting the government website www.ons.gov.uk.

Variations in family structures

Within each type of family structure there can also be huge variations that are linked to families' and children's individual circumstances, as the examples below show.

- Anne-Marie lives with her mother and her mother's partner who is another woman. Anne-Marie refers to them as mum and mummy. Mummy is her biological mother.
- Joseph lives with his father and his partner Tuesdays to Fridays. In this family he has a stepbrother and a half-sister. The rest of the week he lives with his mother and her partner.
- Beyran lives with his foster mum Sally. She has two older teenagers and is a lone parent. He sees his mother on supervised visits every other weekend. He is likely to be adopted in the near future.
- Leo lives with his mother, Jane. She decided she wanted a child and had IVF treatment using a sperm donor to conceive.

How to respect family structures

The key to respecting family structures is not to make assumptions about, for example, the composition of a family or the presence of traditional family figures such as a 'mummy'. In the same way, children may not share the same last name as the parent they are living with or two siblings attending the same pre-school may have different last names. Being aware of the diversity and complexity of family structures should be reflected in your communications both verbal and written. It is essential to find out from parents how they wish to be addressed and how their child refers to them and others who live with them. Respecting family structures is also shown by sensitivity when planning activities which may traditionally celebrate roles such as Mother's day and Father's day as well as when reading stories or simply asking questions about children's weekends or news.

Case study

Respecting family structures

Busy Bees pre-school is a thriving early years setting that is an integral part of the local community. Fran, the pre-school leader, is keen to make sure that all families feel welcome and knows that by making assumptions about children's family backgrounds there is a real danger of making some children and their families feel isolated. One of her members of staff is keen to celebrate Father's day with the children. Fran does not want to dampen her enthusiasm but can see that there may be problems with the activity.

1   Explain why it is important to think about children's family structures when planning activities.
2   Consider ways in which Father's day can be celebrated without causing children to feel left out.

Respecting child-rearing practices

As well as different type of family structures, there are also different styles and beliefs about parenting. In order for the pre-school to be the place where parents feel welcomed and accepted, it is again important to respect the ways in which parents wish to bring up their children. (The only exception here is of course in the minority of situations where parents may be harming their children in some way. In such cases, the rights and safety of the child is paramount and so child protection procedures need to be used.)

Respecting the way in which parents choose to bring up their children is essential as otherwise there is a danger that parents can feel undermined. This in turn can affect their confidence, and when it comes to parenting confidence is often the key. A confident parent is more likely to cope when situations are difficult and a confident parent is also more able to ask for support and advice. It is also worth remembering that there are no 'perfect' parents – only adequate ones, and the view is that most parents fall happily into the 'good enough' grouping.

Examples of the diversity of child-rearing practices may show themselves in some of the everyday routines such as bedtimes, bathing and feeding. Child-rearing practices are often linked to the cultural and even religious heritage of the family. Some parents may, for example, insist that children change clothing to play outdoors or take off their shoes on entry indoors, whilst some mothers continue to breastfeed until their child reaches the age of three years.

Respecting child-rearing practices is often seen in practical ways. For example, it is good practice when caring for a baby to find out how the parent usually settles the child when tired and then ensure that you do the same. This ensures continuity of care which is important for children's emotional development. Where it is not possible to follow the same child-rearing practices when working with children, it is important to explain the reason why and negotiate with parents so that there can be some resolution.

Ways in which parents can participate in the management of the pre-school setting

Pre-schools aim to be parent-led and to respond to local community needs. Their grass roots appeal means that parents are able to shape their local provision. As part of being a learning community for children and adults, the pre-school setting should aim to be responsive to the needs of its local community and to provide opportunities for parents to be involved in the management of the setting (see also Option Unit 3).

- Settings which are a company limited by guarantee or a charity will be managed by a parent management committee. In such settings, parents will have responsibility for the general management of the setting.
- Settings that are run as a private business can offer parents opportunities to be involved in decisions affecting the general management of the setting.

Becoming involved in the committee

The parent management committee of a pre-school has responsibility for:

- the recruitment and management of staff
- ensuring that the setting complies with relevant legislation
- the financial viability of the setting
- the creation and implementation of the policies that underpin the setting's provision.

The management committee is made up of parents whose children attend or have attended the setting. The committee members are elected by the parents whose children currently attend the setting, and manage the setting on their behalf. An important aspect of the committee's role is to involve the pre-school's parents in the setting's decision-making processes.

Involvement in the management of settings run as private businesses

Settings run as a private business can involve parents in decisions about the general management of the setting by starting up a group through which parents' views are represented. Sometimes such groups are called Parent Support Groups or Parents' Forums. The types of activity through which such groups might involve parents in decision making about the management of the setting are:

- involving parents in the review of the setting's policies
- investigating and contributing parents' ideas about appropriate activities
- providing parents with information about the pre-school's curriculum and how it promotes the children's learning.

Attending and voting at meetings

Pre-school settings which are companies limited by guarantee or charities have a legal responsibility to hold an Annual General Meeting. It is at this meeting that:

- elections for the management committee are held
- the management committee reports to the parents on its trusteeship of the setting over the past year
- the management committee discusses with parents its plans for the coming year.

All parents who have children attending the setting have the right to attend the AGM.

Pre-school settings with a Parent Support Group or Parents' Forum can hold an annual meeting at which reports are made on the Group's or Forum's activities. There is no legal responsibility to hold such a meeting but it is a good way for sharing information and decision making with parents whose children attend the setting.

Meetings to discuss and review the management of the setting with parents need not be confined to annual meetings; for example, a meeting might be held to discuss a proposal for the pre-school to participate in an accreditation scheme. Such meetings are an effective means to help parents feel that they are partners in the work of their children's pre-school setting.

Thinking and research

1   How does your pre-school encourage parents to be involved in the decision making process?
2   How do parents find out about how they can be involved in decision making?

Feedback

Parents also provide valuable feedback about the pre-school's service. Parents may make informal comments that influence the pre-school or they may respond to surveys or questionnaires. Staff should also make time for conversation and discussion with parents, as this can provide useful information.

The benefits for children of their parents' participation in the pre-school setting

There are many benefits for children when their parents are involved in the pre-school.

- Firstly, children are able to see that adults are working together and this gives them a greater sense of security and emotional well-being.
- Secondly, children are able to see their parents in a new light and role if they help within the pre-school. This can help children gain a positive sense of their family's identity.

Children who see that their parents engage with organisations are more likely in their later life to model this behaviour.

- Finally, the outcomes for children where parents are actively involved in their education are well researched. Parents are more likely to interact with their children and to provide home activities that support the work of the pre-school in promoting their development. This can help parents and children develop a closer relationship and this in turn can positively affect children's behaviour. Children also gain because their parents become more aware of the benefits of education and are more likely in future to remain engaged and supportive of their children's education.

The benefits for parents of participating in their children's pre-school setting

Parents who participate in their children's pre-school gain in many ways, as shown in the diagram below.

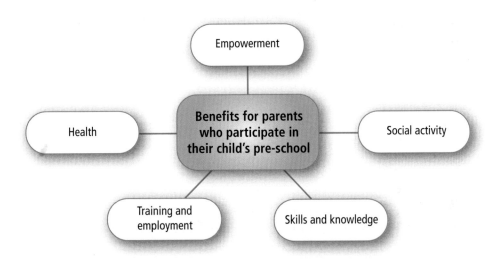

Empowerment

Being able to shape and influence something within their local community helps parents to gain in confidence. From becoming involved in the pre-school, many parents go onto become involved within other aspects of the community. Participating in the pre-school is one way in which parents can gain self-esteem.

Social activity

Many parents find that they make new friends from participating within the pre-school. This is extremely important for parents who are new to the area or are of a different nationality, culture or religion. Participating in the pre-school can help previously isolated families integrate and socialise in a non-threatening and positive context. Fundraising and social events, as well as family learning, can bring adults together and thus help parents to feel that they belong.

Skills and knowledge

Parents who join the pre-school can gain significantly in terms of skills and expertise on many different levels. Firstly, if they join in the sessions they may learn more about the benefits of different types of play activities and ways of promoting learning through interaction. Secondly, parents who become involved become more aware of the curriculum and structure of education. This knowledge can be powerful: it can help parents choose the school that best suits their child or be more aware of how to get help and support for their child.

In addition, parents who join a management committee may learn specific skills and knowledge such as book-keeping, legislation and procedures associated with employing staff or the requirements of health and safety legislation.

Training and employment

Many pre-schools provide family learning opportunities for parents. These can be starting points for parents to improve their own communication, literacy and numeracy skills. From initially wanting to support their own children, many parents get 'hooked' into learning and go on to develop their own skills further. They may take up access courses at local colleges or outreach centres. Parents who volunteer during sessions may go on to take up a career in childcare and education – it is not unusual for such parents to find employment back in the pre-school! Parents who join the committee often find the skills gained there can help them find a route into employment, since they have demonstrated that they can take on responsibility as well as fulfil core tasks such as administration, budgeting and management of staff.

Health

Parents who are involved in their children's pre-school education also tend to report higher levels of well-being. This is linked to the social activity and also the feeling of belonging.

Applying theory to your practice

Ask two parents who are active in the pre-school about the benefits of their participation.

- What do they enjoy about participating?
- Do they feel that they have gained any skills?
- How did the pre-school staff encourage them to participate?

Preparation for assignment

Produce an information booklet that explains how a pre-school can encourage parental participation. The booklet should identify the benefits of parental participation.

The benefits for the pre-school of parents' participation in their children's pre-school

The pre-school is there to support parents and is shaped by parental involvement. The pre-school needs parents to participate so that it can be a resource for the community that responds to the needs of local parents. In this way, parents who participate keep the pre-school focused and alive. Pre-schools also gain from parents' expertise and skills – a parent who enjoys music may bring this into the pre-school whilst a parent who enjoys cooking may come in and take time to prepare food with children. The pre-school in this way can be enriched. The range of activities in the pre-school can also be broadened when there are parent helpers coming into work alongside the staff; for example, a parent may volunteer to be on hand to read stories to individual or small groups of

Parents who participate in the pre-school can help to increase the quality of interactions and the time that can be spent with children.

children or to sit and play a game. By being 'extra' to the child-ratios, parents can help to increase the quality of interactions and the time that can be spent with children. The pre-school also benefits financially through parental involvement. Fund raising activities can provide extra resources, whilst parents are often happy to send in materials, props and other resources.

The benefits for the community of parents' participation in their children's pre-school

There are long-term benefits for the community when parents participate in their children's pre-school setting. The community benefits because parents may, through their experience of being involved with the pre-school, feel more able to become involved in their local community. Their experience of feeling empowered can mean that they feel they have more of a stake in what is happening locally. Parents may, for example, vote at local elections, attend meetings in the community or become involved in projects such as regeneration. The community also benefits if parents have gained skills and knowledge through becoming involved in the pre-school. Parents are often able to transfer their knowledge of being on a committee or doing a specific task within the pre-school outwards into the community. Some parents will also gain qualifications as a result of their initial steps taken by participating in family learning or helping in the pre-school. This means that the pool of local talent can be increased and this benefits the community.

Finally, in areas where there is a low level of expectations with regard to education, the involvement of parents in the pre-school can help. Parents who engage with their children's early education are more likely to continue to be interested and involved with their children's later education. Some parents may become parent governors or join the Parent Teacher Association. If groups of parents engage with schools either formally or informally, the standard and benefits of education locally can improve.

Appropriate curriculum frameworks for children between 0 and 5 years of age

At the time of writing this edition, two frameworks exist in England to support the development and education of young children: Birth to Three Matters and the Foundation Stage. In 2008, these frameworks are to be merged to create the Early Years Foundation Stage (EYFS). This will give England a single framework spanning 0–5 years. Training on the EYFS will begin in early 2007 and you will need to get a curriculum of the EYFS and attend training.

The Birth to Three Matters framework for children under three years

Birth to Three Matters is a curriculum produced by the DfES and Sure Start to help practitioners plan for and focus on the needs of children under three years old. This framework has been well received because it emphasises and celebrates what very young children can do. The current framework takes as its focus the child and steers away from subjects. It identifies four aspects:

- a strong child
- a skilful communicator
- a competent learner
- a healthy child.

The framework also identifies children at different stages of development and play. The following terms are used (see table below).

The different stages of development and play in the Birth to Three Matters framework

Term	Age
Heads up, Lookers and Communicators	0–8 months
Sitters, Standers and Explorers	8–18 months
Movers, Shakers and Players	18–24 months
Walkers, Talkers and Pretenders	25–36 months

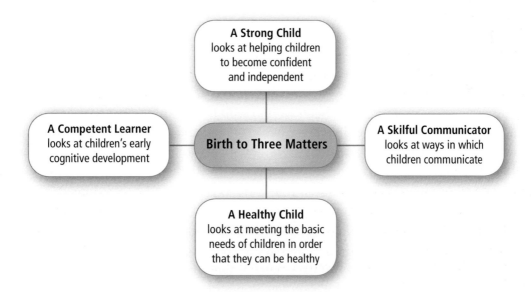

A Strong Child looks at helping children to become confident and independent

A Competent Learner looks at children's early cognitive development

Birth to Three Matters

A Skilful Communicator looks at ways in which children communicate

A Healthy Child looks at meeting the basic needs of children in order that they can be healthy

The Foundation Stage curriculum and its expectations for what and how children learn

The Foundation Stage curriculum was introduced in September 2000 and replaced the previous early years curriculum, known as Desirable Learning Outcomes. The Foundation Stage covers children from the age of three years until the end of the reception year. The aim of this was to provide a more seamless transition from pre-schools into schools for children. Delivering the Foundation Stage is now a statutory requirement for schools and pre-schools who accept a Nursery Education Grant. The Foundation Stage curriculum encourages the use of play to develop children's skills and learning. It also places significant emphasis on the importance of identifying children's needs and planning appropriately, and on working in partnership with parents.

Understanding the principles behind the Foundation Stage

This section looks at the overarching principles upon which the Foundation Stage is based. It also considers the importance of including and making the Foundation Stage accessible to all children and the importance of working with parents. The last pages in this section look at teaching and learning, and the importance of play.

Areas of learning

This is the largest section within the Foundation Stage in which six areas of learning are outlined. Each area of learning is designed to develop particular skills or attitudes. It is worth noting that personal, social and emotional development comes first. This is no coincidence: it is thought that this area of learning underpins a child's development. The six areas of learning are:

- Personal, social and emotional development
- Communication, language and literacy
- Mathematical development
- Knowledge and understanding of the world
- Physical development
- Creative development.

Early Learning Goals and Stepping Stones

Each area of learning includes targets for children to reach, which are referred to as 'Early Learning Goals'. These have been written with the end of the Foundation Stage in mind, by which time most children are five years old and finishing their first year at school. Most early years practitioners are comfortable with the level of these goals, but it must be stressed that they have not been written for the under-threes.

To help practitioners identify the best way to reach these goals with the children in their setting, a series of steps are given, known as 'Stepping Stones'. These break down the skills that children will need to develop in order to achieve the eventual goals. Thus, the experiences and activities of most children in pre-school settings will have been planned according to the Stepping Stone that best matches their development. As a practitioner, it is therefore important to refer to the Stepping Stones closely while 'having an eye' on the eventual goal.

The role of the Early Learning Goals

The Early Learning Goals play an immensely important part in the Foundation Stage curriculum. The idea is that children will all be able to start the National Curriculum in Year 1 with the skills they need already in place. The Early Learning Goals also provide a benchmark so that children who need further support can be identified easily. Reception teachers complete a profile at the end of the school year that shows how children are progressing.

Thinking and research

Find out more about the forthcoming Early Years Foundation Stage by visiting the Department of Education's website (www.dfes.gov.uk).

How the Birth to Three Matters framework and the Foundation Stage curriculum link

The Birth to Three Matters framework and the Foundation Stage curriculum link together fairly well, although the new Early Years Foundation Stage that will succeed them will create a more seamless structure. Currently, they share a similar approach which is to promote children's skills through play. They both also focus on the importance of observing children and then planning on the basis of the observations to meet children's individual needs.

How Birth to Three Matters and the Foundation Stage link to the National Curriculum

Birth to Three Matters	Foundation Stage	National Curriculum
A Strong Child	Personal, Social and Emotional Development	Religious Education Personal, Social and Health Education
A Skilful Communicator	Communication, Language and Literacy	English
A Competent Learner	Mathematical Development Knowledge and Understanding of the World	Mathematics Science Design and Technology Information and Communication Technology History Geography
Creative Development	Art and design	Music
A Healthy Child	Physical Development	Physical Education

How the Foundation Stage links to Key Stage 1 of the National Curriculum

It is worth remembering that children's learning does not happen in a vacuum; they do not know automatically how to do something. Most children are continuously learning or practising skills that will eventually lead them to acquire new skills. This is reflected in the concept of the Stepping Stones. Ideally, you should look at each child and consider the skills and knowledge he or she has gained, then plan to build on the child's existing skills.

The Early Learning Goals for children at the end of the reception year link closely to Year 1 of the National Curriculum. In theory, this should mean that children's transition from reception class to the more formal National Curriculum is smoother.

How to use the Birth to Three Matters framework and the Foundation Stage curriculum to create individual profiles for children

In order to help with planning it is important to assess each child's needs in relation to the framework or curriculum appropriate for his or her age. In this way you can ensure that curriculum plans encompass activities, resources and equipment that will help each child's learning and development. To this end, children should have their own profile. Observations, photographs and work products are used in the completion of the profiles. These need to be used to analyse and identify children's progress and to set possible next steps for their learning and development. In many areas of England, the local early years services have produced profiles for Birth to Three Matters and the Foundation Stage. It is therefore important to check whether these are in place in your area.

Profiles for Birth to Three Matters

In many areas, profiles for Birth to Three Matters are still being created and worked on. Many settings are using the four areas of the framework and then either using the development or points from the component cards on which to base the profile.

Foundation Stage profiles

The commonest approach to creating a Foundation Stage profile is to use the six areas of learning and then list the Stepping Stones and Early Learning Goals. A checklist format then enables you to consider what children have achieved. It is also good practice to either refer to an observation, work product or photograph that illustrates this or to put in some notes. It is important here to note that the Early Years Foundation Stage is set to replace the Foundation Stage by 2008. Look out for training and advice about how to complete profiles for this new curriculum if you work in England.

Observing children during activities is important when completing profiles.

How to create plans for the whole pre-school setting which progress the learning and development of each child

Planning is an essential component in providing for children's care and education. Children thrive when they feel secure and when they are provided with stimulation. In childcare settings, this combination of emotional security and stimulation does not simply 'happen'. Staff need to think ahead about the ways in which they can create this environment. It means actively planning a good routine and layout as well as activities, equipment and toys that will encourage children to play and explore.

Planning is also needed to help staff teams work together effectively to meet children's needs and interests. A good system of planning should create some focus for how staff time is spent so that each member of staff understands his or her role. This role may be working with individual children or being responsible for particular activities.

Creating a curriculum plan is a process that is best done with other colleagues: they may have information about particular children or specific ideas they would like to incorporate. It is also important to involve parents and to think carefully about the interests of each child.

Levels of planning

In order to meet the needs of individual and groups of children, several plans that are interlinked need to be produced.

Long-term plans

Long-term plans provide an overview and direction for a period of time. They are important as they show how the curriculum is to be implemented over time, which helps to ensure that all areas of a curriculum are covered. The length of time that long-term plans cover is variable and depends on the pre-school. Many long-term plans cover at least three months, with some pre-schools producing long-term plans for a year. An example of a long-term plan is given on page 144.

What might be included on a long-term plan?

- When you plan to cover aspects/areas of learning.
- Outlines of how you intend to cover the aspects of learning.
- Special events, outings, festivals and celebrations to enhance children's experiences.

Long-term plan for aspects/areas of learning

Personal, Social & Emotional		Communication, Language & Literacy		Mathematical Development	
Learning intentions	Experiences/ Provision	Learning intentions	Experiences/ Provision	Learning intentions	Experiences/ Provision
Knowledge & Understanding of the World		Physical Development		Creative Development	
Learning intentions	Experiences/ Provision	Learning intentions	Experiences/ Provision	Learning intentions	Experiences/ Provision
Science & Technology History & Geography I.C.T.		Fine motor/manipulative Gross motor		2D & 3D Music & Dance Imaginative Play	

Long-term plans give an overall feel of what is to be covered.

Short-term plans

Short-term plans are used to show how the long-term plan is to be implemented. As with long-term plans, there is considerable variation in the length of time the short-term plan will cover. Weekly plans are probably the most common, but some pre-schools use monthly plans whilst others use daily plans.

What might be included on a short-term plan?

- Learning intentions for individual children and groups of children.
- Information about activities, resources and materials to be provided.
- How the above might be adapted or extended to meet individual children's needs.
- The organisation of the activities, resources and materials, e.g. small groups, outdoors.
- The role of the adults.
- Opportunities for observing individual children.

Week beginning:			Observations to be made on all children but additional observations to be made on the following children:		
Theme/Centre of interest:					
Core Rhyme/Core Book:					

Learning Intentions to focus on for the week					
Personal, social & emotional	Communication, language & literacy	Mathematics	Knowledge & understanding of the world	Physical	Creative

Provision Plan	Monday	Tuesday	Wednesday	Thursday	Friday
Outside					
Creative					
Story Group					

Daily evaluations to include provision, children's responses, developments and future plans

Short-term plans can be used for a day or a week. This is an example of a weekly planner.

The short-term plan should be quite detailed and provide practical information. It should also show the range of activities that are to be offered and how individual children's needs are to be met.

Individual Learning Plans

Individual Learning Plans (ILPs) should be part of developing a profile for children. An Individual Learning Plan is a way of tailoring the curriculum to meet a child's specific needs. This is important because within any large group of children there will be a range of needs, strengths and interests. ILPs are therefore useful to ensure that each child's learning is catered for. As with other areas of planning, there is not a standard format for an ILP, although an example is given on page 146.

Individual Learning Plans should be written using children's profiles which in turn are based upon observations. ILPs provide suggestions for activities, equipment and support that will benefit the individual child. The idea is that children's progress is noted down and, at the same time, working goals linked to the curriculum are recorded. The best person to create an ILP is the key person with whom the child has the most contact and who has also observed the child. The child's key person will also be working in partnership with parents and thus be able to base the plans using their help. The key person can then use knowledge of the child to consider what the child enjoys doing and the best type of learning situations for the child.

Name: Tom McIntosh   Age: 2 yrs 9 months

Date: 14.05.06–29.06.06

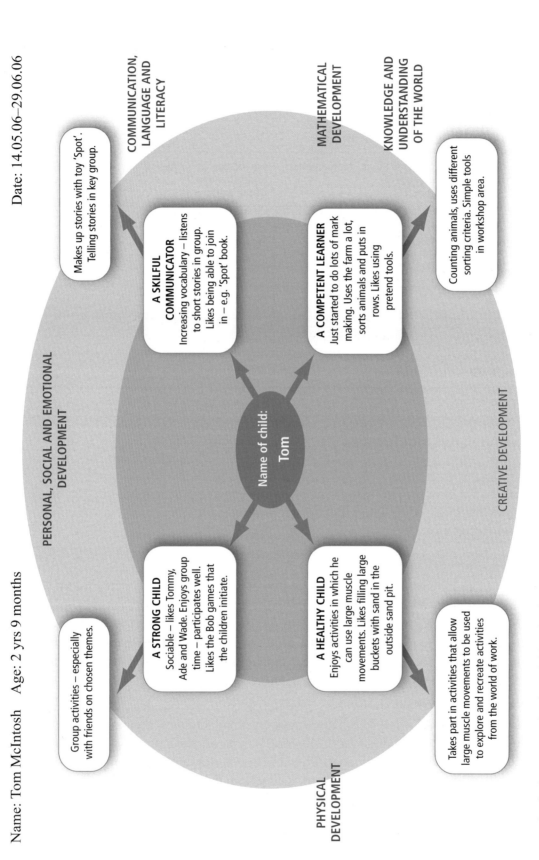

PERSONAL, SOCIAL AND EMOTIONAL DEVELOPMENT

COMMUNICATION, LANGUAGE AND LITERACY

MATHEMATICAL DEVELOPMENT

KNOWLEDGE AND UNDERSTANDING OF THE WORLD

CREATIVE DEVELOPMENT

PHYSICAL DEVELOPMENT

Group activities – especially with friends on chosen themes.

Makes up stories with toy 'Spot'. Telling stories in key group.

A SKILFUL COMMUNICATOR
Increasing vocabulary – listens to short stories in group. Likes being able to join in – e.g. 'Spot' book.

A COMPETENT LEARNER
Just started to do lots of mark making. Uses the farm a lot, sorts animals and puts in rows. Likes using pretend tools.

Counting animals, uses different sorting criteria. Simple tools in workshop area.

Name of child: Tom

A STRONG CHILD
Sociable – likes Tommy, Ade and Wade. Enjoys group time – participates well. Likes the Bob games that the children initiate.

A HEALTHY CHILD
Enjoys activities in which he can use large muscle movements. Likes filling large buckets with sand in the outside sand pit.

Takes part in activities that allow large muscle movements to be used to explore and recreate activities from the world of work.

An Individual Learning Plan for a child under three years old. (Source: Pre-school Learning Alliance)

Good practice

Planning for children

- *Observe and record children's needs*
  Children should be at the heart of any plan. This means that you will need to find out as much as possible about children's needs and interests. Parents and colleagues will play an important role in this respect. As part of this process, you should also refer to children's individual profiles and plans as well as Individual Education Plans where children have Special Educational Needs. (See pages 338–345 for work on IEPs.)

- *Consult with colleagues and parents*
  Parents and colleagues will provide you not only with information about children but also with ideas and thoughts based upon their own experiences. The best curriculum plans are often put together by whole staff teams. This has huge advantages, as particular members of staff may have suggestions for certain areas of learning or development.

- *Refer to the curriculum guidance*
  This next step is crucial, even when you are familiar with the curriculum. Referring to the curriculum guidance ensures that you stay 'on track' and do not overlook any particular learning outcomes. It is also worth looking at the additional material that is provided by the Department of Education and Skills and the Sure Start team and which supplement the curriculum.

- *Record the learning outcomes to be delivered*
  Once you have looked at the curriculum guidance, you will begin to get a feel for the learning outcomes to be planned. You should at this point also look back at previous plans, to see what has already been covered. It is worth considering how effective previous plans have been; it may be that some of the learning outcomes need to be repeated or reinforced.

- *Choose types of play and activities that will achieve these learning outcomes*
  The next step is to think about the activities that will enable children to access the learning outcomes. Choosing the right activities is essential. Curriculum plans can be successful only if the ideas for the activities are interesting and rewarding for children. Try hard to think about how children play and what excites their curiosity. Look for sensory activities and play experiences that allow children to be active, rather than activities that are very adult-directed and structured. You should also think about how the activities can be extended or simplified to meet individual children's needs.

Frequently asked questions

Planning activities for children

 Should everyone in the pre-school be involved in planning?

 Yes. This is important for many reasons but especially because individual children's needs must be met through the planning process and staff will have information about children for whom they are the key person. It also spreads the load if staff work together on planning as they can share ideas and are able in practice to focus activities more accurately.

 How can children's individual needs be incorporated into the curriculum plan?

 You should begin by choosing activities and ideas that build on children's needs, strengths and interests. To do this you should look at children's learning plans as well as the Individual Education Plans. You can use codes to identify those children who will particularly benefit in any activity on your short-term planning. It is also possible to use activity sheets for some activities that the setting provides, which describe in detail how to adapt and extend activities or strategies when working with individual children. These can be very helpful for parent helpers who may not be sure how to make the most of an activity.

 ## Preparation for assignment

- Choose one child with whom you work closely in the pre-school. With relevant permission, contribute to this child's profile through using observations and assessing the child's stage of development.
- In consultation with the child's parent or carer, consider activities that interest this child but will also promote his or her development.
- Think about how these activities may be reflected in the curriculum planning within the pre-school.

How to implement curriculum plans for the whole pre-school setting in ways that appropriately progress the learning and development of each child

From working on the plans, it is important then to implement them effectively. There are several factors that need to be thought about when implementing curriculum plans.

Making sure there is a balance of activities

When implementing plans, it is important to check that there is a balance of activities on offer. Checking that there is a good range of opportunities for children ensures that individual children's play preferences and interests can be met. It is usual for pre-schools working with children aged two years and up to ensure that there is at least one activity from each of the following available:

- play with natural materials
- creative play
- books, stories and rhymes
- songs, music and sounds
- imaginative play
- small and large scale construction
- physical and manipulative play
- puzzles, board games and activities to encourage matching and sorting.

For babies and toddlers, curriculum plans are likely to focus on experiences that you can offer them. Again, over the time that babies and toddlers spend in the setting, it is important that there is a wide range of experiences available. These may include heuristic play or play with sensory materials such as gloop (cornflour and water).

 ## Case study

Snow has unexpectedly come to a pre-school in the city. It is fairly unusual to get snow and the children are very excited. Some have not seen snow before. Whilst some of the children are dressed for the weather, others are not. Barbara, the pre-school leader, quickly consults with staff and some parents. It is decided to put out some of the planned activities but also to take the children outside in small groups so that they can play. The builder's tray (which contains some bark chippings) is quickly emptied so that snow can also be brought inside for children to play with. Some snow is also added into the water tray. Later on, Barbara revises the plans for the next day so that the learning from the snow can be built upon further.

Continued ▶

1   **Why was it important for Barbara and the adult team to be flexible?**
2   **What did the children gain from this session?**
3   **Explain why it is important to revise plans.**

Being flexible

It is always important to monitor children's responses during sessions. Young children's interests do change, and while you may try to plan for their needs, you should realise when an alternative approach is required. In the same way, you may find that an activity that you have planned is a huge success and begins to develop a life of its own. The key here is to remember that the curriculum plan is a tool, not a promise! If children are enjoying learning by a different means to that planned, all is not lost. You simply need to record the changes as they happen. This may require attaching a separate sheet of paper to the curriculum plan, which allows any changes to be noted along with the reasons for them.

The role of the adult

As well as ensuring that a good range of play opportunities is on offer, it is also essential to identify the role of the adult. Adults, as you have seen, are hugely influential in children's learning and the way that they become involved in activities can alter the learning outcomes.

Adult-directed activities

Adult-directed activities are those in which the adult plays an essential role in leading children and teaching them specific skills or knowledge; for example, cooking with children, reading a story or showing a child how to fasten their zip. Adult-directed activities work well when children are active and the adult is responsive to their interest levels. Wherever possible, children should be able to 'follow up' their learning from an adult-directed activity by themselves. This may mean that once they have learnt how to play a simple game or do up a zip for themselves, these materials will be available for them later on so that they can use this new skill independently.

Adult-initiated activities

Adult-initiated activities are those in which the adult has set out materials and resources with a clear idea of the learning intentions in mind for children; for example, putting out tape measures in the role-play area. Such activities prompt children to play in certain ways that will enhance and enrich their learning. Adult-initiated activities can help children to concentrate because, whilst the adult has provided prompts for their play, children still have ownership of the activity.

Child-initiated activities

Child-initiated activities are sometimes referred to as 'free play'. The aim of child-initiated activities is to encourage children to make choices, set their own challenges and literally, play in their own way. Child-initiated activities can encourage children's concentration because children spend longer when they set their own pace for play and therefore tend not to be frustrated. The role of the adult in this type of activities is crucial: the adult has to support and facilitate children's learning rather than lead it. This requires very sensitive observation of children's play so that interventions do not take ownership of the activity away from the child.

Applying theory to your practice

Try out an activity such as the one described below:

- Hide coins in the sand tray and leave out some purses.
- Observe how children play. Do they notice and talk about the coins? Do they use the purses to put money inside?
- How has this type of activity prompted children to learn?

Child-initiated activities encourage children to make choices, set their own challenges and play in their own way.

Monitoring the plan

As well as implementing the plan, it is vital that the plan is monitored. It is important here to emphasise that it is good practice for plans to be changed if needed. Monitoring plans means watching children and considering the learning outcomes for individual and groups of children. It also means reflecting as a staff team on practical aspects of the plans.

How to create and implement curriculum plans in inclusive ways which do not discriminate

When creating and implementing curriculum plans, it is important to think about how inclusive they are. Inclusive plans do not discriminate on the basis of ethnic, linguistic, cultural or family background, gender or ability; they are positive for everyone and help children and their families to feel part of the setting. This means that it is important to take a step back when planning and think about whether the plans really reflect children's interests and family background, and also cater for their specific needs.

Plans should also actively promote positive images and learning in relation to age, gender, disability, culture and religion. This is essential, as children do not simply learn those things that you intend them to – they can learn other things as well, including underlying attitudes. The term 'hidden curriculum' has been used to describe the unintended learning that often occurs. For example, a setting that emphasises only Christian festivals, such as Easter and Christmas, may send out the message that the festivals and traditions of different faiths are not important. In the same way, settings that have a competitive atmosphere may teach that some children are valued more highly than others.

Good practice

Creating inclusive plans

- Have activities, resources and themes been chosen that build on children's interests?
- Do activities reflect and build upon children's home experiences?
- Can activities be adapted, extended or simplified to allow all children to participate?
- Will resources, activities and themes appeal to boys and girls?

To ensure that plans are inclusive it is important to think about the types of activities, resources and theme, if appropriate, that are going to be used. For gender, you may think about whether the activities and resources will appeal to the tastes and interests of boys and girls. In the same way, you must think about how you will be able to adapt, extend or simplify to cater for a range of developmental abilities. To ensure that plans are accessible and inclusive for children in terms of ethnic, linguistic, cultural and family background, you will need to think about whether you are reflecting and valuing things such as a child's home language or a family's celebration of a festival. In the earlier part of this unit (pages 130–2), you looked at the diverse family structures that exist within the UK: these must be thought about when drawing up plans.

Ways in which the pre-school setting can work in partnership with the parents of individual children to progress their learning

It is good practice and essential that parents are involved in their children's Individual Learning Plans and individual profiles. From this, you can tailor activities in the setting to suit children's individual needs and also work with parents so that they can enjoy progressing their child's learning at home. Informally, you might discuss together the type of activities that their child has enjoyed doing in the pre-school and suggest ways in which they might be able to build on this at home. Sometimes it may be possible to lend books, toys or resources that a child has enjoyed using or suggest to parents where it is possible to obtain them; for example, a toy or book library. You may encourage parents to pop in as their child is playing so that they can see for themselves how much their child is gaining and also to see how their child's learning is being extended.

In the same way, you may be able to chat to parents about the type of activities and interests that the child has at home and find ways of extending these in the pre-school. You may find, for example, that a child has been fascinated by the installation of a doorbell so could point out to the child the ring of the doorbell of the pre-school.

Applying theory to your practice

- Describe how you have recently worked alongside a parent in order to extend or build on a child's learning.
- What are the benefits for children and their parents of this approach?

How to work in partnership with parents in the planning and implementation of the pre-school setting's curriculum

Many parents are keen to find out more about how and why their child is learning and so it is essential to involve them in the planning and implementation of the pre-school's curriculum. A good starting point is to help parents understand the frameworks that the pre-school is using so that they can see how the activities and resources are used to support their children's learning. Putting up current plans and talking these through with parents is one way of doing this. Some settings also hold drop-in sessions so that parents can come and see their children in action and staff can talk through the way in which play is assisting their children to learn. Many pre-schools also let parents know what forthcoming festivals, themes and outings are being planned, so that they are able to contribute. This may mean that a parent might plan to do a specific activity with groups of children such as cooking, dancing, making objects or showing children items. Some parents are also interested in providing materials and resources that will support forthcoming events and activities, and thereby enrich children's experiences.

Preparation for assignment

- Produce a reflective account that shows how you have worked with parents to create profiles of their child's ongoing progress.
- How did you ensure that parents felt able to contribute?

Ways in which pre-schools can provide learning opportunities to support parents' participation in the pre-school setting's activities

It can also be helpful to provide a list of suggestions of things that parents can do alongside the pre-school to build on what the child has learnt. Where the role-play area has been turned into a shoe shop, for example, you might encourage parents to point out to their child places in the local area where shoes are sold or let their child try on some 'grown up' shoes at home. In this way parents can enjoy developing their child's learning, and sharing with you their child's reactions. Some parents may also record what they have been doing with their children and share this with you. For example, they may take photographs of the child's birthday or an outing so that you can share this with the child. This is particularly important as young children can find it hard to 'remember' what they do, but once provided with a visual prop or image they often find the words.

Providing experiences that promote all areas of children's learning and development

Ways to progress the development of personal, social and emotional development of children aged 0–5 years

The starting point for all work with children is their personal, social and emotional development. For babies and toddlers it is essential that they have developed a strong relationship with their key person. The Birth to Three Matters framework continually stresses the importance of relationships for babies' and toddlers' learning, growth and development. This is because without strong relationships, babies and toddlers cannot thrive. The focus therefore when working with babies and toddlers is to provide plenty of opportunities for the key person to build a strong bond with the child. From these warm interactions, babies and toddlers begin to develop positive feelings about themselves.

Promoting personal, social and emotional development in the Foundation Stage

This is the first area of development within the Foundation Stage curriculum guidance. This is not accidental: it is recognised that children's emotional well-being and social skills are key ingredients in their later formal learning. Settled, confident children are likely to be able to control their behaviour and be ready for learning.

There are six aspects of learning within this area:

- disposition and attitudes
- self-confidence and self-esteem
- making relationships
- behaviour and self-control
- self-care
- sense of community.

Disposition and attitudes

This aspect of learning is about maintaining and developing children's natural curiosity and motivation. The key to delivering this aspect of learning is to ensure that all activities are enjoyable and stimulating for children. The ability to plan carefully for children's individual needs is therefore important because if a child finds an activity too difficult, he or she may lose confidence and motivation.

Self-confidence and self-esteem

This aspect of learning is about children's inner confidence and sense of identity. Children with self-esteem are more likely to socialise with others, persevere with challenges and try new things. The earliest Stepping Stone is about ensuring that children are able to leave their main carer. You therefore need to think about settling-in policies and organising the routine of the pre-school to help children feel comfortable. Later Stepping Stones focus on encouraging children to talk about their homes and themselves. This means planning activities and times in which adults spend time with children on a one-to-one basis. A child may, for example, want to talk to an adult after he or she has shared a story or whilst helping the adult to prepare snacks.

Making relationships

This aspect of learning is about children learning to socialise with other children and with adults. The focus of your work is to look for activities that naturally encourage children to collaborate, negotiate and enjoy each other's company. Plan games such as picture lotto or activities in which children can play alongside each other. It is also important to realise that true co-operation will not generally occur until children enter the reception class. Adults will therefore need to support children when they are playing together.

Behaviour and self-control

This aspect of learning is about helping children to think about their own as well as other people's needs. It is not about getting children to 'do as they are told'. In terms of working with children, this aspect of learning is about helping children to understand the need and reason for boundaries and limits on their behaviour; for example, saying to a child, 'We need to tidy up so that no one falls over'. To deliver this aspect of learning, practitioners need to think about the daily routines of the pre-school. Ways in which children can learn about behaviour and self-control include tidying up, helping to mend items and clearing away beakers after snack times.

Sense of community

This aspect of learning is about children learning to feel part of a group and respect other people's needs. It is linked with the 'cultures and beliefs' aspect of learning from 'Knowledge and understanding of the world'. The focus is about helping children to appreciate and realise that other children have different needs, interests and strengths. Activities that encourage children to find out more about each other are therefore important, for example, putting up a display that shows photos of children at home enjoying birthdays and family celebrations.

It is important to plan games in which children can play alongside each other.

Ways to progress the development of communication, language and early literacy skills of children aged 0–5 years

Helping babies and toddlers learn to communicate and use language is an essential role for adults.

Encouraging speaking and listening

In Core Unit 1, you looked at the way in which adults help young children to break into language using 'parentese' (see pages 115–6). Helping children to use language to communicate means plenty of one-to-one time with babies and toddlers spent building a good relationship. In addition, you can introduce babies and toddlers to rhymes and songs. These help children to tune into the sounds and rhythm of language. Simple action rhymes such as 'Round and round the garden like a teddy bear' are wonderful at helping babies to enjoy shared communication. The key to encouraging speaking and listening is to ensure that you are responsive to children's early vocalisations and acknowledge them. It is also important to use a running commentary style of speech with babies and toddlers so that they can hear language. For some children who have recognised difficulties in, for example, hearing, you may need to use signs as a tool to help them break into language. The type of signs that are used will depend on the advice of professionals such as speech and language therapists.

Using books with babies and toddlers

You can introduce books to children from an early age. Early exposure to books and images is important in early literacy. Children who enjoy looking at books quickly learn how to turn pages and even babies at nine months can begin to develop favourites. The starting point is often simple picture books that show one object such as animals, clothes or toys. Babies quickly recognise these images and become excited with them. For toddlers, picture books with simple stories are popular.

Good practice

Sharing books with babies and toddlers

- Make the sharing of books a comfortable and pleasant moment.
- Invite babies and toddlers to 'snuggle in'.
- Choose books that are simple but be ready to stop if the child is restless.
- Point to pictures and use expressive language.
- Encourage children to turn the pages themselves and to point out things to you.

Early mark making

Early mark-making experiences are linked to sensory play and also painting. Babies enjoy swishing gloop or liquids on trays, whilst toddlers can enjoy using markers and crayons on paper. The aim of early mark making is simply to let children enjoy the sensation of making shapes with a variety of tools including paint, chalk and crayons. You can encourage children's early interest in mark making by sitting and mark making yourself.

Communication, language and literacy in the Foundation Stage

There are six separate aspects of learning within this area of learning:

- language for communication
- language for thinking
- linking sounds with letters
- reading
- writing
- handwriting.

Language for communication

This aspect of learning is about helping children to develop the skills and vocabulary they need to socialise. Adults will need to model the skills of communication with children. This means actively listening to children and making sure that they get plenty of one-to-one time with a supportive adult. Experiences should be planned so that children can hear new vocabulary in context. There are various ways to plan for this aspect of learning; however, the key is to make sure that children have plenty of personal contact with a friendly and responsive adult.

Language for thinking

While many children 'chatter', they may actually find it hard to express their thoughts or understand concepts. This is because thinking is linked to language (see page 82). This aspect of learning emphasises the importance of children using language to organise their thinking and express their ideas. Activities need to be planned that will give children the vocabulary that is linked to concepts and provide opportunities for them to explain their thoughts. For example, a child may guess what is in a box but the next step is to ask the child what has made him or her come to this conclusion. Young children will also need to hear adults model thinking language. This can be literally sharing your thoughts with a child, for example, 'I think that I will collect up all the buttons made from metal.'

Linking sounds with letters

In order that children can learn to read using a phonic method, they need to listen to letter sounds. In the earliest Stepping Stone, this is simply about encouraging children to discriminate between different types of sounds, for example, a shaker from a chime bar. As well as identifying differences in sounds, children also need to learn nursery rhymes.

This is because rhymes help children to identify the sounds in words. Ideally, you should plan for children to learn a repertoire of traditional and modern rhymes and songs over a period of time.

Examples of rhymes that link sounds with letters include:

- Diddle diddle dumpling, my son John
- Jack and Jill went up the hill
- Five little ducks went swimming one day
- Five little peas in a pea pod pressed.

Reading

It is important in pre-school settings to refer to the Stepping Stones for this aspect of learning. Young children are not expected to have reading books or to practise learning to read! Rather, this aspect of learning is about developing a desire in children for reading, and to enable them to learn about books and how to handle them. This means that story times should be pleasurable for children. Interestingly, the curriculum guidance states that, for young children, the size of the story group should be very small. You should also plan to have an adult available with whom individual children can 'snuggle up' and share a book.

Writing

As with reading, this aspect of learning is not about children being able to compose sentences. The aim is to make sure that children enjoy the experience of making marks and that they learn about writing. One of the best ways of encouraging children to write is to make sure they get a reply! In this way, children can begin to understand the point behind writing. They are often happy to have a go at writing, even if this means just drawing a picture and putting down some marks.

To help children write, you should make sure that there are plenty of examples of print for them to see. It is also important that children are able to sit near and witness adults who are writing. The starting point for most children will be putting down a mark that bears a resemblance to a letter in their name. Thus, children will benefit from playing games in which they can see their written name. In pre-school, it is important not to correct children's writing, as this usually results in children losing confidence and becoming less keen to try.

Starting to write.

Handwriting

Handwriting is the physical skill that allows you to write using pens or other marking equipment. In the Foundation Stage curriculum, stress is laid on developing children's fine manipulative skills in preparation for their eventual writing. Thus, adults need to consider activities that will encourage children to use their hands, such as sorting and pouring activities.

Activities for communication, language and literacy:

- games that encourage children to listen out for sounds
- regular opportunities to learn new nursery rhymes and songs
- exploring sounds made by musical instruments
- role-play, with adults sometimes joining in
- sharing stories and books with small groups of children or individual children
- putting out story sacks for children to recall and enact stories
- making chalk marks and messages outdoors
- large-scale painting, to help children's manipulative skills
- writing notes and messages to teddy.

Ways to progress mathematical development of children aged 0–5 years

Babies and toddlers can develop some awareness of mathematics through practical routines and also play opportunities such as treasure basket and heuristic play (see also pages 164–5). Early mathematics for all children is not about formal teaching but about exposure. For babies and toddlers this may be about 'feeling' number and patterns by, for example, being rocked or gently jogged up and down to the rhyme of 'Humpty Dumpty'. It is also about games such as peek-a-boo where children can literally 'feel pattern', and toys such as stacking beakers so that children learn about size. As with all areas of early development, the role of the adult is key as babies and toddlers enjoy watching and learning alongside adults.

Mathematical development in the Foundation Stage

In the Foundation Stage curriculum, this area of learning is known as 'mathematical development'. It is designed to develop in children a meaningful sense of numbers, shape and measurement. The emphasis throughout the Foundation Stage is making the child see that mathematics is relevant and practical. Thus, worksheets or formal methods of recording are not considered relevant to pre-school children. Rather, the idea is to emphasise the practical side of mathematics so that children gain confidence and insight into what numbers are about. Developing confidence and understanding is now considered very important; previously, many children were taught mathematics formally, which did not necessarily result in confident mathematicians.

Mathematical development is further divided into three aspects of learning, as shown in the diagram below.

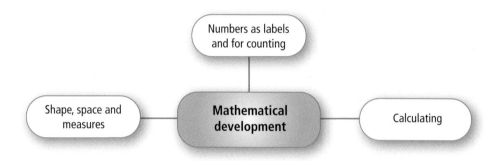

Numbers as labels and for counting

A child's first experience of mathematics often comes through hearing the 'labels'. For example, an adult may count out the number of plates needed for dinner or may tell the child that he or she can have only one biscuit. This aspect of learning is designed to help children learn the 'labels' and then understand what they represent. Thus, children need to hear number rhymes and counting songs as well as hearing adults counting in context. Gradually, children will start using the 'labels' for themselves, although it is normal for pre-school children to mix them up a little. (You may hear lovely snippets of conversations in which, for example, a child reveals that he needs 'twenty hundred'.) It is therefore important for you to work with parents so they understand that, just because a child knows the 'labels', this doesn't mean that he or she is ready to do sums or other formal recording work.

Calculating

This aspect of learning is the starting point for later formal recording. It is about helping children to see how mathematics is used for problem solving. In the earliest Stepping Stones, you need to provide plenty of fun opportunities for children to learn 'more' and 'less', for example, by comparing groups of objects. It is important that children see this in a way that is both practical and meaningful for them. For example, a child may help Teddy to decide if he has enough pots of honey for each of his five friends. Children also need to see how mathematics is used to solve problems. For example, a child may help Teddy to add together all his pots of honey that are scattered around the room.

Shape, space and measures

This aspect of learning helps children to notice shapes and use measures. In pre-school, this learning also happens practically. One of the best ways for children to gain a feeling of shape, space and measure is through constructing things or by problem solving. For example, children may wish to make a car for Teddy to sit in or a hat for him to wear. As well as making things, you can also help children to learn some of the positional language they need to acquire by playing games such as 'Hunt the thimble'. The aim of this type of game is for children to learn to ask questions such as, 'Is it on top of…?' or 'Is it beside…?'

Activities that promote mathematical development:

- stories that involve numbers, for example, 'Teddy goes shopping'
- counting rhymes and songs
- sorting objects into groups
- simple board games that involve rolling dice
- dominoes
- using counting as part of everyday routines, for example, the number of chairs and beakers
- magnetic numbers on metal surfaces
- feely bags containing a set number of objects
- cooking activities in which children measure ingredients, for example, counting out scoops.

Thinking and research

1   Ask five adults about their experiences of mathematics at school. How confident did they feel?

2   How does the advice to do practical mathematical activities with young children link to theories of child development?

Applying theory to your practice

Practical games that involve rolling a dice can be a good way of helping children to enjoy numbers. Children can, for example, roll a dice and then put spoonfuls of sand into a cup – the first to fill up his or her cup is the winner and can make a sandcastle.

1 Explain why this type of activity will help children to enjoy mathematics.

2 Describe how you might adapt this game to meet the different levels of mathematical understanding of the children you work with.

3 Carry out the game with one or two children and evaluate its effectiveness.

Ways to progress the development of knowledge and understanding of the world of children aged 0–5 years

Children need opportunities to explore both the natural and man-made world. For babies and toddlers, this exploration can take the form of sensory play and heuristic play.

Sensory play

Babies and toddlers learn about the world by using their senses, so you should plan sensory activities for these very young children. As with any activity involving babies, supervision is essential. In addition, most sensory play is, by nature, quite messy. The best way of managing the mess is to keep rooms warm and to take clothes off!

Babies learn about the world by using their senses.

Play with water

All children love to play with water, especially as they get older. It is important, however, to remember that children can drown even in small quantities of water; supervision is therefore essential. In warm weather it should be possible to provide a paddling pool and to allow babies to sit and crawl in the water. Nappies should be kept on; if possible, use aqua nappies.

When playing with water, toys that encourage scooping and pouring are especially popular, for example, buckets, jugs and funnels. Water play can also be done as an indoor activity using baby baths or washing-up bowls. Again, even with small quantities of water, supervision is essential.

Play with gloop (cornflour and water)

A mixture of cornflour and water provides a runny and sometimes solid texture for babies to feel and play with. It can be put on trays in high chairs for babies who need support, or in a tray or container on the floor for babies who are mobile. These types of activities stimulate babies' hands and senses and develop physical movements. Gloop is very messy but if left to dry it can be easily removed using a vacuum cleaner. Older babies may enjoy using spoons when playing with gloop.

Play with cooked pasta

Cook pasta such as spaghetti in coloured water and leave it to cool, then give babies helpings of cold pasta for them to eat and play with – they enjoy the sensory feel and taste of the pasta. Babies can play with the pasta while sitting on the floor on a plastic sheet or in a high chair. (Note: food materials have traditionally been used as play materials for babies and young children. However, you should check with parents beforehand that they do not have any objections.)

Treasure basket play

Treasure basket play encourages babies to explore and learn about different objects. It is based upon the idea that babies are naturally curious and that modern, purposely designed toys are limiting. Objects that are 'real' can have far more value because the baby is able to explore them in a range of ways. Treasure basket play was advocated by Elinor Goldschmied in 1994, and in some ways links back to a more traditional way of baby-rearing in which the objects that babies were given by their parents were those that came to hand!

Thinking and research

Borrow a copy of either of the following videos produced by Elinor Goldschmied: *Heuristic Play with Objects* or *Infants at work* (your tutor or local early years team should have one).

How treasure basket play works

A group of natural objects are placed in a basket and given to the baby for him or her to explore. Objects might be chosen because of their texture, smell or shape, for example, feathers, shells or fir cones. Objects made from natural materials are also used such as a wooden spoons, metal scoops and leather wallets. The adult's role is to remain nearby but not to guide the baby. The idea is that this encourages the baby to play in his or her own way and gain his or her own sense of achievement and satisfaction. Treasure basket play should offer endless possibilities because new objects can be included each day for the baby to explore alongside existing ones. When choosing objects for the treasure basket, always check that they are not a choking or suffocation hazard. As with all activities for babies, supervision is essential. Objects will be mouthed by babies as this is a key way in which they will be explored; it is therefore important to wash items before and afterwards.

Applying theory to your practice

Put together a group of objects suitable for treasure basket play. Check that they are not a choking or suffocating hazard. Present them to a baby aged 6–9 months. Observe closely how the baby handles and mouths them.

- What skills is the baby developing?
- What concepts is the baby experiencing?
- What activities could be planned to enhance this baby's interest and learning?

Heuristic play

Heuristic play is usually provided for children once they have become mobile. The aim of heuristic play is again to provide opportunities for discovery and independence. The role of the adult is again to provide reassurance and supervision rather than to direct the child.

How heuristic play works

Groups of objects are laid out in an appealing way. Unlike treasure basket play, objects can be taken from both the natural and man-made world. Containers such as metal biscuit tins, cardboard tubes and plastic bottles are popular with children as they can explore, place things inside and also walk around with them. The key is to provide several of the same item but in different sizes, such as a selection of corks, pegs and spoons. The range of objects that can be put out is endless and this activity remains challenging and interesting for children if you create different permutations. One day a child might be interested in the sounds that objects make whilst another day the same child might be fascinated with putting shells into tins and shaking them.

Knowledge and understanding of the world in the Foundation Stage

This area of learning is perhaps the most diverse in the Foundation Stage curriculum because it encompasses early science, design and technology as well as the beginnings of history, geography, and cultures and beliefs. The key to delivering this aspect of learning is to remember that it is very child-centred. It is also worth noting that the practitioner guidance throughout this area of learning stresses the importance of developing children's language; this is reflected clearly in the Stepping Stones and Early Learning Goals.

There are six aspects of learning within this area of development:

- exploration and investigation
- designing and making
- information and communication technology
- sense of time
- sense of place
- cultures and beliefs.

Exploration and investigation

This aspect of learning is about encouraging children to notice differences, patterns and change. It is the beginnings of early science. To deliver this aspect of learning, you will need to make sure that children regularly get opportunities to handle and sort objects. They will also need opportunities to look at how things work and see things grow. You can contribute to this learning by:

- providing children with different collections of objects, such as keys, buttons and haberdashery
- using magnifying sheets and glasses to help them explore these objects.

Designing and making

This aspect of learning encourages children to solve problems, use tools and learn about textures and materials. As well as the usual construction type of toys, children should be encouraged to use boxes, paper, fabric and other materials. It is also important to show children how to use tools safely. The practitioner guidance lists tools that children should learn how to use, including stapler, scissors, grater and a junior hacksaw!

In addition to construction and junk-modelling type activities, children will also benefit from cooking activities, provided they can use tools and are designing in some way. For example, making sandwiches or salads can be useful cooking activities because there is scope for children to make choices.

Information and communication technology

The focus in the early Stepping Stones is to help children understand about gadgets and the way in which technology is used in people's daily lives. Thus, activities such as encouraging children to turn a tape recorder on and off, or watching what happens when a mobile telephone rings, will cover the outcomes. You should also look out for programmable toys such as floor robots and remote-controlled cars, which teach children about 'cause and effect'. If your pre-school has a computer, it is important to look for good quality software programmes that can develop children's learning and skills. Computers are not absolutely necessary for this aspect of learning, but as computers increasingly become common in children's lives, it is important to find ways

Beans can be used to help children notice different shapes, patterns and sizes.

of helping them to use and learn about their use. Look out for simple programmes that encourage children to be creative, e.g. Paint.

Sense of time

Interestingly, this aspect of learning is closely linked to cultures and beliefs. Both these aspects of learning in the early Stepping Stones are designed to encourage the child to talk about significant events in his or her life and the lives of his or her family and friends. Thus, you need to plan activities that encourage children to think about their experiences both in and out of the setting. A good way of doing this is to use photographs and bring in objects to trigger children's memories. It is also important that you find the time to listen to children, either individually or in small groups.

Sense of place

This aspect of learning focuses on children's local environments, which may include shops, play parks and buildings. The key is to think hard about what children actually see and experience. For example, if you live in an inland town or city, focusing on a topic such as the seaside or farms will not be relevant. Rather, the focus for children's learning is for them to talk about where they live and begin to notice things that they like and dislike about their local environment. It can be very helpful to take photographs of local landmarks, buildings and other sites, because young children find it easier to talk about things that they can actually see.

Cultures and beliefs

This aspect of learning has links to 'sense of time'. It is essential to read the Stepping Stones very carefully because they give clear guidance about the child-centred nature of this aspect. The earliest Stepping Stones are focused on helping children to talk about their families and the feelings and events that are important to them. This is important as the aim is that children first gain a strong sense of their own identity and that of those close to them. It is, therefore, good to look at festivals and celebrations that reflect children's lives as a starting point for young children and then gradually to widen out their experiences.

Ways to progress physical development of children aged 0–5 years

Promoting fine, gross and locomotive movement

An increasing knowledge of how children's brains develop means that this area of learning is particularly important. Physical movements are now known to affect children's cognitive skills and information processing. With babies and toddlers, physical development is promoted through the use of toys and equipment with adult encouragement. The key is to observe children's physical development carefully and provide the right stimulation, space and resources. Everyday physical care routines are also useful in supporting young children's physical development; these include dressing, feeding and washing. A 10-month-old baby might, for example, help by pulling off a hat or feeding him or herself. Using everyday opportunities in this way also promote self-esteem from an early age.

Physical development in the Foundation Stage

In the Foundation Stage curriculum, physical development links to many other aspects of learning within the Foundation Stage, including handwriting, designing and making, responding to experiences, and expressing and communicating ideas.

There are four aspects of learning within this area:

- sense of space
- movement
- health and bodily awareness
- using tools and materials.

Sense of space

Many young children find it hard to get a sense of their position in relation to other people and the objects around them. This aspect of learning, therefore, focuses on helping children to develop spatial awareness. For some children who spend many hours in confined spaces, this is particularly important; it is one of the reasons why outdoor learning is considered so essential. When providing activities it is important to check that all children are trying out a variety of movements as sometimes individual children might be reluctant to try out an activity. This may mean thinking about ways to adapt the activity to ensure that it appeals, for example, asking a child who never goes on a tricycle if he or she would like to take teddy for a ride.

This aspect of learning is about children enjoying space and developing a range of movements. A good starting point is to provide a range of activities that will help children to experience different sensations, for example, balancing, climbing, squeezing into tight spaces and running in large ones. When providing activities it is important to check that all children are trying out a variety of movements and, if necessary, to think about ways of making them attractive to all children.

Children gain from being outdoors.

Movement

This aspect of learning looks at developing children's fine motor as well as gross motor and locomotive skills. Activities that encourage children to try out different movements, such as climbing, swinging and using wheeled toys, will help to cover the Stepping Stones. It is important to check that activities can boost children's confidence, so observations of children's physical development are important. There is also some evidence to suggest that helping children to use cross-lateral movements – those that encourage children to use a left limb at the same time as a right limb, such as marching or crawling – may be beneficial in developing some parts of the brain.

Health and bodily awareness

This aspect of learning is simply about children becoming more aware of the needs of their body. It means that you should help children to think about what they should do if they are feeling tired, hot or cold. Other useful activities include working out how best to wash hands when very dirty, and inviting a dentist or other health practitioner to talk to children.

Using tools and materials

This aspect of learning focuses on developing children's hand–eye co-ordination and fine motor skills when using tools. The starting point is, therefore, to make sure that children have access to a variety of tools. You should also think about the support children may need so that they do not become frustrated. This aspect of learning is likely to be covered in many activities within the pre-school; for example, while children are involved in designing and making or creative development, as well as when children are engaging in play with natural materials such as sand, water and using dough. Look out for adaptations to help children who have particular fine motor difficulties, for example, scissors that work by squeezing. Consider, too, the needs of children who use their left hand.

Ways to progress the creative development of children aged 0–5 years

All children are essentially interested in exploring their environment, so it could be argued that they are naturally creative. In terms of babies and toddlers, safely exploring a range of objects and materials will extend their learning. This is why treasure basket and heuristic play are considered to be so useful.

Imaginative play

In their second year, most toddlers begin to use imaginative play. Providing props such as tea sets, pushchairs and cuddly toys such as teddies will help promote this. Look out, too, for small-world resources such as farm animals, play people and train sets.

Music

One of the first objects that babies often grasp is a rattle. Learning to shake instruments and be responsible for making sounds is exciting and fun for babies and toddlers. Encouraging a love of music and a feel for the beat from an early age can assist in speech and also in learning to read. Look out for music that babies and toddlers enjoy – even non-mobile babies 'dance' by wiggling their bodies!

Painting and mark making

In their second year, toddlers love opportunities to make marks. You therefore need to provide large sheets of paper or white boards for them to experiment. Painting and mark making also encourages gross motor movements.

Creative development in the Foundation Stage

In the Foundation Stage curriculum guidance, the 'creative development' area

Mark making encourages vivid imaginations.

of learning is designed to help children explore different materials and textures, and encompasses music and dance. There are four aspects of learning within creative development:

- exploring media and materials
- music
- imagination
- responding to experiences, and expressing and communicating ideas.

Exploring media and materials

For this aspect of learning, children should be given a wide range of materials, such as paint, dough, clay and fabric, in order that they can learn about them. This aspect of learning should allow children to explore rather than being adult-directed. For example, you may put out a tray of primary colour paints for children to use and encourage them to mix colours. The focus is not about children producing an 'end product' to take home but rather that children learn and enjoy using a large range of materials.

Music

Most children are naturally keen to enjoy and use sounds. To deliver this aspect of learning you will need to provide a range of instruments, including homemade shakers and rattles, and be ready for children to explore the sounds that they make. Activities that encourage children to sing and even make up their own songs are also vital. Look out for music that has a strong beat so that children can learn to play in time to music.

Imagination

Role-play and dressing up is one of the many ways in which imagination can be cultivated. This aspect of learning is designed to help children use their imagination in a variety of ways, including dance. Look out for props that will help children to move to music, and provide a selection of small-world toys and dressing-up clothes for them.

Responding to experiences, and expressing and communicating ideas

In many ways this final aspect of learning is a culmination of the first three. The idea is that children will be able to choose a medium for expressing themselves and focus on creating. This aspect of learning is also about helping children to evaluate and talk about what they are doing. Therefore, it is necessary for children to hear you speak the language that will enable them to do this.

How to enable children to access activities and benefit from them through providing ways that are appropriate to children's age and stage of development

It is important to think about ways in which you can encourage children to engage in the play and learning that has been planned for them.

Working with babies and children under two years

The role of the adult is especially important when working with babies and children under two years of age. Adults are the starting point for these children rather than the activities or other children.

Repetition is important

One characteristic of the very young child's play is the importance of repetition. Playing a simple game of knocking down beakers repeatedly allows the child to learn to predict and anticipate what is going to happen. This understanding contributes enormously to his or her enjoyment of the game. In terms of development, the repetition also allows babies to develop physical co-ordination. This means that adults need to be ready to play a simple game several times over, taking the cue from the baby when to stop.

Modelling play

Sometimes the very young child needs to watch an adult play with an item. This allows a baby to both see its possibilities and learn how to play with it. For example, pushing a button down so that the baby learns that a noise is made might encourage

Knocking down is a favourite game of many young children.

him or her to have a go. Again, as with many other areas of child development, a balance has to be struck between allowing babies to explore for themselves and providing sufficient adult interaction.

Test yourself

How does modelling link to social learning theory?

Encouraging turn-taking

Some games help babies and toddlers learn to take turns. Putting out your hand and saying 'thank you' can encourage a young child to put a toy in it. The game here is to give the object back to the child so that he or she learns that it is returned. Quickly, this movement can become a game in itself, which the child may repeat again and again.

Adults are great playthings

It is often said that the best toy for a baby and young child is an adult. There is a lot of truth in this because adults can adapt their responses to meet a young child's needs.

An adult can rock a baby or take the toddler over to the window to point something out. An adult can build a pile of beakers to knock down or simply play peek-a-boo. No toy designed so far has been able to do all of this!

Working with children under three years

Children at two years of age continue to be interested in adults, but they begin to notice the actions and play of other children too. At two years, children often enter a stage where they begin to know what they would like to play with but sometimes lack the necessary co-ordination or knowledge, and so become frustrated. Again, the role of the adult here becomes essential: children need adults to facilitate their play and to anticipate their needs. Where two-year-olds and older children are together, it is important also to find ways of adapting and simplifying activities so that the younger child can still participate. This might mean looking for larger brushes for a painting activity or holding dough for a child to cut. Many two-year-olds also need some structured support when it comes to playing with others. They may wish to join in a simple game but will need an adult to be 'on their side'. Sometimes you may also need to explain to older children why you might be changing 'rules' or expectations for the younger child.

It is also important to find toys and equipment that meets the needs of two-year-olds. Sometimes they enjoy going back to playing with toys they had as toddlers, so a selection of pop-up toys, trolleys and simple puzzles are needed alongside toys that are for their 'age'. Two-year-olds also need a variety of opportunities as they can become restless; thus providing for their needs may mean being flexible and following their changing interests. For example, after five minutes pouring with jugs, a two-year-old may lose interest; introducing a toy fish at this point might regain the child's interest. The importance of following the child's rhythm and pace is reflected in the Birth to Three Matters framework.

Working with children aged 3–5 years

Whilst some of the principles of working with children under three years remain valid when working with older children, the way you work may have a slightly different emphasis.

Encouraging independence

Encouraging independence should be a key way in which you work with all children, but it is especially important with children aged 3–5 years. This means giving children opportunities for them to select materials and arrange their own ways of playing. This requirement links back to the need of providing a balance between child-initiated activities and adult-initiated activities (see pages 150–1). Independence can also be encouraged through the way that you arrange routines; for example, children may take snacks when they feel ready for them or go to the toilet independently. It also means thinking about the storage facilities that are provided and the way in which you encourage children to tidy up and be responsible for their environment.

Children who do not play with a range of materials

Some children love a particular activity such as sand or playing with cars, and they may spend most of their time with the one resource. This can lead to concerns that a child is not gaining a full range of skills, knowledge and play opportunities. Where this occurs it is worth talking to parents to see what type of play the child enjoys at home and also spending time observing the child. Sometimes children over a number of sessions and also at home are gaining a wide number of experiences. However, if after doing this you are still concerned about the scope of the child's play, it can be worth introducing new materials, concepts or skills using the medium of the play that the child is so enjoying. It can also be worth doing a little advertising at the start of the session: some children go immediately to the same toys because they enjoy them but also feel secure there. Helping children to know what is on offer and also spending time with children whilst they explore a new activity can therefore be worthwhile.

 **Case study**

Aron loved playing with dinosaurs at the pre-school. The first thing he did in the morning was to go and pull them out from the shelves. He would then sit on the mat and one by one line them up and talk to them. He would happily stay doing this for over an hour and would only leave the mat if he could take a dinosaur with him. Aron's mother said that at home, Aron also loved playing with his dinosaurs.

Aron's key person, Sandy, was concerned that over a number of days Aron was missing out on other opportunities, so she decided to incorporate dinosaurs into other activities. She brought in a dinosaur puppet which Aron immediately loved. The puppet loved painting and so Aron started to paint. The puppet also loved seeing toy dinosaurs dancing in the sand tray and so Aron began to take the dinosaurs over to the sand. Little by little, Aron, through the medium of dinosaurs, began to participate in more of the activities.

Giving children time

Time is one of the most important resources in helping children to access and benefit from activities. Children often need time to explore an activity and repeat it. This exploration often means that children gain a better depth of understanding out of activities such as blowing bubbles or making dens. For imaginative activities, time allows children to develop more complex 'plots' and ideas whilst for creative activities, time allows children the confidence to try out, without fear of failure, new ways of working and using materials. In practical terms this means avoiding situations where the routine become so rigid that children have to stop what they are doing before they are ready. It also means that where possible you should share children's interest with parents so that the child can continue an activity at home.

Providing meaningful choices

Children tend to concentrate and learn more effectively where they are given choices and also have selected their own challenges. This means that in the provision of activities you need to provide sufficient materials and encourage children to select their own. Choices have to be meaningful so that children have some genuine ownership over what and how they are doing it. It also means allowing opportunities for children to do things in their own way, for example, making a mountain in the sand tray or a bus in the home corner.

Supporting friendships

At around three years, most children begin to enjoy the company and friendship of other children. This means that you need to ensure that you look for ways of supporting those friendships as children play. This is important as some children try out different activities depending on their friends. You may, for example, organise a board game or a jigsaw puzzle so that a pair of children can play together, or you may set up a letter writing table and see if children wish to write to each other!

Modelling

You have seen that with babies and toddlers, adults need to model how to use toys and even how to play. With older children modelling remains important as an unobtrusive tool to enrich children's play and to help them learn. Modelling may mean sitting with a group of children at the dough table and making an animal out of dough. As children are genuinely interested in adults and what they do, sooner or later children will notice how you are manipulating the dough. Modelling in this way allows children to remain independent but at the same time is a wonderful teaching tool.

How to ensure that children and babies have the space and opportunity to play and move safely and unhindered in ways appropriate to their age and stage of development

Thinking about layout is crucial when working with babies and children. A good layout prevents accidents, uses space effectively and creates a pleasant environment.

Creating safe areas for babies and very young children

Babies' and toddlers' requirements for play and learning are slightly different to that of children over three years old in terms of safety. Firstly, it is important to remember that many of the toys and resources that are routinely put out for children over three years of age are not suitable for younger children and as such often carry manufacturer's warnings. (It is important to heed manufacturer's warnings because if there were a case where a child was injured because those warnings were ignored, the pre-school could be deemed negligible.)

In terms of layout you need to ensure that children are in areas that are suitable for their developmental stage. Where babies are being cared for it is also important to create safe areas for the non-mobile, as accidents can occur where the mobile baby or toddler falls over a non-mobile child or drops something on him or her. In the same way, young two-year-olds can be 'mown' down by older children as their perceptual skills may not be sufficient to move out of the way or to understand the speed of the oncoming child. This means that many pre-schools allocate 'safe' space for younger children where there is increased supervision and also equipment and materials that are suitable for the age range. When thinking about layout for babies and young children, it is also worth bearing in mind that they like to be in sight of their key person. This helps them to feel reassured and, as you have seen, this is reflected in the Birth to Three Matters framework.

Using outdoor areas

When working with groups of children it is useful to consider all available space. Where an outdoor area exists it is essential to use it to its full extent. The outdoor space can be used for physical development and encouraging large-scale movements, but it can also be seen as an extension of the indoor space. Sand, water and imaginative play can be taken outdoors as well as activities for early science and maths. Babies and toddlers also benefit from being outdoors as the fresh air and change of environment is hugely stimulating.

Helping children to move safely

The layout can affect the way children move safely. 'Head-on collisions' where children walk or bang into each other can sometimes be the result of the layout. It is important firstly, to think about how and when children are on the move. In large group settings it makes sense to avoid groups of children, especially of different ages, all moving at the same time, for example, to get coats on. This means that staggering children is helpful as is thinking about the location of things such as coat pegs and other stored items. It is also worth looking at the space between tables and activity areas. It is easy unintentionally to create the 'motorway' effect where children can run in straight lines between different activities. In the same way, it is also important to look at the location of adjacent activities to ensure that they are compatible. Generally speaking, sand, water and paint need to be sited near a source of water and away from role-play areas, whilst book corners and places for construction play and small-world play may be grouped together.

Division of space

Many pre-schools find it helpful to divide large spaces into particular areas. This can help children to focus more easily and, especially for young children, can help them to feel more secure. A large area that is noisy and busy can be intimidating for young two- and three-year-olds. Dividing the environment into areas can also help with supervision and encourage children to play in different ways.

Examples of different types of areas found in early years settings

- *Imaginative play area* – dressing-up clothes, home corners, pushchairs.

Continued ▶

- *Small-world play* – farm sets, dolls houses, playmobil, toys cars, train sets.
- *Creative play area* – gluing, painting, collage, musical instruments, junk modelling, tools, sewing.
- *Exploration* – items for sorting, scales for measuring, magnifying glasses.
- *Literacy* – book corners, mark-making tables, chalks, white boards, story tapes.
- *Natural materials* – sand tray, water tray, peat or mud, pasta.
- *Physical play* – climbing frames, balls, hoops, tricycles, wheeled toys, wheelbarrows.
- *Construction area* – duplo, lego, large wooden bricks, jigsaw puzzles.

Reviewing layout

It is always worth reflecting on the layout of your pre-school. This is especially important if younger children have started to join or where changes to storage, access or equipment have been made. These things can all change the dynamics of the space and

Divide the space into different areas.

so require you to re-consider the layout. To work out whether a layout is effective, it is worth standing back and watching children as they move and play at different points in the session. Also consider keeping an eye on the accident book: are there any areas of the pre-school where accidents frequently take place?

Key questions about layout

- Are there are any areas in the room where children rarely visit?
- Which areas within a room are popular with children?
- Would children benefit from being given more space?
- Are there any areas where children often try and run?
- Are there any areas where children seem crowded?
- Can children access toys and equipment themselves?
- How easy is it for adults to supervise children?
- If there is an outdoor area, is it in constant use?
- How is the outdoor area used?
- How are areas and activities accessible for children who may have sensory or mobility needs?

Ways in which parents can participate in providing the activities offered by the pre-school to promote children's learning and development

Children and their parents can enjoy activities together in and out of the pre-school, and there are many ways in which the pre-school can facilitate this. Firstly, parents can come into the pre-school during sessions and play alongside their children or be involved in specific workshops, such as making cards or painting. It is helpful if the adult team use this as an opportunity to explain how the activity benefits children's learning so that parents can understand more about early education. Parents can also learn more about the activities from being parent helpers and being given the opportunity to set up activities and support them. Being involved in the setting-up of activities can be really helpful – from this, parents can be empowered to repeat some activities at home, for example, making dough or simple finger painting. Some activities also lend themselves to being 'takeaways' – children and their parents might make simple puppets in the pre-school and then use them again at home.

Where parents are unable to come into the pre-school, it is useful if they are given information about the type of activities that their child has done. Some pre-schools are also able to lend out games, books and other materials, so that parents can build on their child's interests.

The learning for parents which can result from this participation

Participating in activities in the pre-school often gives parents the confidence to recreate activities at home or try out new ideas; for example, parents who have made pizza in the pre-school may repeat the activity at home and this may lead to a series of cooking activities in the home. Participation also gives parents skills and knowledge about early education; from this, they may see how to extend their child's play or use materials around the home as toys. Being involved in activities also helps parents to build on their child's existing skills and knowledge. For example, a parent who has seen that his or her child can make a simple sandwich in the pre-school may encourage the child to join in when the parent is making a packed lunch at home.

Promoting the well-being and progress of individual pre-school children

Ways to create profiles of pre-school children's progress

Earlier in the unit you looked at the way in which the Birth to Three Matters framework and the Foundation Stage curriculum are used in developing profiles (page 142). Using profiles is essential as from the profiles you can plan more effectively for children's interests, strengths and needs. Creating profiles should be done by using the tools of observation and also using children's drawings and other items such as photographs, recordings and notes. It is important the profiles are completed by the key person who has spent time working alongside both parents and children. The key person is likely to have a strong overview of the child's interests and needs, and will already have started the process of observation. For profiles to be effective they need to be regularly updated and so it is useful if there is a rolling programme to look at children's progress.

Making the creation of profiles a shared activity with children's parents

When creating a system of profiling children, it is important to ensure that parents are part of the process. Parents are able to see their children in different situations and so may be able to help you compile profiles more accurately. They may, for example, have observed that their two-year-old already points and knows the name of some parts of his body, but this usually happens during the bathtime routine!

The process of compiling profiles begins when parents and their children first join the setting. The child's key person will talk to the child's parents about the child, and this information will be the starting point for the profile. Parents need to know why you create the profiles and their role in their maintenance. It should also be explained that parents have access to the profiles and that their compilation is a shared process. Sharing the profiles means that parents can also celebrate their child's progress and gain more knowledge about his or her learning. Sharing the profiles means taking the time with parents to sit and chat about their child. This in itself should is a valuable activity (see learning for parents on page 181).

How to use profiles of pre-school children's progress to work in partnership with parents to provide appropriate activities

Working on children's profiles should help you to identify activities that will encourage children's learning and development. You may look at children's strengths and interests with parents and consider ways of building on these both at home and at the pre-school. You may, for example, see that a child is just beginning to recognise her own name and suggest to parents that they might like to make a name sign for the child's bedroom; in the pre-school, you might play a game where the child has to find her name amongst two others in the sand tray. In the same way, you may also consider areas of development that need furthering and again look at ways in partnership with parents of working to support the child. A child who is finding it hard to take turns might be helped by playing simple games such as 'Happy Families' that encourage reciprocal actions, and which can be played in pre-school and at home.

How to use profiles of pre-school children's progress to provide a differentiated curriculum

Updating profiles regularly should provide you with ideas of activities for individual but also groups of children. This knowledge needs to be acted upon and should be used when creating plans. You may, for example, look at the short-term plan and consider ways of adapting or extending the activities to meet particular children's needs. The term 'differentiated' curriculum means ensuring that all children are able to gain from the activities and resources. This might mean that for some activities individual children will need extra support, whilst at other times it might mean ensuring that an activity is more challenging.

To make the curriculum differentiated, it is important that the staff in the pre-school meet and discuss how to help individual children and also to 'collate' what is needed for groups of children. It may be, for example, that two or three children would benefit from carrying out an activity in a particular way. Plans should show this differentiation, although in the interests of protecting children's right to confidentiality, it is important that codes are used if children are identified. This is particularly important where plans are on public display.

Example of a plan showing differentiation

Activity	Key learning intentions	Resources	Staff	Support required for individual children	Comments on learning and activity
Role-play 'in the post office'	To reinforce visit to the post office	Forms, stamps, letters, post box, counter and till	Mandy	A and M may need to hear 'script' as did not come on visit	

Appropriate ways to share information from pre-school children's profiles with other professionals and settings

There are many times when it is in children's and their families' interests for information to be shared with other professionals. The starting point is to ensure that parents are happy for information to be passed on and that they understand what exactly is to be shared. This is important as otherwise confidentiality and therefore trust can be lost. The rare exception to this is where there are serious concerns about a child's welfare; in such instances, child protection policies and procedures must be strictly adhered to.

The main reasons why information might be shared with others include the child's move to school, nursery or another setting. By passing on records of children's progress and learning, the setting can prepare for the child more effectively. This should help the child to settle in more quickly and also mean that activities and resources are tailored to meet the child's needs. It is therefore essential that up-to-date and accurate information is given.

It is also useful to contact the people who will be directly working with the child to find out what type of information would best help them. This may include a summative assessment that provides an overview of a child; alternatively, a setting might like to see the child's profile particularly if they are working with the Foundation Stage curriculum. In this way, continuity can be provided. It is also useful to arrange time when the person who will be working with the child can observe the child in the pre-school and meet the parents. This approach has many benefits: children and their parents can meet the new person in a familiar and relaxed environment, whilst the professional can see the context where the child's learning takes place.

The learning for parents that can result from their participation in the creation and use of profiles of their pre-school children's progress

There are many useful and potentially long-lasting benefits for parents if they are involved in the profiling process:

- Parents can enjoy the success and delight of seeing their child progress.
- It helps parents to put the play and learning that the pre-school provides in context: it can help make sense of the planning system and also the rationale behind the provision of resources and equipment.
- It can help parents to see how they might extend and broaden the learning of their child at home.
- Parents are able to see and understand the structure of the curriculum: this has long-term benefits as it makes parents more confident about the education system. This is particularly important for parents who may not have engaged in education before or who are unfamiliar with the English system of educating children.

Involving parents 'behind the scenes' in this way is hugely empowering. It shows parents that education is not a mystery that only some people have the right to find out about.

How to use the profiles of children's progress to review the effectiveness of the pre-school setting's provision

As well as using profiles to look at children's individual needs, it can also be useful to look at them as a whole to reflect on the way you are working with children. You may, for example, notice that children's progress in some aspects of learning and development appears stronger than in others. This may indicate that a setting is overall more confident at delivering some parts of the framework or curriculum; this can be celebrated as a strength. In the same way, you may realise that groups of children are less confident in a particular area and this may give you the opportunity to reflect upon your practice there. From this point it is possible to focus your attention on this area and consider how you might be able to improve practice.

Ways to ensure that all parents have the opportunity to benefit from the learning community provided by their children's pre-school

Ways in which pre-schools can provide learning opportunities to support parents' engagement in the running of the pre-school setting

You have seen that parents should be involved in the running of the pre-school in order that it can meet local families' and children's needs (see pages 128–9). You have also seen that there are significant benefits for parents who take an active part by, for example, becoming members of the committee (see pages 135–6). In order for parents to feel empowered to run the pre-school, it is essential that there are training and learning opportunities open to them. Training and learning opportunities may include:

- access to relevant Pre-school Learning Alliance (PLA) publications
- sessions or short courses in the pre-school led by PLA Development Workers or staff from the Early Years Development and Childcare Partnership (EYDCP)
- information about locally held workshops and courses.

In addition, parents at the outset may need information or sessions that help all of the parents understand the role of the committee, forum or support group.

It is important that parents know that training and support is available as this can be a major factor when parents decide whether to put themselves forward as committee members. Parents may otherwise feel that whilst they may like to be involved, their knowledge or skills may let them down.

Thinking and research

Parents may need support and learning opportunities in order that they can participate. How does your pre-school provide learning opportunities for committee members or for parents who wish to become more involved?

Factors that will influence parents' response to the opportunities to participate in the pre-school

It is important to understand that certain factors might influence whether parents participate in the pre-school. An awareness of these factors may help you to support parents and reduce the potential barriers to their participation. In addition, understanding the reasons why some parents may not participate can also help you to reflect on your own practice and also that of the pre-school. Below is a list of factors that researchers looking at parental participation cite as potential influences on participation.

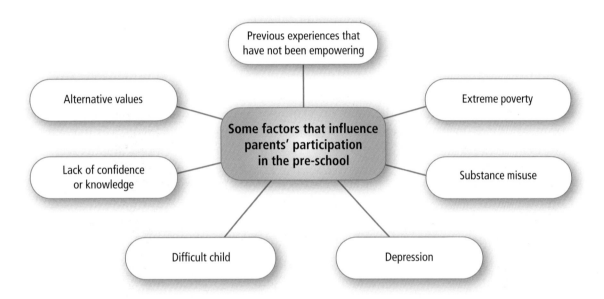

Previous experiences of organisations

A key reason why parents may not become involved is simply because they may not have had experience of being included in the running of other organisations. Many parents' experiences of other organisations, especially educational organisations such as schools, may not have been empowering. They may not realise that the pre-school has parental participation as one of its main aims and that they can be involved in decision making and influence the pre-school's development. Parents may not therefore feel that this is their role and that they can have a stake.

Extreme poverty

Where parents are in extreme poverty they may not necessarily feel able to participate in the pre-school. Poverty can lower confidence and self-esteem. Living in poverty is disempowering. Poverty restricts choices, even ones that otherwise you may take for granted, such as choice of clothing, food and entertainment. Over the long-term, living in poverty means that people have lower expectations of what they can achieve as well as what they may be entitled to. It can lead to social isolation and the feeling of not being part of the community. Living in extreme poverty also drains people of mental and physical energy, and consequently doing anything that may feel like an 'extra' can be daunting.

There are also practical reasons why poverty may reduce participation. Parents may fear that they may be expected to contribute in some way, for example, tea or coffee money, or doing something that has a cost implication, such as making phone calls. Other practical issues include arranging childcare and transport and, if meetings are held in the evening, fear of leaving the home.

Substance misuse

A few parents may be misusing substances such as drugs or alcohol. This can affect their capacity to participate in a pre-school setting. Where parents are battling with this as a problem, it can make them feel ashamed and socially isolated. Substance misuse can also create situations where parents are inconsistent in their participation.

Depression

Depression can be extremely debilitating. Many people who have depression report low levels of energy, tiredness and feelings of isolation. There are many factors that can contribute to depression including poverty, illness and hormones. Depression, as with mental illness, also has a stigma attached and so is often not mentioned.

Difficult child

Parents who have children that they find challenging to parent may not participate. They may find that they are tired and lacking in the energy required to engage. If their child also shows unwanted behaviour in the pre-school, they may feel embarrassed in front of other adults, especially other parents. In such situations, parents may feel it better to keep a low profile.

Lack of confidence or knowledge

Some parents can feel inwardly that they can't participate in the pre-school. They may feel 'that it isn't for them' or that they do not have anything to offer. Some parents also look at others who are engaged in the pre-school and falsely believe that they must be 'better' in some way as they make things look 'easy'. Some parents can also worry about their lack of education or knowledge. This is why it is so important for pre-schools to support parents and help them to build their skills. Parents can also have a fear of the 'unknown' – they may worry that someone might ask them to read or write something because they don't know what will be expected of them.

Alternative values

You have to accept that some parents may not share the same values and vision as you. They may see their role differently and may also have other expectations. Sometimes this can relate back to their experiences of education or previous experiences in another early years setting.

Time

Time can also be a factor for some parents. They may have full- or part-time work and other responsibilities such as caring for a relative. Some parents may also have other commitments in their lives and may not choose to actively engage with the opportunities that are provided. In some cases, it may not be time so much as timing that can be a factor.

Accounting for these factors in the ways in which opportunities to participate in the pre-school are provided

Being aware of some of the factors that can influence parents' decision to participate enables you to consider how best to encourage their participation. Since confidence plays an important factor, a starting point is to consider how you can help parents to feel at ease when they come to the pre-school. The starting point is the commitment shown by staff to partnership with parents. Seeing parents in their own right is helpful in this respect, rather than always seeing them as someone's 'mum' or 'dad'.

Below is a list of some of the key strategies that might be used to encourage parents to participate.

Key strategies that might be used to encourage parents to participate

Chatting to parents	The term 'chatting' can sound inconsequential but it is often the starting point for building relationships with parents. Chatting is potentially non-threatening and so can help parents to see that adults in the pre-school are friendly and warm. Through getting to know parents, you can help them see that opportunities and offers are genuine.
Going at parents' pace	Some parents will increase their participation gradually; this is usually dependent on their increasing confidence and knowledge. Understanding that parents will sometimes need to build confidence before engaging further is important. Persuasion is one thing but pressure is another, so it is important to be sensitive.
Timing	Sometimes the timing of meetings and sessions can be a barrier for parents. Considering flexible timings can be useful, as can thinking about the range of parents' circumstances in order to take into account the needs of working parents.
Childcare	Where parents are caring for several children of different ages, timing, but also childcare, can be an issue. Finding ways for parents if necessary to come with their children is useful to overcome this as a barrier.
Reducing uncertainty	Some parents need to know what they have to do and the format of a session, meeting or event. They may need reassurance that no money is required or that they will not be 'put on the spot'.

Reviewing strategies used by the pre-school setting to encourage parents to participate

It is important for pre-schools to review the strategies that are being used to encourage parents to participate. There are several ways of doing this, as described below.

Auditing

It can be worth doing an audit to look at parental participation. A drop in the number of parents volunteering or an increase in the attendance at meetings can act as indicators as to how well the pre-school is helping parents to participate.

Informal feedback

Talking to parents in an informal way can provide valuable feedback. This is why the key person system is so valuable. As parents get to know their child's key person, so they may feel increasingly able to make comments and provide information. You may hear what they have enjoyed doing and what has worked well for them. In the same way, you may also find out what might have affected their participation.

Questionnaires and evaluations

Questionnaires and evaluations can work well with parents where they feel confident, but it is worth remembering that some parents may not wish to spend time filling in forms. Anything that involves reading or writing can also be a possible barrier and so may affect the information that is collected.

Good practice

Opportunities for parental participation

- Does the pre-school have a parent participation policy which is known and available to all parents and staff?
- Are the reasons why the pre-school offers parents opportunities to participate shared with parents?
- Are invitations to participate given in ways that help parents to feel that they are part of the setting?
- Are newsletters and other written documents available in other languages?
- Are meetings and activities held at convenient times?
- Are meetings and activities always held at the same times?
- Are parents able to bring their children to meetings and social events?

Continued ▶

- Are arrangements in place to help parents with alternative childcare needs, for example, a crèche?
- Are venues chosen that are easy for parents to reach?
- Is there a scheme in place so that parents can share transport?
- When arranging social events, are the costs taken into consideration?
- Are introductions made when a new parent attends?
- Are new parents befriended?
- Are some activities 'drop in' in nature?

Using an understanding of reflective practice to examine the effectiveness of own practice in providing learning communities for pre-school children and their families

The importance of the link between theory and practice for reflective practice

As you have seen in Core Unit 1 (pages 121–4), it is essential that you use reflective practice in order that you can meet children's and their families' needs more effectively. Being reflective also helps you to celebrate your own achievement and to consider ways in which you might be able to increase your effectiveness. For this unit, this means thinking about how effectively you put into practice the principles of the Birth to Three Matters framework and Foundation Stage curriculum alongside ways in which you develop a partnership with parents.

Using reflection to reinforce understanding of the implementation of curriculum frameworks and principles of working in partnership with parents

Taking time to look at the ways in which you plan for children using the curriculum framework is useful. A good starting point is to re-visit the principles behind both the Birth to Three Matters framework and the Foundation Stage curriculum and consider whether you are reflecting these principles in your practice. Note that when the Early Years Foundation Stage is implemented in 2008, you will need to be familiar with its practice and principles.

Reflecting on practice in relation to Birth to Three Matters

Many of the underlying principles of the Birth to Three Matters framework involve relationships. As with the Foundation Stage curriculum, parents are seen as vital in children's early care and education. Birth to Three Matters also stresses the importance of children having a key person so that that through this relationship they can learn. This means that when reflecting on how you implement this framework, you need to focus on how you help children develop this relationship.

Key questions when reflecting on practice in relation to Birth to Three Matters

- How do I ensure that children have a strong relationship with their key person?
- How is the concept of 'competent' learner reflected in the activities planned for babies and young children?
- How do I ensure that children's interests are followed?
- How do I give children responsibility?
- How do I ensure that schedules and routines flow with the child's needs?
- How do I encourage children to make decisions and choices, and also to make errors?
- How do I ensure that children learn by doing?

Reflecting on practice in relation to the Foundation Stage

Whilst play is emphasised as the way in which the Foundation Stage curriculum is delivered, the guidance also focuses on the importance of learning and teaching, and your practice should reflect this. Below is a list of reflective questions based on the guidance in the section 'Putting the Principles into Action.'

Key questions when reflecting on practice in relation to the Foundation Stage

- How do children initiate activities?
- How are children able to learn from each other?
- How do I provide opportunities so that children learn through movement and all their senses?
- How do I give children time to explore ideas and interests in depth?
- How do I help children feel secure so they can be confident learners?
- How do I recognise that children learn in different ways and at different rates?
- How do I encourage children to make links in their learning?
- How do I provide creative and imaginative play activities?
- How do I ensure that activities are challenging but achievable?

(*Source:* Curriculum Guidance for the Foundation Stage QCA 05/00 ref QCA 00/587)

Reflecting on the effectiveness of sessions

As well as looking at individual play opportunities and activities, it is also helpful if you can reflect at the effectiveness of a session. This is particularly important if you have responsibility for the overall running of a setting.

Checklists can be useful tools as a way of reflecting on a session afterwards. Below is a sample checklist that you might like to use a starting point for developing your own.

Example checklist when reflecting on the effectiveness of a session

- Were the adults in the setting aware of the aims and the plan for the session?
- Were the adults aware of their own role and responsibilities for the session?
- What systems do you use to ensure that everyone gets the information that they need?
- How could these systems be changed to make them more effective?
- Do the timings and routine of the setting cause any difficulties?
- Are children 'rushed' or asked to tidy up before an activity has reached its natural end?
- Were there any difficulties with children's behaviour as a result of the timings and routines of the setting?
- How could the structure of the session be changed to address these issues?
- Was there a balance of activities to engage children's interests?
- What was the balance between child-initiated and adult-initiated activities?
- Which activities and resources were the most popular with children?
- What made them popular?
- Was the space in the setting fully used?
- Were there any areas or equipment that were not used effectively?
- What changes could be made to make better use of the space or resources?
- Were there any children who were not engaged or participative during part or all of the session?
- What changes could be made to engage these children's interest?

How to use knowledge about implementing curriculum frameworks and principles of working in partnership with parents to examine own practice in progressing children's learning and development

Evaluating your work with parents

As you have seen on pages 134–8, there are many benefits for everyone when parents are involved in the pre-school. Evaluating your practice with parents means thinking about how effective you are in helping parents to participate and how well you are building real partnerships.

Key questions when evaluating your work with parents

- What systems are in place to communicate with parents who cannot attend the setting?

- How are parents encouraged to pass on their views, concerns and ideas?

- How do you provide opportunities for parents to contribute to their child's profile?

- How do you share your contributions to the profile with parents?

- How do you provide opportunities for parents to share in the decisions about progressing their child's learning and development?

- What strategies do you use to ensure that parents feel comfortable in the setting?

- Are all parents acknowledged when they arrive or collect their children?

- How do you find out from parents about the changing needs and interests of their children?

- How are parents encouraged to participate with their children and in the setting?

- What is the uptake of parents who come and help during the sessions?

- How are plans shared with parents?

- How involved are parents in the planning process?

- How do you ensure that parents feel that they are contributing to their child's learning and progress?

- What systems are in place to help parents learn more about the curriculum frameworks and ways in which they may build on their child's learning at home?

The results of examining own practice in providing learning communities for pre-school children and their parents

Following on from reflection, it is important to consider how to further your practice. There are many ways in which you can further your own practice and sometimes you may decide to use several over a period of time.

Gaining advice

Advice can be sought from your local pre-school worker or the early years advisory team in your area. Talking through your ideas, showing plans and listening to their expertise can be extremely helpful. Being ready to seek advice in this way is a sign of professional competence rather than incompetence, so don't worry about their reaction. As a result of their visit, you may gain suggestions as to training or other sources of information that might assist you.

Training

Training courses can provide you with new ideas and thoughts about practice, and there are increasingly a good number of training opportunities available. A good starting point is the local pre-school development worker as the Pre-school Learning Alliance will arrange courses locally. In addition, early years advisory teams provide training courses at minimal or no cost for all early years settings in their area.

It is important to attend training on areas of your work where you feel that you are strong as well as those areas where you know your knowledge needs to be updated. This is because it is easy to become so comfortable with one way of working that you may be a little blinkered to other possibilities. Sharing training also allows you to share ideas and practice with others, and helps in preventing a pre-school setting from becoming isolated.

Observing the way others work

Sometimes, you can reflect on the way in which you work by learning how other pre-schools engage with parents, create curriculum plans and work with children. Looking at how others work should not be about comparison as this can become too negative. It is about reflecting on others' and your own strengths. Watching other people in this way is sometimes known as shadowing and can help you to see things from a different perspective. Learning how another setting works is particularly useful if you are about to try out a new system or introduce a new project. Learning from others can mean finding out about the pitfalls at first hand and learning how to avoid them. To find a pre-school in your local area that would be willing for you to visit, it is worth first contacting your local pre-school development worker.

Drawing up an action plan

In order to keep the momentum going, it is worth drawing up an action plan for yourself. Such plans are sometimes referred to as Professional Development Plans (PDPs). The idea behind these plans is that they act as a tool for reflection but also help you to focus on ways of furthering your practice. PDPs are also beneficial professionally as they show that you are serious about your career and own development.

Once you have considered the areas in which development might take place, you need to next think about how best you might achieve them. Common approaches include training, asking to take on responsibility or shadowing a colleague. Doing this research is important as it will give you an idea of the timescale in which you might be able to achieve the identified development, and this can affect how you might prioritise.

If they are large areas, you might also need to break them down into smaller steps. You will also need to consider the timescale in which you can achieve them. Setting yourself realistic goals is essential here in order that your plan works. The term 'SMART' is often used when goal setting:

S = Specific
M = Measurable
A = Achievable
R = Realistic
T = Timescale.

The aim of SMART goals or targets is to help people focus clearly on what they want to achieve and to avoid situations when they are unrealistic.

SMART targets

Specific	Try to make sure in your planning that you have thought clearly about what you need to learn, experience or develop.
Measurable	Consider how you will know whether you have achieved this part of your plan. You may, for example, need a qualification or certificate, or want others to recognise that you have become more skilled.
Achievable	When thinking about your plan, make sure that it is possible to complete each target. This will include thinking about how you will organise it and whether it will meet your needs.
Realistic	There is always a danger of being over-enthusiastic and optimistic at the start of any project. Think about how you normally cope and check that your plan will meet your needs and the way in which you learn and work.
Timescale	Thinking about how long each part of the plan will take you is essential. Many people need a start and an end time to help them work effectively. Working out a realistic timescale will help you to remain motivated.

Once you have thought through what you want to develop and when and how, the next step is to record it. Plans should show when and how you intend to implement your goals and how you intend to check your progress. It can also be an idea to record the objectives of each part of your plan.

Below is an example of a personal development plan which may give you some starting points for your own. Remember to adapt it so that it suits your own needs and circumstances.

Personal development plan

Area	Why?	How?	By when?	Update
Heuristic play	To plan for toddlers	Training	Sept 2007	

Test yourself

1 Identify three different types of family structure.
2 Explain why it is important to involve parents when planning activities for children.
3 Describe the benefits of parental participation for the pre-school.
4 Why is it important to refer to children's profiles when planning activities?
5 Why is it important to monitor and be flexible when implementing

Further references and reading

– Tassoni, P. (2002) *Planning for the Foundation Stage* (Heinemann)

– Tassoni, P. and Hucker, K. (2005) *Planning Play and the Early Years,* 2nd ed. (Heinemann)

Pre-school Learning Alliance publications:

* *Learn through play cards*
* *Making their Day: Linking Effective Practice – Providing for two-year-olds in pre-schools and mixed age settings*
* *Parent and Toddler Groups: Self-assessment for Good Practice*
* *Planning a Pre-school Curriculum: Making it work for you*

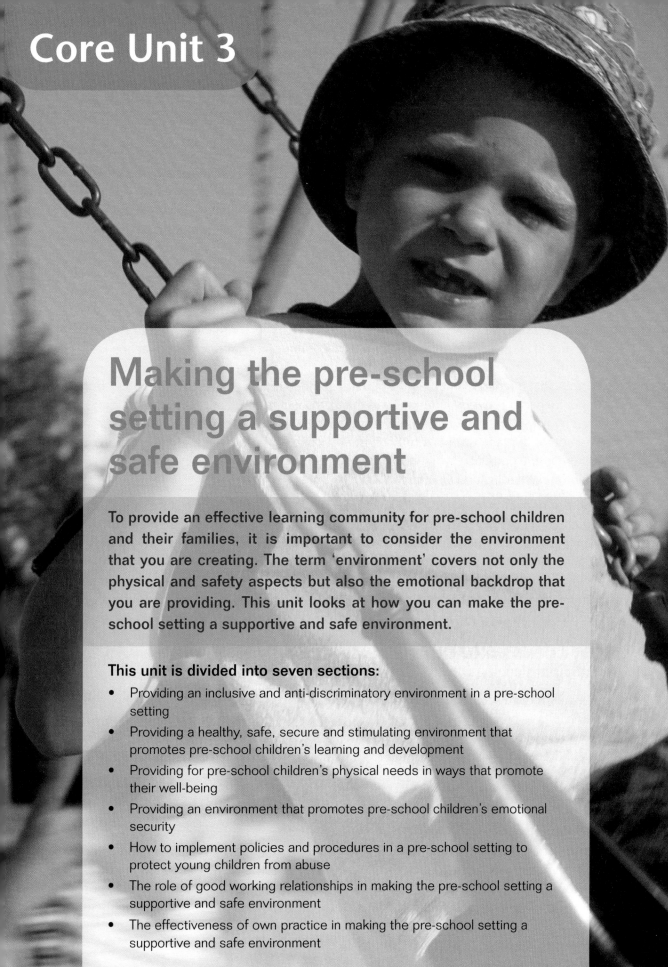

Core Unit 3

Making the pre-school setting a supportive and safe environment

To provide an effective learning community for pre-school children and their families, it is important to consider the environment that you are creating. The term 'environment' covers not only the physical and safety aspects but also the emotional backdrop that you are providing. This unit looks at how you can make the pre-school setting a supportive and safe environment.

This unit is divided into seven sections:

- Providing an inclusive and anti-discriminatory environment in a pre-school setting
- Providing a healthy, safe, secure and stimulating environment that promotes pre-school children's learning and development
- Providing for pre-school children's physical needs in ways that promote their well-being
- Providing an environment that promotes pre-school children's emotional security
- How to implement policies and procedures in a pre-school setting to protect young children from abuse
- The role of good working relationships in making the pre-school setting a supportive and safe environment
- The effectiveness of own practice in making the pre-school setting a supportive and safe environment

Providing an inclusive and anti-discriminatory environment in a pre-school setting

The way in which you work with children and their families reflects society's changing views about equality and fairness. Indeed, it could be argued that the early years sector plays a crucial role because children learn about attitudes from a very young age. For pre-school settings, working in an inclusive and anti-discriminatory way is essential in order to create learning communities. This section looks at the importance of inclusive and anti-discriminatory practice and considers practical ways in which the pre-school provides for it.

What is meant by inclusive and anti-discriminatory practice?

It is an accepted view in society and in the early years sector that every child is special and should be given opportunities to fulfil his or her potential. Inclusive practice is about ensuring that the individual needs of the children and their families are met and that barriers that might prevent them from participating are actively removed. A pre-school might therefore provide information in their prospectus about access to the buildings used by the setting, showing where ramps have been fitted. They might also have procedures in place when a family registers a child for enrolment that the family is asked if there is any particular ways in which the setting can help them to get the most out of their time attending and visiting the setting.

Anti-discriminatory practice is about checking that the curriculum, resources and way in which you generally work do not create barriers and prevent children or their families from participating. Inclusive and anti-discriminatory practice, therefore, means thinking about every aspect of what you do with children and their families and considering whether your actions meet their needs and encourage them to participate in the learning community. It also means being aware of your preconceived ideas about groups of people, and being prepared to think about how these ideas may affect your practice.

Why it is important for pre-school settings to make their practice inclusive and anti-discriminatory?

It is now recognised that adopting anti-discriminatory strategies is a key way in which you can help create a fairer society which everyone in the community can belong to. For pre-schools, inclusive and anti-discriminatory practice increases the participation of children and their families in the local community and so is fundamental to their existence.

The protection of children's rights

Anti-discriminatory practice is also a prerequisite to respecting children and empowering them. This means that there is a strong link between inclusive and anti-discriminatory practice and children's rights. These rights are embedded within the legal framework of the UK as a result of the UK becoming a signatory to the United Nations (UN) Convention on the Rights of the Child (see also pages 201–2). Under the articles of this convention, several key aspects of children's lives are covered and protected. These include, for example, the right of the child to education.

Whilst inclusive and anti-discriminatory practice is at the heart of pre-school practice, it is also important to be aware of the broad effects of discrimination. In terms of society, any discrimination that affects children has long-term effects. Some children may eventually reject the values of the society that has been hostile to them, while other children, whose potential has not been recognised, will fail to contribute to their full potential. The importance of incorporating anti-discriminatory strategies is reflected in the National Standards and the recent Children Act 2000.

Why inclusive and anti-discriminatory practice should be comprehensive

Traditionally, some groups of people are more likely to be discriminated against than others. While quite a lot of attention has been given to gender and race discrimination, it is important to realise that inclusive and anti-discriminatory practice in the pre-school setting must include attention to all types of discrimination shown in the diagram below.

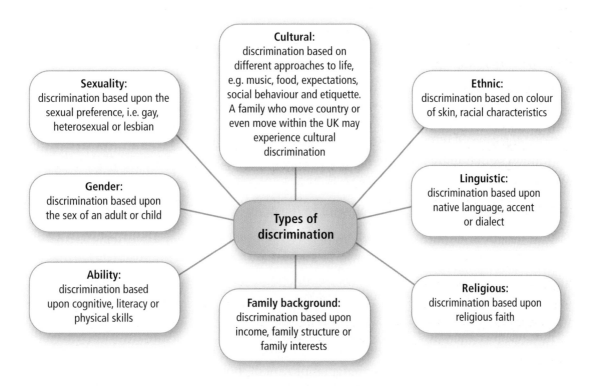

In addition, there are other common types of discrimination such as physical appearance, size and age. Providing an inclusive and anti-discriminatory pre-school means being sensitive to and valuing the differences that make all adults and children unique. By being aware of the possible types of discrimination, you should be able to consider ways of ensuring that children and their families can equally participate in the pre-school.

How to make the experience provided by the pre-school inclusive and anti-discriminatory for children and their parents, and staff

Everyone involved in the pre-school setting benefits from inclusive and anti-discriminatory practice. Children benefit, as they are able to benefit from everything that the pre-school offers, whilst parents and families benefit from being able to participate. The staff team also benefits because working for a supportive organisation is hugely satisfying.

Being aware of hidden messages

A major part of inclusive and anti-discriminatory practice is to consider the 'hidden messages' and values that are part of your setting. Children and their families need to feel that they are not just accepted but actively welcomed and seen as part of the community. Hidden messages are signals that are often negative and can put off children and their families from participating. An example of this might be the types of signs that are displayed on a notice board. Signs that are positive such as 'welcome' or 'thank you for your help' are positive, but ones such as 'Don't bring pushchairs inside' may send out a different signal especially if the notice board is full of other 'Don'ts'. Hidden messages can also be more subtle. For example, families who use a different home language to that of the setting may not feel included if there is no acknowledgement of their language – this might send out a signal that their language is not valued.

Being aware of children's and families needs

A key way in which you can provide a supportive and participative pre-school is to be good at communicating with parents and meeting both children's and their parents' needs. A pre-school setting with a 'can do' approach is helpful here. It means actively looking for ways of removing possible barriers, for example, a parent who needs to drop their child off ten minutes after the session time has started or being aware that a child may need additional support in order to access the sand tray.

The requirements of legislation relevant to inclusive and anti-discriminatory practice

It is essential to understand the requirements of legislation in relation to inclusive and anti-discriminatory practice. This ensures that the pre-school can discharge its legal as well as moral obligation towards children and their families. Key legislation relating to anti-discriminatory practice is outlined below.

Race Relations Act 1976

This Act makes it illegal to discriminate on the grounds of race, colour, nationality and ethnic origin in education and training, employment, housing, and the provision of goods and services including entertainment. The Commission for Racial Equality (CRE) was set up to offer advice and to help enforce the Act.

Example of illegal practices under this Act:

- it would be illegal for a pre-school setting to refuse a child a place because the family were immigrants
- it would be illegal for a pre-school setting to advertise for a 'white' member of staff.

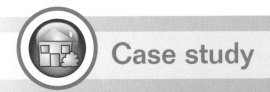

Case study

Leman and her daughter are new to the area. Leman speaks some English but still finds it hard to communicate effectively, although she is well educated. Her daughter Naz is nearly four years old. Leman is in hiding from her husband who abused her. She is pleased to have found somewhere safe to live but finds her neighbours unfriendly. Leman has been advised that there is a local pre-school and one morning goes to visit it. She has not made an appointment. When she rings the doorbell, she finds that a friendly face smiles at her. She says that she is new and wants her daughter to join. The pre-school leader, Pat, asks if she would like to look around. They go inside and Pat makes them feel welcome. Leman notices the posters, photographs and the friendly atmosphere that pervades the pre-school. She notices that other members of staff acknowledge her and her daughter with smiles. This makes a change from being stared at or ignored. Pat talks to Leman's daughter and they all look to see what the children are doing. Leman is invited to sit and watch the children as they play. Leman's daughter wants to join in with the others. Pat smiles and encourages her. Pat asks Leman if she would like to visit again. They use pictures and a calendar to help work out the time and date. Pat finds out what language Leman speaks so that next time she can be prepared.

1   In what ways has the pre-school shown that they are inclusive?
2   How does Leman's daughter benefit from the pre-school striving to be inclusive?
3   Why is it important that the pre-school should be available for all children and their families?

Sex Discrimination Act 1975 and 1986

These Acts make it illegal to discriminate against someone on the grounds of gender. The law also protects people from sexual harassment. There is also a Commission for Equal Opportunities that provides advice and enforces the Act.

Example of illegal practice under these Acts:

*   it would be illegal for a pre-school to refuse to interview a man who applied for a position simply because he was a man.

Equal Pay Act 1986

This Act makes employers pay equal amounts for work of equal value. The Commission for Equal Opportunities provides guidance and enforces this Act.

Example of illegal practice under this Act:

- it would be illegal for a pre-school to pay a male employee more money than a female employee who was doing the same work in the same pre-school.

Children Act 1989

This is a complex and far-reaching Act which enshrines many rights for children. It has had a significant impact on the delivery of care in pre-schools. Under this Act, children's rights and needs are seen as paramount. The Act looks at the importance of involving parents and making sure that families, wherever possible, remain united. Under the Act, establishments including pre-schools and crèches have to be inspected.

Since 2001, much work has been carried out by OFSTED, the inspectorate for children and learners in England. As part of the standards, pre-schools have to show that they promote equality of opportunity and show anti-discriminatory practice for all children in the setting. They also have to show how they identify and respond to children with special needs (Standards 9 and 10).

Disability Discrimination Act 1995

This is the first Act designed to ensure that disabled people are given equal services. It protects individuals against discrimination in several areas, including employment, buying goods and services, and buying or renting property. To allow businesses sufficient time to make reasonable adjustments to their services, the Act was being phased in gradually. The Act also created a National Disability Council to advise and work with the government on matters relating to disability and ways to introduce all parts of the Act. A further Act was later passed creating a commission in response to disappointed campaigners (who felt that a body with statutory powers was essential to make significant progress in addressing discrimination). The Disability Commission now has statutory powers to enforce the Disability Discrimination Act.

Special Educational Needs and Disability Act 2001

This Act is divided into two sections. Part one is a reform of the framework of Special Educational Needs (SEN), designed to strengthen the rights of access of parents and children to mainstream education. This reflects the idea of inclusive education in which children are not 'separated' from their peers because of a disability or particular need. Part two of the Act expands the Disability Discrimination Act 1995 to include education, colleges and universities.

Key features of the Act include:

- the right of children with SEN to be educated in mainstream schools (where this is what parents want and where it is appropriate for the child)
- the requirement of local education authorities (LEAs) to arrange to provide parents of children with SEN with advice and information, and a means of resolving disputes with schools and LEAs
- the requirement for LEAs to comply with orders of the special educational needs tribunal (the independent body that determine appeals by parents against LEA decisions)

'Inclusive education' also means providing a suitable and safe environment for all children's needs.

- the requirement of education settings to tell parents where they are making special educational provision for their child and to allow schools to request a statutory assessment of a pupil's SEN
- the introduction of disability discrimination rights in the provision of education in schools, further education, higher education, adult education and the youth service
- the requirement not to treat disabled students less favourably, without justification, than non-disabled students.

Human Rights Act 1998

The Human Rights Act came into force in October 2000. It has already made a huge impact on current legislation in this country. It requires courts and tribunals to make judgments using certain articles of the European Convention on Human Rights as a starting point. This Act was not designed specifically to protect children but they are accorded the same rights as adults. This means that children have a right to dignity, respect and fairness in the way in which they are treated.

United Nations Convention on the Rights of the Child

In addition to the Human Rights Act, the UK is a signatory to the Rights of the Child Convention. There are five main strands to this Convention:

1. Reinforces the importance of fundamental human dignity.
2. Highlights and defends the family's role in children's lives.
3. Seeks respect for children.

4   Endorses the principle of non-discrimination.

5   Establishes clear obligations for member countries to ensure that each country's legal framework is in line with the provisions of the Convention.

Every Child Matters

This government Green Paper outlined a new approach to ensuring the well-being of children and young people from birth to age 19 years. It laid down five aims for every child, whatever the child's background or circumstances. Each child needs to have the support he or she needs to:

- be healthy
- stay safe
- enjoy and achieve
- make a positive contribution
- achieve economic well-being.

Every Child Matters is about all children being given chances.

This means that all organisations involved with providing children's services will find new ways of working together, for example, by sharing information and working co-operatively to protect children and young people from harm and help them achieve what they want in life. Local authorities have a co-coordinating role under the children's trusts to ensure that this happens.

A 'common core' of knowledge and skills was established for everyone involved in work with children and young people, even if this is only a part of what their work will include. Training will now include:

- effective communication and engagement
- child and young person development
- safeguarding and promoting the welfare of the child
- supporting transitions
- multi-agency working
- sharing information.

Children Act 2004

This Act put in to practice the provisions outlined in Every Child Matters and provided for a new inspection regime.

Recognising and challenging discriminatory practice

It is not uncommon for pre-school settings to have adopted, over a period, practices that are discriminatory. In many cases, the discrimination is not intended but is rather the result of thoughtlessness and lack of consideration. The annual outing may cause financial difficulties for some parents, or the making of Mother's Day cards may make a child who lives with a single-parent father feel awkward. Reviewing how best to make these activities inclusive and accessible for all children is therefore important. Below is a list of areas which you might need to examine to ensure that practice is inclusive and anti-discriminatory.

Session times

Pre-schools serve their local community. The start and end times of sessions may have been set many years ago, when family structures and lifestyles were different. You should consider whether the current session times reflect the needs of parents and their children, or whether they act as a barrier to some families.

Settling-in policies

Settling in can take some time. Consider how flexible your approach is to individual children or whether the pre-school expects all children to follow the same pattern. Anti-discriminatory practice means that individual needs are taken into account and that children are not expected to all be 'the same'.

Accessibility

Accessibility is an issue for many groups of people, including children with mobility needs. Many parents will have younger children in pushchairs; in addition, some parents will use devices to increase their own mobility. Look at how accessible your setting is and consider ways of increasing accessibility. Consult with local voluntary groups as to how best to make your building accessible.

Financial assistance

The ability to pay fees or 'extras' can be an issue for many parents. While pre-schools need to balance their books, consider ways of making payments easier for parents and also whether the 'extras' can be funded in different ways, for example, by applying for grants in the local community or by carrying out fundraising activities. If financial assistance is available for some families, consider how it is offered, and avoid situations in which children are labelled as being from poor families.

Activities

The Birth to Three Matters framework, the Foundation Stage curriculum and the SEN Code of Practice 2001 make it clear that activities need to be planned in accordance with children's learning needs. This means looking for activities that can be simplified, extended or adapted to allow each child to participate at his or her own level. You should therefore avoid situations in which groups of children are seen as 'bright' or 'more able', since labelling children in this way can create stereotypes and also cause discrimination.

Curriculum planning

Familiarise yourself with the type of activities, themes and play experiences on offer. Consider whether they link to the interests of all children or will appeal to certain groups of children only. Think too about the level of involvement from parents and children as their input should help to make plans more reflective of their interests, culture and religion.

Managing children's behaviour

There is an increasing trend to regard children's unwanted behaviour as indicative of the fact that their needs are not being met. For example, children who cannot sit still at story time may be showing that they are tired or bored, or that their language development is not sufficient to cope with the type of story. This is a useful approach to take as it focuses your attention on considering the reasons why children are not able to show 'wanted' behaviour. Punitive or exclusive approaches to behaviour, such as removing children from activities because of their behaviour, are discriminatory and need to be recognised as such. They teach the child that he or she is not valued and do not address the cause of the unwanted behaviour. Seeing behaviour policies as part of anti-discriminatory practices is therefore important.

Test yourself

Why is it important that children that are showing inappropriate behaviour are not excluded or ostracised?

Partnership with parents

The way in which pre-schools work with parents can be an indicator of anti-discriminatory practice. Parents or main carers are key people in a child's life; therefore, the way in which you work with them is crucial. A child whose parents are not valued and respected will come to believe that he or she too is not important. Reflecting on the way in which you communicate with parents is therefore essential. Consider whether some parents are 'favourites': do staff spend more time with them? Think about the way in which parents are addressed, in both speech or writing, and whether these communications contain assumptions about their lifestyle, culture and financial background. It is also important to think about whether feedback from parents is taken seriously, or whether parents who pass comment are considered 'difficult'.

Challenging overt discrimination

Occasionally, you may overhear remarks or see actions that are not appropriate and are potentially offensive or damaging. While it might be tempting to keep quiet, it is worth understanding that, by doing so, you are condoning discrimination. Challenging discrimination is a skill that in many ways reflects your ability to be assertive. This does not mean being aggressive – in many cases, the person who is acting or speaking inappropriately may not realise that he or she is being discriminatory or offensive. Rather, challenging discrimination means gently suggesting to the person that his or her remarks or actions are not appropriate, and explaining why.

In situations where you suspect that people are knowingly being offensive, consider telling them that you find their subject of conversation distasteful and that, if they continue, you may decide to leave their company or (if appropriate) report what they have said. Where you have concerns about a member of staff, it is important to follow the procedure in the pre-schools' anti-discrimination and equal opportunities policy.

Case study

Consider the two situations below.

Situation one

Andrea is listening to a member of staff talking about her recent visit to the emergency department of a hospital with her son. During the conversation, the member of staff uses the term 'coloured doctor'. Andrea realises that the member of staff is not aware that this term is not appropriate. She interrupts the member of staff and gently says, 'I think you mean "black".'

Situation two

A few parents and the supervisor are having a chat about the weather at the start of the session. One of the parents begins to talk about seeing some gypsies at the weekend. The conversation rapidly becomes excited and racist comments are made. The supervisor decides that this conversation is inappropriate and says, 'I am sorry to disagree, but this is a conversation that I find deeply offensive. We are very much committed here to valuing all children and adults, so I must ask that you think about what you are saying.' An embarrassed hush falls and the supervisor brings the conversation back to what the children will be doing in the morning.

1 Why is it important to challenge discriminatory remarks?
2 Why is it important to explain why some comments are not appropriate?
3 Explain why people working with young children must be committed to anti-discriminatory practice.

The role of policies in making the pre-school setting inclusive and anti-discriminatory

Policies are statements that explain a pre-school setting's values, procedures and aims. All policies should reflect an inclusive and anti-discriminatory approach to working with children and their families. This is important as it means that inclusive and anti-discriminatory practice become embedded into the pre-school's way of working. The starting point, however, is to consider the pre-school's anti-discrimination and equal opportunities policy.

Anti-discrimination and equal opportunities policy

Every setting should have a policy for inclusive and anti-discriminatory practice. Policies help by ensuring that everyone in the team is working to the same commitment and intent, and they are a written expression of how this commitment will be translated into practice. Policies also help with practical matters as they should contain procedures to be used if ever the policy is being or likely to be breached.

Standard 9: Equal Opportunities

Standard 9 of the National Standards states that the registered person and staff actively promote equality of opportunity and anti-discriminatory practice. It is about ensuring that children are valued and that the setting actively promotes equality of opportunity. Inspectors will look at your setting's policy and the way in which the pre-school is run, including the activities and resources that are available. You will need to show that children's individual needs are identified and met. It is also important to show the ways in which the setting promotes positive images of culture, ethnicity, gender and disability through resources.

It is important that members of staff read Standard 9 and understand its implications.

As with every aspect of early years practice, the setting's policy should be reviewed and considered regularly. Questions you should ask are:

- Does the policy really work?

- Does the policy reflect current views and attitudes, for example, with reference to the SEN Code of Practice?

As well as being a vital tool to ensure that practice is inclusive and anti-discriminatory, policies are also a requirement in order to achieve Standard 9 of the National Standards and thus registration.

Ideally, you may wish to ask people outside of your setting, such as a pre-school development worker or early years advisor, to comment on your anti-discriminatory practice policy. Sometimes it is easier for someone who knows your setting well but does not work there to notice 'gaps' or areas that require further work. As well as having a policy, pre-school settings also need a procedure to follow when there is a breach of policy.

Drawing up a policy

The policy should be relevant to your setting. This means that, while it may be helpful to look at sample policies, it is essential that your finished policy reflects clearly what is happening in your setting and that everyone in the pre-school understands what it means.

There is no single way of drawing up a policy, but it can be helpful to use headings to structure the document. Below is an example of the type of information that could be used to build a policy.

Statement of commitment

- What are the aims of the policy?
- Who will be responsible for ensuring that the policy is implemented?
- How will the policy be reviewed and when will the review take place?

Admissions policy

- What is your setting's admissions policy?
- How does this reflect the setting's commitment towards equal opportunities?

Respecting children

- How do you help children to settle in?
- How are each child's needs recognised and met?
- How are children actively made to feel welcome and valued?
- How are children encouraged to explore their identity and value that of others?
- How does the behaviour policy reflect the importance of valuing and respecting children?

Involving parents

- How are parents' views about the care of their children respected and acted on?
- How are parents positively encouraged to contribute to the pre-school?
- How is information exchanged with parents, especially those who do not speak the language of the setting?
- How are parents encouraged to provide feedback to the setting?

Resources and activities

- How do resources and activities help to promote positive images of culture, religion, diversity and disability?
- How are activities adapted to meet the needs of all children?
- How do activities and resources contribute to all children's learning?

Staff training and recruitment

- How do new staff find out about anti-discriminatory practice policy and other policies in the setting?
- What training is provided to keep staff up to date with anti-discriminatory practice?
- Who is responsible for monitoring anti-discriminatory practice policy?
- How does the setting ensure that staff recruitment is anti-discriminatory?

Challenging attitudes and inappropriate practices

- What procedures are in place to ensure that inappropriate attitudes, language or practice are challenged?
- What would happen if this occurred?

How to monitor and evaluate the pre-school's inclusive and anti-discriminatory policies and procedures

It is usual for most pre-schools to have a variety of policies and procedures. It is essential that policies are monitored and reviewed regularly so that they do not become outdated or ineffective.

Monitoring policies

It is essential that policies are monitored to check that they are working in the way intended. This means thinking about the way that they are used, considering whether everyone is able to understand them and most importantly whether they are effective. It is useful if one member of staff is responsible for monitoring the policy so that he or she can focus on it and take some responsibility. It is also important when an incident or event takes place to think about whether the policy has been followed and has worked effectively.

Reviewing policies

It is therefore important to review the policies in your setting and check that they reflect current thinking on inclusive and anti-discriminatory practice. For example, you may find that the setting's behaviour policy is not inclusive, or that the policy on working with parents does not emphasise the importance of respecting different lifestyles. It is a good idea for everyone on the staff team to look at the policies and think about whether they reflect the setting's practice. Furthermore, it is important that all staff agree to the policies and are confident that they understand how inclusive and anti-bias practice is reflected in them. Policies need also to be reviewed if there has been any incident, comment or new information that may indicate that they may not be effective or accurate, for example, a new piece of legislation or information as a result of training.

In addition to thinking about policies that directly affect children, it is important to think about policies that affect staff. For example, does the procedure for employing staff reflect anti-discriminatory practice?

Anti-discriminatory policy: key questions

- Do policies reflect the need for pre-school settings to be inclusive?

- Is a member of staff responsible for monitoring anti-discriminatory practice?

- Are parents aware of the anti-discriminatory policy?

- Are parents and others invited to comment about practices in the pre-school?

- How much training has there been on anti-discriminatory practice since the policy was last reviewed?

Links to National Standards

Standard 9 of the National Standards is about ensuring that children are valued and that the setting actively promotes equality of opportunity. Inspectors will look at your setting's policy and the way in which the pre-school is run, including the activities and resources that are available. You will need to show that children's individual needs are identified and met. It is also important to show the ways in which the setting promotes positive images of culture, ethnicity, gender and disability through resources.

Applying theory to your practice

1   How do your pre-school's curriculum plans reflect the learning needs of individual and groups of children?

2   Why is it important that plans are tailored to meet individual children's needs?

Providing a healthy, safe, secure and stimulating environment that promotes pre-school children's learning and development

The pre-school aims to create not only a stimulating environment that children and their families can participate in but also a safe and secure environment. This section looks at some of the key issues in providing such an environment.

How to provide an appropriate physical environment to promote the learning and development of children aged 0–5 years

The term 'environment' is broad. It covers layout, resources, furniture and decoration as well as health and safety. Getting the environment right for children makes a considerable difference. Children who feel comfortable yet stimulated in the environment are able to settle in and enjoy learning. This also has an impact on parents as they can see that the environment will be a safe and secure one for their children. Interestingly, children also respond to the environment that they are in. Behaviour can be improved in responsive, stimulating environments that have been carefully planned.

Key components of an effective environment

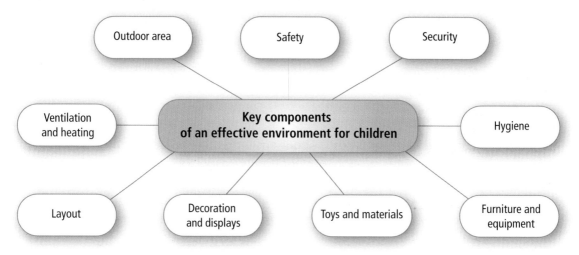

Safety

Safety is of paramount importance when working with children. Parents need to leave their child knowing that he or she is safe. This means that the environment needs to be assessed for risks and staff need to supervise children consistently.

Security

Security is becoming an increasingly serious issue. Children must be kept secure, either from wandering out or from strangers gaining access.

Hygiene

Good hygiene is about preventing germs from spreading and invading the body. Poor hygiene can have devastating results because young children are particularly vulnerable to infections. Food poisoning in a young child can be fatal, while repeated colds can cause ear infections and temporarily affect a child's hearing. Staff therefore need to be aware of how to provide a hygienic environment that is safe for children to play in.

Ventilation and heating

Adequate heating and ventilation helps to meet young children's physical needs. Good ventilation also prevents germs from building up in the air. Interestingly, an overheated room can contribute to children's unwanted behaviour. A comfortable temperature range is 18–21 °C (64–70 °F). Temperatures much higher or lower than this are not considered to be healthy.

Furniture and equipment

Furniture and equipment can play an important part in the daily life of a pre-school. Heavy or poorly designed furniture can mean that the layout of the setting is difficult to change. This can prevent staff and children from carrying out certain activities. For example, a high cupboard will prevent children from being able to put equipment away, while non-adjustable tables might not be comfortable for children to sit at. Another priority is ensuring that sufficient storage exists, since this affects the ease with which children can tidy up and access activities. Children who do not have the opportunity to select equipment and tidy up will not be developing self-reliance and independence.

Layout

The way in which space is used in a pre-school can have a significant effect on how adults and children operate within it. Some layouts encourage children to run between activities, while others prevent staff from supervising children adequately. The setting's layout can also affect how many children are able to access an activity, and thus reduce its appeal. For example, many children enjoy playing in an area that is slightly screened off so that they can engage in role-play more effectively.

Layout is also important in avoiding accidents. Look out for and avoid creating layouts that might encourage children to move at speed in confined areas, for example, a long straight pathway from one end of the room to another. Babies and younger children may also have different needs to Foundation Stage children with regards to layout (see also pages 212–3).

Layout needs to be adapted according to children's stage of development.

Outdoor area

It is very easy to focus on the indoor environment and forget that children need to spend time outdoors. Being outdoors can help children's circulation, physical movement and general well-being. Where possible, play activities should be provided outdoors, as well as the more traditional outdoor equipment such as tricycles, slides and pushchairs. Opportunities for babies and toddlers to be outside also need to be taken into account. Providing easy access and areas which are suitable for these younger children is essential.

Toys and materials

The ability of children to concentrate and engage in play is partially linked to the materials and toys with which they are provided. Toys and materials need to be age and stage appropriate and linked to children's interests. This means providing a range of toys and materials that enable children to learn a variety of skills and also enhance aspects of their development.

It is important that sufficient toys and materials are available to allow several children to engage in the same type of play should they wish. As toys and materials are significant costs in the running of a setting, it is important that decisions about which ones to buy are carefully evaluated and that those that are bought are used well.

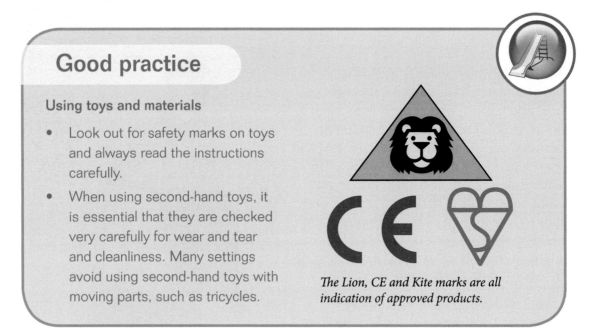

Good practice

Using toys and materials

- Look out for safety marks on toys and always read the instructions carefully.

- When using second-hand toys, it is essential that they are checked very carefully for wear and tear and cleanliness. Many settings avoid using second-hand toys with moving parts, such as tricycles.

The Lion, CE and Kite marks are all indication of approved products.

Decoration and displays

The actual look of a setting can make a huge difference to the way in which children come to settle and behave. Children respond to seeing attractive displays, especially of their own work: it helps them to feel ownership. If children are encouraged to contribute to the care of displays, it can make them feel responsible.

Ensuring that the environment meets the needs of children at different stages of development

As children grow and develop, so their needs change. This needs to be reflected in the pre-school environment.

Identifying the needs of the under-threes

Maintaining safety and hygiene is a priority: young children do not have a sense of danger and, at the same time, they are curious. Toddlers in particular can be determined to explore. It is, therefore, important to be aware of the physical stages of development of each child and to consider how this will affect the child's safety.

- Children who are attempting to walk need to have stable furniture to pull up against, while children who are mobile might attempt to stand on furniture.
- Young children also have physical needs that need to be catered for effectively. Nappy-changing areas must be safe and hygienic, but also pleasant and welcoming for the child.
- Thought should be given to where children will eat and how the layout of the eating area will encourage them to enjoy the experience.

The role of safety equipment

For children under three years of age there is a need to provide safety equipment, especially to keep mobile babies and toddlers safe. (See the table on page 214 for types of safety equipment.) However, safety equipment is not a substitute for good supervision and adults must not be lulled into a false sense of security.

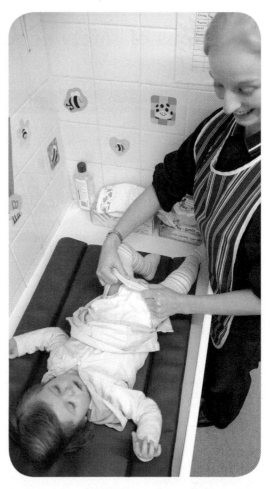

Is your nappy changing area clean and hygienic?

Identifying the needs of children aged 3–5 years

Health and safety remains a key issue in creating an environment because children do not magically become aware of safety when they reach three or four years old. Therefore, some safety equipment may still be required to keep older children safe, for example, plug covers and safety gates. In addition, the provision layout needs to be created with supervision in mind, although this should become increasingly discreet as children mature. Children aged 3–5 years also need to enjoy independence, make choices and create their own play situations. Thus, many pre-schools create areas of provision within their settings to allow children to enjoy playing freely.

The requirements of current legislation relevant to providing a healthy, safe and secure environment

The environments that pre-schools, nurseries and childminders provide are regulated to ensure that all children are safe and receive a good standard of care. The current regulations are linked to the Children Act 1989. This Act provides for the registration of all childcare providers who care for children for longer than two hours at a time.

Types of safety equipment for children under three years of age

Type of equipment	Purpose	Precautions
Reins and harnesses	These are required for outings and for babies and toddlers in high chairs.	Care must be taken that these fit snugly but not too tightly. Staff should always position a harness so that it can easily be undone if the child chokes.
Safety gates	These prevent children from moving into areas which might be hazardous, for example, stairs and kitchens.	Look out for gates that are easily opened by adults. Safety gates may be needed in rooms with older children.
Plastic corners	These are used to prevent toddlers from walking into the corners of furniture.	
Plastic plug covers	These are used to prevent children putting their fingers into live electric sockets.	Plug covers are also needed to protect older children.
Latches and window locks	Latches prevent children from having access to cupboards and drawers that may have dangerous contents. Window latches prevent children from falling out.	Some latches are easier to use than others.
Fire guards and radiator covers	These prevent children from touching hot radiators or gas appliances.	Make sure these are securely in place.

The National Standards

Since September 2001, the Early Years directorate at OFSTED has taken on this inspection role. The inspection takes place each year and providers are currently inspected against the set of National Standards, of which there are 14. Collectively, the standards cover all aspects of children's care, including safety, food and drink, and child protection. A chart showing the National Standards, which includes an OFSTED descriptor of each standard, is found on pages 215–6.

Health and safety legislation

In addition to the National Standards, there exists legislation about health and safety. There are two key pieces of legislation that affect health and safety in early years settings:

- the Health and Safety at Work Act 1974
- the Children Act 1989.

More information on these Acts is given on pages 216–8.

The National Standards

National Standard	Title	Descriptor
Standard 1	Suitable Person	Adults providing day care, looking after or having unsupervised access to children, are suitable to do so.
Standard 2	Organisation	The registered person meets required adult to child ratios, ensures that training and qualification requirements are met, and organises space and resources to meet the children's needs effectively.
Standard 3	Care, Learning and Play	The registered person meets children's individual needs and promotes their welfare. The registered person plans and provides activities and play opportunities to develop children's emotional, physical, social and intellectual capabilities.
Standard 4	Physical Environment	The premises are safe, secure and suitable for their purpose. They provide adequate space in an appropriate location, are welcoming to children, and offer access to the necessary facilities for a range of activities in order to promote children's development.
Standard 5	Equipment	Furniture, equipment and toys are provided, which are appropriate for their purpose and help to create an accessible and stimulating environment. They are of suitable design and condition, are well-maintained and conform to safety standards.
Standard 6	Safety	The registered person takes positive steps to promote safety within the setting and on outings and ensures proper precautions are taken to prevent accidents.
Standard 7	Health	The registered person promotes the good health of children, takes positive steps to prevent the spread of infection and adopts appropriate measures when children are ill.
Standard 8	Food and Drink	Children are provided with regular drinks and food in adequate quantities for their needs. Food and drink is properly prepared, nutritious and complies with dietary and religious requirements.
Standard 9	Equal Opportunities	The registered person and staff actively promote equality of opportunity and anti-discriminatory practice for all children.
Standard 10	Special Needs	The registered person is aware that some children may have special needs and is proactive in ensuring that appropriate action can be taken when such a child is identified or admitted to the provision. Steps are taken to promote the welfare and development of the child within the setting in partnership with the parents and other relevant parties.
Standard 11	Behaviour	Adults caring for children in the provision are able to manage a wide range of children's behaviour in a way that promotes their welfare and development.
Standard 12	Working in Partnership with Parents and Carers	The registered person and staff work in partnership with parents to meet the needs of the children, both individually and as a group. Information is shared.

Continued ▶

National Standard	Title	Descriptor
Standard 13	Child Protection	The registered person complies with local child protection procedures approved by the Area Child Protection Committee and ensures that all adults working and looking after children in the provision are able to put the procedures into practice.
Standard 14	Documentation	Records, policies and procedures that are required for the efficient and safe management of the provision and to promote the welfare, care and learning of children are maintained. Records about individual children are shared with the child's parent.

The Acts are designed to enable further legislation to be passed to update their provisions; these updates take the form of regulations. One example is the 1997 Fire Precautions (Workplace) Regulations, which made it compulsory for workplaces to have 'running men' symbols to help people see where they should go in the event of a fire. The changing nature of health and safety means that pre-schools must stay up to date with current regulations; ignorance of regulations is not considered a defence in law.

Health and Safety at Work Act 1974

This Act was designed to protect employees so many of its provisions apply to workplaces in which there are five or more members of staff. The Act gives duties to both employees and employers.

- *Duties of employees*
  The Act is clear that employees must follow the setting's health and safety procedures and use the health and safety equipment provided. Employees should not put others at risk by their actions, for example, by failing to report a faulty plug when there is a procedure to do so.

- *Duties of employers*
  The Act places significant duties on employers. Employers have a duty of care towards their employees and must take every reasonable step to consider their health and safety and to minimise risks. This means providing adequate training and protection and carrying out risk assessments. Under this Act, settings with five or more employees must have a health and safety policy that explains how risks are to be minimised. Most pre-schools appoint a senior member of staff to be responsible for health and safety.

Test yourself

To whom would you report any concerns that you have about safety?

Significant regulations under the 1974 Health and Safety at Work Act

Regulation title	Description
Control of Substances Hazardous to Health Regulations (COSHH) 2004	These regulations look at the storage and use of chemicals and other hazardous materials. In pre-school settings, this might include cleaning products and the disposal of nappies. The regulations require settings to assess the risks and then write a procedure for managing the risks, for example, locking bleach in a cupboard and providing gloves.
Reporting of Injuries, Diseases and Dangerous Occurrences (RIDDOR) 1995	Workplaces must provide an accident report book for their employees (the 1989 Children Act regulations require an accident book for noting down injuries to children). Any injuries to an employee that mean that he or she cannot work for three or more days must be reported to the Health and Safety Executive.
Fire Precautions (Workplace) regulations 1997	Workplaces have to show how they would evacuate the building and carry out practices. Signs showing what to do in the event of a fire must be placed in every room. (Note that the 1989 Children Act also requires settings to have an evacuation procedure.)
Health and Safety (First Aid) Regulations 1981	Every workplace must have a first aid box and appoint at least one trained first aider to be responsible in the event of an accident. The contents of the first aid box are left to the discretion of the workplace. (Note that the 1989 Children Act requires that any medication given to children is recorded.)

Children Act 1989

This Act is designed to protect children and to give them legal rights. It is a wide-ranging piece of legislation because the idea was to combine many existing pieces of legislation into one Act. As part of the Act, people who care for children, such as childminders, and settings caring for children, need to be inspected. OFSTED has carried out this inspection role since September 2001.

Regulations that detail the standards of care for children come under the Children Act and include several relating to the health, safety and welfare of children. These regulations need to be dovetailed into your pre-school's compliance with the 1974 Health and Safety Act. Some of the key regulations that you will need to comply with and that OFSTED is likely to check during their visit are shown in the chart on the next page. Note that simply following these regulations alone is not sufficient to meet the requirements of an inspection.

Examples of regulations linked to health and safety under the 1989 Children Act

Links to National Standards	What you need to do
Suitable person	OFSTED must be informed about people who may come into contact with the children, such as staff, volunteers and people who live on the premises.
Organisation	You must have procedures in place if a child is lost or a parent fails to collect their child. You must keep a record of the names and details of anyone who will be in regular contact with the children.
Physical environment	OFSTED must be informed if any changes are made to the premises or the way in which they are used.
Safety	You must have a policy in place which shows the procedure in the event of a fire.
Health	A record has to be kept of all medicines administered to children. A signed record of accidents must be kept in the setting. Serious accidents that result in injuries or death to children must be reported to OFSTED. You must report all notifiable infectious diseases to OFSTED.
Working in Partnership with Parents and Carers	You must keep records of the name, address and date of birth of each child, and the name, address and telephone number of a parent. You must have a complaints policy for parents to use.
Child Protection	A policy must be in place that shows how children are to be protected from abuse and the procedure to be followed in the event that abuse is suspected.
Documentation	Records that link to the regulations must be kept for at least two years following the last entry. OFSTED must be informed of significant changes or events, for example, members of staff leaving, a change of use of premises, longer opening hours, etc. Records as required by the National Standards must be kept on the premises. (See the National Standards on pages 215–6 for the comprehensive list.)

Thinking and research

Finding out information about current health and safety regulations

You can find out more about health and safety by contacting the Health and Safety Executive (HSE). This is a government agency that advises on health and safety

Continued ▶

and has the power to investigate and bring prosecutions against employers. They have a helpline and publish information leaflets. Contact www.hse.gov.uk or telephone HSE Infoline on 0845 345 0055.

You can also find out more about accident prevention by contacting the Royal Society for the Prevention of Accidents (ROSPA) at www.rospa.org.uk.

How to use risk assessment procedures to ensure the health and safety of pre-school children and adults

It is impossible to create an environment that is totally free from risk. Yet even if this were possible, it would not be beneficial for children as they do need to explore materials and toys as well as the environment in order to learn. This means that pre-schools need to look at ways of evaluating and managing risks through a process called risk assessment.

Carrying out risk assessment

Risk assessment means thinking about what children are likely to be doing, working out the level of risk and then considering strategies to minimise the risks. Risk assessments are also used to evaluate the risk of activities for staff members. Sometimes risk assessments are seen as ways of preventing activities, resources or equipment from being used. This can lead to an environment that is not sufficiently stimulating for children and this in turn can become a risk: children who are bored often show poor behaviour including aggression.

Forms for risk assessment need to be drawn up and reviewed as part of the pre-school's health and safety policy. Risk assessments need to be reviewed as a number of factors can affect their validity; for example, the pre-school might take in younger children or new pieces of equipment might be bought.

Example of a risk assessment form

Activity/Resources/Area	Risks to be assessed	Remedies
Steps leading to entrance	Danger of falls, especially when wet. Danger of children pushing each other when playing on them.	Install a grab rail. Supervise children. Restrict numbers on steps.
Tricycles	Danger of falls and collisions between children. Create one-way system so that children do not cycle towards each other.	Create a designated area for tricycles. Provide cycle helmets.
Treasure basket play	Danger of choking and suffocation. Danger of cross-infection.	Check size of objects using safety gadget. Provide each baby with his or her own treasure basket. Wash items after use.

How to maintain a hygienic environment in a pre-school setting

Good hygiene is essential in early years settings:

- young children are more vulnerable to infections because their immune system is still developing
- repeated illness in children can affect their overall development since they miss out on play and activities
- children in groups are particularly vulnerable to food poisoning, colds and other infections because bacteria and germs can spread easily.

Good hygiene is about preventing the possible spread of infection. This is becoming particularly important as many strains of bacteria are now becoming immune to antibiotics.

It is thought that, given the right conditions, a single bacterium can produce a colony of 250,000 in six hours.

Understanding how germs are spread

A host of organisms can infect the human body. Major groups are bacteria, viruses, fungi and parasites, such as worms and nits. Understanding how these organisms infect people can be helpful when thinking about prevention.

Inhalation

Some germs, for example, colds and influenza, are airborne and are breathed in. Keeping a window open to provide ventilation can help prevent airborne infections.

Inoculation

Some germs infect people because they enter through the skin via cuts, grazes and other wounds. Covering cuts with plasters can prevent infection from gaining an entrance.

Ingestion

Some bacteria, viruses and parasites, such as threadworms, cause infection when a person swallows them. This is an easy way for germs to enter babies and young children, who frequently put their hands in their mouth. Remember that babies explore objects, such as toys, by putting them in their mouth and so objects that are mouthed in this way will need cleaning.

Maintaining cleanliness

You will need to have a regular routine of cleaning in order to maintain a high standard of cleanliness in the setting. It is important that staff understand their responsibilities in relation to cleaning and are ready to mop up spills where necessary. You will also need to make sure that all staff who prepare food have had training, for example, a basic food hygiene certificate.

Using cleaning products

It is not advisable to use cleaning products when children are around. Some cleaning products, especially aerosols and sprays, can trigger breathing difficulties in children with asthma. There is also the danger that products left unattended may be swallowed or spilt.

When using cleaning products, it is essential to read the instructions on the packaging because some products must be used with gloves. Take care to ensure that different cleaning products are not mixed because some products can produce strong chemical reactions when combined. Under the COSHH Regulations 2004 (see page 217), cleaning products must be risk assessed.

Routine cleaning in the pre-school setting

Area/item	Method
Hard floors	Wash with disinfectant every day and during the day if there are spills. Floors in wash areas and kitchens need particular attention.
Carpeted areas	These should be thoroughly vacuumed and arrangements made for them to be shampooed regularly.
Toilets, hand basins, sinks	Bacteria favour damp conditions to multiply and so these areas need to be cleaned at least once a day to prevent the spread of infection. Attention should be paid to handles on toilets and doors in these areas.
Door handles	Frequently used door handles should be wiped each day with disinfectant.
Tables	Tables should be wiped over at the end of each activity with disinfectant. If they are used to serve food, they should be cleaned at the beginning and the end of the meal. The legs of the table should also be given attention.
Chairs	The backs and sides of chairs are often handled and if they are used at food tables can become dirty. Chairs should therefore be wiped over frequently.
Bins	Bins should be emptied regularly and covered over. Separate bins are needed for waste paper and for soiled waste materials. Waste materials such as nappies should be put in a bag and then put into a covered bin. This bin should be out of reach of children.
Feeding equipment	Beakers, plates, cutlery – anything used to serve food – must be cleaned thoroughly. Staff should wash their mugs properly as dirty mugs are a common cause of infection in staff rooms.
Toys and frequently handled equipment	Wipe down with disinfectant and rinse if necessary. Pay particular attention to objects such as pencils if children suck the ends, and toys that babies put in their mouth.
Cuddly toys, bedding and soft furnishings, such as cushions	Surprisingly high levels of bacteria can build up on fabrics. This means that cuddly toys, bedding and cushion covers, etc. need to be washed regularly – at least weekly. Toys that are not easy to clean should be discarded.
Outdoor areas	Check that animals, including birds, have not fouled. Make sure that equipment is clean and wipe it if necessary. Cover sand pits to avoid parasitic infection and always check for fouling before use. Remove any litter. Wear disposable gloves while cleaning outdoors.

Using protective clothing

It is important to use gloves and protective aprons when cleaning. This includes nappy changing, sorting out 'accidents' and also first aid. Protective clothing helps to prevent the spread of infection provided the clothing is removed afterwards. Wearing aprons that have been used for earlier nappy changing might spread infection.

Test yourself

Where disposable gloves are provided for cleaning, changing nappies, etc., why do you have a legal duty to wear them?

How to implement and review procedures for handling emergencies and first aid

Procedures for emergencies

All staff should understand what to do in an emergency. This is not only a requirement for registration; it also makes common sense. Regular fire drills and evacuation procedures should be practised so that both staff and children become familiar with them. Signs should also be clearly displayed to act as reminders but also to provide visitors with information. Evacuation and assembly points need to be clearly indicated.

The responsibility for organising practices should lie with a designated member of staff. This is usually the person who has responsibility for health and safety within the setting.

Case study

Caroline is health and safety officer for the Busy Bees pre-school. She has decided to call a fire drill. She deliberately does not tell anyone except the supervisor so that she can find out how well the procedures are working. The staff team talks about the practice afterwards.

1 Explain the importance of regular fire drills.

2 Give two reasons why staff should not always know that a fire drill is going to happen.

3 Why is it important to evaluate the procedures for emergencies?

Ideally, some practices should be carried out without warning at different times of the day and with the assumption that fire has broken out in different places. This allows procedures to be tested in realistic conditions and ensures that part-time members of staff are involved. A record of each practice should be kept.

Once a practice is finished, staff should be encouraged to give feedback. Such feedback can be invaluable: problems can be ironed out or suggestions for improvement considered. Such comments and notes should be added to the practice records. In cases where a practice has not gone as smoothly as hoped, it is essential to repeat the practice within a short space of time. New members of staff should also be given training in evacuation procedures and it is usual for them to sign to show that this information has been given.

Good practice

Emergency evacuation

- Is one member of staff designated for fire safety?
- Are frequent practices carried out?
- Are fire alarms and fire safety equipment regularly checked and recorded?
- Are new members of staff aware of the procedures for evacuation?
- Are notices and signs relating to evacuation clearly displayed?
- Who is responsible for contacting emergency services?
- How would emergency services be contacted?
- Is there regular liaison with fire prevention officers?

Reviewing evacuation procedures

- How were parents/visitors alerted to the fire?
- What was the overall evacuation time?
- Did everyone evacuate? If not, why was this?
- Were any problems encountered, for example, blocked or locked exits?
- Were registers taken and were they accurate?
- Did everyone meet at the appointed location?
- Was the location of the evacuation point appropriate?
- How did the children react?

Procedures for first aid

While serious accidents are, thankfully, rare in pre-school settings, staff must know the procedure for handling accidents whether serious or minor. It is a requirement that each setting has a designated person for first aid, although ideally everyone in the setting should at least have a basic first aid qualification. It is also useful to keep a record of when staff attended training, since first aid qualifications need to be regularly renewed. Signs also need to be displayed that show the name and location of the nearest first aider. As most first aid training focuses on the needs of adults, it is important also to learn about first aid with babies and young children (paediatric first aid). This is a requirement of National Standard 7.9. Some local authorities provide training via their early years teams or keep a register of trainers that deliver paediatric first aid as part of the training course.

Good practice

Implementing first aid procedures

- Is a member of staff designated for first aid?
- Are there signs showing where first aid kits are to be found?
- Do all members of staff know where the first aid kits are situated?
- Are first aid kits checked regularly?
- Are first aid kits out of reach of children but accessible for adults?
- Do staff understand the importance of filling in the accident book?

Appropriate responses to accidents and injuries

While every effort should be made to prevent accidents, it is also important that everyone knows what to do if a child has an accident. This section looks at how to respond to an accident. While this information might be helpful, it is not a replacement for attending a basic first aid course. Such courses will give you practical experience of how to administer first aid correctly. In addition, techniques for first aid do change, so you should always take refresher courses. Being trained in first aid has the potential to save a life and so learning resuscitation and also how to put children in a recovery position is vital. To remain the qualified first aider for your setting, you will need to keep your qualification up to date. Currently this means taking a 12-hour course every three years.

Responding to an accident

It is important to respond to every accident with care. What might seem a simple bump to the head might later result in concussion. If you are the nearest adult when an accident occurs, you should remain calm and take the following steps.

1 Keep calm
- *This reassures children and helps them to follow your instructions.*
- *It prevents further accidents.*
- *It allows you to assess the situation more accurately and make the right decisions.*

2 Look out for any further dangers
- *What was the cause of the accident? Is this still a danger?*
- *Do other children need to be evacuated?*
- *Does the casualty need to be removed to prevent further injury?*

3 Assess the extent of the injury
- *Is the child breathing, talking?*
- *Can you see bleeding?*
- *Is the child in great pain?*

4 Decide on the type of help required
- *Is emergency help required?*
- *Is a first aider's assistance required?*

5 Summon help
- *Is it safe to ask one of the other children to get help?*
- *Can help be summoned by calling out?*
- *Is there a telephone or other means of getting help?*

Responding to an accident.

When to contact emergency services

Emergency services should always be contacted if any of the following apply:

- the child has stopped breathing
- you cannot find a pulse
- the child has difficulty in breathing or the skin and lips are turning blue
- the child is vomiting blood
- the child is unconscious or not responding
- the child is bleeding profusely

- where a child has a pre-existing condition (for example, asthma, diabetes, sickle cell anaemia, specific allergies resulting in anaphylactic shock) and the parents have alerted the setting to the need for emergency medical intervention.

It is essential not to waste time before contacting an ambulance if a child's condition causes concern. It is always better to err on the side of caution than wait to see if the child's condition improves.

Basic first-aid procedures

General points	Fractures, dislocations and srains
<ul><li>Call or shout for help.</li><li>Stop any treatment and follow **ABC** if a child stops breathing: 1) check **A**irways for obstructions; 2) look to see if the child is **B**reathing; 3) take a pulse to see if blood is **C**irculating.</li><li>Do not give food or drink to children who have had a major accident.</li><li>Remain calm and reassuring.</li></ul>	<ul><li>It is not always easy to spot that a child has a fracture, but signs may include: – loss of movement and power – swelling – awkward angle of limb.</li><li>Keep the child still and get a first aider to come and help you.</li><li>If a leg is thought to be broken, tie bandages around both legs above and below the fracture to keep the leg still.</li><li>Use a scarf or bandage to make a sling to keep an arm still.</li></ul>
Poisoning	**Choking**
(Children may not look well, begin vomiting or you may see what has been taken.)<ul><li>Ask the child what he or she has eaten or drunk, if this is possible.</li><li>Watch for signs of losing consciousness.</li><li>Do not make the child vomit or give any drinks.</li><li>Take the suspected poison with you to the hospital so the appropriate treatment can be given.</li></ul>	<ul><li>Hold the child so that his or her head is downwards. This can be over your knees.</li><li>Slap firmly five times between the shoulder blades.</li><li>Repeat if necessary.</li></ul>
Cuts and wounds	**Burns and scalds**
<ul><li>Direct pressure needs to be applied to the wound with a clean pad. If it is a large wound, try to press the edges together.</li><li>Do not remove anything from a deep wound as you may cause more bleeding.</li><li>Tie a bandage around the pad – firmly but not too tightly.</li><li>If blood comes through, apply another pad and bandage over the top.</li><li>Keep applying pressure for about 15 minutes.</li><li>Lay the child down and raise the injured part so that it is higher than the heart.</li></ul>	<ul><li>Cool down the affected area immediately using cold water or any harmless liquid (e.g. milk) if you are not near water.</li><li>Do this for at least 10 minutes.</li><li>Keep talking to the child and explain what you are doing.</li><li>Do not remove clothes that have stuck to the skin or put on creams of any kind.</li><li>Cover the area with a clean cloth, e.g. a teacloth (do not use anything like a fluffy towel).</li></ul>

If you decide that emergency services need to be called, make sure that either you do this or another responsible adult does – sometimes in the confusion of an accident everyone thinks that someone else has made the call. While waiting for the emergency services to arrive, you should try to get the help of a trained first aider.

Information that the emergency services will need

Keeping calm is essential when contacting the emergency operators. In order to dispatch help they need clear information and will therefore run through a series of questions. The type of information required includes:

- type of emergency help required
- your name
- location of where you are telephoning from
- location of incident and any landmarks
- cause of the accident
- symptoms and signs of injury
- age of the child.

Before or once the emergency help has arrived, you should refer to the child's admission details and emergency contact details. This is important as the child might be allergic to some medicines or the child's doctor may need to be contacted.

Resuscitation

Resuscitation should be carried out *only* if you have been trained to do so. If you have not, summon a first aider immediately.

Dealing with minor injuries

Fortunately, most pre-school staff will only ever tend to minor injuries (see table on next page). When children have had a knock, bump or graze, it is good practice for them to be seen by the first aider in the setting. This is important as children will need to be assessed carefully. The accident book should be filled in and signed, regardless of whether any treatment was necessary. You should also ensure that parents are informed of the accident and ask them to countersign the accident book. This is vital because it is one of the regulations of the Children Act 1989.

Accident reports

It is a requirement that records are kept of any injury a child sustains in the setting, regardless of how superficial. In addition, an accident record book is required for staff and other adults. It is a good idea to look regularly at where and how accidents are taking place because the setting's layout or a certain piece of equipment may prove to be the source of a problem. Records must be promptly filled in after any incident and must be signed by the member of staff who treated the child. Parents should also be given information about the accident. This might mean providing a slip with information or asking parents to sign the accident record book. Serious accidents have to be reported to OFSTED. Separate accident books are required for staff members and serious accidents have to be reported to the Health and Safety Executive.

Treating minor injuries

Injury	Treatment	Check for
Bump to the head, e.g. falling over or running into another child	Apply cotton wool squeezed in cold water. If the bump is bad, apply wrapped crushed ice.	Drowsiness, vomiting or headaches – these could indicate concussion.
Nose bleed	Tip the head forward. Pinch the soft part of the nose just below the bridge. Wrapped crushed ice can be put on to the nose if needed.	Seek medical attention if the bleeding continues for more than half an hour or if it is mixed with clear fluid.
Grazed skin	Rinse the wound with clean water. Allow to heal in the air.	
Bruises and trapped fingers	Apply cotton wool squeezed in cold water or wrapped crushed ice.	Run a hand gently over the limb to check that nothing feels lumpy, which might be a sign of a fracture.
Vomiting	Do not leave the child. Reassure him or her. Offer a sip of water to take away the sour taste.	If vomiting occurs after a bump to the head, medical attention is needed as this is a sign of concussion.
Insect stings	Reassure the child. Try to remove the sting by scraping it out with a finger nail. Do not squeeze the sting. Use a wrapped ice pack to reduce the swelling.	Urgent medical help is needed if the sting is in the mouth or if the child starts to look ill. Some children are allergic to stings.

Key questions when reviewing first aid procedures

- Is the accident book filled out promptly and signed each time?
- Are emergency contact details kept up to date?
- Does a 'spot check' of the first aid kit reveal any deficiencies?
- Are procedures for first aid emergencies displayed?
- Are first aid qualifications still valid?
- Do staff wear protective gloves and handle waste products safely?

How to implement and review procedures for responding to illness, handling children's allergies and administering medicines

In order to care for children effectively it is important to have procedures for when they are ill, have allergies or need medication. Procedures need to be written down and provide clear guidance so that any member of the adult team knows how they should respond. As with all procedures, it is important that new members of the adult team are given sufficient time and explanation to familiarise themselves.

Responding to children's illness

Children's high metabolism means that they can quickly go down with an illness, so they may become poorly while in your care. It is important that you are vigilant because children want to be with their parents when unwell and you also need to avoid the spread of infection. A quick response is especially important because some infections, for example, meningitis, can quickly take hold of a child and getting prompt medical attention can save lives.

The better that you know a child, the easier it is for you to identify quickly that he or she is feeling poorly. Parents can also help you when settling in children as they may share with you some of the specific ways in which their child shows that he or she is not well, for example, pulling on an ear lobe. This information is especially important when caring for babies and toddlers who may not otherwise be able to communicate their feelings.

 Case study

Raj is eight months old. He is a little fretful and keeps pulling and rubbing his ears. He has also not been feeding well. He has rings under his eyes and is generally unhappy. He wants to be carried, which is unusual, but he does settle. His key person, Sam, decides to contact Raj's parents at work to let them know that he looks poorly and to find out how he was in the night. It turns out that he had not slept well and his parents feel that he is teething. His father is unable to leave work straight away as he has a meeting but they agree that he will pick up Raj early and that Sam will call again if Raj shows signs of distress.

1 **Why was it important for Raj's parents to know about their child's well-being?**
2 **How can a key person system benefit a child who is tired or not feeling well?**
3 **Why is it essential to inform parents as soon as a child shows signs of being unwell?**

General signs that a child may not be well include:

- lack of appetite
- poor skin – colour pale or greyish
- rings around the eyes
- fretfulness
- tiredness
- difficulty in participating and concentrating
- requests for a comforter or needing the reassurance of an adult
- vomiting
- headache
- flushed cheeks
- wetting or soiling.

Avoiding the spread of infection

If children are feeling poorly it is important that you take steps to minimise the risks of spreading infection to others. This means that you should take the child away from other children while waiting for the parents to collect him or her. It is therefore a good idea for settings to consider having in their layout an area in which poorly children can wait. Some children will want to lie down, while others will be happy just to stay in the company of a familiar and reassuring adult. If toys or other equipment are used to entertain the child while he or she is waiting, it will be important for these to be washed once the child has left.

Good practice

Avoiding the spread of infection

- Make sure that the sick child does not come into contact with other children.
- Wash any toys or equipment that a poorly child has handled once he or she has left.
- Keep windows open in the setting to increase ventilation.
- Make sure that all children wash their hands before eating and after using the toilet.
- Make sure that all equipment in the setting is cleaned thoroughly.

The table below shows common childhood illnesses and how to treat them.

Common childhood illnesses and how to treat them

Illness	Incubation	Signs and symptoms	Treatment	Complications
Common cold	1–3 days	Running or blocked nose; sneezing; headache; lethargy; temperature.	Keep up fluid intake. Rest and sleep.	Ear infection; bronchitis.
Chicken pox (Varicella)	10–14 days	Groups of red spots with raised white centres that become itchy on trunks and limbs; slight fever.	Calamine lotion to relieve itchiness. Nails could be cut short to prevent scratching.	Scars caused by spots becoming infected.
Ear infection		Pains, e.g. earache, headache; persistent or intermittent vomiting.	Seek medical attention. Antibiotics, paracetamol.	Temporary hearing loss (sometimes permanent where children have repeated infections).
Food poisoning	½–36 hours	Diarrhoea, vomiting.	Fluids only for 24 hours. Seek medical assistance after 24 hours.	Weight loss; dehydration; in severe cases, death.
Gastroenteritis (inflammation of the stomach lining)	7–14 days (bacteria); ½–36 hours (virus)	Nausea, diarrhoea, vomiting.	Keep up fluid intake. Seek medical advice if symptoms are severe.	Weight loss; dehydration; in severe cases, death.
German measles (Rubella)	14–21 days	Mild symptoms include a pink rash on head which spreads to trunk and limbs, sore throat and slight fever.	Rest if needed.	No complications, but can cause serious problems for an unborn baby if a pregnant woman is infected. (Children are at their most infectious a few days before symptoms show until one day after symptoms disappear.)

Continued ▶

Illness	Incubation	Signs and symptoms	Treatment	Complications
Measles	8–14 days	At first: fever, runny eyes, sore throat and cough. Red rash (often blotchy) appears, often starting from the head and spreading downwards.	Rest, plenty of fluids and paracetamol if needed to treat fever.	Ear and chest infections; in rare cases, encephalitis (inflammation of the fluid around the brain).
Meningitis, viral and bacterial	2–14 days	Fever; severe headache; nausea; stiff neck; blotchy skin rash that can look like bruising; drowsiness; dislike of light. Babies may arch back and their cry is high-pitched. Symptoms develop rapidly.	Urgent and immediate medical attention. Antibiotics and observation.	Deafness; brain damage; death.
Mumps	14–21 days	Fever, headache. Difficulty in swallowing with swollen face and glands in neck.	Keep up fluid intake; rest; paracetamol for pain relief if necessary.	Meningitis orchitis (inflammation of the testes in young men).
Tonsillitis		Very sore throat with pain on swallowing; fever; earache; headache.	Antibiotics and rest.	Ear infection; deafness (rare).
Whooping cough (Pertussis)	7–21 days	Spurts of violent coughing with child taking in a deep breath (a 'whoop' sound made); vomiting.	Antibiotics in early stages; rest, reassurance and food after coughing attacks.	Nosebleeds; pneumonia; brain damage.

Providing reassurance and comfort

All children will need reassurance and comfort if they have had an accident or are feeling unwell. They will also look to you to remain calm and will often react according to the cues that you give them. Talking in a calm way and reassuring the child will be hugely helpful, as will giving the child a cuddle and letting him or her know that he or she is safe. It is also a good idea to talk to the child about what is happening, because not understanding can be very frightening.

All children will need reassurance and comfort if they have had an accident or are feeling unwell.

It is normal for children to want to be with their parents when they are feeling unwell or after an accident; some children can feel unsettled after a slight bump. Contacting parents promptly if a child is unwell or has had an accident is important because parents know how best to comfort and respond to their child.

Children's allergies

Some allergies can be extremely serious and have been known to be life-threatening. This means that you need good systems to collect information from parents and also procedures to avoid situations arising where children might be put at risk. Many parents whose children have serious allergies are happy to have a photograph of their child in a prominent place to act as a constant reminder about the foods that their child can and cannot have.

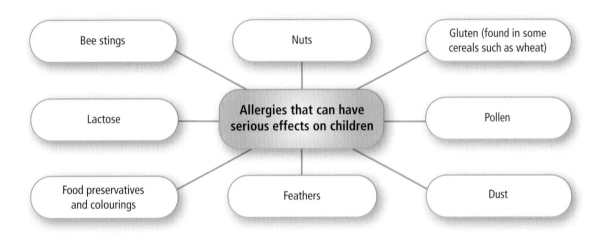

Bee stings — Nuts — Gluten (found in some cereals such as wheat) — Lactose — **Allergies that can have serious effects on children** — Pollen — Food preservatives and colourings — Feathers — Dust

Good practice

Dealing with children's allergies

- Check labels on any purchased food products to check for suitability.
- Check before serving any food and drink that it is suitable for each child.
- Always double check if you are unsure about whether a food is suitable.
- Ensure that you know what action needs to be taken if a child is exposed to 'his or her' allergen.
- Make sure that children's epi-pen, inhaler or other medication to counter the effects of an allergen are stored in an accessible place.

Administering medicines

Some children may need medication during the pre-school session, especially if they have medical conditions such as asthma or diabetes. By agreeing to administer medicines you can play an important role in helping children to participate in the pre-school. As medicines are hazardous substances, procedures for administering them have to be strictly followed. It is also important that parents understand the procedures and the reasons behind them. For specific children's health needs, you must be trained by a qualified health professional who knows about the child's condition.

Good practice

Administering medicines

- Make sure that a form is filled in for each medicine that a parent wishes you to administer.

- Ask parents for information about how to use items such as epi-pens or inhalers if you are not sure.

- Check the date on any medicine but especially those that are only used occasionally, such as inhalers and epi-pens, in case of expiry.

- Read the form carefully to check the time, dosage and other instructions for administering the medicine.

- Wash your hands.

- Always use the measure that is provided with the medicine, e.g. a 5 ml spoon rather than a teaspoon.

- Record the date and time that you gave the medicine.

Storing medicines

- Clearly label and store each child's medicine.

- Follow the storage instructions for medicines, i.e. liquid antibiotics may need to be kept in the fridge.

- Keep medicines out of reach of children.

- Make sure that other members of the adult team are aware of where inhalers and epi-pens are kept in case of emergencies.

How to work in partnership with parents to implement procedures for the arrival and departure of children

Registration is an essential part of keeping children safe: for example, it is important to know how many children are in the setting at any one time in case there is a fire or other emergency. It is also a requirement of the National Standards that a daily record is kept showing the hours that children have attended. This means that good procedures have to be in place in order to record children's arrivals and departures. Working in partnership with parents in this respect is essential. It is by involving parents and helping them to understand the importance of keeping records that the procedures remain effective. The starting point for this is to explain to parents why the registration and collection procedures are so important in terms of keeping their children safe. It is also important to review practice regularly and to check that the procedures for signing children in and out of the pre-school are working well. Talking to parents and seeking their views and ideas on how to make the process more effective is vital.

Arrivals

It is important to have a good routine established for when children arrive at the pre-school. In additional to the emotional benefits for children to know what to expect, it also makes registration more effective. Some pre-schools have a system whereby parents 'sign' in their children as they arrive, while others have a system in which parents find the name card for their child and encourage the child to post it in a box. Whilst these systems are helpful, it is still important for a member of staff to record children's arrivals so as to keep an overview.

It is useful to create a registration area that is large enough because several parents may arrive at once. It is also important for staff to be available for parents as this is the time when information often needs to be shared and relationships built. Keeping a notepad handy is often a good idea so that important messages can be written down. It can also be useful to have a supply of forms so that if a child has some medication, parents can fill in the consent form. In the same way, any changes to collection arrangements need to be written down.

Departures

At the end of each session it is essential that the right child goes home with the right person. This can be extremely important information, especially when there are child protection issues or court orders. Most settings have a system whereby parents come into the hall or room at the end of the session and personally collect their child. This can work well because it avoids situations in which children are hanging around near an entrance. It also means that parents can talk to their child's key person and find out more about their child's learning.

It is important during departures that a staff member supervises the entrance door to the pre-school as it is easy for a child to 'escape' if there is a lot of coming and going during this time. During this 'departure' period, it is important to have a system for noting which children have left.

Signing out before the end of a session

As well as having a system of registration when children arrive, it is important to have a system for signing out children who leave before the end of a session. This means that if an evacuation were necessary, time would not be wasted in looking for a child who had already left. Ideally, information about who has signed out should be recorded alongside the register so that the information is together.

Visitors' book

Parents who are staying to help or visitors, including those on official business such as early years advisers, should be signed in and out of the premises. Again, this is important in the eventuality that an evacuation of the building is required. Visitors should also be given a badge identifying their status. This should help to prevent a situation in which, for example, a visitor attempts to take a child and in doing so is unchallenged by another adult.

How to maintain pre-school children's safety on outings

Outings are enriching experiences for children. They allow children to see different environments and to have their attention drawn to new features. Outings are also good opportunities for parents to participate in their children's learning and so, whilst being hard work to organise, are extremely satisfying. Safety has to be considered throughout and so outings have to be carefully planned.

Planning an outing

It is important to visit at first hand any new location and to do a 'dry run' without any children in order to be able to carry out a risk assessment. Below is a list of factors to consider when thinking about the location of the outing.

Key questions when planning an outing to a chosen location

- What will it be like if it rains or is cold?
- How easy will it be to supervise children?
- How good are the toilet facilities?
- Where will you eat?
- How accessible is it for pushchairs or wheelchairs?
- Are there any roads or other hazards such as rivers nearby?
- Are there any visible hazards such as litter bins or steps?
- Will members of the public be present and if so how will you keep children together?
- How long will it take to go around or do the activities?
- How helpful are the staff?

Before the outing

Before an outing can go ahead, parents must give their consent. Without a signed consent form, children cannot be taken from the pre-school. This means that plenty of time must be allowed to get forms back in. It is also essential to organise sufficient supervision and to make sure that throughout the outing the ratios of adults to children can be maintained following the National Standards guidance. It can be useful to exceed the guidance in case any adult is ill on the day or has to drop out beforehand. Children will always benefit from having plenty of adult support.

During the outing

Where volunteers or parent helpers are joining the outing, it is important to brief them beforehand so that they understand their role. They will also need a list of the children that they are to supervise and clear instructions as to what they should do in an emergency situation. During the outing, it is important for children to be easily identified, for example, by bibs or the name of the pre-school on stickers. For child protection reasons, it is important not to identify children by name on stickers.

Good practice

Organising an outing: before the outing

- Make sure that consent forms have gone out in time and check that they are returned.
- If minibuses or coaches are being used, check that seatbelts are provided.
- Check that sufficient adults are coming on the trip.
- Confirm all arrangements in writing and phone again the day before, e.g. the venue and transport arrangements.
- Arrange a meeting with all adults accompanying the children.

During the outing

- Keep a register before going out of the pre-school and at several points during the outing.
- Provide clear instructions for helpers and volunteers, e.g. where to meet, what they need to do.
- Take with you the contact details of all children.
- Make sure that you have first aid kit, extra money, spare clothing, mobile phone, etc.

Case study

Meadow View Pre-school has planned an outing to the local park. Before the trip Mo, the pre-school leader and a parent from the committee, went to look at the park and its facilities and to carry out a risk assessment. The outing was explained to parents and slips were given out so that consent could be gained. Parents were invited to come along as helpers. Mo organised a short meeting before the outing to explain what the children would learn from the trip and also how the children were to be grouped and organised to avoid any incidents. Mo and the staff team also worked out an alternative plan in case the weather was bad, but this was not needed. The outing went well and the photographs of the children playing in and exploring the park were put out for everyone to look at afterwards.

1 Explain some of the reasons for the success of this outing.

2 Why is it important to explain the learning intentions behind outings to parents?

3 Why is it useful to have some alternative plans in place for outdoor visits and outings?

Providing for pre-school children's physical needs in ways that promote their well-being

Providing for babies and pre-school children's physical needs, including the security provided by having a key person

Types of physical care needs

Meeting the physical needs of babies and pre-school children is an important part of providing a stimulating learning environment. Babies and children cannot flourish if their basic needs are not looked after. The types of physical care needs that are common are:

- nappy changing
- toileting
- hand washing
- providing food and drinks.

Nappy changing

Nappy changing and toileting help children to feel comfortable and are linked to their emotional security. Prompt nappy changing helps babies and toddlers to move more easily and also avoids the potential risk of painful nappy rash. With older children, swift nappy changing helps them to feel better in themselves.

Toileting

The ability to go to the toilet is a fundamental right for children which is linked to their dignity and as well as their physical comfort. Worrying about going to the toilet can affect children's concentration and their ability to settle in. This means pre-schools must pay attention to the quality of the toilet arrangements: they should be clean and attractive areas in which children are encouraged to take responsibility for themselves. Adults in the pre-school also need to understand the balance between safety and the importance of privacy.

Hand washing

Hand washing is a major way of preventing infection from spreading in pre-school. For children, it is also a pleasurable and potential learning experience. Children enjoy washing their hands and gain pleasure from doing so independently or with some adult support. Hand washing is often one of the early skills in helping children to become self-reliant.

Providing food and drinks

Babies and children need food and drink for their growth and development. For babies, the process of weaning is also linked to the development of their speech and language, since chewing, biting and swallowing help to 'muscle' the tongue and mouth. For older children the provision of food and drink can help them to learn about food, socialise and develop their self-reliance skills.

Thinking and research

Using articles and the Internet, find out about the process of weaning babies onto solid foods.

- What is the current recommended age for children to begin this process?
- What are the dangers of beginning the weaning process early?
- What types of foods should be avoided?

The role of the key person in providing individual babies' and children's physical care

Babies and children need a key person as this has been shown to be essential in promoting their overall development. On pages 264–5 of this unit, you will look at the role of the key person in providing for babies' and children's emotional security. Here, the focus is on the key person in relation to meeting physical needs.

The aim of a key person system is that children and their parents are able to have a strong relationship with one member of the team who gets to know them and their needs. In terms of physical care needs, the key person system is a highly effective one as it personalises the care that is provided. Children benefit from having their physical needs met by a key person especially where the physical care is intimate, for example, nappy changing. For babies, where physical care such as feeding is linked to emotional security, the key person is essential. This means that it is now considered to be good practice for babies and toddlers to be fed and changed by their key person. With Foundation Stage children, the key person should be involved at meal times and snack times and be available for their key children if they need support. As the key person also works closely with parents, up-to-date information can be exchanged effectively. Again, this is essential in caring for babies and children who cannot otherwise communicate that they are still hungry.

How to provide for babies' and pre-school children's nutritional and dietary needs

Food and drink plays an important role in the healthy development and growth of children. Understanding how best to meet the nutritional needs of children of different ages is therefore essential when providing snacks and meals for children. As with other areas of working with children, it is important to remain up to date about how best to provide food and drink for children. There have been some significant changes in the past two years with, for example, the advice that children should have five portions of fruit and vegetables a day and that babies should not be weaned until six months old.

Meeting babies' nutritional needs

Over the course of their first year, babies' nutritional needs change. This is reflected in the amounts and type of foods that they need. Babies begin life completely reliant on milk, taken either from the breast or the bottle, and finish their first year able to feed themselves finger foods.

Types of milk

For the first six months, babies require only milk. There are essentially two forms of milk: human and manufactured (formula milk).

- *Breast milk*
  The choice whether to bottle-feed or breastfeed depends on the mother. Breastfeeding is considered the best start for babies because the milk is 'designed' for them. It is possible for a mother to express milk and freeze it so that a baby in group care can continue to have her breast milk. If a mother chooses this option, it is essential to be supportive. Expressing milk and giving it in a bottle is not always completely glitch-free. Sometimes babies can resist taking a bottle or refuse to return to the breast. It can therefore be useful for mothers to seek advice from their health visitor before the baby is left in group care. Bottles and teats, etc. should be sterilised (see diagram opposite).

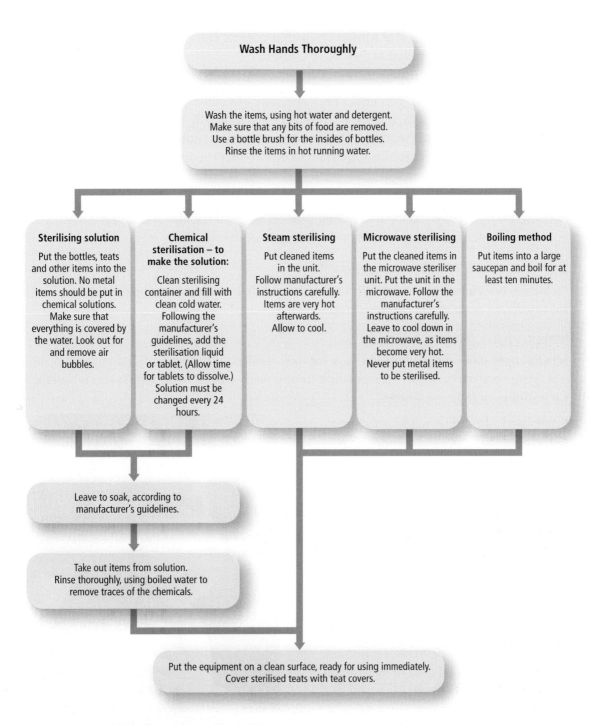

Wash Hands Thoroughly

Wash the items, using hot water and detergent.
Make sure that any bits of food are removed.
Use a bottle brush for the insides of bottles.
Rinse the items in hot running water.

Sterilising solution	**Chemical sterilisation – to make the solution:**	**Steam sterilising**	**Microwave sterilising**	**Boiling method**
Put the bottles, teats and other items into the solution. No metal items should be put in chemical solutions. Make sure that everything is covered by the water. Look out for and remove air bubbles.	Clean sterilising container and fill with clean cold water. Following the manufacturer's guidelines, add the sterilisation liquid or tablet. (Allow time for tablets to dissolve.) Solution must be changed every 24 hours.	Put cleaned items in the unit. Follow manufacturer's instructions carefully. Items are very hot afterwards. Allow to cool.	Put the cleaned items in the microwave steriliser unit. Put the unit in the microwave. Follow the manufacturer's instructions carefully. Leave to cool down in the microwave, as items become very hot. Never put metal items to be sterilised.	Put items into a large saucepan and boil for at least ten minutes.

Leave to soak, according to manufacturer's guidelines.

Take out items from solution. Rinse thoroughly, using boiled water to remove traces of the chemicals.

Put the equipment on a clean surface, ready for using immediately. Cover sterilised teats with teat covers.

Step-by-step guide to the sterilisation of babies' feeding equipment.

- *Formula milk*
  Formula milk is given with a bottle, so is often called bottle-feeding. Formula milk is made of cow's milk that has been modified to allow the baby to digest it. Ordinary cow's milk should not be given to a baby until he or she is at least one year old.

There are several brands of formula milk that parents can choose, and it is important to use the brand of milk that they have chosen.

- *Soya milk*
  Some babies are allergic to cow's milk and may therefore be given soya milk as a substitute. The decision to feed a baby soya milk is usually made because the baby is showing an allergic reaction. However, this decision should be made only after consulting a doctor. It is also important to ensure that the right brand of milk is given to the right baby.

Whatever type of milk is chosen, it is essential that bottles and teats are sterilised because milk provides the ideal breeding ground for bacteria. You should always wash your hands before touching bottles and feeding equipment.

Sterilising bottles and feeding equipment

As babies are vulnerable to infection it is essential that feeding items are properly sterilised (see diagram on previous page).

Making up a bottle feed

Most parents who choose formula milk for their babies will use powdered milk because it is cost effective. However, it is possible to buy ready-mixed milk, which can be useful for journeys or if time is limited.

Bottle-feeds should be made according to the manufacturer's instructions. It is important to follow these carefully and not adapt the formula milk in any way. Putting too much powder in a bottle can cause babies to gain too much weight, while insufficient powder can mean that babies lose weight or become distressed.

Feeds are usually made in batches for the day and then refrigerated. Any unused bottles must be thrown away after 24 hours. It is important to ask parents about how much feed needs to be made up because they will have a good idea of how much and when their baby feeds.

How to feed a baby

Feeding is a pleasurable time for babies. It is also an important emotional time in which the baby feels secure and can build an attachment to the person feeding him or her. It is therefore good practice for the baby's key worker to feed the baby so that a good

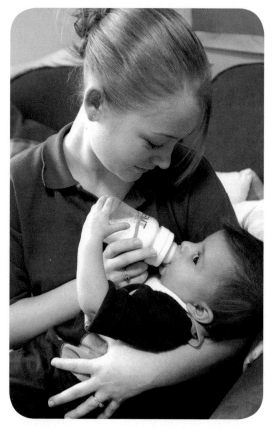

When feeding a baby, it is important to adopt the 'natural' position.

relationship can develop. It is important to adopt the 'natural' position of a mother suckling a child at the breast. This gives the baby support, but also allows him or her to look directly into the face of the key worker.

The amount of milk taken at each feed needs to be recorded to enable you to check that the baby has had sufficient amounts over the course of a day. Most babies are now fed 'on demand', which means that their own pattern for feeds is respected. As babies self-regulate and learn to take only as much as they are hungry for, it is important not to force a baby to finish a bottle. The ultimate test as to whether a baby is gaining enough nutrition is to check his or her weight and consider how settled the baby seems.

Bottle-feeding a baby: a step-by-step guide

- Change the baby's nappy if required.

- Wash your hands.

- Warm the bottle by using a bottle warmer or by standing it in a jug of hot water.

- Collect tissues and bibs, etc. so that everything is to hand.

- Make sure that the bottle is at the correct temperature.

- Check the flow of the milk.

- Angle the bottle so the teat is completely covered with milk.

- Talk to the baby as he or she is feeding.

- Allow the baby to take breaks and suckle gently.

- Wind young babies by sitting them up and gently rubbing their backs.

- Do not force the baby to take more than he or she wants.

- Throw away any unused feed.

Weaning

Weaning is the process by which babies move from taking only milk to eating proper foods. This is an essential process because milk alone will not provide the nutrients required by the growing baby after six months. It is therefore important that at six months the process of weaning begins.

When to begin weaning

It is now suggested that babies are not weaned until they are six months old. This is to prevent digestive difficulties and allergies. Parents who wish to begin weaning earlier should consult their health visitor for advice.

There are a few signs that babies are ready to wean. These include the baby seeming much hungrier or becoming unsettled. In addition, the baby may begin to wake during the night when previously he or she slept through. The baby's weight may also stop increasing or the baby may even begin to lose weight.

Introducing babies to weaning

Babies have to learn to take food from a spoon. For some babies this comes easily, while other babies need to be coaxed. The first spoonfuls are usually baby rice mixed with a little of the baby's usual milk. Baby rice is usually recommended because it is unlikely to cause an allergic reaction.

The best time to introduce the first spoonful is when the baby is not tired and is not too hungry. Put a bib on the baby and have some tissues to hand. Feed the baby some of their usual bottle and then put a little mixture onto a spoon, just touching the baby's lips. The baby will hopefully suck the food from the spoon. If the baby becomes distressed or repeatedly spits the food out, it is important to remain calm and simply try again another day.

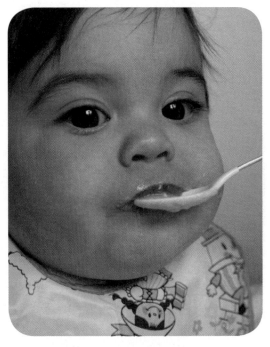

Babies soon learn how to feed from a spoon.

Increasing the range of foods

Once a baby has grown used to taking from a spoon, it is important to build up a range of foods that he or she can eat. Foods should be introduced one at a time so that any allergic reaction is detected. Foods should be fairly liquid in form so that the baby can swallow them easily. Most foods are therefore puréed and either water or the baby's usual milk added, to make a smooth consistency. The amount of food should be built up gradually so that by around six months the baby is having three meals a day. During this time, the amount of milk the baby takes will gradually lessen, although it is recommended that the baby should continue to have between 500–600 ml of milk a day.

When preparing foods, you should not add any sugar or salt. This may make the food seem bland to you but it will still be tasty for the baby. Salt must be avoided because it can affect the baby's kidneys, while sugar can lead to dental decay and cause babies to become overweight.

If commercial foods are chosen by parents, it will be important to check that they are suitable for the age of the child and not past their best-before or use-by date. It is also essential to read the manufacturer's instructions about storing jars.

Introducing water

Babies will become thirsty once they begin to take solid foods. This means that cool boiled water should be offered as well as bottled milk. If babies do not drink sufficiently there is a danger that they will become constipated. A record should therefore be kept of the amount of drink as well as food that a baby consumes. Never use bottled mineral water with babies unless a medical practitioner has been consulted because it contains high levels of minerals such as salt.

Frequently asked questions

Drinks for babies

 Should babies be given juice and other drinks?

Over the past few years, dentists have been concerned about the number of babies and young children with serious dental decay. While cooled boiled water is considered the best drink for babies, there are also many baby juices and drinks on sale. To prevent dental decay and gum disease, dentists advise that these drinks be given in cups. Using bottles and beakers means that babies and toddlers are likely to have repeated sips and their gums will therefore be repeatedly exposed to the natural sugars and acids in these drinks. The current advice is to use these drinks sparingly and to encourage babies to become used to drinking water, which is a healthy habit.

7 to 9 months: introducing lumpy foods

The next step in the weaning process is to provide babies with foods that are both more varied and more textured. Instead of puréeing food so that it is smooth, foods can now be mashed or minced. This encourages the baby to learn to chew a little, which helps the tongue and jaw to develop and is important for later speech.

The baby should now be starting his or her feed with solid food and finishing with milk. It is still important for the baby to have sufficient milk during the day (the recommended amount is 500–600 ml). While full-fat cow's milk can be used in cooking, it cannot be used for a baby's main drink and formula or breast milk should still be used. It is also recommended that babies should have two or three servings of starchy foods, such as rice and potatoes, every day. Unless the baby is known to have an allergy, wheat-based foods such as pasta and bread can also be introduced into the diet. When introducing new foods, it is still important to watch out for allergic reactions, the symptoms of which might include diarrhoea or skin conditions.

At this stage, feeding becomes a little messy because babies want to play a more active part in the process. They may try to grab the spoon or the food. This is to be encouraged, so provide an extra spoon for the baby and cover him or her as well as you!

9 to 12 months: introducing finger foods

This is the final phase of weaning. Babies should be starting to feed themselves because their hand–eye co-ordination is sufficiently developed to allow for this and they are used to chewing and swallowing. The baby should also be eating a good range of foods that provide him or her with a balanced diet. Foods can be cut into small pieces that the baby can pick up, for example, small pieces of toast with cheese or chopped banana. Milk should continue to play a vital role in the baby's diet, and he or she should have at least 350 ml of milk a day. If a baby is reluctant to drink this much milk, the amount of other dairy products in the diet should be increased.

The safe preparation of food

It is essential that high standards of hygiene are in place when providing food for babies. Most settings continue to sterilise feeding equipment beyond the recommended six months in order to avoid any possible cross-infection. It is also important to throw away all unused foods after they have been served to babies.

Introducing finger foods.

Good practice

The safe preparation of food for babies

- Use separate spoons, bowls and other feeding equipment for each baby.
- Use separate face cloths and towels to clean each baby afterwards.
- Throw away all unused food that has been served.
- Store foods correctly.
- Make sure that formula milk powder and jars of baby food are not past their use-by or best-before date.

Keeping babies safe

Babies should never be left unattended with food or drink because there is a danger that they might choke. Ideally, all staff should know what to do if a baby begins to choke. It is also important to keep an eye on a toddler who may wish to 'share' his or her food with a baby.

Providing for children's physical needs

Food and drink are essential in meeting children's physical needs. Food is required to give energy and help the body grow, while water is required to maintain the body's vital organs. Children who are hungry or thirsty will find it harder to concentrate and so providing for children's dietary needs is essential. The importance of food and drink is reflected in Standard 8 of the National Standards (see below). While pre-schools cannot be completely responsible for children's diets, you do have a duty to ensure that the food and drink that you serve them are healthy and nutritious. This is currently a 'hot' issue because it is reported that a significant proportion of young children are overweight.

National Standard 8

Children are provided with regular drinks and food in adequate quantities for their needs. Food and drink are properly prepared, nutritious and comply with dietary and religious requirements.

How nutrients are used by the body and examples of foods they are found in

Nutrient	Benefits to the body	Example of foods
Fats	Energy; also needed for the body to absorb vitamins A and D	Butter, olive oil, margarine, vegetable oils; fats are also present in meat, fish and dairy products
Carbohydrates	Energy	Bread, pasta, flour, potatoes, sweet potatoes, plantains and bananas, vegetables
Proteins	Energy, growth and repair	There are two types of proteins: proteins that are found in meat, fish, soya and dairy products can be absorbed by the body, while proteins found in vegetable products such as peas, beans and lentils need to be eaten in combination with other food so that the body can take in the protein, e.g. beans on toast; lentil and barley soup.
Mineral elements	There are many minerals needed in a balanced diet. The role of some has not yet been fully identified.	Traces of mineral elements are found in many vegetables, particularly if eaten with their skin.
Iron	Helps blood to carry oxygen.	Red meat, broccoli, spinach, plain chocolate, egg yolk.
Calcium and phosphorous	Used for maintaining and repairing bones and teeth.	Milk, cheese, yoghurt and other dairy products. They are also added to white flour.
Fluoride	Used for maintaining and repairing bones and teeth.	Sea fish; added into some water; often taken in by the body through toothpaste.
Vitamins	Many diseases are caused by lack of vitamins, even though the amounts needed by the body are very small.	
Vitamin A	Healthy skin; growth and development; needed for maintaining good vision.	Fat-soluble (found in fats); dairy products; cheese; margarine; apricots; fatty fish.
Vitamin B-group	Growth and development; appetite; helps release energy from other foods; good for the nervous system.	Bread, flour, meat, yeast, pasta, rice, noodles; added to some breakfast cereals.
Vitamin C (fragile; easily destroyed by cooking process)	Needed for forming bones, teeth and blood vessels; needed for skin.	Fresh fruits and green vegetables, e.g. oranges, kiwi fruit, potatoes, blackcurrants, cabbage. *Continued* ▶

Nutrient	Benefits to the body	Example of foods
Vitamin D	Needed for bones and teeth.	Dairy products, e.g. milk, cheese, yoghurt; fish; added to margarine.
Vitamin E	Not completely understood but links to fertility and protection from cancers and heart disease.	Vegetable oils; green leafy vegetables; milk; nuts.
Vitamin K	Helps blood to clot.	Green vegetables, e.g. spinach, broccoli, peas.

Children's dietary requirements

Children's dietary requirements are not quite the same as those for adults. Firstly, this is because children are developing their tastes. You should therefore be careful not to give them the taste for high fat, salty or sugary foods. You also need to be aware that in relation to their body weight, children actually need proportionally more energy than adults do. This is because children are growing and are generally more active. As a child's stomach capacity is less than that of an adult, children should be given foods that are nutrient dense. For children under three years of age, this includes full-fat milk. It also means that low-fat diets, which may be safe for adults, should not be followed unless medical advice is sought.

A balanced diet

Eating healthily is always a question of balance. It is not just a question of dividing foods into 'bad' and 'good' because too much of any one type of food is likely to cause problems. This is because foods are composed of nutrients and the body needs a range of foods in order to get the correct mix of nutrients. Each nutrient has a specific role to play in the body. There are five nutrient groups in total; meals that are nutritious will contain nutrients from all five groups. The chart on pages 248–9 describes the benefits to the body of each nutrient group.

Sample weekly menu for young children

	Day 1	Day 2	Day 3	Day 4	Day 5
Mid-morning	Diluted orange juice Banana	Water Grapes	Milk Cheese straws	Milk Raisins	Water Satsuma
Lunch	Pitta filled with tuna and sweetcorn Fresh lychees Water	Turkey curry with rice Yoghurt Water	Macaroni cheese Broccoli Ice cream and fresh fruit Water	Shepherd's pie Carrots and peas Blackcurrant fool Water	Trinidad fruit stew (made with plantains) Banana and custard Water

Providing nutritious snacks and foods

To ensure that children are getting sufficient nutrients, you should consider the nutrients that are in different types of food when planning menus or snacks. You should also consider the way in which the food is prepared because part of the food's goodness, for example, vitamins, can be lost during the cooking process. Generally, to retain the maximum amount of vitamins it is a good idea to serve fresh fruit raw and vegetables lightly steamed.

When planning a menu for children, it is worth thinking about how easy the food is for children to manage. Look out for foods that do not require endless chewing and think about the ease with which children can feed themselves.

Using children's appetites as portion guides

Children themselves are generally good indicators of how much they can eat. Children who are very hungry are sometimes about to have a growth spurt, while children who are fighting infections may be off their food. This means that wherever possible children should be encouraged to serve themselves; providing that a good range of food is available, they should get the nutrients they need. If puddings or desserts are served, it is important that these are as nutritionally sound as other parts of the meal, for example, yoghurt and fresh fruit. It is not a good idea to 'label' these as treats otherwise children will learn the hidden message that the main course is a chore.

Applying theory to your practice

- What types of snacks are provided in your pre-school?
- Why is it important that they are nutritious?

Five-a-day campaign

The importance of fruit and vegetables is increasingly recognised, and it is suggested that children and adults should aim to eat five portions of fruit and vegetables a day. This means that instead of biscuits, many pre-schools provide fresh fruit and vegetables, for example, carrot sticks. To find out more about the five-a-day campaign, visit www.5aday.nhs.uk.

Foods to avoid

- *Salt*: children should not be given salty foods, such as crisps, or have salt added to their food. Too much salt can affect the kidneys and lead to long-term health problems.
- *Raw or partially cooked eggs*: eggs are perfectly safe provided that they are completely cooked. Eggs that are only partially cooked, for example, boiled eggs with runny yolks, should be avoided because there is a risk of food poisoning.
- *Foods that are high in fats and low in other nutrients*: while young children do need fat in their diets, it is important that they do not acquire a taste for high-fat processed foods, such as chips, pies and crisps. Learning to like such foods simply stores up problems for later in life because they are low in other nutrients. Cheese, milk and yoghurts, which do contain fat, are considered to be good for children.
- *Sugar:* you should avoid encouraging children to develop a 'sweet tooth'. While it is good to provide children with foods that are naturally sweet, such as melons or pineapples, it is not a good idea to include too many foods with added sugar. Too much sugar in a child's diet can cause obesity and dental decay. It also stores up problems for the future because children will find it harder to enjoy fresh fruit and drinks that are plain. It is for this reason that many dieticians do not recommend giving children foods that contain artificial sweeteners: while they do not contain any calories or sugar, they do teach children to enjoy sweet tastes.

Ideas for healthy snacks

You should aim to provide children with snacks that are nutritious and easy for them to eat. It is good practice to involve children in the preparation of snacks, an activity which can be planned and prove rewarding for all involved.

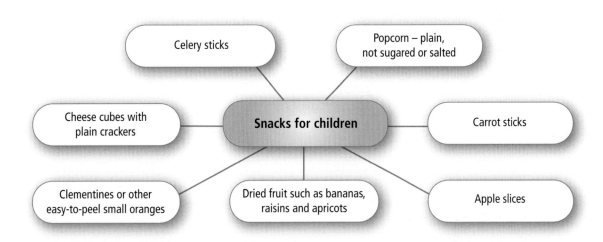

Attitudes towards food

Children learn about food partly from the adults around them. Therefore, if you want children to enjoy their food and eventually choose foods that are good for them, they need to see you eating healthily. This means that adults should try to sit with children at snack and meal times. It is also important to avoid comments that may teach children to dislike certain foods or to become worried about their body shape.

Finishing everything up

Many dieticians feel that children should not be cajoled into finishing their food on the plate. While gentle encouragement to eat is fine, children should not be made to sit at a table or refused other foods as a punishment. The idea is that children who are taught to finish everything even when they are not hungry, may later find it harder to control their eating habits because they have learnt not to follow their appetites.

Encouraging children to taste new foods

Some children can be resistant to the idea of tasting something new. This can lead to them having quite restrictive diets that lack balance. Pre-schools can play an important role in helping children to taste new foods.

- *Cooking*
  Where children are involved in some of the preparation and design of the meal, they are more likely to taste their food. This can be an opportunity for family learning as children and their parents do a little cooking together.

- *Serving foods*
  It is good practice for children to serve their own foods. This has many benefits as not only are children more inclined to taste something new if they feel in control over the portion, but they are also learning about portion size. It can also be a good way of encouraging children to socialise as they pass each other dishes.

- *Role modelling*
  Parents and adults play a huge role in helping children to acquire positive eating habits. You can encourage children to try out new foods by showing your own willingness to 'have a go'. This coupled with some praise has in studies been shown to be highly effective.

Religious and cultural dietary needs

For some families, food plays an important role in their culture, religion or social beliefs. A good example of this is the increasing trend for some families to eat only meat and poultry that has been reared ethically, or to insist that fruit and vegetables are organically grown. Such beliefs have to be respected and you will therefore need parents to specify how best to meet their child's dietary requirements. The chart opposite shows some of the common food restrictions related to religion, although it is essential to find out more information from parents.

Food allergies

Some children can be allergic to certain foods, and in extreme cases an allergic reaction can be fatal. This means that care needs to be taken when preparing and serving food to ensure that children do not eat foods that trigger a reaction. You should also check the ingredient label on purchased food products before giving them to children.

Examples of religious and cultural dietary needs

Food	Muslim	Jew	Sikh	Hindu (mainly vegetarian)	Rastafarian (mainly vegetarian although take milk products)	Vegetarians	Vegans
Lamb	Halal	Kosher	Yes	Some	Some	No	No
Pork	No	No	Rarely	Rarely	No	No	No
Beef	Halal	Kosher	No	No	Some	No	No
Chicken	Halal	Kosher	Some	Some	Some	No	No
Cheese	Some	Not with meat	Some	Some	Yes	Yes	No
Milk/yoghurt	Not with rennet	Not with meat	Yes	Not with rennet	Yes	Yes	Soya and other substitutes
Eggs	Yes	No blood spots	Yes	Some	Yes	Yes	No
Fish	Halal	With fins, scales and backbones	Some	With fins and scales	Yes	Some	No
Shellfish	Halal	No	Some	Some	No	Some	No
Cocoa/tea/ coffee	Yes	Yes	Yes	Yes	Yes	Yes	Yes
Fast periods	Ramadam	Yom Kippur					

If in doubt about any food, always check and err on the side of caution. Parents tend to have up-to-date advice and some may prefer to bring in their own snacks and foods to avoid any confusion. Your pre-school should have a procedure in place that helps staff to identify those children who have specific dietary requirements, and this may be checked at inspection.

On the next page is a chart of some of the more common food allergies. Note that this is not a comprehensive list and therefore it is vital that information is exchanged with parents.

Some common food allergies

Food	Reaction and recommendation
Nuts	Some children have violent reactions to nuts and products that contain nuts, such as marzipan. The advice is to avoid giving nuts including peanut butter to all children below the age of five years.
Gluten	Gluten is found in wheat and other flours. Products such as bread, biscuits and pizzas are not suitable for children with this allergy.
Lactose	Some children are unable to digest lactose found in dairy products. Foods such as milk, yoghurt and cheese are not suitable for children with this allergy. Parents should be asked about substitute foods.
Chemicals and preservatives	Some children have strong reactions to preservatives and colourings found in manufactured foods.

Diabetes mellitus

Diabetes is a medical condition in which the body has difficulty regulating the amount of sugar in the blood. If a child in your setting has diabetes, it is essential for all staff to follow the child's diet and eating patterns. Going without food or drink for a period, or being given foods that are high in carbohydrates and sugars, can have severe effects on the child. Usually, parents are able to give advice as to when and what their child should be eating. It is usual to find that children with diabetes require frequent snacks so that their blood sugar levels can remain stable.

Good practice

Children's diet and eating habits

- Do staff sit and eat with children?
- Are children encouraged to serve themselves?
- Are staff aware of the specific dietary needs and allergies of children?
- Is food chosen which is nutritious?
- Are children able to follow their own appetites?

How to exchange information with parents about babies and pre-school children's dietary needs and feeding patterns

It is important to work alongside parents in discussing and exchanging information about meeting children's dietary needs. Parents know their children well and also may have their own views about how they wish their children to be cared for. Some parents also find it helpful to gain support and information about healthy eating, especially as obesity in childhood is a 'hot topic'.

Finding out about babies and children's requirements

In order to successfully share the physical care of children, it is important to find out about individual babies' and children's requirements. It is especially important to find out about dietary allergies as well as cultural and religious restrictions and preferences. This may include food sourcing, for example, organic foods and halal meat, as well as food preparation, i.e. keeping separate dishes for cooking meat and fish.

It is also useful to find out about children's food preferences, experiences and attitudes towards food. When caring for babies, you also need to know about their usual feeding patterns so that you know how much and when they take their milk.

Sharing information with parents

As well as finding out about children's needs, you also need to share information with parents. This is especially important when you are caring for babies and children who come for longer sessions that include meals. Parents will need to know if their children have tried and enjoyed new foods such as vegetables and also whether they have eaten well. This is especially important so that parents can provide additional food if their child has not been hungry. It is also worth noting that children who are 'off' their food may sometimes be fighting an infection. For babies, it is important to keep a daily record for parents that show the times of their feeds and how much milk has been taken. As babies are introduced to new foods during weaning, it is also important to report their likes and dislikes and also any reactions to foods.

The nature of babies' and pre-school children's personal hygiene needs and how to provide appropriately for these including nappy changing and toilet training

Good personal hygiene is important in keeping babies and children healthy and comfortable. Personal hygiene in pre-schools is likely to range from bathing of

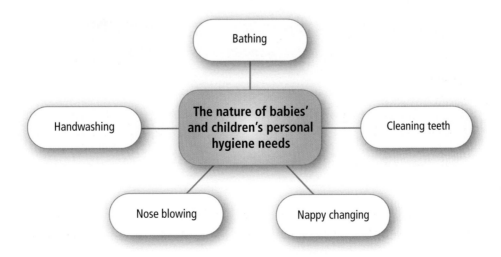

babies through to accompanying children to the toilet as they become increasingly independent. In addition, some children with learning or medical conditions may continue to need significant support in terms of their personal hygiene, i.e. nappy changing. The best person to carry out children's personal hygiene needs, especially those of a more intimate nature such as nappy changing, is the child's key person.

Personal hygiene needs of babies

Babies have sensitive skin and great attention needs to be given to their personal hygiene.

Washing and bathing

During the course of a session, it is likely that babies will need, as a minimum, their face and hands washed. It is important to discuss with parents which skincare products, if any, should be used. You should also ask parents whether they have any preferences about how skincare should be carried out, for example, some parents may prefer that their child's hands are washed under running water, while other parents may prefer to use baby oil.

Drying babies' skin

Babies' skin is more sensitive than adults' skin. This means that after washing and drying a baby's hands and face, care must be taken to dry the skin properly in order to prevent

Good practice

Bathing a baby: a step-by-step guide

- Clean baby first using cotton wool and water or baby wipes (with parents' consent).
- Prepare fresh clothing, nappy and towels before putting baby in bath.
- Clean baby's face and neck gently using face cloth. Dry carefully afterwards.
- Add cold water first followed by hot water. Make sure that the water is warm but not hot – the ideal temperature is 36–38 °C (97–100 °F). Test using your elbow before putting the baby in.
- Support the baby by putting your arm around his or her back and using your hand to support the underarm (see illustration).
- When the baby is washed, wrap in towel and dry thoroughly. Make sure that his or her skin is dry before putting on nappy and clothes.
- Do not wipe the baby's face with water from the bath.
- Do not let the baby drink the bath water.
- Watch out for signs that the baby is getting cold, i.e. blue lips, shivering.

it from becoming chapped. This is best done by gently patting the skin rather than rubbing it. Some babies' skin can be dry and parents may therefore ask that you use lotions or oils.

Bathing

It is useful for a baby bath to be kept in pre-school as some babies may need a bath if their nappies have leaked and their clothing and skin is soiled. Removing faeces from their skin is important to avoid nappy rash and also infection.

Nappy-changing

Nappy-changing plays a key part in caring for babies' skin. It is important to change nappies regularly to prevent nappy rash and possible infections. A separate nappy-changing area is recommended to prevent the spread of infection, although the National Standards do not necessarily insist on this being a separate room.

Preventing nappy rash

Although nappy rash is quite common in babies, it is distressing for them and every step must be taken to prevent it. One of the best ways of preventing nappy rash is to change nappies frequently and put the baby on a towel without a nappy for a short time each

Good practice

Changing a nappy: a step-by-step guide

1 Get the entire equipment ready before taking the nappy off.

2 Wash your hands and put on gloves.

3 Remove the baby's clothes from the lower part of the body and undo the nappy.

4 Using tissues or cotton wool, wipe the faeces off the baby's bottom and place the dirty nappy and tissues into a nappy sack.

5 Using wet cotton wool or baby wipes, wash the baby's bottom from front to back. Throw each piece of tissue away after one wipe. Do not pull a boy's foreskin back during washing.

6 Dry the baby's bottom with tissues or cotton wool.

7 Apply a barrier cream (if parents have asked for this)

8 Put a clean nappy on and dress the baby.

9 Clean the mat, remove and dispose of the gloves, and wash your hands.

Don't forget to talk to the baby during nappy-changing. Babies also like a chance to kick their legs while the nappy is removed.

day. It is also essential that a baby's skin is completely dried after bathing and nappy changes. Putting a nappy onto a damp bottom will increase the likelihood of nappy rash.

Although there are several causes of nappy rash, it is usually aggravated by ammonia in a baby's urine that has an acidic effect on the skin or by bacteria in the baby's stools. Other causes include:

- sensitive skin
- poorly fitting nappies
- allergic reaction to detergent, bubble bath or other skin products
- baby wipes that contain alcohol
- dietary changes.

Upon the first signs of redness, blisters or soreness, it is essential to take the following measures:

- change the baby's nappy more frequently
- allow more air to the baby's skin, for example, allow time without the nappy on after each nappy change
- some parents may ask you to use a barrier cream.

If the nappy rash does not improve, it is important that medical advice is sought promptly.

Noting changes to stools

It is important to note any changes in the baby's stools or the frequency of urination. Stools that are particularly hard may indicate constipation while a baby whose nappy is dry may not be taking in enough fluids. Diarrhoea should also be noted because this can be caused by food intolerance or an infection. It is important to talk to parents about any changes that you see because they may wish to seek medical advice.

Care of babies' teeth

Many babies will have their first teeth at around six months old. Once a baby's teeth have appeared, it is important that they are cleaned. This needs to be done gently because gums can become sore and irritated. A soft brush should be used along with toothpaste designed for babies; adult toothpaste is not recommended. Brushing teeth should take place after meals and each child should have his or her own brush.

Teething

When teeth are coming through, the gums can become sore and swollen. Parents often report an association with teething and nappy rash. Signs that babies are teething include:

Hot red patches on a child's cheeks may be a sign of teething.

- the desire to chew on items
- irritability
- stronger smelling urine
- a red patch on the baby's cheeks.

To help babies cope with the sensation, it can be helpful for them to chew on something soft, such as a specially designed teething ring. Products to rub onto gums should not be used unless parents have given their permission.

Nappy changing children

As well as babies, toddlers and some older children may need nappy changing. The essential steps do not change from those outlined above, but your approach might need to change.

Toddlers

Toddlers can become increasingly bored and frustrated when they need to have their nappy changed. It is therefore important to ensure that this is a pleasurable and also speedy experience. Providing books or toys that they can hold as well as involving them in the process will help. It is also useful to give toddlers 'notice' that you will need to change their nappy rather than taking them away from an activity without explanation.

Older children

Older children can become embarrassed that they are in nappies. This means that you need to ensure their privacy and also encourage them to be as active in the process as possible. Encouraging older children to come and tell you when they need their nappy changed can be empowering and is also one step on the way to toilet training.

Toilet training

Children can be toilet trained only when they are physically ready for it and also motivated to learn. There is no magic age: some children are ready quite early on at around 18 months, whilst others take longer – anything up to three years.

Signs that a child may be ready for toilet training include:

- becoming aware that he or she has soiled or wet his or her nappy
- the nappy is dry for long periods
- a growing interest in toilets and potties
- sufficient language to express the need to go to the toilet.

In addition, a child's body must be sufficiently mature. This takes longer for some children than for others.

Observing a child's co-ordination

In some countries, early years practitioners look at whether the child's co-ordination is sufficiently developed by watching how the child walks up steps. Children who are able to use alternate feet as opposed to putting one foot on a step and then another are thought to be physically ready for toilet training.

Working with parents

How and when toilet training takes place will need to be agreed with the child's parents. The key is to ensure that the child is relaxed and ready; a favourite potty from home may be required. Regular exchanges of information are also necessary so that parents and practitioners can assess whether the toilet training process is working.

Once it has been agreed to begin toilet training, it is important not to pressurise the child. Telling a child that he is, for example, 'a big boy now' may backfire if you discover after a few days that he is not actually ready; this situation may knock the child's confidence. A low-key approach is therefore worthwhile: simply show the child where the potty is and give the odd reminder. If the child is ready to use a potty, there will be few accidents. Forcing a child to stay on a potty is not usually effective because it stresses the child. This can cause the muscles involved in passing urine or motions to fail to relax sufficiently to allow anything to happen.

Good practice

Toilet training

- Check that the child is physically ready and motivated.
- Avoid pressurising the child.
- Give the child the odd reminder.
- Make sure that the potty is nearby.
- Make sure that the child's clothes are easy for him or her to remove.

Taking children to the toilet

It is essential that children can go to the toilet when they need to. Children will find it hard to wait if they need to go because their bodies are still developing. Ideally, children should be encouraged to have free access to the toilets. However, if this is not possible because of the layout of the building, children should be escorted there. You also need to consider how to manage situations in which children encounter other people. It is also a requirement that the child's need for dignity and privacy is respected. This means that a toilet door should be closed if a child wants it to be closed. The requirement to treat children with dignity also means that it is not good practice to force children to go to the toilet.

Coping with accidents

Many young children wet or soil themselves at one point or another. Sometimes this is because they are fighting an infection; at other times it may simply be because they were too preoccupied to notice their body's signals. Whatever the reason, it is essential that you react in a warm and calm way. This prevents situations in which children who have had an accident are too frightened or embarrassed to tell an adult.

Good practice

Taking children to the toilet

- Make sure that the toilets are clean and attractive.
- Ask children if they wish to have the door closed.
- Reassure children that you are on hand should they need assistance.
- Encourage children to do as much as they can for themselves.
- Wash your hands too!

After an accident, control should be given back to the child wherever possible. Encourage the child to do as much of the changing and washing as possible because it will help the child to feel independent. It is also important that you are sympathetic and reassure the child that many children have accidents. You can also ask children if they would like you to remind them to pop to the toilet next time. Where children are having regular accidents, it is important to talk to the child's parents. This is because there are many reasons why children may have a toileting accident, including bladder infections, stress and illness. When dealing with children's accidents, it is recommended that you wear disposable gloves to avoid contracting any infections.

Good practice

Dealing with accidents

- Reassure the child.
- Take the child to a discreet place where he or she can change easily.
- Have a bag of spare clothes and make sure that they are attractive.
- Encourage the child to choose the clothes into which he or she will change.
- Provide a towel and cloth so that the child can wash.
- Encourage the child to do as much of the changing as possible.
- Rinse through clothing and pop it in a discreet bag.
- Discreetly clean any equipment, chairs or items that the child was using at the time of the accident.
- Inform the child's parents at the end of the session.

Case study

Jonathan was having a lovely time in the water tray. He is four years old and is usually good at getting himself to the toilet in time. Today he has wet himself and is upset. He looks about for help and his key person sees him and comes over. She takes him to the toilets and gets the spare clothes bag down from the shelf. She lets him choose what to change into. He takes off his clothes and his key person encourages him to wash himself. She talks matter of factly about other things and he is quite happy. Afterwards she put his damp clothes in a bag and washes her hands. Jonathan goes back to the water tray and is soon playing again. His key person writes a quick note ready for the childminder who collects him today.

1   Why did having the assistance of his key person help Jonathan?

2   Why is it important to give children as much independence as possible in these situations?

3   Why is it important to share information with the parents or others who care for the child?

Hand washing

Hand washing is a key way in which you can reduce the spread of infection. Children need to be taught how to wash their hands using soap and warm water (the temperature should be at least 63°C (145°F) to kill germs). Children should also learn how to dry their hands thoroughly because warm, wet hands spread germs. It is important that children see adults washing their hands so that they can model their behaviour. You should therefore be seen washing your hands before you eat or after a messy activity.

Making hand washing fun

Children are more likely to learn to wash their hands if the experience of hand washing is enjoyable for them. Look out for soaps that are attractive and allow plenty of time for children to enjoy the sensation

When hand washing, allow plenty of time for children to enjoy the sensation of running water and soap.

of running water and soap. Praise children who remember to wash their hands. You may like to develop a hand-washing rhyme or song for your setting.

Nose blowing

Nose blowing may not seem very important, but it is crucial in terms of preventing painful ear infections and cross-infection in general. Young children have great difficulty in blowing their nose. They therefore need first to be taught to wipe their nose. As wiping is not as effective as blowing, children may need to wipe their nose frequently. Once a young child can wipe his or her nose, you can encourage him or her to have a go at nose blowing. Some children find this a little frightening and you may need to reassure them.

As with hand washing, nose blowing needs to be made as fun and interesting as possible. Consider having attractive tissues and praise children when they fetch a tissue for themselves. It is also worth carrying a packet of tissues with you so that you have some constantly to hand. Tissues should be disposed of immediately, preferably in a bin with a lid. It is also good practice to wash your hands after nose blowing.

How to provide for babies' and pre-school children's physical needs through a partnership with their parents

Pre-schools have a justly earned reputation for working closely with parents. In relation to providing for babies and pre-school children's physical needs this is essential. Parents must leave their babies and children feeling confident that their needs will be met. Building a relationship with parents where information can be shared is therefore a major part of that. The sharing of information needs to be a two-way process as both parents and adults working in the pre-school will have knowledge and expertise.

Firstly, parents know about their own children and their physical needs, for example, how to care for their hair and skin. Parents will also have their own preferences about their child's physical care, and these might be linked to the family's cultural, religious or social beliefs or views. It is important to record this information down and to check from time to time that it remains correct, since children's tastes or their need for a certain type of diet or skincare may change.

As well as gaining information from parents, adults in the pre-school also need to share information about how the pre-school organises physical care. As adults in the pre-school are likely to be in contact with other professionals and attend training, the practice in the pre-school will reflect this. Adults in the pre-school can also be a source of support for parents because, whilst all children are unique, many problems such as those associated with toilet training, will have been encountered many times before. Sharing expertise in this way can therefore be of added benefit to children and their families.

Providing an environment that promotes pre-school children's emotional security

The importance of emotional security to babies' and pre-school children's learning and development

Feeling secure, safe and happy are important requisites in terms of babies and pre-school children's learning and development. For babies, the amount of crying and also their weight gain can be linked to their need for emotional security. Thus settled and contented babies are more likely to thrive and develop. For pre-school children, feeling secure and settled allows them to fully participate and gain from the experience of the pre-school. Feeling emotionally secure gives children confidence, helps them to concentrate and allows them to socialise with other children. The importance for emotional security has been increasingly recognised and appears in two of the aims of the recent Every Child Matters framework (see page 112).

The role of the key person in providing for babies' and pre-school children's emotional security

One of the main ways to help children achieve emotional security in the pre-school setting is to ensure that they have a key person. A key person is someone with whom each child develops a strong relationship. The importance of babies and young children having a 'surrogate' relationship in the absence of their parents has been the focus of several pieces of research. As parents normally provide children with emotional security, babies and children need someone else to take on this role when their parents are not present. The term 'surrogate' does not mean that the attachment or relationship with the key person replaces the strong relationship that children have with their parents, as this is a unique and enduring bond. Instead the relationship with the key person provides a temporary 'safe base' for children whilst their parents are not with them. Babies and children recognise their key person as someone to whom they can go for reassurance and a cuddle, as well as to act as a playmate and protector. Where children's speech is still developing or they are unable to use speech, a key person will be able to understand what the child is trying to communicate as they get to know the child. This is especially important when caring for babies as a key person will quickly tune in to the cries and body language of a baby.

As well as getting to know the child, the key person also works closely with parents so they can jointly meet the child's needs. Whilst the focus is often on the needs of the child when their parents are not present, it is also important to remember that parents too have a unique bond with their child. A pre-school's key person system can help reassure parents that their child will have someone to rely on and to look after him or her in their absence.

How to work in partnership with parents of babies and pre-school children to implement settling in procedures which promote their emotional security

The strong bond between baby or child and parent means that separation needs to be handled extremely carefully. Babies and children can find it hard to leave their parents and parents can find it difficult as well. It is important to remember that nature did not intend for parents to leave their young offspring 'with strangers' and so there is a biological response to separation as well. By working closely in partnership with parents and using a key person system, babies and children can leave their parents and benefit from the learning environment.

Working with parents to identify a settling in plan

Babies and children will find it easier to settle in if a plan has been agreed with parents. Babies and children do not like sudden changes and so working out with parents how to approach the separation works well. As all children are different, arrangements for settling in will need to be tailored. There are factors that will affect the settling in plan. They include the age of the child, the child's previous experience of being left as well as whether the child already knows any of the adults or children in the pre-school. It is also important to discuss with parents how they are feeling about leaving their children as parents who are feeling anxious are likely to transmit this anxiety to their children. This means that settling in arrangements for a child who has an older sibling in the pre-school are likely to be different to those of a child who has always been in the company of his or her parents. By agreeing a plan together that meets the needs of both child and parents, the settling in process is likely to be smoother.

Using a key person system for settling in

From the start of the settling in process, the key person will play a pivotal role. The key person needs to talk through how best to help the child settle in with the parents. The key person will also need to spend a little time finding out about the ways in which the parent usually comforts the baby or child, and finding out about his or her favourite toys and activities. It is also important that the key person spends some time in the company of both child and parent(s) as young children use their parents' reactions to gauge whether a person is safe. By talking together, a powerful signal is being sent that the key person is 'safe'.

It is important that the child meets and interacts with their key person several times before being left for any significant time, although it can be useful for parents just to pop out of sight to gauge how well the key person relationship is coming along. Once a relationship has been established between key person and child, the parents can start to leave. Most pre-schools working with parents agree a system of providing feedback, which might be another member of staff popping out to let parents know that their child is fine.

Case study

It is Bozena's first session at the pre-school without her father. Bozena is three and a half years old and speaks only a little English. Her key person, Helen, has

Continued ▶

spent some time with Bozena and her father and now knows a few essential words in Polish. Helen has also learnt that Bozena loves playing in the role-play area and also with dough. Helen also knows that Bozena is very unsure in group situations. Bozena and her father visited the pre-school four times before Helen and Bozena's father felt that Bozena was sufficiently familiar with the pre-school for him to leave for an hour. Helen and Bozena's father agreed that he would wait outside for the first ten minutes in case Bozena became distressed and that Helen would ring him on his mobile. Helen has been playing with Bozena and a couple of other children at the dough table. Bozena looks very happy and is already beginning to play with another girl.

1   Why is it important that Helen understands a few key words in Polish?
2   Explain why the settling in process needs to be tailored to the needs of individual children?
3   Why is it important to work closely in partnership with parents when settling in children?

How to help babies and pre-school children make transitions within and from the pre-school setting in ways that promote their emotional well-being

There are times when babies and pre-school children will need to change room, building or leave the pre-school. In some cases, a key person may also leave. It is important that babies and children are supported during these changes as the old adage 'children are adaptable' is not entirely true!

Introducing children to new adults

One of the most effective ways in which you can help children cope with significant changes is to introduce them to the adults who will be responsible for their care. For babies and toddlers, this means that the adult who will be taking on their care needs to spend a little time in the company of both the child and the key person. This needs to take place in the same way that the original relationship with the key person was built up – bit by bit, so that the child is familiar and confident with the new adult. In situations where babies and toddlers are moving to a different room, their existing key person may make frequent trips into the new room so that the child can become more familiar with their new key person.

Introducing children to other children

From three years, many children are starting to develop friendships and are increasingly becoming interested in other children. This means that for older children, helping them to cope with changes may be about helping them become used to other children. One way of helping children make relationships with each other is to play some structured games or activities. This means that children might sit next to each other and be engaged in a joint task. This can help children get to know each other as a pre-cursor to playing together. Another strategy is to find out about children's interests and use them as a way of helping them play with other children.

Familiarising children with a new environment

Where children are changing room or going to school, it can be helpful to familiarise them with their new environment. Using the principle that the key person acts as a 'safe base', children will often cope better if they have spent some time in the new environment in the presence of their key person. This is why many pre-schools will take groups of children to the primary school before children are due to start.

Talking to children about changes

It can also be helpful to talk to children about the changes that are to take place, although before doing this it is worth sharing information with parents. With some children who are already anxious about change such as going to school, talking about it can create more anxiety especially if the change is not an immediate one. Talking about change also has to be done in the context of children's ages and stage of development, as some children get confused about how quickly a change is to take place.

How to communicate with babies and pre-school children in ways that promote their emotional security

The way in which you communicate with babies and pre-school children can make a significant difference. Babies and children respond well to adults who are warm, confident and responsive to their needs. Communicating with babies and pre-school children means thinking about your body language and tone of voice as much as the actual words that are used. This means that it is good practice to get down to babies' and pre-school children's level in order to make eye contact and also to avoid children feeling that they are being crowded or stood over. Responding to babies and pre-school children means smiling if this is appropriate, not rushing them into communicating with you, and looking for props such as cuddly toys or simple repetitive games such as peek-a-boo that might facilitate communication. When communicating with children, it is important to use this as an opportunity to value them and show them warmth. This might be done using terms of traditional endearment that are appropriate, such as 'yes, you can, love,' as these can signal to children that they are liked.

As well as thinking about the way in which you communicate directly with individual children, it is also important to think about how you gain the attention of other adults and children. Calling over to another adult or calling for all children's attention can sometimes sound like shouting and be unnerving for some children. Using techniques to attract groups of children's attention, such as gently ringing some sleigh bells, are therefore worth exploring.

Good practice

Communicating with babies and children

- Be responsive to babies' and children's moods and interests.
- Get down to their level.
- Allow babies and children time to respond.
- Make eye contact and physical contact where appropriate.
- Keep your tone of voice warm.
- Smile and use positive body language.

How to work in partnership with parents to promote the emotional security of babies and pre-school children

Parents act as the long-term providers of their children's emotional security. Working in partnership with parents is therefore important. Parents can help you to support their children because they know and understand their children. They may, for example, be able to tell you about situations in which their child responds well or finds things difficult. Sometimes this can be some of the practical but nonetheless essential details, such as a child disliking going to the toilet when other children are around.

If you have a good relationship with parents, you will also be able to share information that might have an impact on the child's needs, as even the smallest changes in children's lives can have an impact on them; for example, a brother's hamster has died or the child is moving to a new flat. The key person system allows such information to be shared as parents can get to know their child's key person and should feel that the information they provide is valued in a non-judgemental way. The key person system also means that parents know that someone is taking a particular interest in their child's well-being.

How to implement policies and procedures in a pre-school setting to protect young children from abuse

How protecting children from abuse promotes their human rights

It is a sad fact that some children are abused by adults. Sadder still are the cases in the past where professionals in the sector have failed to act on the signs that children are being abused, even when children try to tell them. In some cases this has been the result of ignorance, whilst in others children have been let down because of a lack of procedures. Today, child protection is taken very seriously in pre-schools and it is recognised that protecting children is linked to protecting their human rights. This section looks at ways of recognising and responding to abuse, but as child protection advice and procedures can change over time, it is important that you remain up to date by going on training courses and looking at the latest publications from organisations such as the NSPCC (National Society for Prevention of Cruelty to Children) and the Pre-school Learning Alliance. It is also important to find information for your local area procedures by contacting your Local Safeguarding Children Board (see also page 276).

The relevance of the UN Convention on the Rights of the Child

Children have a right to grow up without fear of exploitation or abuse. This right in enshrined in the UN Convention on the Rights of the Child, to which the UK is a signatory. Being a signatory means that these rights are embedded in UK legislation and can be seen in, for example, the 1989 Children Act and 2004 Children Act.

The types of abuse from which children may suffer and the indicators of these

There are four types of abuse that are usually cited, although children can be subject to more than one type of abuse at once, for example, neglect alongside emotional abuse.

Types and definitions of abuse

Abuse is often categorised into four types:

- physical abuse
- emotional abuse
- sexual abuse
- neglect.

Many children will suffer more than one type of abuse and all types of abuse can have long-term effects. Some children will learn from being abused to become abusers, while others will find it hard to trust others. Children can also fail to achieve their academic potential because being relaxed, comfortable and secure are important prerequisites for learning.

Physical abuse

Physical abuse causes physical harm to a child. It may involve hitting, shaking, throwing, poisoning, burning, scalding, drowning or suffocating. Physical harm may also result when a parent or carer feigns the symptoms of or deliberately causes ill-health to a child. This situation is commonly described as 'factitious illness by proxy' or 'Munchausen Syndrome by proxy'.

Emotional abuse

Emotional abuse is the persistent emotional ill-treatment of a child such as to cause severe and persistent adverse effects on that child's emotional development. It may involve conveying to a child that he or she is worthless, unloved or inadequate, or valued only in so far as he or she meets the needs of another person. It may feature age or developmentally inappropriate expectations being imposed on the child. Emotional abuse may cause a child frequently to feel frightened or in danger, or it may involve the exploitation or corruption of a child. Some level of emotional abuse is involved in all types of ill-treatment, though it may occur alone.

Sexual abuse

Sexual abuse is forcing or enticing a child or young person to take part in sexual activities whether or not that child is aware of what is happening. These activities may involve physical contact, including penetrative acts such as rape and buggery, and non-penetrative acts. Sexual abuse also includes non-contact activities, for example, forcing children to watch or participate in the production of pornographic material, getting children to watch sexual activities or encouraging children to behave in sexually inappropriate ways.

Neglect

Neglect is the persistent failure to meet a child's basic physical and/or psychological needs. It is likely to result in the serious impairment of the child's health and development. It may involve a parent or carer failing to provide:

- adequate food, shelter and clothing
- protection from physical harm or danger
- access to appropriate medical care or treatment
- adequate responsiveness to a child's basic emotional needs.

(Adapted from *Working Together to Safeguard our Children*, Department of Health, 1999.)

Recognising signs of abuse, including in very young children who cannot use verbal communication and children who use alternative forms of communication

Adults working with children need to understand the physical and behavioural signs that a child is being abused. Early years practitioners are in a good position to observe children and thus notice changes in their well-being. This is important because not all children will communicate that they are being abused on account of their age, not speaking English or having a communication difficulty. Some children will also not report abuse because they may not realise that they are being abused.

As well as looking out for the behavioural and physical signs of abuse, it is essential that you have a good understanding of child development. This may alert you to a child's development being atypical. Whilst it is important that signs of abuse are acted upon, it is also important that judgments are suspended because some behavioural and even physical indicators of abuse may have other causes.

Signs of physical abuse

While most young children will have the odd bump or scrape, children who repeatedly have bruising and injuries may be suffering from physical abuse. In some cases, violence against a child can escalate and result in fatal injuries. Some children are given a cover story by their abuser to explain their injuries to others; the child might be threatened with further violence if he or she does not use the story. The fear factor partly explains why children may not reveal that they are being harmed.

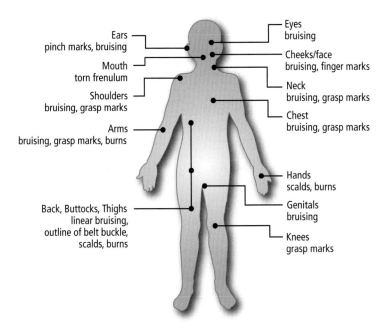

Ears
pinch marks, bruising

Mouth
torn frenulum

Shoulders
bruising, grasp marks

Arms
bruising, grasp marks, burns

Back, Buttocks, Thighs
linear bruising,
outline of belt buckle,
scalds, burns

Eyes
bruising

Cheeks/face
bruising, finger marks

Neck
bruising, grasp marks

Chest
bruising, grasp marks

Hands
scalds, burns

Genitals
bruising

Knees
grasp marks

Physical signs of abuse in children.

Children who have been physically abused are more likely to show aggressive behaviour towards other children, especially those who are younger. This is one way in which the child can feel empowered.

What you should do if you have concerns that a child is being physically abused

If a child has a physical injury it is good practice to ask the child how it happened. You should also mention it to the parent. You should be concerned if the child is reluctant to tell you how the injury occurred or if the parent is defensive. You should also be concerned if the child's and the parent's version of what happened is very different. Usually, children are quite keen to show off their 'war wounds' and tell you about them. In the same way, most parents will, on arrival, mention any injuries that a child has.

Signs of physical abuse in children

Physical indicators

- Unusual-shaped bruises (these might reflect the shape of an object or fingers).

- Bruises and marks on the body not associated with accidental injury, for example, on the chest.

Continued ▶

- Burn and scald marks (including small burns from cigarettes).

- Bite marks.

- Fractures or swellings.

- Cuts to the face.

- Black eyes.

- Difficulty in walking; stiffness.

Behavioural indicators

- Showing aggressive behaviour towards others.

- Aggression shown in role-play, for example, hitting a teddy in the face with a pan.

- A child is withdrawn and quiet.

- A child is reluctant to be with a parent or a particular adult in the setting.

- A parent or carer appears to be very aggressive with a child.

- A child does not take part in or is excluded by a parent from activities involving undressing, for example, dressing in costumes for a concert.

Signs of emotional abuse

Emotional abuse accompanies other forms of abuse because they result in children's emotional development and mental health being at risk. Emotional abuse alone can be hard to detect because there are no outwardly physical signs in young children. In older children you may see self-harm, substance misuse or eating disorders. There are, however, various behavioural indicators of emotional abuse in young children.

Children who are 'hungry' for unconditional love and affection are very vulnerable. They may be targeted by paedophiles who often recognise that the child's need for love may outweigh his or her reluctance to participate. Children who are emotionally abused also lack confidence. This can mean that the child is reluctant to try out new activities for fear of failure or humiliation.

Behavioural indicators of emotional abuse in children

- Attention-seeking behaviours, for example, a child is extremely clingy or deliberately provocative.

Continued ▶

- The child is eager for affection and may seek it inappropriately, for example, by approaching strangers.

- Telling lies to gain sympathy or attention.

- Regressive behaviour, for example, baby talk or thumb sucking.

- Tantrums beyond the age when most children have ceased to have tantrums.

- Difficultly in socialising with peers.

- Tearfulness, lack of confidence and poor self-worth.

Signs of sexual abuse

Sexual abuse is not always easy to detect because the child may not realise that the actions of the adults are inappropriate. In addition, there may not be any outward physical signs because injuries can be internal or hidden by underwear.

Sexual abuse can be hard to detect because some of the adult perpetrators are extremely clever. They can gradually gain a child's trust (this is called grooming) and over a period include increasingly sexual acts in their relationship with the child. For example, a kiss on the cheek becomes one on the lips. Sexual acts are also sometimes integrated with ordinary play and care activities, for example, bedtime and bathtime, or rough-and-tumble. Some children are told that activities are 'special' and 'secret'. Others may be threatened with violence if they tell another person, or told that something nasty will happen to a family member or person that they care for if they tell.

Signs of sexual abuse in children

Physical indicators

- Bruises, scratches and injuries that are not likely to be accidental, for example, bruising to the inner thighs.

- Difficulty in walking and sitting.

- Fear of going to the toilet.

- Complaints of pain when passing stools or urine.

- Genital or urinary tract infections.

- Soiling or dirtying when the child has previously been clean and dry.

Continued ▶

Behavioural indicators

- Regression in behaviour, for example, using comforters, rocking or thumb sucking.

- Inappropriate sexual behaviour, for example, undressing other children, exposing themselves, sitting on the laps of people they do not know, trying to fondle adults.

- Showing sexual behaviour in imaginative play, for example, making dolls 'have sex' or putting a doll to bed and taking its clothes off afterwards.

- Knowledge of adult sexual behaviour, for example, knowing the colour of semen.

- Unwillingness to be with a particular carer.

Signs of neglect

Neglect causes children to be at risk of accidents and infections and can prevent them from learning. In severe cases, neglect can result in a child's death. Parents can sometimes neglect their children because they have health problems or are not coping with their parenting role. Sometimes, neglect is the result of ignorance, for example, not understanding that a fruit-only diet will fail to provide sufficient nutrients for a child.

Signs of neglect in children

Physical indicators

- Frequent accidental injuries (these are often the result of a lack of supervision or safety equipment).

- Children who are underweight and hungry.

- Children who are untidy and dirty, including their clothing.

- Children who are tired (this can be due to a lack of nutrition as well as inadequate sleeping arrangements).

- Children with frequent low-grade infections that go untreated, for example, nits, colds, influenza, coughs and earaches.

Continued ▶

Behavioural indicators

- Children may steal food and drink.

- Children who take significant responsibility for younger children.

- Children who are reluctant to go home at the end of sessions.

- Children who mention that they are often left alone.

Looking for changes in behaviour patterns

As well as being aware of signs that a child is being abused, you should look for significant changes in a child's behaviour. This can occur as a result of abuse commencing. A child who previously was settled, happy and confident may quickly become withdrawn or aggressive. In some cases, behavioural changes are a response to other things in a child's life, such as the birth of a sibling or the illness of a family member. Therefore, while changes should be noted and acted upon, it is important not to jump to conclusions. This means that changes to a child's behaviour should be mentioned to parents as a starting point. Most parents will readily provide an explanation. If, however, you continue to have concerns, you should follow the written procedures in your setting.

You should also be aware of changes in children's behaviour towards adults working in the setting. Abuse can happen in care and education settings. This means that you should keep an eye out for children who appear reluctant to be with a particular member of staff.

Recognising changes in children's behaviour as signs of possible abuse

Look out for children who:

- become aggressive

- become withdrawn

- begin to show sexual knowledge

- are more clingy than usual

- are reluctant to join their carers or parents

- try to avoid being with a particular member of staff or adult in the setting

- change their behaviour on particular days, for example, after a weekend with another family member or on days when a certain person is in the setting.

The requirements of legislation, codes of practice and local guidelines for responding to abuse, including lines of responsibility, and alerting and reporting procedures

The Children Act 1989 and 2004

There are two key pieces of legislation with reference to the protection of children: the Children Act 1989 and the Children Act 2004.

The 1989 Children Act was a comprehensive Act that covered family law as well as child protection. It is under this Act that pre-schools and other settings caring for children have to be inspected. This Act also gave a clear direction as to the priority of professionals working with children in the well-quoted phrase 'the welfare of children is paramount.' The 1989 Children Act also attempted to bring agencies together to prevent further fatal cases of child abuse where children were left unprotected. Sadly, the death of Victoria Climbie in 2000 showed that there were still much more work to be done. An enquiry known as the Laming Enquiry looked into the circumstances around her death and its recommendations were taken up in a government green paper called Every Child Matters. This has now become a programme for change and in 2004 a further Children Act was passed in order to implement this programme.

The Children Act 2004 places a duty on local authorities to ensure that every child, whatever the child's background or circumstances, has the support he or she needs to:

- be healthy
- stay safe
- enjoy and achieve through learning
- make a positive contribution to society
- achieve economic well-being.

More details about the Every Child Matters programme can be found at the following web site: www.everychildmatters.gov.uk.

Local Safeguarding Children Boards

In terms of child protection, Every Child Matters has meant that local authorities are required to form Local Safeguarding Children Boards (LSCBs); these replace the Area Child Protection Committees (APACs). From Spring 2006, LSCBs will co-ordinate local work to safeguard and promote the welfare of children. They will also develop local policies and procedures for child protection. Boards will be composed in a similar way to the former Area Child Protection Committees and so will include senior managers from all the key agencies that work with children and their families, including police and probation services.

Working Together to Safeguard Children

In 1999, the Department of Health issued a key document entitled *Working Together to Safeguard Children*. It was as a result of this work that each local authority formed an Area Child Protection Committee. Working Together to Safeguard Children is a key document in relation to child protection. It is to be revised in Spring 2006 (at the time LSCBs are formed); this means that you should ensure that you have a current copy of it within the pre-school.

The role of written policies in enabling pre-school settings to protect children from abuse

The Children Act 1989 requires that pre-school settings should have a policy in place that outlines how children are to be safeguarded from abuse. The policy also has to outline the procedure to be followed in the event of an allegation of abuse or neglect. It is important that you have read your pre-school's policy so that you are confident that you know what you should do in the event of concerns about a child. It is essential also that written policies are followed as some of the procedures are linked to safeguarding children.

National Standards

In order for pre-schools to be registered they have to comply with Standard 13 of the National Standards. This standard is wholly about child protection.

Good practice

Child protection: key questions

- Is there a policy in place that outlines the procedures for reporting suspected abuse?
- Does the policy comply with the procedure designated by the LSCBs?
- Does the policy include a procedure to be followed if an allegation is made against a member of staff or other adult?
- Is there a member of staff responsible for child protection and liaising with other agencies?
- Are staff aware of the signs that might indicate abuse?
- Is staff training held regularly to update knowledge about child protection?

How to follow procedures for responding to disclosure by and suspected abuse of pre-school children

Responding to a child's disclosure of abuse

Sometimes children will seek out the support of adults to prevent abuse from continuing. In other cases, children may unintentionally say something that is significant to an adult. The term 'disclosures' has been used to describe these types of event; however, this term is now used less frequently in court because the defendant's solicitors can then infer that adults have encouraged or led the child to make a claim. The latest guidance from the Department of Health warns adults working with children to be aware that the way in which they respond to a child who they suspect has been abused can affect the later outcomes.

What to do if a child tells you about abuse

There are some simple but essential rules to follow if a child tells you about abuse or says something that is of concern.

Good practice

Responding to a child who tells you about abuse

Do:

- Reassure the child that you believe what he or she is saying.
- Listen to the child carefully, but do not ask questions as this may jeopardise a police investigation.
- Tell the child that you will do everything you can to protect him or her.
- Tell the child that you will need to talk to other adults in order to help him or her.
- Reassure the child that he or she is not in trouble and that he or she has acted properly.
- Make notes in pen immediately after the conversation has finished and before talking to anyone else. Write down only what the child has told you. Do not speculate or add any comments. Include the date and time, and then sign the notes.

Do not:

- Promise the child that you will be able to keep what he or she has said a secret. This is important because the child can feel let down later and will not trust other adults.

Continued ▶

- Question the child or pass any comment other than to reassure the child.
- Make notes while you are with the child *or after* you have discussed what has been said with another adult.
- Add additional information into the notes later.
- Talk to other people about what has occurred, other than the designated person for dealing with child protection in the setting.

What happens next…

If you have concerns about a child you should let these be known to the designated person in your setting. This may be the pre-school leader or another senior member of staff. This person may then seek further advice from Social Services or the NSPCC, or may go on to make a referral. If you are the designated person in your setting, you should follow your Local Safeguarding Children Board's guidelines. Once a referral has been received, the social worker will decide on the next course of action, dependent on whether the child is seen as being at risk of significant harm.

The Department of Health has produced a flow chart to show the process that should take place once initial concerns have been expressed; this can be accessed at the Department of Health website (www.dh.gov.uk).

Stereotypical assumptions about abuse

It is important to be aware of some of the stereotypes around abuse. The stereotypes can lead to abuse not always being identified. Stereotypes about child abuse can prevent people from identifying a problem and can lead to false assumptions. Research on child abuse shows that the following stereotypes are common but inaccurate.

- *Stereotype 1: strangers abuse children*
  Many people believe that child abuse is carried out by strangers. Surprisingly, this is not borne out by the statistics on child abuse: the majority of abusers are people known to the child. Abusers may be family members, friends or even adults working with children. Cases in which strangers abduct and abuse children do occur, but these represent only a small number of abuse cases.

- *Stereotype 2: abuse occurs in poor families*
  This stereotype is dangerous because it can mean that children from more affluent families are not thought to be at risk of abuse. Sometimes children from wealthy families who have been abused are not believed because of this stereotype.

- *Stereotype 3: abuse occurs in single-parent families*
  Plenty of stereotypes abound about single-parent families. Because child abuse occurs across the social and income spectrum, it is unfair to assume that children from single-parent families will be abused. Focusing on single-parent families can mean that other children at risk of abuse are not identified.

- *Stereotype 4: only men abuse children*
  While statistically, more men sexually abuse children than do women, this does not mean that women do not sexually abuse children. Stereotypes about women as nurturing and 'safe' can mean that children who have been sexually abused by women are not believed. In addition, it is also important to recognise that older children and siblings can abuse younger children.

Avoiding jumping to conclusions

Many people fear that by reporting their concerns, they may create problems for the child and his or her family. Whilst it is important to understand that sometimes what children say or show in their behaviour is not always linked to abuse, it is important not to jump to conclusions about what might be happening. The task of further investigation and hence decision making will be the eventual responsibility of professionals working in child protection.

Confidentiality

It is important that any information given to you whilst suspect abuse concerns are investigated remains confidential both during and afterwards. This means that you should not discuss the issues or information that you have been given with anyone other than the authorised persons. Breaching confidentiality can jeopardise children's safety; it may also lead to a prosecution being unsuccessful which may allow an abuser to continue.

How to respond appropriately to parents and other family members in situations of suspected abuse of pre-school children

It is in the interests of the child for both parents and family members to have good working relationships with those who work at the pre-school, especially the child's key worker. If trust is breached because parents feel that they are being judged, the parents may decide not to continue bringing the child into the setting. This is not in the child's interest if abuse is taking place. Nor is it in the pre-school's interest if no abuse is taking place and the parents talk unfavourably about the atmosphere in the setting.

When the parent is implicated in the abuse, there can be a conflict between working in partnership with parents and ensuring that the child's welfare is protected. The guidelines from *Safeguarding Children* (2003) suggest that when a referral is made a discussion takes place as to how much information parents should be given. The clear message is that you should always remember to put the child's welfare first. It is therefore useful to seek advice about how to work with parents from the professionals dealing with the child's referral.

Gaining information from parents

Where initial concerns are expressed about a child, it may be appropriate to talk to parents about how the child sustained an injury or the child's behaviour. However, until abuse is confirmed and the perpetrator identified, it is essential not to pre-judge parents because some behavioural and physical signs are not the result of abuse.

Confidentiality

Once a child has been referred, any relevant information about the child coming from the parents might need to be passed on. It is therefore important that parents understand when talking to you that you may not be able to guarantee the confidentiality of any information that they give you. Making sure that parents know this can help prevent situations where parents feel that their trust in you has been betrayed. Whilst parents need to know the limits on your ability to keep information confidential, it is important that they know that you will not pass on any information about the suspected child abuse to anyone other than those involved in the referral case. Parents need to know that other parents and staff members will not be judging them and that they and their family will not become a subject of gossip.

The range of services and other professionals who will be involved with pre-school children who have been abused and their families, and how to work effectively with them

There is a multi-agency approach to child protection. This means that when abuse is suspected or identified, several professionals may become involved to support the child and the family. The extent of involvement depends on the nature of the abuse and the needs of the child and his or her family.

Social Services and social workers

Social Services and social workers will be involved in cases of child protection and abuse. Social workers may have a variety of roles including directly supporting children and their families as well as undertaking assessments to consider whether a child is safe within a family.

Police

The police may be involved in order to investigate child abuse and, if appropriate, bring a prosecution. Specific units within the local police service are responsible for this work

Psychologists

Child psychologists may assess children's emotional needs and make recommendations as to how a child and his or her family may be best supported. Educational psychologists may also support children in terms of helping their behaviour and learning.

Therapists

Children and their families may be involved in specific therapy. Some children may be referred to play therapists so that through the medium of play, they can explore and release their emotions about what has happened to them. Family therapists may work with the whole family to explore the dynamics of the relationships within them.

Drug and alcohol counsellors

Where substance misuse is a factor in abuse, adults within the family may need counselling and support.

Psychiatrists

In some cases of abuse, a parent's or family member's mental health may be a factor. Referrals may therefore be made for psychiatric support.

Primary Care Health Team

The Primary Care Health Team, which may include the family doctor and health visitor, will also support the family and the child in terms of their health needs.

Foster carers

Where children are not staying within their birth family, they may be placed in foster care. This means that you may have a child who comes to the pre-school as a temporary arrangement whilst in foster care. Building good relationships with foster carers is therefore important so as to help children settle in and find ways of helping them cope with the changes.

Working with other professionals

As you have seen, there are many people who may be involved with the child and the family. Working effectively with them means identifying at the start their role and also clarifying with them how this might link to your work with children and their families. It is particularly important to find out the boundaries of confidentiality so that you are giving information only to those who ought to have it. If you are unsure about passing information on to a professional, it can be useful to ask the person to put the request in writing. At the start of any investigation of child abuse, Social Services or the police will often request information about the child or the family. This information may help with making an assessment of the situation, providing evidence of a criminal assault or creating a child protection plan. It is important to find out what exactly is required bearing in mind that accuracy and clarity is extremely important. You may also be asked to go to a child protection conference in which decisions about how best to help the child are made.

How to implement working practices that protect pre-school children and the adults who work with them

It is essential that you remain aware that members of staff and other adults in the setting might be potential abusers. This sounds rather drastic; however, thinking in this way can help you to establish safeguards that will protect children from abuse and adults from potential allegations. The National Standards provide clear guidance as to the importance of 'suitable people' being with children. This means that new staff need to be cleared by the Criminal Records Bureau and that OFSTED has to be informed of any changes to staff in the setting.

You should also consider your practice with children. It is easy to overreact and withdraw any physical contact between adults and children; however, this is unfair on young children who sometimes need physical reassurance. The key is transparency and respecting children's cues. This means that staff can cuddle children but this should be done openly rather than hidden from others. It also means that you need to respect children's wishes. This means encouraging a child who wants to slip his or her hand into yours, but equally encouraging the child to let go when he or she is ready to leave.

Good practice

Ways of reducing opportunities for abuse

- Make sure that members of staff or volunteers working regularly with children have clearance from the Criminal Records Bureau.
- Maintain a visitors record book and make sure that visitors wear a badge.
- Do not allow students or visitors to have any unsupervised contact with children in the setting.
- Do not shut doors when alone with children.
- Take cues from the child as to how much physical contact he or she wants.
- Encourage children to take as much responsibility and control as they are able to for their personal hygiene.
- Respect children's need for dignity and privacy when they are changing or in the toilet.
- Be aware of children's reactions to colleagues.

Supervision of visitors and other adults in the setting

It is essential that all visitors including trades people, such as builders, are supervised when they are in the building and not allowed to have unsupervised contact with children. This should include parent helpers and volunteers unless they have been police checked. While young children may have some understanding of not talking to strangers, they will not necessarily understand that a person who has come to fix the floor or help serve snacks is still a 'stranger'. To save potential embarrassment, it is therefore important that a sign or a notice is clearly displayed at the entrance which states that this is the setting's policy.

Ways which are appropriate to pre-school children's age and stage of development to help them to respect their bodies and protect themselves from abuse

As well as understanding the signs of abuse, it is important to understand the ways in which you might protect children from abuse. A key way of doing is this is by finding ways of empowering children. Empowering children means encouraging them to take control and become as independent as possible. This can give children the confidence, which in turn may help them to either avoid abuse or tell an adult about it.

Keeping secrets

One way in which abusers control children is by telling them that they have to keep secrets. This means that you should talk to children about secrets and surprises and teach them that they are allowed to break secrets. This means that it is not good practice to tell children that they have to keep a secret – even if it is a good one.

Helping children to feel confident about their bodies

Children need to feel as early on as possible that they have some rights over their bodies. In practical terms, this means encouraging children to feel that they can be private when they go to the toilet or that they can have control over who touches them and where. This means that whilst you are happy to cuddle or hold hands of children, it is at their invitation and that when they no longer need physical reassurance you are quick to let them go. Working in this way with children sends out subtle but powerful messages about having rights over your body.

Helping children feel valued

It is important that children learn that they are loved for being themselves, exactly as they are. This is unconditional regard and gives children confidence. Abusers can sometimes make children feel responsible for the abuse and that they have deserved it in some way. Other abusers confuse the child by making their love conditional on the child accepting or doing things for them. Statements that use adult authority to encourage children to do things should therefore be resisted, for example, 'Will you pick it up for me? There's a good girl', as they teach children that obeying adults is the way to being loved and gaining approval.

How to identify own effectiveness in implementing strategies to protect pre-school children from abuse

By its very nature, child abuse is often secretive and hidden from view. This means that you may not always know that you are 'missing' children who are being abused. Identifying your own effectiveness thus becomes more difficult, but by reviewing your overall practice and knowledge, you may be able to see where you need to take action.

Good practice

Key questions: identifying own effectiveness in protecting children from abuse

- When did I last read the child protection policy of the setting?
- Do I know what I should do if I have concerns about a child?
- When did I last attend child protection training?

Continued ▶

- Am I aware of the local structure of child protection?
- Do I ensure in my practice that children are empowered, for example, given privacy?
- Am I available for children when they need to talk?
- Do I observe children and consider their development?

How to use identification of own effectiveness to decide on and take action to develop own effectiveness in implementing strategies to protect pre-school children from abuse

There are many ways in which you can work on improving your effectiveness in relation to child protection. Firstly, it is important to remain up to date with policies and procedures. There has been significant changes as to the way in which child abuse cases are meant to be handled. Keeping up to date means reading bulletins and magazines as well as attending regular child protection training, especially training that is locally organised. This is because currently there is a focus on bringing local professionals together when dealing with child protection.

Since children sometimes do not directly report abuse to adults, it is essential that you remain alert as to the possibilities that a child is being abused. This is often shown in terms of a child's behaviour and development. Using observations and linking these to normative and behavioural development is therefore essential. Re-visiting your knowledge about normative development can therefore be useful, as can attending training to reinforce your knowledge.

The role of good working relationships in making the pre-school setting a supportive and safe environment

The importance of good working relationships between all of the adults involved in pre-school children's care and education

The pre-school is a large partnership between staff, parents, the local community and other professionals supporting children and their families. Good working relationships can make this partnership hugely successful and rewarding. Where there are good working relationships between all of the adults, everyone including children benefit.

How the staff in the pre-school setting can work as an effective team

For pre-schools to be effective learning communities for children and their families, it is important that the staff can work together as a team. Teamwork requires a variety of skills.

Leadership

Teams that are working well together often have an effective leader. The pre-school leader often sets the tone for successful partnerships not only with other staff but also with parents. Pre-school leaders need to support members of the team, provide clear direction and also facilitate communication. Newly-appointed pre-school leaders can find it helpful to attend training relating to these management skills.

Supportive

Whilst the pre-school leader may set the tone of teamwork, the team itself has to pull together and be supportive of each other. Support is based on respect and valuing each other and being ready to work towards the common good. Supportive teams make not only good working conditions but are also the basis for friendships.

Communication

Good teams communicate well. This means that everyone in the team knows what they need to do and also have known what is happening during a session. Meetings can play a major part in this as they provide a structured way of talking about planning, activities and the needs of children. Meetings do not always have to be formal or even long. A pre-school team may gather around at the end of the session to briefly talk through and evaluate the session. Meetings that require more time might be held in someone's home. Teams that meet regularly find that they are more in tune with each other and have a good understanding of what is happening. Written forms of communication such as planning, notes and reminders are also useful tools. Communication between staff needs to be respectful, positive but also open.

Roles and responsibilities

Effective teams are good at understanding their roles and responsibilities. Staff know what they are responsible for doing and how this fits into the successful working of the pre-school. Clear roles and responsibilities can avoid confusion and also the potential for conflict, for example, two members of staff both thinking that they are meant to be getting snacks ready. This is why meetings and clear direction from the pre-school leader can be helpful.

How staff can create effective relationships and partnerships with pre-school children's parents

Seeing parents as equal and valued partners in their child's education has been a long established value of the pre-school. Effective relationships and partnerships between parents and the pre-school is of reciprocal benefit (see also Core Unit 2, pages 135–8). Creating an effective relationship with parents is therefore in everyone's interests.

Effective relationships are based upon trust

Pre-schools understand that effective relationships are built on trust. If parents feel that they cannot trust you, they will not wish to exchange information with you or feel that they can participate in the pre-school. Trust is based on honest communication and is often built up over time. Parents need to know that they are being told about their child and their child's progress and this is why involving parents in building their child's profiles and the planning is so important. Trust also means being aware of the importance of confidentiality which is why pre-schools have policies about storing personal information and passing on information.

Effective relationships are based on valuing parents

Parents need to feel that they are welcome and that the pre-school setting values all parents. Parents, like children, can quickly sense if they are welcome by observing body language. Simply smiling and acknowledging parents is a good starting point. It is also worth remembering that while there are differences between parents and staff in their roles and approaches, for example, to child-rearing, that you are united by wanting the best for the child. A key way in which pre-schools show that they value parents is by involving them at all levels in the running of the pre-school. When parents are able to become involved in the pre-school and are contributing to its success, a powerful signal is sent out about respecting parents and the skills that they can offer.

Effective relationships are based upon good communication

Effective relationships require good communication skills. This means thinking about all ts of communications that are used in the pre-school.

Face-to-face contact

Many parents enjoy having some time to talk to members of staff. Face-to-face contact is a quick and easy way to exchange information and offer a response. It is therefore a key way in which you can establish and maintain an effective relationship with parents. Interestingly, face-to-face contact can be seen on the surface as 'chatting' and informal, but the reality is that it offers parents opportunities to ask questions, put forward suggestions and become more involved in their child's pre-school. Frequent face-to-face contact with parents also means that pre-school staff can often pick up on any worries that parents have as they 'know' the parents. 'Knowing' parents means also that relationships between parents and adults in the pre-school are usually 'warm' and therefore this facilitates working with parents as equal partners.

In order to communicate well with parents, staff need to listen as well as talk. Active listening skills, which are used in counselling, can be very helpful. It is therefore worthwhile to read up on active listening skills or, better still, attending a basic counselling course.

Written communications

As well as face-to-face contact, relationships with parents can also be maintained by communicating in writing, for example, a pre-school may send a copy of the planning home for each parent. Written communication alone is rarely sufficient to create a 'warm' relationship in the way that face-to-face contact can, but it can be a good way of keeping in touch. Any written communication needs to be legible, clear and accurate. The tone of the writing is also important and it is useful to check that it is 'warm'. You must make sure that you do not exclude groups of parents who may not have English as their first language. This means checking whether a translation is appropriate. It is also important to bear in mind that some adults have difficulty in reading. That said, there are some advantages to written communications such as notes and letters. Parents at their convenience can read these and they also provide opportunity for parents who cannot come into the setting to remain in contact.

The role of good communication and respect for individuals in creating effective working relationships and partnerships

As you have seen both with parents and staff teams, communication plays a vital role. Good working relationships are based upon successful communication. This prevents misunderstandings or, in extreme cases, situations where there is confusion or a lack of confidence and trust.

There are four types of communication:

- verbal
- non-verbal
- written
- visual.

Each type of communication has particular benefits and so thinking about which communication methods are best suited to a particular situation is important.

Verbal communication

Verbal communication includes face-to-face contact as well as by other means such as telephone. It is important to recognise that verbal communication is a powerful tool because it is an immediate method of communication. People can respond quickly to what has been said and this can be useful as it allows for clarification, immediate agreement or further explanation. Verbal communication does, however, rely on adults' ability to listen, understand and process words. This is often where there can be difficulties and it is easy to find examples of two people who have heard the same words but come away with different messages!

Non-verbal communication

Non-verbal communication is powerful and includes body language, facial expressions such as smiles, and signs. Good non-verbal communication can put others at their ease as well as communicating that you value others. Non-verbal communication can also underline verbal communication and make it more effective, for example, smiling as you agree with someone or tilting your head to show that you are listening. Being aware of others' non-verbal communication is also important. A parent may say something but his or her body language may present a different message, for example, a parent who says 'I'm alright, really' but who is actually upset.

Written communication

Written communication includes reports, letters and plans. Written communication can be an effective method of providing information as it gives people time to read and process information. It is also useful as written communication can be looked at again for reference.

Visual communication

Visual communication might include photographs, posters and even cartoons. Visual communication is not a major way of communicating but it can be extremely useful alongside written communication, for example, a photo alongside text to show how children enjoy learning from playing with sand.

Good practice

Making communication effective

- Think about the best communication method for the situation.
- Consider the needs of individuals, e.g. translation, interpretation, sign language.
- Think carefully about the impact of your communication.
- For face-to-face communication, monitor responses and adapt your communication style accordingly.
- Remember that non-verbal communication is particularly powerful. Think about the impact of body language, gesture and facial expressions on others.

Respect for individuals

Whatever communication method is used, it is important that there is always an underlying respect and awareness of others. Respect for others is characterised by thinking about what others are trying to communicate. This means listening and reading carefully. It also means thinking about the impact that your communication might have on others, especially when they might not always share the same attitudes and values as you.

There are also practical ways in which you can show respect for others whilst communicating. Some of these are very basic but do show inherent respect. They include listening carefully to what others are saying, avoiding interrupting others or speaking over them, and being on time and prepared for meetings. Respecting others also means trying to be prompt when replying to letters and messages.

The effectiveness of own practice in making the pre-school setting a supportive and safe environment

The importance of the interplay between theory and practice for reflective practice

As with all areas of your work with children and their families, it is important to think about your own practice and ways in which you might become more reflective. The starting point for this is, of course, to have a good knowledge of the theory for providing a supportive and safe environment for children. In this area of your work it is also important to understand that there are often new guidelines and advice for procedures such as food handling and child protection. This means that you need constantly to monitor your practice and adjust it according to new developments.

Using reflection to reinforce understanding of what makes the pre-school setting a safe and supportive environment

Reflecting on practice using the theory as a basis can help you to gain an understanding of what makes the pre-school a safe and supportive environment. A good way of doing this is to stand back a little and notice what is being done in your pre-school to create the safe and supportive environment and then see how this links to the theory. Below is a chart that you could use to see how the theory links to the practice of your pre-school.

Reflection on practice

Area	Practice	Links to theory
Registering children	Children are registered as they come into the setting.	Registration is a requirement of the National Standards. Registering children means that if there is a fire, we can ensure that everyone is evacuated.
Recording accidents		
Collection of children		
Key person		
Risk assessment		

How to use an understanding of the factors that make the pre-school setting a supportive and safe environment for babies and pre-school children to identify the effectiveness of own practice

It is important to look at one's own practice and to consider its effectiveness. As you have seen in the previous units, this means that you need to be objective and analytical.

Below is a list of questions that relate to parts of this unit which you might like to use when considering your effectiveness. Note that this is not intended to be a comprehensive list and you will need to add to it.

Key questions when considering effectiveness of own practice

Inclusive and anti-discriminatory practice

- Do I understand what is meant by inclusive and anti-discriminatory practice?

- How do I ensure that the activities that I plan for children reflect inclusive and anti-discriminatory practice?

- Do I ensure that children are given individual attention and that their individual needs are met?

- How do I ensure that children are given positive image of other people and children?

Stimulating and safe environment

- Do I understand and use the procedures when children are ill or have accidents?

- Do I understand and use the procedures for administering medicines?

- How do I help parents to understand the importance of adhering to procedures for collecting children?

Providing for children's physical needs

- Do I understand and use the procedures when providing food and drink for babies and children?

- Do I know what constitutes a healthy and balanced diet with regard to the latest nutritional guidelines?

- Do I work with parents to understand and meet their children's dietary preferences and needs?

- How do I ensure that children's skincare and toileting needs are met?

- How do I work with parents in order to ensure that we share information and work together to meet children's physical needs?

Continued ▶

Providing an environment that promotes children's emotional security

- Do I understand the impact of an effective key person system on children and their families?

- Do I have strong relationships with those children and their families with whom I act as a key person?

- How do I build and maintain relationships with children and their parents as a key person?

- Do I understand and follow the settling in procedures of the pre-school?

- How do I ensure that children who are going to move from or within the pre-school are supported?

Good working relationships

- Do I communicate in a respectful way to all adults in the pre-school?

- Do I understand the significance of good working relationships and their impact on children and their families?

- Am I able to put my point of view across in a calm and thoughtful manner?

- Do I listen to others effectively and consistently?

How to use an identification of own effectiveness to decide on and take action to develop own practice in making the pre-school setting a supportive environment for babies and pre-school children

Once you have considered your strengths and weaknesses in your practice, the next step is to consider how best to further your practice. You have seen in Core Unit 2 how to develop a plan that can help prioritise areas and also act as a focus (pages 143–8). This area of working with children is often tied to legislation and regulations. This means that you must continue to update your knowledge base as this often informs practice.

Training courses

Training is a key way in which knowledge can be updated and you can ensure that your practice is current. Look out for professional development courses run in your local area by a range of providers including the Pre-school Learning Alliance (PSLA), your local authority and groups such as St. John's Ambulance or the NSPCC.

The Internet

The Internet can be a useful source of information, especially about changing regulations in relation to health and safety. It is, however, important to use sites that are likely to contain accurate and information relevant to where you work. The following is a list of sites that might be useful:

- www.hse.gov.uk – this site is run by the government organisation responsible for enforcing health and safety legislation.
- www.ofsted.gov.uk – this is the website for OFSTED and contains information about inspection procedures and also how to meet the standards of care.

Test yourself

1 What is meant by the term 'inclusive practice'?

2 Identify two pieces of legislation that deal with inclusive and anti-discriminatory practice.

3 Explain why it is essential for parents to understand the arrival and departures procedures for the setting.

4 Give four benefits for parents and children of the key person system.

5 Explain why it is essential for settling-in plans to be individual to children and parents.

6 Identify four types of abuse.

7 What are LSCBs?

8 Explain why visitors must not have unsupervised contact with children.

9 What are the benefits of team work in the pre-school?

10 List four ways in which staff can work together as a team.

Reading and references

The bulk of the references given below are websites because much of the information and advice around food, safety and child protection periodically changes. This means that it is essential to keep up to date.

- www.wiredforhealth.gov.uk – guidance on infection control.
- www.surestart.gov.uk – for up-to-date information about diet and nutrition and other aspects of babies' and children's care.
- www.everychildmatters.gov.uk – for up-to-date information about child protection and other information about Every Child Matters.
- www.food.gov.uk – the Food Standards Agency website.
- www.dh.gov.uk – the Department of Health's website.
- *Working Together to Safeguard Children* – at the time of writing this is the latest guidance about child protection. It is published by the Department of Health.

Working to support parents with literacy, numeracy and language needs in a pre-school setting

It is estimated that 11 million adults in the UK have one or more areas of literacy, numeracy or language skills where their level is below that expected of an 11-year-old. For some parents, watching their children learn and wanting to encourage them will create new opportunities for their own learning. Working with parents and children together brings to fulfilment the aim of pre-schools to be learning communities and a valued resource within their community.

This unit is divided into four sections:

- Why engaging in support for parents with literacy, numeracy and language needs is an important activity for pre-school settings
- How to make available to parents opportunities to develop their literacy, numeracy and language skills
- How to enable parents to access support to develop their literacy, numeracy and language skills
- Reviewing the activities undertaken by the pre-school setting to enable parents to develop their literacy, numeracy and language skills

Why engaging in support for parents with literacy, numeracy and language needs is an important activity for pre-school settings

Many adults need a second chance in order to gain literacy, numeracy or language skills that they have missed out on during their childhood. Some adults may have developed a need for these skills as an adult. Current figures suggest that one in five adults have relatively low levels of either literacy, numeracy or language skills.

Pre-schools are excellent places for parents to gain the confidence and knowledge they need in order to get this second chance. This means that as part of the remit of the pre-school to provide education for young children, it can also be to help parents benefit from learning. This is the idea behind the concept of the pre-school as a learning community.

What are literacy, numeracy and language needs?

Having a need in one or more of the above areas may affect an adult's ability to function well in everyday life. Usually, adults who realise that they have a difficultly find ways of avoiding situations when these skills may be called upon, for example:

- they may always pay in cash as they may not have felt confident enough to open a bank account
- they may seek private help from a family member or friend who has more secure literacy skills to complete forms.

Such difficulties may mean that some adults find it harder to gain employment or when in employment may not take up further opportunities for fear that their skill level may be identified. In addition, adults with literacy, numeracy or language needs can find themselves isolated. This is because in order to avoid situations where their difficulty may be noticed, it can seem easier to 'opt' out from close relationships or social activities than suffer the stress of this difficulty being realised by others and reliving the fears and frustration of their school years.

Reasons for literacy, numeracy and language needs

There are many reasons why some adults have not gained these skills at a proficient level. Interestingly, many adults who have missed out on skills have actually gained competence and capability in elements of literacy and numeracy simply through living, and usually surprise themselves at how well they can learn. It is also not unusual to find that adults excel in some other areas; for example, an adult may have a gift for music, mechanics or mentally adding up numbers but find it hard to do simple written calculations. There are also many examples of successful individuals who have struggled with one area of their learning but still managed to run their own businesses with ease. Common reasons for literacy and numeracy needs are described below.

Absence from school

Some adults' early education may have been disrupted and therefore they fell behind with either the teaching of literacy or numeracy. Missing out on learning a basic concept in mathematics can have a particularly profound effect on later mathematical learning because the missing concept is essential in understanding those taught and built upon later. Absence may have occurred for a variety of reasons, not least family circumstances, i.e. a member of the family needed the person to be at home or because of ill health. Some may also have changed schools as their family moved to find work or within their work role, for example, families where the main breadwinner is in the military or because of their lifestyle, i.e. travellers.

Hearing/visual impairment

Some adults may have had hearing loss or visual impairment during childhood. Hearing loss, especially if undetected, can affect a child's speech or ability to hear the sounds in words; this is crucial to being able to read and spell. In the same way, a child who has an undetected visual impairment may miss out on being able to read words.

Learning difficulty

There is now an increasing awareness that some children may have learning difficulties that require particular methods, strategies or styles of teaching. Some adults may in their childhood have had a learning difficulty that resulted in their not being able to access the teaching and learning. For example, it is only in recent years that the specific learning difficulties of dyslexia or dyscalculia have been recognised in schools and local education authorities. Many older people may have these difficulties but they remain undiagnosed. Such people will not have had the opportunity to learn strategies that children are taught in schools today.

Relationship with teacher

Some adults fared badly in school because their school did not meet their needs or the relationship with their teacher was not satisfactory. Relationships with teachers are core to children and young people's success and achievement. This sometimes mean that adults reflect back and realise that they did not try hard or 'gave' up due to the lack of encouragement given.

Bullying

Some adults may have been prevented from learning effectively if they experienced bullying. This may have resulted in absenteeism or simply affected the child's confidence.

Home circumstances

You have seen that parents play an important role in the educational outcomes and achievements of their children. Some adults may reflect back and realise that their home situation was less than ideal in supporting their schooling. A family bereavement, illness or breakdown may have resulted in them being unable to concentrate at school or caused them to miss out on the opportunities provided.

Reasons why there may be language needs

In terms of language, it is common to find that adults may be second language users and be reasonably proficient in their home language. The opportunity to learn and use English may not have been available, for example, local classes were held in the evening but the parent was doing night shifts, or other family members were proficient in English so 'took over' everyday tasks that required English. Whilst some adults with language needs also have difficulties in reading or writing, this is not always the case. Some may have achieved higher qualifications using their home language. There are some adults whose language needs mean that they find it difficult to talk in the company of others and use language to express their emotions, thoughts and needs.

Case study

Lutfi and Aysel have come to the UK with their three young children from Turkey. They are keen to make friends and integrate into the local community. Their English is limited and they are finding it a problem to communicate with other parents in the pre-school beyond smiling and simple phrases. This is becoming a source of frustration for them as they can see that it will be hard to develop proper friendships. They are both highly qualified and Lutfi has a degree in electrical engineering but sometimes they notice that other adults treat them as if they were children! Aysel feels welcomed by the pre-school staff and today she asks if they know whether any English classes are available locally. The pre-school leader says that she will try and find out.

1 Explain the benefits for this family if Lutfi and Aysel can learn English.

2 Why is it important to recognise that an adult may have strengths as well as areas of need?

Common examples of literacy, numeracy and language needs

Literacy	Numeracy	Language
Reading	Using coins and notes	Speaking and listening
Spelling	Managing a budget	Vocabulary, grammar
Writing	Borrowing and saving money effectively	Pronunciation

The links between parents' literacy, numeracy and language skills and children's acquisitions of these skills

It is increasingly recognised that parents' skills, confidence and attitudes to learning have a significant effect on their children's success and achievement. A piece of research carried out by Sacker et al in 2003, showed the balance between the effects of schools and parents on children's achievement. At the age of seven years, parental influence was almost six times as important as the school's influence and remained higher until children were in their teenage years. This means that children whose parents are able to engage with their child's early education and find ways at home to promote language, literacy and numeracy will have many advantages in terms of achievement as their input has a significant impact on the child. The expression 'parents as first educators' is therefore completely deserved.

Engaging with early education does not mean that parents should undertake a relentless programme of formal literacy or numeracy education with their child. This would be unlikely to be successful and is likely to be counter-productive in that it could endanger the quality of the child–parent relationship. Engagement with early education means playing with children, encouraging them in their play activities, and asking them interesting questions about what they see and feel. It is clear that understanding the world from a child's perspective is a vital skill.

As well as parental engagement, parents' skill levels are also important. Studies show that children whose parents have good levels of language, literacy and numeracy are more likely to acquire these skills. One piece of research showed that children aged ten years who were struggling with reading had parents whose own literacy rates were low. The reasons behind this are complex as most parents value these skills. Possible reasons, however, might include modelling, whereby parents are able to show a child what to do through the way they talk, reason, read or write. For example, a two-year-old may take an interest in mark-making after seeing a parent holding a pen whilst writing a shopping list. In the same way, a child might pretend to play with money after seeing a parent check his or her change in a shop. Parents who are skilled in these areas may also notice and take pleasure in seeing their children trying out their early skills; for example, a three-year-old may pretend to read the newspaper and the parent may smile and comment to encourage the child. Sharing books and introducing a child to the enjoyment of books and stories is an important key activity that parents can instigate and make a part of their daily family life.

Later, as children become of school age, parents who are confident in their own skills may feel able to ask questions about how their children are getting on without worrying that they may be put on the spot or not understand the answer. They may also recognise where their child has difficulties and seek out early support. For example, parents who are comfortable with reading will be happy to engage in the reading process in an interactive way, listen to their child read, talk about stories, model reading skills and encourage the child to read their school and other books at home. Parents who enjoy reading themselves can share their enthusiasms and this is infectious. The enjoyment of reading is a continuation of the joyful physical games that parents play with babies and toddlers. They may also encourage their children with writing and learning things such as spellings. This support at home has enormous impact on children's confidence and interest as well as their performance.

The factors which can influence parents' expectations for their role in promoting their children's literacy, numeracy and language skills

With relatively few exceptions, parents regardless of their income, culture, lifestyle or religion want the best for their children. Parents want their children to be happy, achieve and be successful. Having said this, there are factors that might influence the way that parents contribute towards their children's early learning.

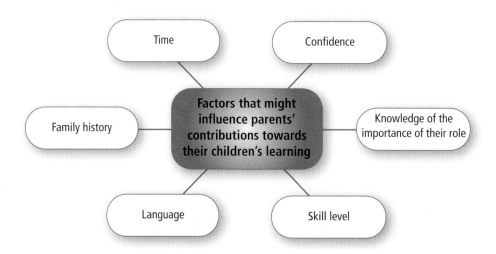

Confidence

Confidence is often critical in many aspects of parenting. Some parents may not feel confident in their own abilities and worried that they may 'teach' their children incorrectly and that it is best left to the pre-schools and schools. Parents who are more confident are better able to support their children and will be more likely to ask for resources and ideas from the pre-school staff to further their children's skills.

Knowledge of the importance of their role

Some parents may not be aware of the importance of their role in helping their children to develop early skills. Parents may enjoy being with their children but not see how much influence they have on their children's later development. They may not see that they have normally been key to their children's development of physical skills like standing and walking, and to the acquisition of verbal skills. They may not see that this significant role continues through into later childhood, in partnership with children's other educators.

Skill level

Some parents may have limited skills in literacy and numeracy and so may not feel able to support their children. They may also be concerned that their children will, as they become older, become aware of the limits of their skills and so may prefer to avoid any literacy and numeracy activities.

Language

Some parents whose home language is not English may be unsure about how best to help their children learn English. They may have concerns that helping their children to count or read in the home language might be disadvantageous to their children in learning English.

Family history

Some of the ways in which parents raise their children link back to their childhood experiences. Parents who were read a bedtime story when they were young are more likely to read one to their children. Parents who played simple games such as 'I Spy' are able to play them with their children because they can remember them. The link between childhood experiences and parenting means that some parents naturally promote early literacy, numeracy and language skills in their children and do so without even thinking about it. Parents who have not had these experiences in their childhood may not carry them out with their own children simply because they have no knowledge of them. This, of course, does not mean that they are not caring and loving parents!

Time

Time can be an issue for an increasing number of parents who work, especially if they are on a low income and have several part-time jobs. They may believe that it takes a lot of time to help children with early literacy and numeracy and not realise that many early concepts can be done as part of everyday tasks.

Applying theory to your practice

Do you remember playing games as a child or being read a story? With whom did you do this?

How pre-school settings' role in promoting children's language, literacy and numeracy can support their ability to contribute to supporting parents with literacy, numeracy and language needs

Interestingly, the way that you work with children in promoting early language, literacy and numeracy can indirectly support parents in a range of ways. A good starting point here is to be aware that many adults with skill needs have appalling memories of their time at school and so associate learning language, literacy and numeracy with fear, misery and humiliation. These negative feelings are often very strong and can consequently be a crucial factor in preventing adults from seeking help even when it is offered.

The pre-school has an important role to play in changing parents' negative perceptions and feelings about language, literacy and numeracy. The pre-school should be a non-threatening environment which encourages involvement and is friendly and supportive. This environment can help parents to revisit their old fears of literacy and numeracy and see, via their children, that learning can be fun and enjoyable, thereby allowing them to explore new ideas and opportunities and enhance their lives. This is the fundamental idea behind the Pre-school Learning Alliance's campaign 'Changing life, changing lives'.

Thinking and research

Find out more about the Pre-school Learning Alliance's work in relation to family learning by visiting their website: www.pre-school.org.uk.

By planning and carrying out activities that promote children's knowledge and skills, the pre-school creates a learning culture that emphasises the importance of language, literacy and numeracy. Parents are able to see that their children enjoy learning and this can help some parents to feel that learning does not have to be dull, laborious or frightening. Parents can also see how staff work with their children and that they are supportive, patient and help to make learning fun. This can help parents to gain trust in staff members, which can be a crucial factor in deciding whether to join a course or seek help.

As well as putting language, literacy and numeracy on the map, pre-schools also help parents' confidence and knowledge by sharing their plans with them and encouraging them to help out with activities. Finding out about what their children are learning and being a part of it can again give parents confidence. Some parents also realise that they may have missed out on these experiences as a child and this may help them to understand why they have found some areas of learning difficult. This can also make them more determined to ensure that their own children do not have the same problems and so decide to learn more about supporting their children.

Parents whose home language is not English

Whilst some parents have difficulties with literacy and numeracy, some parents may need support with their English. Parents who do not speak English can feel isolated from others within the community and limit their circle of friends to people who can speak their language. For these parents, seeing their children learn English can be a source of pleasure and again the pre-school provides a backdrop for this to happen. By watching staff interact and work with their children, this helps parents to feel that they may like to stay and help in the setting. This is an important first step in terms of gaining support for learning English.

The importance of recognising the boundaries of the pre-school setting's role in contributing to supporting parents with literacy, numeracy and language needs

Helping parents with literacy, numeracy and language needs requires a sensitive and skilled approach. It is therefore important to understand the boundaries of the pre-school's role.

First, it is important to understand that the pre-school is there to be a support for parents, not a source of pressure. This means that whilst you might be keen to encourage parents to become more involved with or to join in activities, you must be sensitive and respect their wishes. For many parents, the journey towards actively seeking support is a slow one and a common expression that adults use is 'the time just felt right to do something'.

Confidentiality is also essential and parents have the right to know that anything that they say or they do with regards to their literacy, numeracy and language needs remains confidential and is not discussed with others without their permission. This is particularly important to remember when contacting others such as literacy tutors or community development workers.

The pre-school is there to be a support for parents, not a source of pressure.

Finally, you must be aware of your own skills and ability to help parents. Getting support for literacy, numeracy and language requires great trust and confidence. Mustering this can be hard so it is essential that parents' experiences of gaining support are positive, since this will often be the starting point for them. It is, therefore, always important to think about the extent to which the pre-school will be able to assist a parent and to know where to enlist further advice so that parents' experiences remain positive.

How to make available to parents opportunities to develop their literacy, numeracy and language skills

How to identify parents who may need support for their literacy, numeracy and language skills

A surprising percentage of the adult population has difficulty in one or more areas of literacy, numeracy and language skills. For literacy alone, estimates currently run at 7 million. The word 'estimates' is used here because many people are not ready to admit or realise that their skills are limited. Sadly, a skill deficiency has significant consequences on not just earning power but also confidence. Many people with one of the above skill needs find it hard to come forward for help. Fear of being judged as 'stupid' or simply memories of failing at school can prevent adults from seeking support. Some adults therefore go to quite extreme lengths to avoid being put in situations where others may guess that they have a difficulty. As you will see later on, this in itself has serious consequences for the way in which you may support these parents. There are, however, some indicators that might suggest that parents may benefit from some support.

Possible indicators that parents may benefit from support with their literacy, numeracy and language needs

Literacy	• Reluctance to read or write in front of others, e.g. saying ' I'll do it when I get home.' • Forms or other information requiring writing not taken or returned. • Lack of time, glasses or a pen used as a reason to avoid reading or filling in a form. • Not knowing what is happening, e.g. did not realise that setting was closed although sign displayed. • Older children in the family write messages, letters or read.
Numeracy	• May have difficulty in understanding and using money, e.g. may produce a bank note so as to be sure to have sufficient or exact change (so as not to be short changed). • May have difficulty in managing family finances.
Language	• Encourages child to talk or uses them to interpret. • May not chat or talk to staff or other parents. • May leave the child to come into pre-school alone. • May not answer the phone or door. • Appears frightened or withdrawn when contact is made. • Simplified speech relying on signs and gestures.

The importance of and ways of responding to parents as people with a range of interests and skills

Whilst you might identify that some parents may have a difficulty in one or more areas of literacy, numeracy or language, the best way you can support them is by valuing them and helping them to gain in confidence and trust. Knowing how to spell, write or read a bank statement are useful skills but do not make any of us better people. Most adults have plenty of other skills and talents and it is important that you focus on these. Many of the support programmes in place begin by using adults' strengths and interests as building blocks for learning. By talking to parents and helping them feel welcome in the pre-school, you may encourage them to realise their own strengths. By being involved in the pre-school, parents will see that they can learn new skills, even if to begin with this is just learning how to make dough.

Responding to parents who share their need with you

You have seen that parents who have some needs in relationship to their literacy, numeracy or language skills may try hard to avoid others knowing about these needs. Adults often fear that others will be shocked or think less well of them as a result of what they perceive as a deficiency. They may also feel that disclosing or revealing a need will make 'an issue' of it. This means that if parents do seek help or share their need with you, it is essential not to overreact and to show warmth and good listening skills. For some parents, telling someone else about their need will be a relief but may also open some emotional floodgates. Some adults, for example, have not even told their partners and close friends about their feelings and may have led a 'double life'. Finding somewhere to talk out of the way of others and being positive is essential. You may need to reassure parents that they have taken a step in the right direction and also that you will find with their permission ways of helping them further.

Afterwards, some parents may look to see if the information they have given you will change your attitudes towards them. This means that if parents have talked to you or sought help for their need, your response towards them needs to show that you value them and continue to see them as equal partners in their children's education. Parents need to hear you chatting to them as you did before and talking to them about their children as you did before. Parents may also need to see that you are careful in front of others and that you are discreet about acknowledging their need. You may, for example, wait for others to leave before asking them if they would like you to fill in a form.

How to be sensitive to parents' feelings about their need for support for their literacy, numeracy and language skills

The range of feelings that parents might have about getting support can be complex and vary from individual to individual. The extent and intensity of these feelings can depend on their experiences to date and particularly those that they had during their childhood. Common feelings include embarrassment, aggressiveness and anxiety.

Embarrassment

It can be embarrassing for an adult to realise that he or she has not developed skills which others take for granted. Parents who have older children may also realise that their older children may have 'overtaken' them in terms of knowledge. Adults may feel 'silly' for not having knowledge.

Aggressiveness

It can be easy for complex feelings to be substituted by aggressiveness or hostility. Being uncooperative and difficult to approach can be a learnt response in order to 'feel' strong or to prevent others from probing further.

Anxiety

Beginning the journey towards developing skills is not easy, especially where parents have had previously negative experiences. This means that many parents may have strong feelings of anxiety and may question their own capabilities. They may also question whether the support offered is suitable. It is important to provide reassurance and let parents know that their feelings are not unusual. Anxiety may show itself in physical symptoms such as headaches, a flare up of eczema or a stomach upset. Anxiety may also mean that parents, if not reassured, may decide at the last moment not to attend.

How to ensure that all of the pre-school setting's staff are committed and able to contribute to the support offered to parents

You have seen that parents who have needs are likely to have quite strong feelings and concerns, and they will need the staff team to be supportive and reassuring. This means that everyone in the pre-school team must show commitment to the idea of supporting parents and understand what is involved. The extent of the pre-school's involvement will of course vary from setting to setting. In some pre-schools it may be decided to begin by extending open mornings and encouraging parents to come and carry out activities alongside their children. Other settings may begin the process by finding out more about services and support in their area or by funding a member of staff to take a qualification in adult learning.

The first step in the process is to talk together and gain ideas about what is possible and also likely to be of interest to parents. Staff who work directly with parents may already have some ideas as a result of getting to know more about their interests and listening to their comments. It is important that the journey towards providing support for parents is a comfortable one for everyone. Common fears for staff include the idea that they will in some way be 'teaching'. This is rarely the case as the starting point for most support is simply to encourage parents to enjoy learning alongside their children and to provide specific activity days and events where this can happen. Where parents want to go on further with their learning, most pre-schools then enlist the help of other agencies (see pages 308–10) which may result in the provision of a tutor, information about schemes and services or further training for staff.

It is reassuring for staff to understand that there is plenty of support available for pre-schools embarking on the process of supporting parents, which is provided from a number of sources including the Pre-school Learning Alliance. It is also worth looking at the training materials and resources from the 'Step into Learning' programme: this was a funded project that aimed, through the intermediary of early years settings, to engage parents and promote literacy, numeracy and language skills. The development project has come to an end but the training resources are available online; to access them go to www.surestart.gov.uk/stepintolearning.

It is also useful for staff to know that there are many potential benefits for their own personal and professional development. In some cases, staff may use the support facilitated by the pre-school to enhance their own literacy, numeracy or language skills or to take a journey of their own towards gaining further professional qualifications.

Confidentiality

One of the key issues for the staff team is confidentiality. The staff team must agree on how sensitive pieces of information gained from parents or from working with them are to be handled or stored. Everyone must understand that breaching a parent's rights to confidentiality may have devastating consequences and may lead the parent to avoid further support.

Preparation for assignment

Prepare an information booklet that helps pre-school staff understand the importance of identifying and supporting parents who may have literacy, numeracy and language needs.

How to enable parents to access support to develop their literacy, numeracy and language skills

The role of the pre-school setting in signposting parents to sources of support for developing their literacy, numeracy and language skills

When thinking about parents with literacy, numeracy and language needs, it is important to remember that these needs are closely linked to confidence. Whilst in other areas parents may feel confident to seek advice and support (for example, going to a garage and getting a car fixed), getting help with literacy, numeracy or language is different. Being unable to read fluently, cope with money or ask simple questions has traditionally carried a stigma. This means that support in these areas requires strong levels of motivation but also the courage that comes from confidence. This is where the pre-school setting can be of assistance as parents see it as a place where adults are respectful, friendly and non-judgemental. From this nurturing environment, parents may become interested in finding out more about what is on offer. The pre-school therefore has a role in 'signposting' sources of support.

The term 'signposting' means acting as a source of information that will help parents who are interested in taking their first steps towards further learning. The way in which signposting takes place can be anything from posters on notice boards and leaflets in racks through to staff mentioning specific open days or events to parents. In order to be able to signpost services and sources of help to parents, it is important to build good relationships with others in the community and also to be aware of local and national strategies. It is also important for staff in the pre-school to be aware of current approaches to helping adults, i.e. building on interests, making sessions relevant and enjoyable, and above all avoiding situations where adults feel they are back at school!

National and local strategies for enabling adults to progress their literacy, numeracy and language skills

There are now many projects available that support adults who wish to work on their literacy, numeracy and language skills. The importance of helping adults with skills is seen as important not only on a personal and social level but also in economic terms. Adults who are confident with their skills are more able to work at a higher level and thus this benefits not only their family and local community but also the country as a whole, as there is demand for skilled workers. This link means that most support is funded and is either available at no cost or at a subsidised rate through the current government initiative known as 'Skills for Life'. In addition, in some areas additional funding is available from sources such as the European Social Fund or through money set aside for social and economic regeneration.

As initiatives and projects can vary from area to area, it is important to find out what is available locally. It is also worth noting that sometimes organisations, projects and initiatives are 'rebranded' or re-organised to reflect different sources of funding or approaches. This is why as well as current strategies, key national organisations have also been listed below. Note that this is not a comprehensive list and that it is likely that there will also be a range of initiatives within your local area.

Skills for Life

This is the government initiative launched in 2001 which highlights the importance of helping adults with their literacy, numeracy and language skills. Skills for Life set targets for improving levels of adult education in key population groups and also identified routes and organisations that would help deliver the targets. Funding was also set aside in order to fund projects. To find out more, visit www.sflqi.org.uk.

Pre-school Learning Alliance

The Pre-school learning Alliance has a department that advises on family learning. The department can provide wide-ranging support including training, advice about funding as well as training materials for family learning. More information can be found online at www.pre-school.org.uk.

Jump Start

Jump Start is one of the current family learning programmes that the Pre-school Learning Alliance has developed. Jump Start are workshops that focus on literacy and numeracy. Parents are able to learn about how literacy and numeracy are taught in early years settings; they gain ideas about how to help their children at home and they also carry out activities alongside their children. More information can be found online at www.pre-school.org.uk.

Cache Level 1 Award in Getting Started in a Pre-school Setting

This is an introductory programme for parents who are becoming interested in a career with children. The programme can give parents a level 1 qualification and is designed to be a starting point from which parents can go on to take other pre-school qualifications. The Getting Started programme lends itself to supporting literacy and helps parents to identify for themselves their own needs.

Get On

This is a national campaign which raises awareness of getting support reading, writing and numeracy skills; more information is available online at www.dfes.gov.uk/get-on/.

Move On

This is a project that is designed to help adults improve their literacy and numeracy skills and also to gain an initial qualification; more information is available online at www.move-on.org.uk.

National certificates in literacy and numeracy

These are certificates that recognise adults' skills in literacy and numeracy. These were launched in 2001 as a way of motivating and celebrating adults' achievements. Tests can be taken online at www.dfes.gov.uk/readwriteplus.

Basic Skills Agency

This organisation is largely funded by the government and its aim is to improve levels of literacy, numeracy and language skills in the general population. It is a good source of information and has an excellent publications section which includes videos. Recent initiatives include 'Step into Learning'.

Learndirect

This is a national confidential helpline (telephone 0800 100 900) which provides information about local courses and support. Calls are free. Training organisations and colleges register information with Learndirect which is then passed on by the telephone operators. Note that the operators will not know the local area, and if a project or group has not registered with Learndirect they will not be on the system. More information is available online at www.learndirect.co.uk.

Department of Education and Skills

This is the government department that deals with education, skills and training. Their website should provide a range of links for organisations and current initiatives; visit it online at www.dfes.gov.uk.

Learning and Skills Council (LSC)

The Learning and Skills Council is responsible for the funding and training of all post-16-years education except higher education. This includes vocational training such as NVQs as well as basic skills training. Each regional area will have its own office and your local LSC should have a list of local training providers offering literacy, numeracy and language skills to whom they provide funding. It is also useful to approach your local LSC when in the design stage of any project. If the project fits their criteria it may be that funding will be made available. Find out more online at www.lsc.gov.uk. The LSC also runs an initiative known as 'Next Steps'; to find out more visit the LSC website.

Learning and Skills Development Agency (LSDA)

The LSDA was spilt into two in April 2006:

- its policy and strategic work have moved to the Quality Improvement Agency for Lifelong Learning (QIA)
- its programmes, research, training and consultancy projects are now delivered by the Learning and Skills Network (LSN).

LSN is relevant to trainers in this context. It aims to provide training and staff development programmes that support quality improvement for schools, colleges and training organisations. To find out more about the Learning and Skills Network, visit www.lsneducation.org.uk.

National Institute for Adult Continuing Education (NIACE)

This is a charity whose aim is to promote lifelong learning in the adult population. The NIACE website provides information about training and projects, and also has good links; visit www.niace.org.uk to find out more.

Adult Learners' Week

Adult Learners' Week encourages parents, families and adults to celebrate their learning. The week usually takes place in May. Events are organised locally by community organisations such as pre-schools and colleges. Details about this annual event can be found on the NIACE website (www.niace.org.uk) as they help to organise it.

Further Education Colleges

Most colleges provide a range of adult courses that usually include literacy, numeracy and language support. A dedicated team of tutors usually organise these courses, some of which are likely to be run in the community rather than at the college. The term 'outreach' is sometimes used where tutors help adults take the first steps by working directly with them in places that are familiar to them, such as the community centre, school or even public house!

Adult and Community Learning Services

In each area, the local education authority (LEA) will be providing support for adults through its Adult and Community Learning Service. To find out how these services are delivered locally, you will need to contact your local education authority. Some local education authorities have contracted their work to colleges, voluntary organisations and even some private training providers.

BBC

The BBC has a useful website where there are games and quizzes, information and search facilities to make local contacts. To find out more visit www.bbc.co.uk/raw.

Bookstart

This is a project that encourages parents to share books with their babies and young children. Bookstart produces packs for parents which include free books and resources. The Bookstart website (www.bookstart.co.uk) has a section for early years settings and professionals.

Sure Start

Sure Start is the government-funded health and childcare initiative that looks at ways of connecting services for parents with the aim of improving the health and education of young children under the age of five years. To find out more about your Sure Start projects in your area, you can visit their website (www.Surestart.gov.uk).

Literacy Trust

The Literacy Trust is an organisation that promotes literacy within the UK. Their website (www.literacytrust.org.uk) provides masses of information about all aspects of language and literacy and is a useful starting point for research, publications and to find out more about other organisations.

Thinking and research

Choose two of the organisations listed on pages 308–10 and research which approaches and initiatives they are currently offering.

Local agencies providing support to enable adults to progress their literacy, numeracy and language skills and how to assess their suitability for providing support for parents

You have seen that there is a range of organisations and strategies available. It is important to understand that this is an area where fresh initiatives are used in order to gain interest. This means that it is essential to find out what is available in your local area. Places to look out for information include your local library, college and education authority, as well as talking to Pre-school Learning Alliance development workers.

The terms 'basic' or 'life' skills are often used in relation to literacy, numeracy and language needs. It is important to be aware of this term as it is often used by those providing support and help for adults and so may be the key phrase that will help you find contact numbers. As provision can vary enormously from area to area and is not always 'joined up' (because initiatives may be funded from different sources), you may find that you have to contact several people.

Once you have identified possible sources of help, it is essential to do some preliminary investigation. This is to prevent situations where parents who may already be a little anxious about getting support make a fruitless phone call or visit and then lose heart. By finding out what is available first, pre-school staff will be able to pass on information with more confidence. To help assess suitability it is worth understanding current approaches to working with adults.

Approaches to working with adults

Firstly, the aim is always to make sure that adults lead their learning. This means finding out what parents want to learn and what interests them. A parent may, for example, be keen to find out more about how to help their child learn to read, or want to know more about computers as they are thinking about buying one.

The second principle is that adults need to learn at their own pace and develop their confidence. This means that most adults usually learn in small groups and that activities are tailored very much to their needs and interests.

Finally, learning situations must be enjoyable. This means that tutors must be approachable, friendly and work in partnership with adults rather than as 'teachers'. A good example of this is they way in which adults may decide to develop their IT skills, as the case study on the next page shows.

Case study

Learning based on interests

Gary has been thinking about learning more about IT as he has just bought a computer for the family. He enjoys using it and thinks that it will be good for his children once they get to school. He also has a digital camera and loves taking pictures of the family together.

The pre-school organised a session for parents about digital photography as the pre-school had bought a camera for the children and the staff to use. The session was open to all parents and Gary was pleased that there were quite a few other dads there. At the end of the session Gary had learnt how to edit his photos and also how to make the most of the camera. Gary had not been to any sort of classes since he left school and was surprised how much he enjoyed it. As part of the session there was also information about other courses in the area. Gary has decided to sign up for a longer course that will even give him a qualification.

1 Why is it important that learning links closely to the interests of adults?

2 Why might short 'taster' courses be of interest to some parents?

3 Why is it important that the pre-school acts a signpost for further courses and information?

Good practice

Factors to consider when assessing suitable support for parents

- Is there an initial assessment or advisory interview?
- Is it possible to meet the tutor before attending the group?
- Is it possible to attend a session to get a feel of the group before joining?
- Where does the group meet?
- How many people are there in the group?
- Who is the group aimed at?
- What is the age range of the people within the group?

Continued ▶

- Are there men and women in the group?
- What time does the group meet?
- Is it possible to gain a qualification?

There are a growing number of learning opportunities provided via IT or computer-based programmes, for example, in Learn Direct centres. Learners can expect there to be a tutor on hand if they need to ask questions.

Information that might be useful to gain

In many areas, there are already established groups in place. Finding out more about the groups and the way that they are run can be helpful in finding out their suitability.

How the pre-school can create and maintain links with local agencies providing support for literacy, numeracy and language skills

It is useful to build a network of contacts locally so that you can provide accurate and up-to-date information to parents. It also means that local agencies know of the

Learning more about computers and gaining IT skills is a popular starting point for many adults.

pre-school's interest and therefore can approach you with possible ideas for funding and projects. In the same way, it also means that you know which organisations may be able to support you either financially, with a venue or with tutors, if your pre-school wants to promote a project.

Finding out about services in your local area can seem daunting if you are starting from scratch, but as you make contacts you will find that your knowledge of provision in the area will keep growing. Many people find that the name of one person organising provision leads onto another.

Further Education College

This is a good starting point as most Further Education colleges will have an adult education department. They may offer leisure courses as well as basic skills courses. Many colleges also provide outreach workers that visit community settings.

Local Education Authority/Adult and Community Learning Centres

In some areas there are adult education centres which will deliver a range of courses. The way to find out about what is available is by contacting your local education authority. If you are not sure about their phone number, go into your nearest school as they will have a central number.

Children and Family Services/Early Years Team

Contacting your local Early Years Team can be a helpful step to find out what is available locally in terms of family learning. Where Early Years Teams fit in, the structure of local or metropolitan services can vary. Look under 'Children and Family Services' or 'Education Department'. The Early Years Teams may be able to signpost you further to other departments that might be useful, such as the EMAS team (see below) or in some areas the Family Learning Team.

Libraries

A call or visit to your local library is also useful. You may find brochures from colleges and adult education centres as well as projects run by the local library. Many organisations use the library notice board as a way of flagging up their services

Community centres

It is worth visiting the local community centre as again, many projects use centres as their base for delivering support. Find out if there is an outreach worker or a community development worker that you can talk to.

Ethnic Minority Advisory Service (EMAS)

These are teams that can be contacted via the local education authority or department. They aim to promote the education and welfare for ethnic minorities including traveller families. This can be a good starting point for finding out about services for parents who may have English as an additional language.

Regneration/ Strategic Partnerships

Some areas have a Regeneration Team or Strategic Partnership, which is involved in the economic and social regeneration of an area. Contacting their office may help you to find out what funding is available but also what is already happening in your local area.

Connexions

The Connexion team is responsible for supporting and advising young people aged 13 to 19 years (and up to 25 years if they have a learning difficulty). This might be useful if you have young parents. In addition, your local Connexions team should have contact details about career advice and also people who are involved in Skills for Life provision. To gain the contact details for your local area, call the national helpline on 0808 0013219.

Job Centre Plus

Literacy, numeracy and language needs can all be potential barriers to employment. This means that job centres are now helping people gain these skills through a variety of different projects. Calling into you local job centre may again give you contact details for services in your area.

Sports and leisure facilities/football clubs

As adult education is linked with areas of interest, it is worth calling into your local leisure complex to see if there are any contact details on their notice boards. It is also worth contacting the local football club as football clubs were identified as possible partners in the government's Skills for Life strategy.

Local Learning and Skills Council

It can be useful to contact the local learning and skills council. Find out your nearest office by using the national website (www.lsc.gov.uk).

How to create and use opportunities to share information with parents about sources of support for the development of literacy, numeracy and language skills and encourage them to take up the support

There are many ways in which you can help parents to find out about opportunities to support their literacy, numeracy and language skills.

Creating opportunities within the pre-school

You have seen that one of the principles of supporting adults is to look for activities that are of interest to them. Parents as a group, either via the parent management committee or as individuals, may have suggestions as to what they feel they would like to know more about. This can often be the start of a journey! Parents may like to find out more about their children's learning or what happens when their children go to school. One-off workshops or events may be the starting point but if successful, these may lead to other things. Taking on board such suggestions and then, if necessary, seeking support from outside of the pre-school is often an effective starting point for parents to come together and learn. The advantage of creating opportunities within the pre-school is that parents come together and are familiar with each other. Some events and courses may also be of interest to staff members as well. This takes away any stigma attached and creates a learning community.

Case study

'We had already started off with a literacy course, but then some parents said that they wanted to find out more about numeracy. I contacted the local adult education co-ordinator who set about looking for a tutor. The group is going well and has grown. The group is made up of some parents, a couple of staff members and others who are friends of parents. Some parents focus on how to help their children with their maths at school, whilst others are keen to do a qualification that will help them to go on.'

1 Explain why it is important to follow parents' interests?

2 Consider reasons why group sizes are often small to begin with.

3 Explain why many adults prefer to learn with people that they 'know'?

Inviting others in

A good partnership with other services might mean that development workers and co-ordinators from other services might be invited into the pre-school. The local co-ordinator for adult education or a tutor from the college may be invited to provide advice or to hold drop-in sessions. Drop-in sessions at a pre-school can be popular because they provide parents with the opportunity to try something without actually having to make a firm commitment. This can be helpful as a first step. Whilst literacy, numeracy and language skills might be the focus, it can be good to create other learning opportunities as this helps parents to associate the pre-school with learning, i.e. a session by a dietician about 'fussy eaters' or by a health visitor on 'sleeping through the night'.

Providing crèche or extended places

Some parents may find that childcare is an issue in helping them to attend an event. This means that you may support an event or group by being able to provide a crèche for those parents who attend or by providing additional places in the pre-school. Some types of training such as 'Step into Learning' also work by encouraging parents to learn and practice skills with their children. The pre-school can host such events or be directly responsible for their organisation.

Notice boards

One effective way of helping parents to find out what is available is to use the notice board and then to draw attention to it. This can be helpful for general learning events, although it is important to remember that parents with significant difficulties in literacy or language may not be able to access written information on a notice or poster. You may therefore need to help them find out about it by talking to them or by introducing them to the person who will be organising it. For additional language users, it is useful to get notices and posters translated. It is essential that information on noticeboards is kept up to date and is also relevant to parents' needs.

Leaflets

Leaflets can be an effective way of letting parents take away information to look at and think about. Leaflets need to be current, attractive and reflective of parents' interests and needs. As with using notice boards, it is important to remember that not all parents will find it easy to access information. Leaflets may need to be translated for some parents. Discreetly offering the option of reading it or explaining the contents might be useful for some parents.

Word of mouth

Talking to parents about what is available is perhaps one of the most effective ways of passing on information. This needs to happen sensitively so that parents do not feel that they are being 'targeted'. This is why strong relationships are a key element in helping parents. Some parents will need time to take their first step and so it is important not to pressurise parents into doing something that they are not ready for. Word of mouth between parents is also effective. Social events that help parents come together can therefore be a way in which parents that have already engaged in further learning recommend it to others.

Making initial contacts alongside parents

If something is of interest to parents, you may ask whether they would like you to find out more about it first. Ideally, it is best to do this alongside parents so that they can be involved in the process and ask questions. You might, for example, phone a help line whilst the parents are with you. This may be particularly important for parents who are additional language users.

Accompanying parents

For some parents, the first few steps of their journey to gain support are the hardest. Meeting a tutor or attending a group for the first time can be daunting for some parents. This means that you may encourage parents by offering to be there with them as they take their first steps. In some cases, the course or group may be of interest in any case. At other times, you may be able to find someone else within the pre-school who is also interested in finding out more or attending a group, and so your role may be to put parents in contact with each other.

Some parents may prefer staff to make the initial enquiries.

Showing ongoing interest

An additional way in which you can support parents is to show an ongoing interest in their learning. This can be a source of encouragement and can help parents to share any anxieties or 'glitches' that they are having. For example, a parent may be finding an aspect of learning difficult and may ask you if you can flag this up on his or her behalf. Having someone in the background to act as a supporter can sometimes make the difference between success and failure. It is not unusual after the initial burst of enthusiasm for adults returning to learning to find it difficult to maintain the momentum. Having someone to help you reflect on how far you have come and what you have achieved so far can make a significant difference.

As well as benefiting parents, finding out about what they are doing can be helpful in terms of signposting services for others. Knowledge about the type of activities that parents undertake, their enjoyment and practical factors such as timing and group size, etc., can help you to target support more effectively.

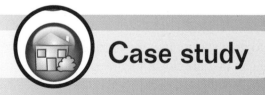

Case study

Kelly's learning journey

Kelly missed a lot of her secondary education. She had to move school when she was 13 years old because of her parents' divorce. She found it hard to find new

Continued ▶

friends in the new school and became increasingly unhappy. She started to miss odd lessons and in the end only attended PE as she liked the teacher and knew that she wouldn't need to do any reading or writing, which had always been difficult for her.

Since leaving school, Kelly has had a series of jobs but has always handed in her resignation if it looked liked there was a possibility of her needing to write or use a computer. This is unfortunate since Kelly is very good at working with people and taking the initiative, and she has often been put forward for promotion.

Kelly now has three children and wants to have a 'proper career'. She has been helping in the pre-school and has enjoyed some of the sessions that they have put on for parents. Kelly knows that some of the pre-school staff have 'worked' their way up and are now qualified. Following a chat and a suggestion from the pre-school leader, she is now about to do the CACHE level 1 'Getting Started' course. She is a little nervous but is also quite excited too. Helping in the pre-school has helped Kelly to feel more confident and she knows one or two of the other people who are in the group.

1 How has Kelly benefited from the support of the pre-school staff?

2 Why is it important that pre-schools actively find ways of supporting parents with literacy, numeracy and language needs?

3 Consider the potential benefits to Kelly, her family and the community of her returning to learning.

Reviewing the activities undertaken by the pre-school setting to enable parents to develop their literacy, numeracy and language skills

Why it is important for the pre-school to review the effectiveness of its practice in supporting parents with literacy, numeracy and language needs

You have seen that one in five adults will have areas that need developing in terms of their literacy, numeracy and language needs. You have also looked at the benefits for parents of developing their skills in terms of confidence and empowerment, as well as to assist in gaining employment. You have also seen the links between parents' skill levels and their children's later achievement in education. This means that there is a powerful case for ensuring that all pre-schools see themselves as learning communities. It is therefore essential as part of the development of the pre-school that thought is given to the effectiveness of current provision for parents and ways to extend it further. This process needs to involve the whole pre-school including staff, committee members and tutors, as well as the parents themselves.

How to review the practice of the pre-school, including that of individual members of staff, in supporting parents with literacy, numeracy and language needs

Whilst this unit has specifically focused on ways of signposting and helping parents to begin their own learning journey, supporting parents also means ensuring that they can access information about the pre-school and their children's learning. Supporting parents also means ensuring that the pre-school is a place where they feel relaxed and become part of the learning community. Sadly, some parents may be so worried of being 'put on the spot' to read something or fill in a form that this forces them to keep their distance. This has significant implications as, for example, a parent may therefore not come to a 'Jump start' session because he or she may feel that he or she has to write something down, or may not volunteer to come into the pre-school for fear that he or she may be asked to read a story to children. Since involving parents in the pre-school is often one of the first steps for parents, it is worth reviewing approaches that are taken as part of the everyday practice and running of the pre-school.

Showing parents that you understand

The starting point for reviewing ways in which you support parents is to consider the messages that parents are gaining. Do parents feel there is an assumption that everyone involved in the pre-school is literate, numerate and fluent with English? Or are parents getting the message that staff in the pre-school have not made these assumptions and are available to them if help is needed in a discreet way?

Applying theory to your practice

Look at the pair of statements below which show the difference that can be made in approaches.

- 'There are leaflets over there about the course.'

- 'We have some leaflets about the course, but I can tell you about it if you prefer.'

- 'You will need to fill in the medical form if you want him to go on the trip. Can you bring it back tomorrow?'

- 'This is the medical form that we need to fill in. You can take it away, but I know that some parents like me to go through it with them and give them a little help. Do you want a hand with it? It's easy for me because I do these all the time, but when you are not so used to them it can be harder.'

- 'Thanks for offering to help out on Saturday. I thought you might like to sell and look after the money on the tombola. Gill was coming, but she isn't now

Continued ▶

so you would be by yourself. You don't mind that do you? There's not too much mental arithmetic to do. If the numbers end in a '0' or '5' the person wins, and tickets cost 10p each.'

- 'Thanks for offering to help out on Saturday. Is there anything you fancy doing? Some people like to be together on a stand for moral support with the money. We need someone on the tombola, but with all those numbers not everyone wants to do it. We also have face painting, making drinks and supervising the obstacle course.'

  1 Which statements are the most encouraging for parents? Give reasons for your choices.

  2 Explain why it is important that communications with parents do not make assumptions.

Encouraging parents to take the first steps

As well as showing that assumptions are not made, the pre-school also needs to think about how parents are encouraged to take the first steps towards gaining support. Think about how some of the statements above made it easier for parents to acknowledge that they might need support.

Good practice

Encouraging parents to take the first steps towards gaining support

- How does the pre-school encourage parents to 'drop in' and see what their children are learning?
- Are social events structured in a way which means that parents with literacy, numeracy and language needs will not worry about being 'put on the spot'?
- How does the pre-school flag up information about services that might be of benefit to parents?
- Are staff aware of the importance of not making assumptions about literacy, numeracy and language needs?
- How does the pre-school maintain its links with others in the community that might support parents?

Written information

Today, a surprising amount of information is written down. Whilst this suits many parents, it can be a significant barrier for others. It is therefore worth looking at how written information is used and considering ways of supplementing it so that parents who have difficulties in either reading or understanding can have access to the information. Where written information is absolutely essential, consider keeping the language simple, sentences short and the print size large and clear. Adding pictures or symbols can also help people to gain some sense of the meaning. It is also important to avoid using 'jargon' or acronyms, i.e. 'PSE', as not all parents will understand its meaning. Whilst written information plays a role in providing information, remember that the spoken word is often more powerful. Draw attention to new notices and help parents by reminding them about events and changes to routines as they come into the pre-school.

Good practice

Using written information

- Think about translating information to ensure that it reflects the languages used by parents.
- Use print rather than joined up handwriting.
- Make sure that print is large enough.
- Add pictures, photographs or symbols.
- Take time to 'talk' through what is written.

Applying theory to your practice

Look around the pre-school and consider how information is being presented. Is there an assumption that parents will be able to read?

Expecting parents to write

As well as thinking about the amount of written information in the pre-school, it is also worth remembering that some parents may find it hard to write letters and fill in forms.

A parent may not complete a form saying that his or her child can go on a trip or may not write a comment to go into the child's profile. In addition, parents may be concerned that if they help out in the pre-school, they may be asked to write things such as a list of children who came to the activity.

Why it is important and how to include in the review of the setting's practice the parents whose literacy, numeracy and language needs are being supported

You have seen in earlier units that feedback from parents is always important. It can help you to shape aspects of the work you do in order to develop the pre-school further. In terms of literacy, numeracy and language needs, gaining feedback from parents is particularly essential in reviewing the setting's practice. The experience of many pre-schools is that uptake of initial sessions that support parents can be quite low, but that they build as the pre-school gains experience and develops as a result of feedback

Feedback is especially important after a session or event has been held and the most frequent way in which information is gained is by simply talking to parents; however, remember that some parents with language needs may prefer to write or talk in their own language. It is also important for parents to feel that they can share with you aspects that you need to develop further, and that you encourage them to be honest and frank with you.

Below is a list of questions that might help you to plan for future support. It may also be important to gain feedback from others such as outreach workers or Skills for Life tutors about ways in which the pre-school can develop further its practice.

Questions that encourage feedback from parents

- What did parents enjoy most?

- What did parents say that they got out of the session/workshop/event?

- Are there other things that they would like the pre-school to do now?

- How easy was it for parents to attend? (Information, timing, venue, nerves, etc.)

- What helped parents to make the decision to come?

- Was there anything that nearly put them off coming?

- How would parents suggest that the pre-school lets parents know about future events?

- Do parents have any suggestions for ways in which the event might have been organised/structured differently?

Test yourself

1 Explain the importance of pre-schools supporting parents with literacy, numeracy and language needs.

2 Describe one major initiative designed to support parents with language, literacy and numeracy needs.

3 Identify ways in which children's achievements in literacy, numeracy and language are linked to their parents' achievements in these areas.

4 Explain why it is essential for pre-schools to have good contacts with local agencies that provide support for parents.

5 Why is it important for pre-schools to review activities that support parents' learning?

Further references and reading section

Pre-school Learning Alliance publications:

* *Adults learning in pre-schools* (B012)
* *Nutritional Guidance for the Under Fives* (A400)
* *Looking at Learning Together* (A200)
* *Parental Stake in Pre-school Education* (A136)
* *What do we mean by maths?* (A130)

Basic Skills Agency publications:

* *Literacy and Social Inclusion: The Handbook*
* *Count and figure it out together* – a pack to encourage family numeracy designed for parents to use with their children aged 3–5 years.
* *Fun with…* – a series to encourage parents and children to play together in different situations, e.g. outdoors, with games.

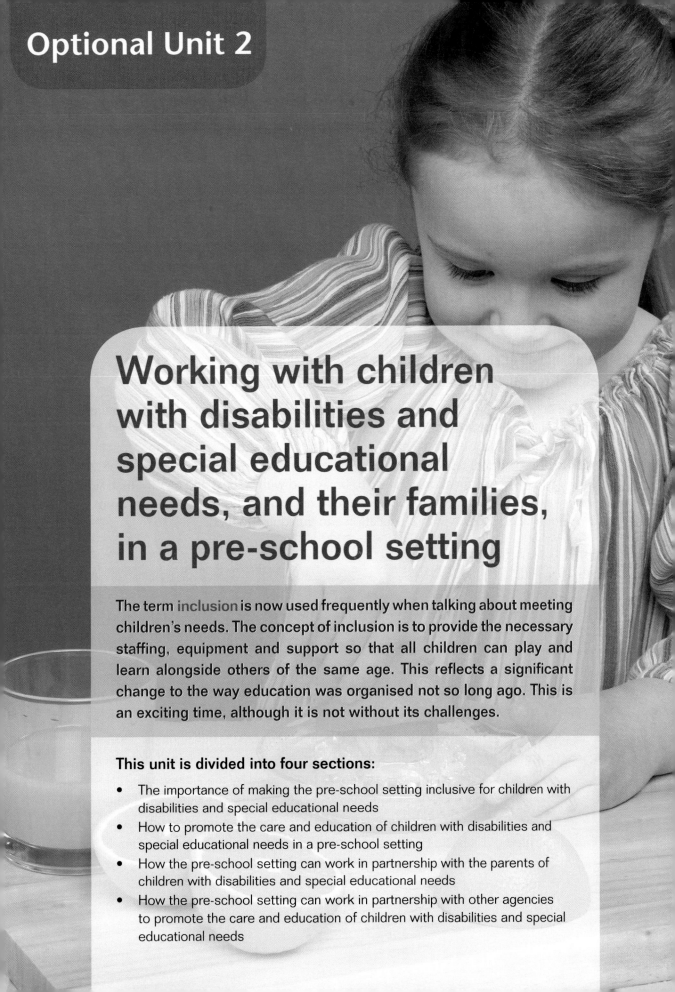

Working with children with disabilities and special educational needs, and their families, in a pre-school setting

The term inclusion is now used frequently when talking about meeting children's needs. The concept of inclusion is to provide the necessary staffing, equipment and support so that all children can play and learn alongside others of the same age. This reflects a significant change to the way education was organised not so long ago. This is an exciting time, although it is not without its challenges.

This unit is divided into four sections:

- The importance of making the pre-school setting inclusive for children with disabilities and special educational needs
- How to promote the care and education of children with disabilities and special educational needs in a pre-school setting
- How the pre-school setting can work in partnership with the parents of children with disabilities and special educational needs
- How the pre-school setting can work in partnership with other agencies to promote the care and education of children with disabilities and special educational needs

The importance of making the pre-school setting inclusive for children with disabilities and special educational needs

Previously, children who were in any way different from their peers were segregated and seen as a 'problem'; they may have been sent to a 'special school' or educated at home. For many children this meant that they were unable to achieve their potential because expectations of children with any disability were low. Such segregation was a reflection on a society that could not cope with diversity. As a result of campaigning and influences, such as the Warnock Report (1978), today's view, enshrined by the SEN Code of Practice 2001, considers that all children are entitled to learn alongside their peers and that the expectation that all children can achieve their potential should be high. This means that pre-schools are welcoming more and more children who may not before have had such opportunities.

The promotion of children's rights as a basis of making the pre-school setting inclusive for children with disabilities and special educational needs

The idea behind inclusion is that all children have basic rights regardless of their gender, lifestyle, religion or disability. These rights are legally enforceable because in 1991 the UK signed the United Nation's Convention on the Rights of the Child and have incorporated these rights into current legislation. Under this convention, children have many rights including the right to education and also to be treated with respect and dignity. Inclusion therefore means thinking about the potential barriers that might prevent children from having equal access to pre-school education and thinking about how best to remove them.

Key terms associated with disabilities and special education needs

- Impairment refers to the loss or abnormality of development or growth, for example, a hearing impairment means that a person has a loss of hearing.

- Disability refers to the restrictions that an impairment causes, for example, a person with a hearing impairment has a disability in hearing.

- Handicap refers to the disadvantage that the person has in relation to others in certain situations. Note that the person is not himself or herself 'handicapped' – he or she is being handicapped by the situation. For example, a person with a hearing impairment is being handicapped when announcements are broadcast in an airport because he or she has a hearing disability. This person's disability does not prevent him or her from reading the signs and getting onto the aircraft, so he or she is not handicapped all the time.

Whilst this unit looks specifically at the needs of children with disabilities and special educational needs (SEN), it is important to understand that inclusion is about fairness for *all* children. An inclusive setting, therefore, strives to meet the needs of all of its children and their families. This might mean thinking about how best to help a family who is new to an area as well as how to support a child whose family is on a low income.

Defining disability

One of the key issues when looking at the needs of children with disabilities and special educational needs is the language and terms that are used. Language is such a powerful tool that it terms and expressions can create their own problems. A good example of this is the word 'spastic'. Whilst once it was a medical term to describe the stiffness of limbs, it became a term to label groups of children and adults and was finally used as an insult. In addition, nobody likes to be labelled and pigeon-holed, and a strong message when working with children is to always remember the individual rather than his or her disability or medical condition.

Frequently asked questions

Using the right language

Q **I am afraid of getting it wrong when talking to parents about their child.**

A The key is to be sensitive to your language and, if you are unsure, to gain information directly from support groups or even parents. Your focus should always be about the individual child rather than any condition or disability that he or she may have.

Defining special educational needs

The term special educational needs (SEN) is in itself quite controversial. Some organisations consider it a redundant term because all children have needs and therefore you should automatically look for ways to meet their needs without labelling them. While this is a powerful argument, the difficultly arises in that currently the National Standards, the SEN Code of Practice 2001 and other guiding documents use this term. Defining children with SEN is therefore in itself potentially difficult. However, for the purposes of this unit, the term special educational needs will be used to identify children who need extra support in order to access the curriculum alongside other children.

Thinking and research

The guiding document that needs to be used in pre-schools is the SEN Code of Practice 2001, which is available free of charge from the Department of Education and Skills publications section.

Look at the introduction to the SEN Code of Practice 2001. How has the problem of definition been overcome by those compiling the code?

Social and medical models of disability and their effect on the inclusiveness of the pre-school setting

Two models of disability are often cited: medical and social. Both models reflect attitudes towards disability and so subsequently affect practical approaches taken towards children and their families. By understanding the two models it is possible to reflect on the inclusiveness of the pre-school setting and to work effectively with children and their parents.

The medical model

In past years, educational practice was based on the medical model. The key feature of the medical model is that it sees the child who has different needs as being imperfect. The focus is therefore on curing or changing the child to become as 'normal' as possible. Where this was not possible, these children were 'segregated' from other children.

The medical model sees such children and their families as helpless and thus in need of sympathy and charity. This way of thinking is reflected in much of the language that is no longer appropriate (see also page 327).

Operating a medical model of disability in a pre-school would mean that children whose needs were different to other children's might be excluded. They might have to 'sit out' during some activities or be expected to 'sit still' even though the activity was relevant or appropriate. A medical model of providing extra support would be one that is not fully integrated into the routine, curriculum planning or layout. Children might be 'pulled' out of play to come and do something different, might have to sit somewhere else to have their snack, or have to wait for a certain piece of equipment to be taken out of a cupboard. A medical model of disability highlights differences between children and so children can learn that they are not the same as others. It also means that other children notice and focus on the disability.

The social model

Inclusion reflects the social model of disability whereby children are accepted and valued for who they are. Instead of seeing children who have different needs as a problem, the focus is on changing practice to accommodate and meet their needs, for

A social model of disability means that children's needs are taken into consideration when reflecting on the layout of the pre-school setting.

example, changing the physical layout of the pre-school. The social model of disability is also about empowerment. Children and their families are seen as equal players in education, and their interests, thoughts and views are therefore considered to be valuable. The social model of disability has had an impact on the type of organisations that help children and their families, as well as the way in which they work.

Operating a social model of disability within a pre-school means that children's needs are taken into consideration during the planning and also when reflecting on the routines and layout of the setting. A social model of disability should feel that the needs of the children are being met 'seamlessly' rather than being bolted on as an after-thought. A social model of disability in practice means that other children also benefit. They may play alongside and benefit from some of the additional strategies and support that is being provided.

How to create an inclusive culture in the pre-school setting, including identifying and overcoming barriers to inclusiveness

Creating an inclusive culture in the pre-school is an essential part of getting it right for children and their families. An inclusive culture should be one where everyone visiting, using the service and also working with the setting feels welcome and at ease. It means thinking carefully about the needs of everyone and avoiding making assumptions. It is often the assumptions that are made that can unwittingly cause problems. Simple examples include the assumption that all children are mobile or that all adults are comfortable with reading English. Building an inclusive culture therefore means reflecting on the routines, practices and traditions of the pre-school and then considering whether adaptations need to be made. In some cases, specialist equipment needs to be obtained, but quite often inclusivity is more about attitudes and creativity rather than purchases!

The term 'reflective practice' is often used in the context of educational practice. Reflecting on what you do and the reasons behind your actions can often reveal whether the pre-school provision is meeting the needs of children with disabilities and their families. The policies of the pre-school should also reflect the concept of inclusion and so everything from admission policies to behaviour policies need to be reviewed to ensure that they are not based on any unrealistic assumptions.

Applying theory to your practice

In what ways do you feel that your pre-school demonstrates inclusive practice?

How to work within legislation and local guidelines to make the pre-school setting inclusive

Over the past few years, several pieces of influential legislation have been passed in an attempt to combat the discrimination that disabled children faced in education (see also pages 200–1). The latest pieces of legislation have moved further towards the concept of inclusion. It is important for pre-schools to keep up to date on changing legislation because grants and funding could be removed from settings that fail to comply with the recommendations. Currently, guidance on interpreting the legislation relating specifically to children with special educational needs is provided by the SEN Code of Practice 2001. (The previous Code of Practice is no longer valid.)

Special Educational Needs and Disability Act 2001

This Act is divided into two parts:

- The first part of the Act strengthens the rights of parents to send their children into mainstream education. The SEN Code of Practice 2001 (see below) is a product of this legislation.
- The second part of the Act extends the 1995 Disability Discrimination Act and prevents education establishments from denying access to a child because of a disability. This legislation is quite powerful because it means that parents can take a pre-school to court if their child is denied a place because of a disability. Pre-schools are required to make

reasonable adjustments to the physical environment so that children who are not mobile or who have more complex needs can have access.

SEN Code of Practice 2001

At the time of writing, this is the latest Code of Practice to be issued for professionals. It is a product of the Special Educational Needs and Disability Act 2001. The SEN Code of Practice is essential reading and replaces the guidance in the previous Code of Practice. It explains the duties and responsibilities of pre-schools and outlines the procedures to be adopted in order to identify and work with children who have special educational needs. It is essential that you have a copy of the Code of Practice as it is a useful reference. There should also be a copy available in the pre-school.

The SEN Code of Practice is a DFES publication available free of charge from the order line 0845 6022260 or DFES Publications, PO Box 5050, Sherwood Park, Annesely, Notts, NG15 0DJ; ISBN 184185-537-6.

Fundamental principles of the SEN Code of Practice

The SEN Code of Practice begins by outlining its guiding principles. These are entitled 'Critical Success Factors' and can be found at the front of the Code. It is important to understand that the Code is founded on the key assumption that all practitioners will aim to meet the needs of all children through their daily practice and will, for example, change layouts, differentiate activities or use a variety of resources to this end. Children whose needs can be met by making simple adjustments in this way are not considered to have special educational needs. This means that children who have a medical condition that is not affecting their ability to learn or who have English as an additional language are not classified as being with special needs.

Case study

Fatima has diabetes. She is given an insulin injection before coming to pre-school in the morning. She requires no additional resources or support, although staff make sure that she has her snack on time.

- **Would Fatima be classed as having a special educational need?**

Special educational needs policy in pre-schools

To ensure that the requirements of the SEN Code of Practice 2001 are complied with, every pre-school must have a policy for SEN. This policy should show how children's needs are identified and met. As with the other types of policy that a pre-school may have, there is no single way in which SEN policy should be written. The following information, however, is likely to be included:

- a statement of commitment
- the roles and responsibilities for SEN in the pre-school
- the identification of children with SEN
- involving children
- involving parents in meeting children's needs
- the procedure for meeting children's needs, including Individual Education Plans (IEPs)
- training staff to help meet children's needs.

When drawing up a policy it may be useful to use the publication *Pre-school Learning Alliance (2005) Policies for Early Years Settings*, which contains a sample SEN policy.

Responding to children's needs

The SEN Code of Practice 2001 stresses the importance of identifying children who may have particular needs as early as possible. Previously, once a pre-school recognised that a child might have a learning need, specialists were contacted immediately and a 'statement' was eventually drawn up via the local education authority. This practice has now changed: the SEN Code of Practice has introduced a 'graduated response'. The aim of this approach is to encourage early intervention and to avoid labelling children from an early age.

Early Years Action

Early Years Action is the first layer of the graduated response. It is used only after the following conditions have been met:

- the pre-school has thought about ways of differentiating the curriculum for the child
- the pre-school has assessed their practice
- the child continues to give cause for concern.

The aim of this layer of response is to provide 'in house' support that is carefully targeted. This means that the special educational needs co-ordinator (SENCO – see also pages 333–5) and parents will meet together to share concerns and draw up an Individual Education Plan (IEP). The SEN Code of Practice suggests that, for most children, this targeted support will be sufficient to meet their needs.

Early Years Action Plus

Early Years Action Plus is the second layer of action. It means that other professionals outside of the pre-school will be contacted to advise and assess the child's needs. It is important here to note that under the SEN Code of Practice parents have to give their consent before outside help is sought. In most circumstances, pre-schools also need to show what steps they have already taken to meet the child's needs. Individual Education Plans will continue to be used, but it is likely that other professionals will also provide help with drawing up and reviewing IEPs. If further help is required that cannot otherwise be funded, a statutory assessment may be requested in order that the child can have a statement (see below).

Statutory assessments

Where children's need are complex and cannot be met through using the Early Years Action and Early Years Action Plus phases, a statutory assessment may be requested in order for the child to gain a statement of needs. Statements are legally binding documents that detail the support to be provided for children by the local education authority. Before a statement can be obtained, a statutory assessment is made of the child's needs. This is a thorough and potentially costly and time-consuming process. The aim of the SEN Code of Practice is to cut the number of statements: it is hoped that, by putting resources into the graduated response system, only children with complex needs will require a statement.

The role of the Special Educational Needs Co-ordinator in making the pre-school setting inclusive for children with disabilities and special educational needs

Under the SEN Code of Practice 2001, every pre-school must have a member of staff who is responsible for co-ordinating support for children with special educational needs. This role is known as the Special Educational Needs Co-ordinator (SENCO). The SENCO will have several responsibilities, which include meeting with parents, observing children and supporting colleagues.

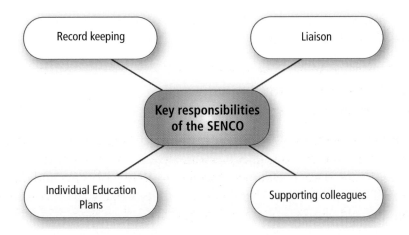

- *Liaison*
  SENCOs are responsible for liaising with other agencies, professional as well as parents. This is a crucial role.

- *Supporting colleagues*
  SENCOs should take on an advisory and supportive role in the pre-school. They may provide training, suggest training opportunities and provide advice for staff members. They may also suggest strategies for others to try or may work alongside colleagues.

- *Individual Education Plans*
  Where children require IEPs, the SENCO is responsible for ensuring that they are produced, used and reviewed. The key person may draw up the IEPs and the SENCO may provide guidance or they may be jointly produced.

- *Record keeping*
  The SENCO is responsible for maintaining children's records in the setting. Records have to be accurate and comply with the Data Protection Act.

While a SENCO may advise the other adults in the pre-school about how best to meet a child's needs, he or she will not necessarily work with individual children. This is to avoid situations where children are 'taken out' and find themselves being separated from their peers. This means that whilst the SENCO will be responsible for implementing the setting's special educational needs policy and carrying out some of the liaison work with other organisations and parents, the main thrust of responsibility for meeting the child's needs remains with practitioners. The Code of Practice therefore expects that all practitioners should be responsible for meeting children's needs. This means that whilst the SENCO has an important role in co-ordinating the setting's SEN policy, everyone in the pre-school has a role to play in ensuring that it is an inclusive setting.

Good practice

Starting points for SENCOs

- Form or join a network of other SENCOs in your area.

- Contact the early years/SEN advisory team in your area.

- Subscribe to organisations offering support for SENCOs, such as the National Association for Special Educational Needs (NASEN).

- Look out for training opportunities for team members and yourself.

- Visit education shows.

- Look for ways of making contact with parents before their child first joins the setting, so that you can talk to them about any adaptations or support that their child will need.

- Devise a brief information sheet for new members of the team to help them understand your role.

Continued ▶

- Ask for a regular slot at team meetings to update colleagues.
- Set up a resource shelf for team members, e.g. books, articles, blank IEPs.
- Make sure that other members of staff can understand how and where records are stored.
- Keep an effective diary and highlight dates where reviews, updates or meetings are required.

The Pre-school Learning Alliance

For pre-schools that are members of the Pre-school Learning Alliance, further support is also available. The Pre-school Learning Alliance has an Inclusion Officer based in its national centre and, in some areas, local support staff with responsibility for special educational needs. They also provide a range of publications and training courses on SEN and have a special educational needs helpline (020 7014 9346).

Preparation for assignment

Write a leaflet that explains to parents:

- the role of a SENCO in your pre-school
- the role of other professionals that support the pre-school in ensuring that children's needs are met.

How to promote the care and education of children with disabilities and special educational needs in a pre-school setting

Sources of information about particular disabilities and special educational needs

In order to support specific children and their families, it can be helpful to gain further information – although learning more about a disability is no substitute for getting to know the individual child and his or her family. Even twins with the same disability will each have their own personality, preferences and therefore needs. Having said that, researching further and finding out about the types of support available should help you to work more effectively.

There are many sources of support available. The first port of call will therefore be to talk to the child's parents, who will have developed strategies to meet their child's needs at home and are 'experts' on their child. The parents may have spent hours already in waiting rooms and reading up about their child's disability or medical condition. Tapping into this knowledge is essential because asking parents to advise you will enable you to meet the child's individual needs. As well as information that can be gained directly from parents, there are also support and campaigning groups for most of the common disabilities and types of special educational need. A search on the Internet can provide you with the contact details of such groups as well as information from a range of sources. A word of caution, however: it is important to check that you are reading information from a reputable source. (Some starting points for further research are provided at the end of this unit.)

The effect of developmental delay and impairment, including the importance of early recognition and intervention

The SEN Code of Practice 2001 stresses the importance of identifying as early as possible children who require extra support in their learning. This is because a developmental delay in one area of a child's development can impact on his or her overall development. For example, a child who is not fully hearing may have difficulty in concentrating, socialising and guiding his or her behaviour. Finding out about children's development is therefore important as a way of checking that you are meeting their needs.

Self-esteem

Whilst the effects on a child of developmental delay or unidentified delay can vary, a common effect is the development of low self-esteem. Throughout childhood, children develop both a concept of who they are and expectations of themselves. One of the key dangers of not identifying and supporting children who have additional needs is that they may not realise their own potential. A child who finds it hard to sit still at story time because he or she cannot hear the words of the story may come to believe that he or she is unable to concentrate; a child who cannot remember the letters in his or her name because he or she is not seeing them clearly may come to believe that he or she is not a writer. While these are simplistic examples, they illustrate the importance of making sure that children do not learn about failure because of inadequate support.

Good practice

Checklist for hearing impairment

- Does the child have frequent coughs and colds?

Continued ▶

- Does the child often fail to respond to his name or instructions when engaged in an activity?
- Does the child watch other children to know what to do when instructions are given?
- Is the child withdrawn or does he or she appear to be in his or her own world?
- Is the child's speech muffled or unclear?
- Do parents report a lack of interest in watching television or listening to story tapes?
- Does the child appear to study a speaker's face intently?
- Does the child try and be close by to an adult during story or other such times?
- Does the child lack concentration during language-based activities?

How to use observation and assessment to progress the learning and development of individual children with disabilities and special educational needs

The starting point when considering how best to work with children with special educational needs or disabilities is to observe them. By observing children closely, you can focus on areas of need and consider how the child responds in a variety of situations. Ideally, observations in a setting should be ongoing for all children because the early years' Foundation Stage makes it clear that you plan according to children's interests and stages of development.

Good practice

Key questions that might be helpful when identifying children's needs

- In what situations does the child need further support?
- How does the child respond in these situations?
- Does the child have any particular interests?
- What are the child's strengths?
- Are there any strategies or situations that appear to be helpful?

In order to assess children's needs, it is likely that several observations and assessments will be carried out. As you have seen, children's responses can vary enormously (see Core Unit 1, pages 106–7). Observations will help you to decide whether further individual planning for children is needed in the form of Individual Education Plans.

Observation methods

It is a good idea to use a range of observation methods to find out more about the child. Some pre-schools also find it helpful to use more than one observer because you can sometimes focus on different aspects of a child's development and in this way come to different conclusions. It is also essential to ask parents about what they see of their child at home, which can sometimes reveal a different perspective. In some cases, carrying out a focused observation can provide you with a new approach to try with a child.

Individual Education Plans

Individual Education Plans (IEPs) are action plans that are drawn up where children's needs are seen to require extra support. They are a key tool that the SEN Code of Practice 2001 requires that practitioners use.

When are Individual Education Plans necessary?

It is a mistake to think that an IEP will be necessary for every child. The key test as to whether a child needs an IEP is whether you need to provide very different or extra support to help that child. The Code of Practice is clear that for all children it is good practice to adapt environments and your practice to meet their needs. IEPs are necessary only when further support is required. This means that a child with a medical condition such as epilepsy is not likely to need an IEP because these types of conditions do not usually affect children's learning and overall development. In the same way, a child who wears a hearing aid may not need an IEP because he or she will be able to participate fully once adjustments are made to activities and the environment.

It is important to think carefully about whether an IEP is necessary. You may otherwise be snowed under by paperwork and fail to use time that should be spent focusing on children effectively. The guidance given by the Code of Practice is described below.

Creating an IEP

If an IEP is considered necessary, the next step is to organise a meeting in which parents and practitioners can discuss how best to help the child. At this meeting a discussion about the child's needs should take place followed by consideration of those targets that might be recorded as a focus for further work with the child (see pages 339–40).

People involved in writing the IEP

Once the observations have been carried out, it is important to talk through with parents what has been learnt. This is a key feature of drawing up a successful IEP. It is also important that the child's key person or a practitioner with responsibility for the child is involved. The idea is that these people should be able to tailor the plan of action to best suit the child. The person who should co-ordinate the creation of the IEP is the Special Educational Needs Co-ordinator (SENCO), although he or she may not necessarily write it.

Information to be recorded

There is no standard format for IEPs, but the following information is usually recorded:

- the child's name and date of birth

- the date of the IEP
- the date and level of support, for example, Early Years Action Plus
- a brief summary of the child's area of need
- the child's strengths and interests
- the targets the plan is to cover
- how the targets are to be measured
- the teaching methods and strategies to be adopted
- the staff who are to be responsible for the implementation of the plan (this might be more than one named person)
- the date the IEP will be reviewed
- signatures of parents and staff.

Writing the IEP

The IEP should not be a lengthy document. It is important to remember that an IEP is a short-term action plan; it is not designed to provide a long-term overview. However, it does help to focus practitioners and parents on short-term targets and priorities that will help the child. Many pre-schools have developed a format so that the information can be fitted onto an A4 sheet of paper. There are also software packages that can be used to write IEPs on computers; however, these need to be carefully evaluated as they may not have been written with the very young child in mind.

The first pieces of information that are recorded on an IEP, such as the child's name, are straightforward. Other pieces of information require more thought, as detailed below.

- *Areas of need*
  This section should simply outline the child's current needs or areas for support. The section should be quite short and focused on why the child needs additional or different support. For those children who have many needs, it is important to identify which aspect the IEP will be working on.

- *Setting targets*
  As part of the creation of the IEP, some targets are set. These targets allow practitioners and parents to focus their work on developing particular skills in the child. Ideally, targets should be small and very achievable. This allows everyone, including the child, to feel a success. Targets are like small stepping stones that will help the child on his or her journey. Each IEP builds on the last; the aim is thus for the child to complete his or her journey little by little.

The acronym SMART is used in relation to setting targets. It is helpful because it serves as a reminder to ensure that targets are realistic.

S – specific
M – measurable
A – achievable
R – relevant
T – time-bound

IEP targets should be SMART targets

Specific	As you have seen, targets are small steps. The key is to break down anything you would like the child to achieve into small skills. For example, if you feel that it would be helpful for the child to use a pair of scissors, a first target might be to focus on the child being able to hold the scissors correctly.
Measurable	To help you monitor the effectiveness of the IEP, targets should be measurable. If they are not, how will you be able to check that the child has made progress and is ready for the next target? Thinking about the measurability of a target can help to make the target more focused.
Achievable	Targets must be achievable otherwise all involved – the parents, the child and the practitioners – can become despondent and lose motivation. Choosing targets that are relevant is therefore important. Ideally, the targets should concentrate on helping the child rather than the setting. You should consider what targets will best help the child to access the curriculum and meet his or her needs. Parents may have different views about what is relevant; for example, they may want their child to achieve a skill that will help the child at home.
Relevant	IEPs are short-term action plans. This creates a sense of urgency which means that they are less likely to be forgotten. The IEP should state when it will be reviewed. Most pre-schools will draw up IEPs every six or eight weeks.
Time-bound	The six- or eight-week target time is a useful average for the amount of time in which a target should be achieved.

The SEN Code of Practice suggests that IEPs might have three or four targets. This number may be too great if a child attends few sessions, so you may wish to reduce the number of targets.

Teaching methods and strategies

As well as deciding on targets, it is important to record how targets are likely to be achieved. This is an essential part of the IEP because targets alone will not help the child. You will need to consider how best to support the child and how this support will be provided.

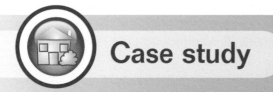

Case study

Shona is four years old. She was a premature baby and her physical development **is giving her parents and practitioners cause for concern. She sometimes shows signs of frustration during activities and finds it difficult to concentrate. The Special**

Continued ▶

Educational Needs Co-ordinator and Shona's parents have decided to draw up an Individual Education Plan that will focus on Shona's fine motor skills. This is because they believe these skills to be the underlying reason for Shona's frustrated behaviour and poor concentration. Shona's parents are keen to play a part at home.

1 Explain why Shona's frustrated behaviour may be linked to her physical development.

2 Why is it important that parents and the pre-school work together to draw up an IEP?

3 Suggest two types of activities that might benefit Shona.

Storage of IEPs

The parents and the SENCO should sign the finished IEP. It should then be kept in a safe place because it is a confidential document. It is not appropriate for an IEP to be put on display or left in a place where adults who are not directly involved with the child might see it.

Amending an IEP

IEPs should be seen as working documents therefore an IEP should be checked regularly and, if necessary, amended. For example, it might be that because of a child's absence the timeframe is no longer appropriate. Changes to the IEPs can be penned in and the date of the amendment should be added. It is good practice to let parents know that an IEP is to be slightly amended. If significant changes are required, it is better to draw up a new IEP.

Implementing the IEP in the pre-school

The time and effort that has been put into writing the IEP will be wasted if no further action is taken. Children's IEPs should therefore be considered when planning activities and staff deployment. It is the role of the SENCO to ensure that the IEP is effective, although this can happen only if all members of the team are aware of its significance. Some settings integrate children's IEPs into their planning by adding extra notes or a column so that it is clear how the activity is to meet the child's needs (see, for example, the daily planning sheet illustrated on the next page).

Reviewing IEPs

It is an important part of the process that IEPs are reviewed. Carrying out a review means that you are far more likely to carry out the suggested activities and observe children's progress closely. When a review is due, it is important to observe the child closely once more and consider what progress he or she has made. It is also important to pool together information from colleagues and parents.

Daily Planner: Monday

Adult-directed activities

Staff member	Activity and area	Focus	Individual needs	Comments
Dianne	Making stretchy dough – messy play area	Experimentation, measuring and noticing changes to texture	Rubber mat for C.K. to stop bowl from slipping	More self-raising flour needed for tomorrow
Andraya	Name treasure hunt – outdoor area	Name recognition and searching skills	Put red sticker on L.C.'s card. Encourage to find himself. Repeat	L.C. found his name easily. Repeat tomorrow perhaps without sticker?
Toni	Sandcastles – sand tray	Sizes of buckets and quantities of sand required	J.K. may need thin plastic gloves. Plenty of encouragement	Extend this with flags tomorrow?

Activity and resources/materials

Gloop – pink	Water tray – shells, pebbles and boats	Role-play – suitcases, clothes and luggage labels	Writing – postcards, envelopes and stamping machine	Dough – shells, pot pourri
Jigsaws	Farm animals + small cardboard boxes	Outdoors – large cardboard boxes		

This daily planning sheet shows how children's individual needs will be met.

Once information has been collected from observations, colleagues and parents, a meeting with parents should be arranged. The discussion should focus on the 'whole' child as well as on those needs identified in the IEP. After the child's progress has been considered, a decision needs to be made as to whether a further IEP is required. The key issues here are whether the child is making progress and whether such progress can be sustained by simply differentiating the curriculum. If the decision is made to draw up a further IEP, the same process is followed as previously. In situations when no IEPs are required, it may be helpful to explain to parents that this does not mean that their child will be left to 'fend' for him or herself. No IEPs may be needed for children showing slower progress than their peers but whose needs can be met by adjusting the setting's activities and daily routine.

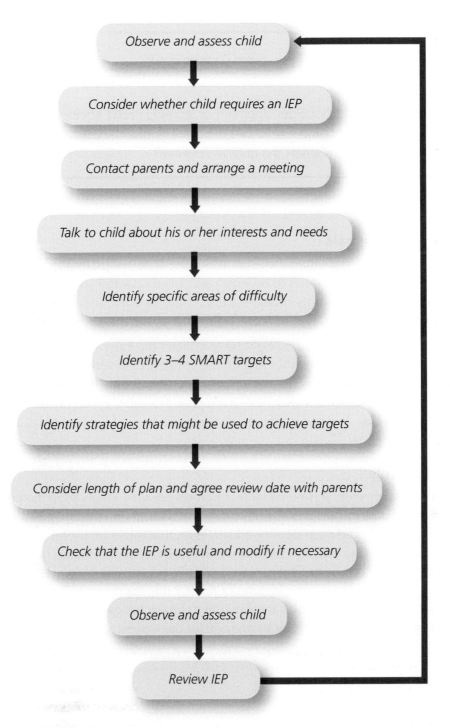

Observe and assess child

Consider whether child requires an IEP

Contact parents and arrange a meeting

Talk to child about his or her interests and needs

Identify specific areas of difficulty

Identify 3–4 SMART targets

Identify strategies that might be used to achieve targets

Consider length of plan and agree review date with parents

Check that the IEP is useful and modify if necessary

Observe and assess child

Review IEP

The stages of writing an IEP.

Preparation for assignment

Choose one child whose development or learning needs additional support. With relevant permission ask to see the child's Individual Education Plan. How will this plan aim to support the child's progress?

Involving professionals

Where children's progress remains a cause for concern, it will be important to consider whether other professionals need to be involved. This discussion should take place with parents and the review meeting might be a good time for such discussion. Remember, parents should be asked for their consent before any professionals are contacted.

The first port of call in many areas might be to contact the Early Years Advisory Team, although in some areas it is possible to gain direct referrals to services such as the Speech and Language Team. In some cases, parents may decide to seek help by contacting their GP or health visitor. The involvement of other professionals outside of the setting means that, in terms of the 'graduated response', children will be accessing Early Years Action Plus.

Involving parents

As you have already seen, it is essential that parents are fully involved in the creation of IEPs. Parents are able to give you a better picture of their child, and they may also have some targets in mind and have developed strategies that might be useful when working with the child. Involving parents can also mean that those skills that are being developed with the child in the setting can be encouraged at home, for example, encouraging a child to put on a coat. During the lifetime of the IEP it is important to have frequent contacts with parents. This enables information to be exchanged about the effectiveness of the strategies and helps everyone to prepare for the review meeting when the IEP is revisited.

Involving children

The SEN Code of Practice makes it clear that even the youngest children should be involved in the IEPs. This is to avoid the idea of the child as a 'passive object'. Very young children can be involved by asking them what they enjoy doing. Understanding and building on children's interests is an extremely effective way of helping them to progress. Once children's interests have been identified through observations or, ideally, by asking the child, teaching strategies should be organised accordingly. For example, a child who particularly enjoys playing with dough and whose target looks at building scissors skills, may be shown how to use scissors to cut into dough.

In addition to thinking about children's interests, it may be possible to ask children directly about what they would like to achieve. Sometimes a child may say that he or she wants to be able to do something by him or herself, or to do something that he or she has seen another child do. When children find it hard to communicate, it can be useful to use a prop such as a teddy and ask the child to show us 'what teddy would like to do'; this sometimes helps children to express what they really would like to do.

Case study

Helena is three years old. Her speech is slightly delayed as she often lets her twin speak for her. She understands well but she still needs to be encouraged to talk rather than to simply point at objects. Her vocabulary also needs to be built up as she tends still to generalise words, for example, using 'coat' for all types of clothing or 'dog' for all animals. Her mother finds it hard to give her individual time as she also has two other children. She says that Helena especially enjoys animals and plays a lot at home with a farm set. Helena also enjoys touching and exploring new objects.

1 Think of two possible targets that might be used in drawing up an IEP.

2 Describe two activities that will help Helena to achieve these targets.

3 Explain how the adults in the setting might work with Helena to achieve the targets.

How to ensure that children with disabilities and special educational needs are able to participate fully in and benefit from all of the pre-school setting's activities

Areas of need

The SEN Code of Practice 2001 recognises that children may have one or more areas of need. The avoidance of identifying particular 'conditions' or 'disabilities' is deliberate because labelling can lead to children being stereotyped. The Code of Practice lists four areas of need:

- communication and interaction
- cognition and learning
- behaviour and social and emotional development
- sensory and physical development.

Supporting children's communication and interaction

As you saw in Core Unit 1 (pages 48–52), communication and language is a significant skill that most children are able to learn reasonably easily. This is not the case for a few children who may need additional support. The chart opposite shows some common reasons why this may be an area of need for some children.

Language can affect behaviour

The ability to make yourself understood and to interact with others is crucial. Children who have communication and interaction as an area of need can show behaviours that are linked to frustration. They may be more aggressive or attention-seeking than other children of their age. It is important to see these types of behaviour as by-products of children's unmet needs and not to focus on them. Instead, you should concentrate on finding ways of helping these children to communicate their thoughts and wishes and develop their language skills.

Being a language partner

Children who have communication and interaction as an area of need will often benefit from spending time with a responsive adult. The aim of the adult is both to act as a language partner to help the child develop language and interaction skills and to 'read' the child effectively. Children who know that they will be understood are far more likely to attempt to interact. Language partners tend to work well because children do not feel under pressure to talk. Children are thus more likely to respond because they are not afraid of saying the wrong thing or not enough.

Good practice

Being a language partner

- Make good eye contact with the child.
- Smile and express genuine pleasure when the child tries to interact.
- Avoid asking the child lots of questions and develop a 'chatty' style.
- Acknowledge the child's communications by answering or responding rather than simply giving praise.

Using visual means of communication

Children whose language skills are still developing often need visual as well as verbal cues. These help children's comprehension and allow them to take in more information. Visual cues are particularly useful for situations in which children may find it hard to concentrate, such as story time. Having a visual cue helps children to understand and focuses their

Difficulties
Children may not be able to choose a medium that is appropriate, e.g. they may throw an object rather than use words or a gesture to show their feelings. Children may also have difficulties in encoding information using words because words are abstract symbols. Children may not have the vocabulary to put their thoughts into words.

Difficulties
Children may not be able to process their thoughts and feelings.

Difficulties
Children may not be able to respond to others or they may need plenty of time.

Stage 1 Information
The sender has to decide what he or she wants to convey.

Stage 7 Response
They may then wish to send information themselves in which case the cycle continues.

Stage 2 Encoding
The sender chooses a medium in which to send the message. This can be using spoken language, written, non-verbal or visual.

Stage 6 Feedback
The receiver of the information may show some reaction. Sometimes the sender of the information may not see the feedback, e.g. if a letter is sent.

Stage 3 Transfer of information
At this point, the information is sent out.

Stage 5 Decoding of information
The information is now interpreted.

Stage 4 Reception of information
The receiver now hears or takes in the information.

Difficulties
Children may not be able to show appropriate feedback; they may laugh or smile when the message being sent is sad or serious.

Difficulties
Children may not have the receptive vocabulary to understand the meaning. Children may not be able to understand the gesture or tone of voice. Children may not be able to process the information effectively.

Difficulties
Children may not be able to see the gestures or fully hear the sounds. Children may not be able to read what has been written. Children may not be able to remember what is being said.

Difficulties
Children may have difficulty in using speech, e.g. a child may have a stutter or have difficulties with pronunciation.

The interaction cycle.

Using a puppet can aid communication skills.

attention. Many educational psychologists therefore suggest using props with children and also trying to explain what is happening by using pictures or picture timetables.

Puppets

Many children enjoy puppets. Sometimes children who are reluctant to talk will say something to a puppet or cuddly toy. This is because they do not worry about being judged or getting something wrong. Puppets can also be used to model language because you can say something to the puppet and the puppet can then respond.

Hearing loss

Some children may have communication and interaction as an area of need because they are not fully hearing. It is important to recognise the signs that children are not hearing as this can be extremely frustrating for them. Hearing loss can affect a child's enjoyment of activities and his or her ability to play with other children.

Good practice

Strategies for supporting children who may not be fully hearing

- Always turn to the child so that he or she can see your face clearly.
- Make sure that the lighting allows the child to see your face.

Continued ▶

- Do not cover your mouth with your hands.
- Check early on that the child understands the conversation.
- Use visual cues such as props and pictures to help the child follow what is happening.
- Consider the use of quiet areas for some types of activities.
- In group situations, make sure that the child is close by.

Dysfluency

Many children will have some dysfluency (stammering) in their speech when they first begin to put sentences together. For most children, it is simply a phase in which their thoughts travel more quickly than their words. Children may stumble over the initial sounds of words, particularly if they are under pressure to speak quickly. Understanding how to help children relax while speaking is important, because if children feel stressed a vicious cycle can develop in which they stammer more. This can sometimes lead to children not talking in group situations.

Good practice

Strategies to reduce stammering

- Avoid situations in which children compete to talk first, for example, group situations in which children are asked a question and the first to put their hand up can speak.
- Avoid situations in which children cannot take their time, for example, circle time in which other children wait their turn.
- Reduce the speed at which you talk and make sure that the child feels that you have plenty of time in which to speak.
- When speaking, make sure that you are on the same level as the child.

Checklist to help children with communication and interaction

- Do children have time with a language partner?

Continued ▶

- Are visual cues provided to help children?

- Are story times organised according to children's language needs?

- Are group times 'competitive' in nature?

- Are staff aware of the importance of helping children to relax?

- Are staff aware that some behavioural responses are the result of frustration?

Supporting children's cognition and learning

Cognition is about the way in which you process and use information, and how you learn to perceive and understand the world. It is linked closely to language, so some children who have communication and interaction as an area of need may also need extra support with cognitive development. There are many components to cognition, which includes attention, concentration and memory. It is not fully understood how information is processed and learnt, but it is clear that physical development and language play a part in children's early years.

Helping children to concentrate

Concentrating is far more complex than most people realise. The starting point is to understand that the brain is bombarded by information all the time. For some children, this means that they cannot stay focused because they are easily distracted by new information, for example, seeing another child walk nearby or hearing their name. As the brain matures, it becomes more efficient at ignoring information that is not required and children find it easier to settle and focus their attention.

Good practice

Helping children to concentrate

- Avoid passive activities – encourage children to be active in their learning.

- Build on children's interests – when activities have meaning and relevance for them, they are more likely to be able to learn.

- Use sensory activities that stimulate the brain – such as sand and water play.

- Remember that children find it hard to concentrate when they are tired.

To help children concentrate use sensory activities that stimulate the brain, such as sand play.

It is also worth recognising that children find it much easier to process information when it is presented to them in a way that engages their senses and allows them to be active. Using language alone for most children is quite difficult. This is why young children find it very hard to sit still and simply listen passively.

Encouraging children to make connections

Children find it easier to concentrate and learn when they build on previous knowledge and experiences. This is because it helps them to make connections. It is therefore a good idea to repeat games or activities but with variations. It is also important to encourage children to talk about what they think will happen next and encourage them to remember what they have done before. This helps children to use knowledge they have gained to build new learning. Helping children to find similarities between previous situations can also help them adjust to new situations; for example, saying to children, 'Do you remember how we washed our hands before when they were dirty?'

Understanding that young children often use language to organise information

As you saw in Core Unit 1 (page 82), language and thought are interconnected. It is therefore important to encourage children to talk aloud if they wish because this is often a key way in which they acquire information. Sometimes, children talking aloud in situations, for example, circle time, are interpreted as them not being able to listen. The reality is that talking aloud often shows the contrary: the child is thinking and therefore talking about the information they have learnt.

Good practice

Supporting children's cognitive development

- Make sure that activities are active.
- Look out for sensory activities to help children learn.
- Encourage children's language and do not prevent children from 'thinking aloud'.
- Help children find connections between current and past experiences.
- Make sure that planning reflects individual children's experiences.
- Remember that young children may need to see things rather than imagine them.

Supporting children's behaviour and social and emotional development

There are many reasons why children may find it difficult to show 'appropriate behaviour'. If you are serious about inclusion, it means that your approach to guiding children's behaviour is based on the understanding that most behaviour reflects a child's unmet needs. If you take this approach, it may mean that you need to reflect upon what the child's behaviour is telling you. This approach challenges the traditional ways of managing children's behaviour: instead of focusing on how the child's behaviour is causing you difficulties, you need to think about the how the child can be helped to show alternative behaviours.

Modelling behaviour

You can sometimes help children to show appropriate behaviour by acting as a play partner and modelling behaviour. Children can then learn how to respond to others in a comfortable way. The use of puppets and cuddly toys can also help some children to model behaviour.

Taking a pro-active approach to children's behaviour

Children can sometimes learn habits of behaviour that mean the behaviour is likely to continue. You, too, can become trapped in a cycle of responding to these habits. It is therefore helpful to take a step back and consider why the child is showing the behaviour and what happens when he or she does. This approach can be quite revealing. Sometimes children have learnt that they will gain immediate adult attention from a certain act. This attention serves as a reinforcement (see Core Unit 1, pages 76–7) and the child will go on to repeat the behaviour. If you analyse the child's behaviour, you may sometimes realise that the child's basic need is for adult attention and that he or she has simply learnt to gain it in an inappropriate way. A pro-active approach to such habits of behaviour is therefore to look for ways of giving the child attention, thereby reducing his or her need to seek attention inappropriately.

In the same way that adults can become trapped in responding to a child's cycle of behaviour, so can other children. Sometimes, other children might refuse to play alongside a child or will 'tell tales'. In such situations, you may need gradually to introduce the child into play with others. This might mean asking the child to choose another child to carry out an adult-directed but pleasant activity, such as cooking. Helping children to interact in structured situations can be very helpful.

Checklist for a pro-active approach to children's behaviour

- What play activities engage and interest the child? Are these being provided?
- Are the activities suitable for the child's stage of development?
- What level of support does the child need and is this being received?
- What situations cause the child to seek adult attention?
- Does the child have opportunities to feel in control?
- Does the child need adult support to help him or her play with other children?
- How are the child's underlying needs being met?

Supporting children's sensory and physical development

Children who have a sensory impairment or whose physical development is atypical will need extra support in order to enjoy experiences and benefit from the learning environment. There is a strong link here to cognition and learning, so sometimes a need in this area will link to children's cognitive development.

Using a multi-sensory approach

All children, regardless of whether they have Special Educational Needs, respond well to sensory materials and experiences. For children who have sensory and physical development as their area of need, a multi-sensory approach is essential. Specialist equipment is often available on loan from toy libraries. It is important not to 'exclude' other children from using such equipment because all children will benefit from playing with it. A multi-sensory approach helps a child to compensate for a particular impairment.

Helping children who dislike tactile materials

Some children dislike putting their hands in sensory materials such as sand and water. It is important to understand that this is not likely to reflect attention-seeking behaviour but rather that the hands of some children are over-sensitive. This is referred to as being tactile defensive. Children who find it hard to cope with sensory materials will need support, and the following strategies might be useful.

Good practice

Strategies for supporting children who are tactile defensive

- Do not dismiss children's fears.
- Do not force children's hands into things; this can make them feel panicky.
- Avoid making an 'issue' out of a child's reluctance to handle things; some children can then learn to use this as an attention-seeking device.
- Ask parents about materials that the child enjoys at home.
- Choose activities and games that encourage children to touch large-scale things with pressure, for example, bouncing on a trampoline, trampling on wet sand, wearing wellington boots or wringing water out of fabric.
- Look for materials that are firm for children to explore, for example, dried beans and marbles.
- Encourage firm movements using tools, for example, cutting dough with knives, printing into wet sand with forks, drawing with sticks.
- Consider putting sand or dough into plastic bags so that children can play with it through the plastic.
- Introduce materials that are more tactile, such as cornflour and water, only as children become more confident.
- Model language so that children can learn to express what they are feeling.
- Look for ways of helping children to remain in control; for example, while playing in the sand, allow them to wipe their hands on a towel at any time. The knowledge that they can do this can help children to gain confidence.

Children who show little response to touch

While some children overreact to touch, others show little reaction. These children particularly benefit from daily sensory activities. It is also a good idea to build on their favourite sensory activities by incorporating them into other activities. For example, a child who likes playing with cornflour and water might enjoy mark-making activities in the same tray.

Throwing bean bags into hoops, to promote physical development and co-ordination skills.

Developing co-ordination

The ability to co-ordinate movements is something that it is easy to take for granted. For some children, co-ordination is difficult and you may need to help them by looking at strategies to develop co-ordination or by making activities more accessible for them. As with other areas of need, advice should be taken from parents and other professionals working with the child.

Using the range of specialist equipment and systems available to promote the learning and development of children with disabilities and SEN

As you have seen when looking at the four areas of need, you may sometimes need to support children by using specialist equipment and systems. This is an area in which you often need to be guided by parents and other professionals. Any piece of equipment chosen, for example, equipment to help a child to stand during activities, must be appropriate for the child's needs. In the same way, if concept boards or a visual signing system is used, it is essential that you seek advice otherwise the investment in terms of time and money may be wasted.

Case study

Jack was finding it hard to finish a jigsaw puzzle. When he put a piece in, the whole jigsaw puzzle often slipped away from him. His co-ordination was such that he could not put one hand down to act as a stabiliser. The supervisor looked at the difficulty that Jack was having and came up with the idea of putting the jigsaw onto a sheet of rubber matting. This allowed Jack to finish the puzzle without any further adult help.

1 **Explain why this adult support was better than helping Jack to finish the puzzle.**

2 **Why is it important to look for ways of allowing children to be independent?**

3 **Describe why this approach illustrates what is meant by inclusive practice.**

Being ready to improvise

One of the skills in helping children who have one or more areas of need is to think creatively. This requires a 'can do' attitude! For example, a suction cup normally used for holding tea towels may be perfect as a lower coat peg or apron peg for a child who is not able to stand up.

Looking for accessibility

Children who have difficulty with standing or mobility do not necessarily have special educational needs. This is because they are able to learn alongside other children once adaptations or adjustments are made to the physical environment. You should therefore think about the layout of the provision and consider ways in which children might be able to do the same or similar tasks as other children. For example, instead of having to stand at a water tray, water might be provided on a table or other surface that is at a better height. It is important here that all children in the pre-school are invited to play with any new provision because otherwise the child might become isolated.

In some cases, children may be using special equipment such as a standing frame. Standing frames are used to allow children to stand as they take the child's weight. The key when using specialist equipment is to gain information directly from the paediatric occupational therapist or physiotherapist working with the child. Find out why a piece of equipment is used and also how and when it should be used. You should also learn about how to check that it is safe and properly working. Some pieces of equipments, for example, may require routine maintenance.

Communication systems

There are many different systems available to support communication with children. Suggestions as to what to use are usually made by speech and language therapists in conjunction with parents.

Picture representations

Picture representations help children to communicate with you by allowing them to point to a picture if they cannot take you directly to the object they want. It is also helpful for you to use picture representations to show children what is going to happen next. Commercial systems of picture representations are available and are based on an 'exchange system'. The exchange system helps children to learn that communication is a two-way process. The child learns to choose a picture and give it to an adult and the adult then returns the communication by giving the child a further picture or symbol. Training is normally provided for staff using these types of systems with children.

Sign representation

Some children may need signs to support spoken language. Makaton is a well-known system that is used alongside the spoken word (see also page 51); this helps children's language because the gestures reflect the meaning of the spoken word. This helps children who have difficulty in comprehending the meaning of speech. Children using Makaton may have a learning difficulty and it is this rather than a sensory impairment, such as deafness, that is affecting their communication. Makaton is not a language in itself and so must not be confused with British Sign Language. The decision to use Makaton or another signing system will be made by speech and language therapists in conjunction with the child's parents.

How the pre-school setting can work in partnership with the parents of children with disabilities and special educational needs

The importance of the partnership between the pre-school setting and the parents of children with disabilities and special educational needs

The SEN Code of Practice 2001 strengthens parents' rights and encourages a much closer involvement with them. This approach should pay dividends: before, parents frequently felt very left out of the process and practitioners were often unsympathetic to their feelings or unappreciative of their knowledge of their child. This approach was not in the child's interests because parents' knowledge was unused. For example, for situations in which children were involved with several professionals, it was often only the parents who had a direct overview of what was happening.

How to work in partnership with parents

The key to working with parents is to ensure that good relations are established from the start. This is good practice regardless of any particular needs the child may have. It is also important to share immediately with parents any concerns or observations that you have about their child, rather than 'store them up' for later. This is crucial because the SEN Code of Practice states clearly that parents must be involved with the drawing up of Individual Education Plans and that parent's consent has to be given before any professionals are contacted. It also avoids situations whereby a parent whose child has been in the pre-school for a while is suddenly faced with an avalanche of information. This can make parents feel quite defensive, cross and cheated, especially if they have asked after their child and nothing has been said.

Seven key principles when working with parents

The SEN Code of Practice outlines seven key principles that you should adopt when working with parents. These principles are sound ones and should be followed in relation to all children regardless of their individual needs.

1 *Acknowledge and draw on parental knowledge and expertise in relation to the child.* This principle is about recognising that parents really know their children. They may also have contacts with support organisations and other professionals.

2 *Focus on children's strengths as well as areas of additional need.* There is a danger that when children have particular needs, practitioners focus only on these. It is essential to remember the 'whole' child otherwise parents may feel that their child is seen as a 'problem'.

3 *Recognise the personal and emotional investment of parents and be aware of their feelings.* Parents do not see their child in terms of developmental milestones or key learning intentions. Their focus is on the whole child and on nurturing their offspring. This principle reminds you to be sensitive to the emotional tie that exists between parents and their children.

4 *Ensure that parents understand the procedures, are aware of how to access support in preparing their contribution, and are given documents to be discussed well before the meetings.* While some parents may have quite a lot of knowledge as to the procedures of identifying and supporting children's special needs, others may not. This can put parents at a serious disadvantage and, as a result, they may be unable to participate fully.

5 *Respect the validity of differing perspectives and seek constructive ways of reconciling different viewpoints.* Parents may not always agree about whether their child has particular needs or with the strategies that are being suggested. Confident practitioners are able to understand that views may differ while others may see this as a direct challenge to their expertise. Conflict is not helpful to anyone and rarely meets children's needs. By respecting and actively taking on board parents' views, it should be possible to find positions of compromise.

6 *Respect the differing needs that parents themselves may have, such as a disability or communication and linguistic barriers.* Some parents may have particular needs. If you are not sensitive to these, they may create a barrier to effective communication and information-sharing. This means being ready to take a flexible approach when organising meetings and sharing information, for example, some parents may wish to bring a friend or an interpreter to a meeting.

7 *Recognise the need for flexibility in the timing and structure of meetings.* It is easy to pay lip service to involving parents. If parents are to be truly involved, you must ensure that you choose meeting times and places that everyone can attend.

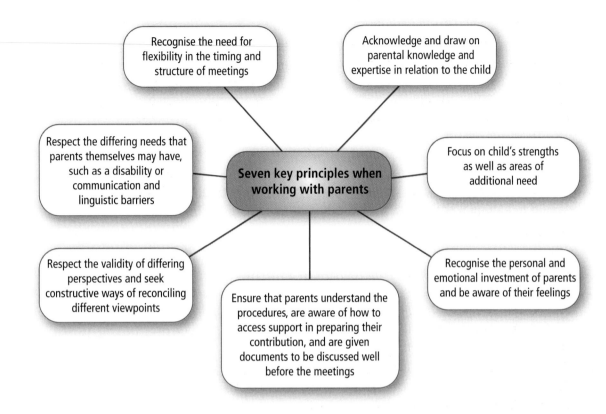

Recognise the need for flexibility in the timing and structure of meetings

Acknowledge and draw on parental knowledge and expertise in relation to the child

Respect the differing needs that parents themselves may have, such as a disability or communication and linguistic barriers

Seven key principles when working with parents

Focus on child's strengths as well as areas of additional need

Respect the validity of differing perspectives and seek constructive ways of reconciling different viewpoints

Ensure that parents understand the procedures, are aware of how to access support in preparing their contribution, and are given documents to be discussed well before the meetings

Recognise the personal and emotional investment of parents and be aware of their feelings

Case study

Sophie has complex learning needs. She is four years old and her mother Wendy is delighted with the way that the pre-school is supporting her needs. The SENCO and Sophie's key person spend time talking through what they are doing and Wendy feels that they can really share ideas. She likes the way that staff listen to her and do not treat her as just Sophie's mum but as a person in her own right. Wendy is also pleased with the way that the pre-school co-ordinates and shares information with other professionals such as Sophie's speech and language therapist. She feels that everyone works as a team together in Sophie's best interest. She is sad that Sophie will soon be moving on to school, but has decided to spend time helping out in the pre-school once Sophie has settled in because she thinks that she may eventually take up a career in working with children.

1   Why is it important that pre-schools work alongside parents to meet children's needs?

Continued ▶

2   **Explain why it is important for the pre-school to work with other agencies and professionals.**

3   **Consider why it is important for staff to remember that parents have their own needs too.**

Recognising the varied ways in which parents and other family members might respond to having a child with a disability and special educational needs

The way in parents and other family members respond to having a child with disabilities and special educational needs can vary enormously. There is no standardised reaction to having a child with special education needs or a disability; indeed, many parents report that their own feelings can change on a day-by-day basis according to how tired they are feeling and how others including professionals are working with them.

Denial

Some parents and family members can find it hard to accept that their child has any difficulties during the process of identification. Accepting that your child has difficulties and particular needs requires a huge re-adjustment emotionally. Some parents talk about the process of 'letting' go and almost mourning for the child that they thought they had; you might hear phrases such as 'When I see a child of Manjeet's age, I often think about how Manjeet might have been and what she would have been like.'

Guilt

Few parents of any child are not prone to reporting feelings of guilt. For parents who have children with disabilities or SEN, there may be specific thoughts such as whether they were in any way responsible for the disability or special educational needs. Parents may also feel guilty about any other siblings in the family who may not be getting the same level of attention as the child with the disability or special educational needs. Where children's needs are particularly physically or mentally demanding, parents can also feel guilty about moments where they have been unable to remain patient. Some parents also feel guilty when others step in to help. Sending a child for respite care may be accompanied not only with relief but also feelings of letting down the child.

Worry

Some parents talk about how they become worried about their children's future. Some children may, for example, have shortened life expectancy or may not in the longer term be able to live an independent life. In the pre-school years, parents may be worried about whether their child will have friends or be able to join in and attend mainstream school. Other worries might be more practical such as financial concerns. Some parents may find it hard to work if they also need to provide care for their children.

Love

Finally, it is important to recognise the immense love and dedication that most parents and their family members have for their children. Love pushes parents to seek out new information, remain patient and above all see their child as a unique individual. Remembering that for parents their child will always be 'David' rather than a boy with Down's syndrome or 'Monika' rather than a deaf girl is therefore paramount.

Ways through which the pre-school setting can work with the parents of children with disabilities and special educational needs to promote their learning and development

You have seen that working with parents is essential. Working closely with parents means that children's learning and development can be promoted. This is a two-way process. Parents might like sometimes to build on an activity at home that has particularly engaged the child, whilst you can learn from parents about a technique that they are trying out at home, for example. The spider diagram below shows some of the ways in which you can work with parents.

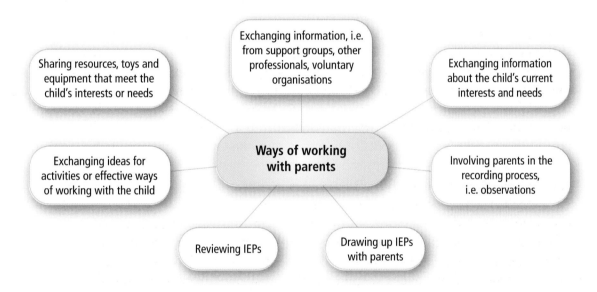

How the pre-school setting can work in partnership with other agencies to promote the care and education of children with disabilities and special educational needs

The range of other professionals and agencies who may be involved with children with disabilities and special educational needs and their families

Most children's needs can be met within the pre-school by simply focusing on the child's needs and (in some cases) reflecting on your practice. However, some children will need additional support from other professionals. The idea of collaborative working between different groups of professionals is not new. The Children Act 1989 sent a clear message that this was expected when it stated that children were considered as being 'in need'. Children with 'special needs', an umbrella term that encompasses children with special educational needs, are categorised according to the Act as being 'in need'. In many areas there currently exists a range of services for children with special needs.

Understanding your local services

The range of services for children and even the titles of these services vary enormously from one local authority to the next. This means that it is essential that you find out about what is available in your area and develop a list of contacts for your pre-school. In the same way, the system for referring children can vary. In some areas, speech and language units will accept direct referrals; in others, referrals may need to come via a family doctor or health visitor.

This section looks at what is likely to be available in most parts of the country; however, it can be thought of as a general overview only. In many cases you will come into contact with professionals via a child's family because the parents may have a long-standing involvement with these services.

Special Educational Needs advisory teams

Most local education authorities will have teams that support teachers and others involved with children with special educational needs. In some areas these teams might be referred to as 'Inclusion Support' or 'SENCO Area Teams'. The differences in title again reflect the local nature of provision. In some areas, advisory teachers will visit pre-schools to help support SENCOs; in other areas, they will also help with the creation of IEPs. Many SEN advisory teams provide training for pre-school settings, so it can be helpful to check what support is available in your area.

Speech and language teams

Each area will have a Speech and Language Team. This service is usually funded by the health service, although many speech therapists work closely with education departments. Many speech and language teams will allow a direct referral if parents have given consent.

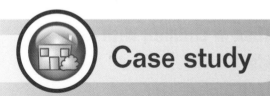

Case study

Michael is now three years old. He was a premature baby and has complex needs. The social worker that supports his family is looking for a suitable pre-school place for him. She has visited Farley Bank Pre-school and is impressed with its

Continued ▶

warm atmosphere and the commitment of the staff. She arranges for Michael and his mother to visit and meet the pre-school leader Joan with her. Joan shows them around and finds out about Michael's interests and his needs. It is decided that Michael will begin the process of joining the pre-school over the next few weeks and that he will need his own support worker that will be provided by the pre-school, but funded by the local authority. To help the pre-school meet Michael's needs, the social worker also contacts the sensory impairment team who are already working with Michael. They arrange a visit so that they can help Joan and her team prepare for Michael. Michael's mother is delighted and says to Joan 'I can't tell you what this all means to me. At last Michael may have someone to play with apart from me.'

- **How might Michael benefit from joining the pre-school?**
- **How might the pre-school gain from Michael coming to join them?**
- **Why is it important for pre-schools to work alongside other professionals?**

Sensory impairment team

Most education services will have a team that supports children with visual or hearing impairments. As with other services, the title of this team may vary from area to area. Most teams will employ specialist staff who visit the pre-school and family to advise how best to meet the child's needs. This team may be able to advise on layout and equipment when working with children with sensory impairments. Most sensory impairment teams will also have strong links with the speech and language team.

Educational psychologist service

Educational psychologists look at and identify children's learning and development. In cases where a child's needs are complex and a statutory assessment is required, educational psychologists will be involved. As demand on their services is high in most areas, it is unlikely that a referral will be made as a first port of call because usually a member of the SEN team will assess the child first.

Parent partnership services

In order to strengthen parents' rights, the SEN Code of Practice asks that every local education authority has a parent partnership to assist those parents who have a child with special educational needs. The aim of the service is to support parents and provide independent advice. Parents should be told about this service when you first discuss the possibility that their child has special educational needs because many parents find this service very helpful.

Health visitors

Health visitors are qualified nurses with specialist training in health promotion. It can sometimes be very helpful to talk to a child's health visitor but this must be with parental permission. Health visitors can refer children to other services and have a good knowledge of children's health issues.

Physiotherapy services

Physiotherapists are part of the health service. They may be involved in the care of children who have medical conditions or are recovering from surgery. Physiotherapists will provide advice and guidance to parents – and, if appropriate, to settings – about exercises and movements that might help the child.

Social Services

The Children Act 1989 gave local authorities the duty to provide for 'children in need'. This means that children who have complex or severe needs will be provided with a social worker. The social worker's role is to assess and check that the child's needs and those of his or her family are being met.

Paediatric occupational therapy services

Paediatric occupational therapists work with children to maximise their physical movements with the aim of helping them to become as independent as possible. In addition to working with children they are likely to work directly with the family. In early years settings, they may advise on how best to make the layout accessible for the child.

Portage

Portage is a home-based teaching service for children under five years which is organised locally. Portage teachers or volunteers visit the home regularly and work with parents to devise a structured programme to build children's skills. The parents then implement the programme, with encouragement and advice being offered by the portage team.

Local and national sources of information which could help the pre-school setting to promote the learning and development of children with disabilities and special educational needs

There are many sources of local and national information that can help you to meet the needs of children and their families. A good starting point is to talk to some of the professionals from the services that are available in your area. It is also worth building a directory of national organisations so that you can act as signpost for parents and colleagues who wish to gain further information. Below are some examples of organisations that provide information and support for parents and professionals.

Department for Education and Skills

The DfES has a wide range of published materials to support early years practitioners and parents. Look out for a series of leaflets that are designed for parents. Most of the publications are free and can be ordered either by telephone or via the DfES website (www.dfes.gov.uk).

Contact A Family (CAF)

This national organisation provides factsheets on disabilities and special educational needs, but also acts as a gateway for other organisations. It aims to support parents but also provides information for professionals. Parents can use CAF to find out about local support groups but also families in their area who also have children with similar needs. To find out more, visit the organisation's website at www.cafamily.org.uk.

National Association for Special Educational Needs (NASEN)

NASEN is an organisation that aims to promote the education and advancement of all those with special educational needs. It is a useful organisation as it provides training, information and has branches across the UK; the organisation's website address is www.nasen.org.uk.

Toy libraries

Toy libraries lend a wide range of toys and equipment to parents but also to early years settings. Toy libraries provide specific toys and equipment for children with special educational needs and disabilities as well as toys that all children will enjoy. The way the service is run can vary, with some libraries being staffed completely by volunteers whilst others are funded and run by the local authority. To find out details of your nearest library contact the National Association of Toy and Leisure Libraries (www.natll.org.uk).

The importance of staff in the pre-school setting understanding their role, responsibilities and competence when working with other professionals

There are many facets to working successfully with other professionals. Firstly, it is important that procedures within the pre-school are set up so that everyone knows who is responsible for liaising with which professionals. These procedures should be outlined in the SEN policy and, in general, the SENCO should take the lead. It is also essential that, following meetings with other professionals, information is shared with those responsible for working with the child and, where appropriate, the parents. In some pre-schools a slot is created in every staff meeting so that staff can be updated; the use of a 'standing item' on the agenda shows a commitment to SEN.

Respecting the contributions of other professionals

When many professionals come together to help a child, each person will have his or her own contribution to make. It is a like a jigsaw, with each person holding a piece of the puzzle. This means it is important to understand the roles and perspectives of other professionals so that an overall picture can be formed. Sometimes, the perspectives of other professionals mean that they have different priorities from you; for example, a professional with a health background will consider a child from the perspective of health, while a practitioner from a pre-school may be more aware of the child's learning and education.

Looking for ways to integrate practice

Many professionals may have limited time to work directly with children; for example, a speech and language therapist may see a child for half an hour once a week. For their work to impact upon the child, professionals may ask pre-schools to integrate exercises or ways of working into the child's day. It is extremely important that this co-operation occurs because it will help the child to make progress and will also meet his or her medical needs.

Being ready to use others' expertise

Other professionals often have considerable expertise and experience that you can find helpful. They may be able to provide you with training or ideas as to how to work best with children.

Record-keeping

As part of your work with other professionals, you might be asked to keep records that are additional to those usually kept in the pre-school, for example, a record of a child's exercise programme or certain achievements. It is always useful to discuss with other professionals how they wish the information to be presented and exactly what is required.

Explaining your work

Some professionals may find it helpful to understand the work of the pre-school. It can therefore be helpful to invite those professionals working with the child to come into the setting to see the child and the way in which you work. This gives other professionals an insight into your areas of expertise, as well as the constraints under which you work. (Note that professionals can come and observe a child only if the child's parents have given their consent.)

Understanding the limits of your competence

As a practitioner, it is important that you recognise your strengths but also your professional limitations. This means that you should let others know if you have not been trained to carry out certain work, for example, to administer injections. It is also important when presenting your views of the child's needs that this is done accurately and factually. Furthermore, if you are required by another professional to carry out observations, you must be ready to check how they would like them to be completed. This is because your day-to-day work often has a very different focus from that of most other professionals.

How pre-school settings can create a partnership relationship between the setting, parents and other professionals

It is increasingly recognised that where parents, adults in the pre-school and other professionals can work together, not only do the children benefit but so do the adults. Working in a collaborative relationship means that information is shared and communication is more relaxed. This has benefits as consistency of care and approach is often essential in helping children. The case study below shows how one pre-school was able to create such a partnership.

Case study

Moshe is nearly four years old. His parents and the SENCO are concerned that his speech is not progressing as they had hoped, even though he is receiving more individual support in the pre-school. After a review meeting with Moshe's parents, it was decided to contact the Speech and Language Team. The pre-school had already built up a good relationship with the team and so it was decided that the SENCO would make the initial contact. Once the team had been contacted, the SENCO phoned Moshe's parents to let them know that he had been referred.

1   Why is it important that parents give their consent for a referral to take place?
2   Explain why early identification can benefit children.
3   Why is it helpful to develop a directory of local contacts?

Preparation for assignment

Design a leaflet for new members of a pre-school team about the SEN Code of Practice 2001. The leaflet should contain:

- an explanation of the term 'inclusion'
- an outline of the principles behind the Code of Practice
- a description of the role of the SENCO
- an evaluation of how the Code of Practice affects the pre-school's everyday practice.

Test yourself

1   List two key pieces of legislation relating to children with special educational needs.

Continued ▶

2   What does IEP stand for?

3   What is the role of the SENCO in a pre-school?

4   Outline the two-stage approach to identifying and working with children with special education needs.

5   Name two other professionals who might have a role in helping children with identified needs.

6   What is meant by the term 'medical model of disability'?

7   Explain the importance of working from children's interests when drawing up an IEP.

8   Evaluate the importance of working with parents when drawing up an IEP.

Further reading and references

- Tassoni, P. (2003) *Supporting Special Needs: Understanding Inclusion in the Early Years* (Oxford: Heinemann)
- Pre-school Learning Alliance (2002) *Role of the Special Educational Needs Co-ordinator*
- Pre-school Learning Alliance (1999) *Inclusion*
- Pre-school Learning Alliance (2005) *Special Educational Needs Code of Practice for Early Years Settings*
- Pre-school Learning Alliance (2005) *Working Towards Better Practice: SEN and Impairments*

Pre-school Learning Alliance publications are available from its website (www.pre-school.org.uk) and from its mailing house telephone number 0870 603 0062.

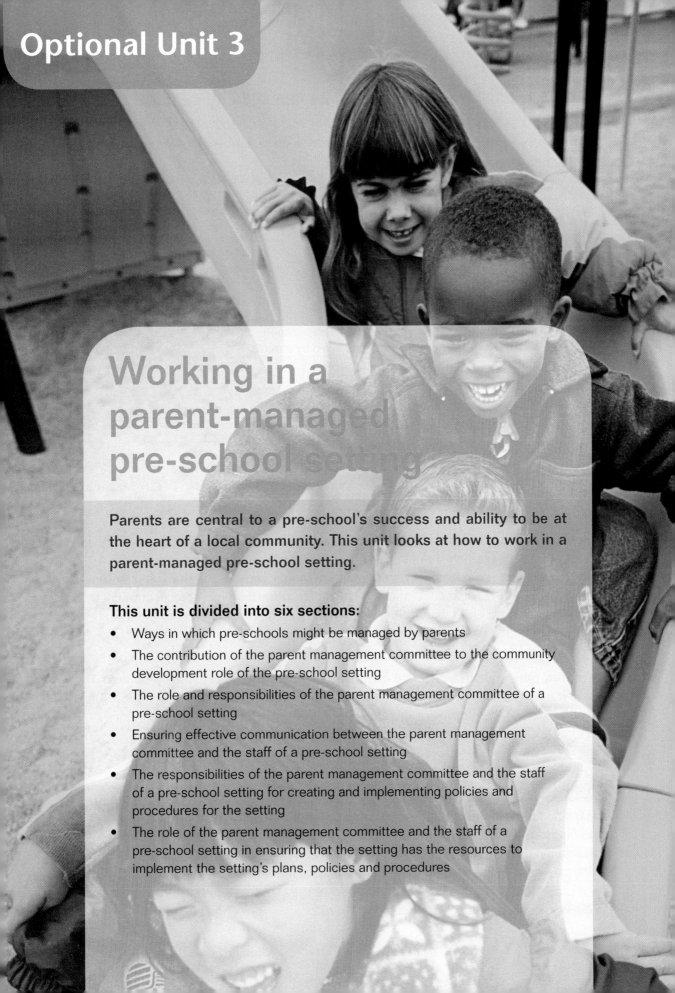

Working in a parent-managed pre-school setting

Parents are central to a pre-school's success and ability to be at the heart of a local community. This unit looks at how to work in a parent-managed pre-school setting.

This unit is divided into six sections:

- Ways in which pre-schools might be managed by parents
- The contribution of the parent management committee to the community development role of the pre-school setting
- The role and responsibilities of the parent management committee of a pre-school setting
- Ensuring effective communication between the parent management committee and the staff of a pre-school setting
- The responsibilities of the parent management committee and the staff of a pre-school setting for creating and implementing policies and procedures for the setting
- The role of the parent management committee and the staff of a pre-school setting in ensuring that the setting has the resources to implement the setting's plans, policies and procedures

Ways in which pre-schools might be managed by parents

It is important to know how your pre-school is run and managed. There are several ways in which parents may run or contribute to the running of a pre-school depending on how the pre-school has been set up to run.

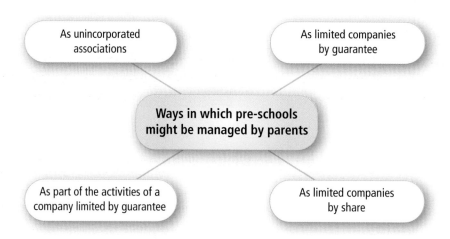

Pre-schools run as unincorporated associations

Pre-schools run as unincorporated associations usually have charitable status. They will have a constitution which stipulates who can be members and how the association is to be run. Most pre-schools have adopted the model constitution drawn up by the Pre-school Learning Alliance. Under this constitution most of the membership will be parents who have a child within the pre-school. Others, for example, people from the local community, can be associate members.

The pre-school is run by a committee consisting mostly of parents who have been elected by other parents. Associate members can also be elected to the committee. The committee acts as the employer of the staff who run the pre-school and is responsible for all aspects of the running of the pre-school. Committee members are in theory personally liable if the pre-school runs into financial difficulties.

Pre-schools run as limited companies by guarantee

Pre-schools run as limited companies by guarantee usually have charitable status. This means that those running the pre-school have limited liability if the pre-school runs into financial difficulties (unless it can be shown that this has happened deliberately or through negligence). Pre-schools run in this way usually adopt the Pre-school Learning Alliance model memorandum and articles of association. These create the structure for a parent-managed committee who in turn runs the pre-school on similar lines to pre-schools run as unincorporated associations.

Pre-schools run as part of the activities of a company limited by guarantee

Some pre-schools are actually part of larger organisations with charitable status, for example, a community group may run a pre-school as part of its work. In this situation the overall legal responsibility of the pre-school is that of the organisation, but a sub-committee may be set up under the direction of the management committee or team that runs the organisation. This may then consist of parents who manage the pre-school, but it will report to the management committee or team.

Pre-schools run as limited companies by share

Pre-schools run as limited companies by share are usually run for profit and are privately owned, often as small businesses. The owners can choose to create a structure for parents to provide feedback and support in the form of a parent support group or parent forum.

Thinking and research

Find out how your pre-school is operated.

The contribution of the parent management committee to the community development role of the pre-school setting

The parent management committee of a pre-school setting as a model of community participation

The pre-school plays an important role in the local community. It acts as a resource for parents who want their children to benefit from early years childcare and education. It is also a resource for parents, providing a focus where friendships can be made and support obtained. Learning, both formal and informal, goes on in pre-schools.

Parent management committees are a key way in which this important resource can respond to the needs of the local community. As parents are users of the resource they can, through the parent management committee, actively shape how the pre-school works. Their knowledge as local parents and their contacts with local parents and services means that they have knowledge as to the current needs and wishes of parents. This means that the pre-school can grow and be developed by the community and for the community. In practical terms, this means that the pre-school may offer services such as extended hours in response to local demand or provide an outlet for other groups such as a toy library. When parents move on as their children become older and new committee members take their place, the pre-school keeps rejuvenating and this means that it remains in contact with and at the heart of the community. The important role played by the parent management committee means that every pre-school develops its own identity and flavour which is a reflection of the local community.

The role of the parent management committee in enabling all of the children's parents to be stakeholders in the pre-school setting

The term 'stakeholder' is commonly used to reflect the idea that parents have a vested interest in the way that the pre-school is run. Whilst not all parents will be members of the parent-managed committee, their voices, ideas and wishes still need to be taken into account by the parent management committee. The ways in which parent-managed committees engage with other parents can vary from pre-school to pre-school and will be both formal and informal. Formal events will include invitations to the annual general meeting and newsletters; informal contacts might include committee members getting to know parents by being available at the start or end of pre-school sessions (see pages 381–2) or holding informal social events where parents' views can be discovered in a relaxed way. Parent management committees need to be proactive in enabling parents to be stakeholders, so that the committee can be sure that it is being representative of parents' views. To this end, pre-schools may sometimes undertake research, such as questionnaires or surveys, to help them gain more feedback about the role and activities of the pre-school.

The potential benefits for committee members, other parents and children that can arise from belonging to a parent-managed pre-school setting

A parent-managed pre-school benefits everyone concerned with the pre-school, including the children.

Benefits to committee members

Committee members benefit both socially and professionally by serving on a parent-managed committee.

- Firstly, they are able to meet with others who share an interest in their children's education. From this starting point, many close friendships are made and these usually endure beyond the pre-school.
- Committee members can build on their existing skills as well as learn new ones. These skills are often transferable, such as budgeting, recruitment, and health and safety management. This means that some committee members may use these skills and knowledge later on to take up employment or other voluntary work in the community.
- Learning new skills and knowledge and developing a strong circle of friends helps people's confidence and self-belief. This is incredibly powerful and many committee members feel that they are empowered in other areas of their lives. They may go on to take up employment, further training or try out other roles within the community. Committee members also feel that their interest in their child's early education equips them later on to work alongside other professionals such as teachers, or even to train in teaching or social work themselves.

Parents can gain skills and confidence from being part of the management committee.

Case study

Sarah was a committee member of her children's local pre-school. Here she talks about how this has helped her.

'I had worked before having children, but when you give up work to care for children you can quickly lose your confidence. I was surprised about how quickly that happened even though I knew that I was learning new skills as a mother. Things change quickly so that even my computer skills had become out of date. I joined the committee and eventually became responsible for fundraising. You become friends quickly with other committee members and I liked the way that you can share thoughts and ideas about your children's education. Through being on the committee, I felt that I was keeping up to date and also learning a lot of skills. When my children started school, I applied for a post working as a fundraiser for a local hospice charity. I know that my experience as being a fundraiser for the pre-school helped me to get the job. It showed that I was capable of getting along in a team as well as the experience of putting on events. I still support the local pre-school and meet up with those friends that I made during my time on the committee.'

1   How has working with the pre-school benefited Sarah?

2   How did the pre-school benefit from Sarah's participation?

3   Explain how the local community has benefited.

Benefits to other parents

As well as committee members, other parents also benefit from a parent-managed pre-school. A parent management committee encourages other parents to feel that they can become involved and participate in the pre-school. Since committee members are often parents they are not removed from what is happening in the pre-school. This means that other parents are more likely to feel that they can make suggestions, pass on any concerns and generally know that their voice counts too. It is also easier for a parent to ask another parent who is a committee member for information or advice and vice versa. Overall this means that parents are able to be active in shaping the feel of 'their' pre-school.

Parents whose children attend a parent-managed pre-school also find it easier to join in the activities of the pre-school as they 'know' the people who will be there, for example, attending family learning or fundraising events or the annual general meeting. Parents are also likely to become more involved in their children's education and, as you have seen in Core Unit 2, this can affect their confidence and ability to parent effectively.

Benefits to children

Children benefit from a parent-managed pre-school as they gain from additional activities and resources. Parent-managed pre-schools are cost effective as the organisation and administrative costs are low. This in turn means that there may be more money available for new equipment or higher staffing levels. Parents may also feel more comfortable in the pre-school and so may spend time there as a volunteer or be involved in organising additional activities such as outings. Overall, this means that children's experiences in the pre-school are enhanced.

There are also emotional benefits for children. A parent-run pre-school is likely to reflect parents' ideals and values about early education. This means that children are likely to pick up on the harmonious atmosphere that can be created: a true partnership between home and their pre-school setting. Children also learn from an early age about community participation and are able to see that their parents can take on responsibility.

Preparation for assignment

1   Talk to three parents who are committee members or part of a support group.

   • What do they enjoy about being involved?

   • What benefits have they personally gained?

   • How did the pre-school encourage them to be involved?

2   Write a report based on your interviews.

The role and responsibilities of the parent management committee of a pre-school setting

The role of the management committee as trustees in companies limited by guarantee and in unincorporated associations

As you have seen in the introduction to this unit, there is more than one way of organising the legal structure of a pre-school as a charity. Wherever possible, it is strongly recommended that a management committee consisting mainly of parents is responsible for the running of the pre-school, and that the models advised by the Pre-school Learning Alliance create a legal framework for this to happen. Committee members in their role become 'trustees' and so are literally entrusted with the running of the pre-school. This includes the employment of staff, the management of the pre-school's assets, health and safety, and running the pre-school's financial affairs including insurance and keeping records. Committee members therefore take on considerable responsibility – where the pre-school's status is that of an unincorporated association, this can include personal liability. This is one reason why many pre-schools are increasingly becoming limited companies by guarantee, which means that committee members would only be liable for a token amount (usually £1).

The function of 'memorandum and articles of association' and 'constitutions' in defining the role and responsibilities of the parent management committee

In order for a pre-school to operate effectively, everybody needs to understand his or her role, responsibilities and scope of powers. This means that written rules must exist that help those who are running the pre-school to know what they can and should be doing. For pre-schools that operate as a company limited by guarantee, these documents are the memorandum and articles of association. Pre-schools that run as incorporated associations will have a constitution. These documents serve as the actual basis for running the pre-school and are legally binding. They are extremely important as they help those running the pre-school to understand what they are entitled to do in terms of their powers, how money can be used, and how decisions about the pre-school are to be made.

Memorandum

A memorandum outlines the overall purpose and scope of the pre-school. The information that is generally included in a memorandum is described below. A model memorandum is provided by the Pre-school Learning Alliance, to help its members work within a framework that has already been approved by the charity commission.

Information included in a memorandum

- *Name* – this is the legal name of the pre-school. Bank accounts, records and other administrative documents relating to the pre-school must use this name.

Continued ▶

- *Registered office* – this is the address that is given.
- *Objects* – these are the aims and purpose of the pre-school.
- *Powers* – these are the powers that the pre-school can use in order to achieve their objectives, for example, to hire premises.
- *Benefits* – the extent to which directors can gain personal financial benefit from the pre-school.
- *Limited liability* – the legal status of the pre-school.
- *Guarantee* – the extent to which the directors are personally liable (usually just for £1).
- *Dissolution* – what is to happen to the assets of the pre-school should for any reason it closes or wishes to change its legal status.

Articles of association

Articles of association provide the basis for operating the company; for example, under the Pre-school Learning Alliance's model, this is a system of membership with an elected committee.

The model articles of association provided by the Pre-school Learning Alliance is based on their model constitution (see below), as this over time has performed well and has encouraged parents to be actively involved in the running of the pre-school.

Constitution

Pre-schools that operate as unincorporated associations will have a constitution, which sets out the aims and powers of the pre-school. Similarly to the articles of association, it also sets out who can become members and how a committee is to be formed and run. The Pre-school Learning Alliance has a model constitution that most pre-schools which are unincorporated have chosen to adopt.

Charitable status and tax

An organisation that has charitable status is exempt from Corporation Tax and may be entitled, where it owns property, to generous relief from Local Authority Business Rate (up to 80 per cent mandatory and a further 20 per cent discretionary). It is also able to raise funds from the general public.

If an organisation does not have charitable status it must act as a small business (company, sole trader or partnership) and pay tax on profits, even if little profit is made. This would include activities that generate funds but are not childcare, for example, holding a sale or event. Organisations, whether charities or business-based, are not exempt from VAT.

Key points for a parent management committee

Where your pre-school has adopted either the model articles of association or the model constitution of the Pre-school Learning Alliance, it is useful to understand the following points.

- The committee must consist of a Chair, Treasurer and Secretary.
- The committee must meet at least three times a year.
- An Annual General Meeting must be held each year at which audited accounts are presented.
- Staff of the pre-school are paid and therefore cannot be on the committee although they can attend meetings. They can, however, be members and so therefore have the same voting rights as other members. They should declare an interest and withdraw from any discussions about staff pay.
- The committee acts as employers of the pre-school staff.
- 60 per cent of the committee should be made up of parents (although arrangements are in place where this is not possible via the Pre-school Learning Alliance).

Applying theory to your practice

Find out how your pre-school is run.

1 When was the last annual meeting of the pre-school?
2 Draw a flow diagram that shows the structure of the pre-school management.

The responsibilities of the parent management committee of a pre-school setting

Key responsibilities of the parent management committee

As you have seen, the parent management committee has considerable responsibility for the structure and smooth running of the pre-school's affairs.

Holding meetings

Meetings are essential not only for the smooth running of the pre-school but also are required to fulfil the legal duties, i.e. holding an Annual General Meeting.

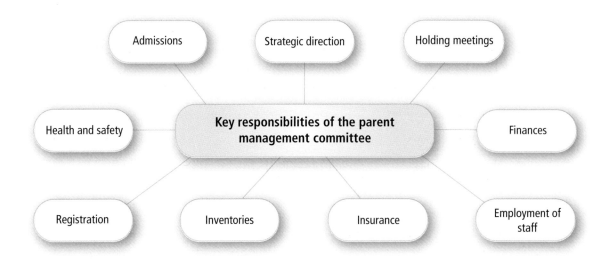

Finances

The management committee is responsible for controlling the financial affairs of the pre-school. This includes paying staff, rent or mortgage and business rates, as well as generating income through grants, fundraising and collecting fees. Sufficient funds must at all times be available to meet the expenses of the pre-school. This means that a good system of book-keeping and accounting is required. Annual accounts have to be prepared and a return prepared for submission to the charity commission. In addition, pre-schools that are run as charitable companies limited by guarantee must send a return to Companies House.

Employment of staff

This is a major responsibility for the committee. As an employer, the pre-school must abide by all employment legislation including legislation governing sick pay, holiday entitlement and maternity/paternity leave.

Insurance

Pre-schools have to take out a range of insurances. These include public and employer's liability insurance. These insurances cover the pre-school in case of any accidents in the pre-school. In addition, pre-schools will need insurance that covers their equipment and resources in case of theft or damage, as well as building insurance if the building is owned. For insurance to be valid it has to be current and also sufficient to cover the cost of replacement. Pre-schools also have to abide by the terms of the insurance, for example, taking reasonable care to lock premises.

Inventories

Pre-schools must know what they own for a range of reasons, for example, to be compensated in the case of a theft. This means that inventories covering equipment and resources must be kept up to date. Inventories also help pre-schools to check that the amount of insurance cover they are buying is sufficient.

Registration

Pre-schools have to be registered with several organisations including HM Revenue and Customs and OFSTED. The committee holds the ultimate responsibility for the implementation of the National Daycare Standards as they apply to that setting.

Health and safety

The pre-school as an employer and also as a provider of services must comply with all health and safety legislation, including the Health and Safety (First-Aid) Regulations 1981 and the Fire Precautions (Workplace) Regulations 1997 (amended 1999).

Admissions

The committee is also responsible for controlling admissions of children into the pre-school. This is important as the total numbers of children attending a session must not exceed the number that the pre-school is registered for. Also, sufficient staff must be available to meet the adult–child ratio requirements.

Strategic direction

As well as ensuring the smooth running of the pre-school, the committee is also responsible for ensuring its future by:

* developing the pre-school to meet the needs of current users

* looking to the needs of future families.

This might mean looking at new activities for the pre-school, such as offering out-of-school care, or thinking about buying premises.

Case study

The committee of the pre-school considered the physical condition of the pre-school's premises and decided that it was important that they be upgraded. This was thought to be important to ensure that the pre-school would continue to attract parents and to be a popular facility for the community. The pre-school did not directly own the building but it was agreed that the Chair would approach the owners as she worked part-time for them. Each member of the committee had a role in getting the task started. One member of the committee worked as a probation officer and thought that he might be able to see whether some of the work could be done as part of the Community Service programmes that were run. Two members of the committee had close links with a DIY shop and it was agreed to see if the paint might be donated or discounted. A further member of the

Continued ▶

committee had a sister who worked as an interior designer and offered to contact her about choosing colours. The committee agreed to meet again a month later so that they could agree a further plan of action.

1 Why is it important that responsibility is shared between committee members?

2 Why does the pre-school benefit from a parent-managed committee?

3 What are the benefits for the local community?

The tasks through which these responsibilities can be carried out

As you have seen there are several responsibilities that are required of the committee. However, when it comes to the tasks associated with the committee, these may be carried out by or delegated to the pre-school staff or other parents. This helps to spread the load whilst at the same time allowing others to build their expertise and take the initiative. It is important though that where tasks are delegated, the committee has a reporting system in place to ensure that they are completed. This is essential as the committee remains legally responsible for the pre-school, i.e. if the insurance monies are not paid, the committee might be seen as negligent.

The way in which tasks are divided will vary according to each pre-school, and sub-committees might be created to focus on some of the tasks, for example, a fundraising committee or a committee to look into extending session times. (See 'Thinking and research' activity opposite.)

The importance of sharing with the pre-school setting's parents information about the management committee's role and responsibilities and how these are being fulfilled

Parent management committees have great potential to shape the pre-school to meet the changing needs of local families. However, this can only be done if the parent management committee stays in close contact with parents within the pre-school.

Parents who understand the nature and structure of the committee will find it easier to know how best to pass on information or ideas. They will understand how decisions are made and how to influence the decision-making process. Parent management committees that are good at sharing information with parents also find that they are supported in their work as parents take on some of the tasks. It also becomes easier to encourage new members to stand for election to the committee. This is important, as there is a natural turnover of members as each year some members will leave as their children move onto school. This is a democratic process but can only be so if there is sufficient interest from other parents to vote or to stand for election. Parents who understand the role of the committee are again more likely to use their vote or to become involved in the election.

Thinking and research

Write a list of the type of responsibilities that your pre-school committee undertakes. Then consider how and who fulfils the tasks that are required; you may wish to complete a chart like the one started below.

Responsibilities of pre-school committee

Responsibility	Task	By whom
Organising the annual general meeting and other meetings		
Managing admissions	Keeping a record of enquiries, contact details and a list of places	
Managing finances	Book-keeping Preparing accounts annually Reporting on the pre-school's finances Preparing a budget Applying for grants	
Fundraising		
Employing staff		
Providing equipment and resources		

Ways to share this information with parents

Meeting with parents

Face-to-face meetings are one of the most effective ways of helping parents to understand the role of the committee and what is happening within the pre-school.

The term 'committee' may in itself seem very daunting and formal, but this can change when a new parent meets another parent who is friendly and 'happens' also to be a member of the committee. Many pre-schools have a system where a committee member welcomes new parents and their children on their first visit and talks them through the role of the committee. In addition, many committee members will spend time in the pre-school and so get to know parents as they drop off and pick up their children. They may also, in this way, get to know parents who are volunteering or spending time helping their children to settle in. When a committee member is in the pre-school, it can be helpful for the pre-school leader and staff to introduce them to parents that they have not met before. This helps to show parents how staff and committee work together.

Handbook or prospectus

Many pre-schools give parents a handbook or prospectus which gives parents information about the pre-school. Information includes sessions times, how the pre-school is run and also arrangements for admitting children. The prospectus is a good way of helping new parents find out about the committee and how it works. It can be helpful for a member of staff to talk through the prospectus with parents so that they can feel free to ask questions but also to assist those parents who may not find it easy to read written information.

Notice boards

It can be helpful for parents to see who's who in a visual way on the committee. Photographs of committee members along with a brief description of their role can be an effective way of helping parents to find out about the committee. Notice boards can also be a way of helping parents to read about decisions that are to be taken or have been taken. Some pre-school committees also write a brief synopsis of 'latest' news from the committee.

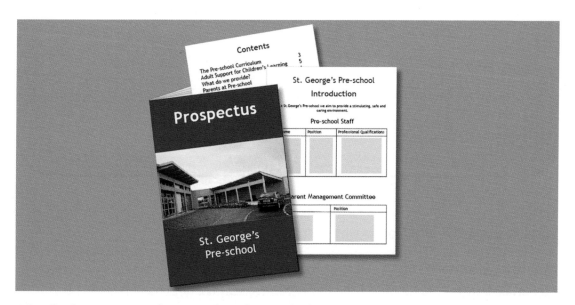

A handbook gives parents information about the pre-school.

Newsletters

Newsletters are another way of providing parents with information about the committee and its activities. Contact details for the Chair, Treasurer and Secretary can also be provided. Newsletters can be combined with details about the pre-school's activities including planning. As with other types of written information, it is important to remember that not all parents will be able to access text – some may have sight problems, difficulty with reading or understanding English (see also Optional Unit 1).

Websites

An increasing number of pre-schools are developing websites. These can be useful for parents who find it difficult to come into the setting but still want to keep up and find out more. They may be able to download newsletters, planning and other documents. Websites can also be a way of exchanging information as parents can make comments directly. It is important, however, to remember that not all families will have access to the Internet and some may have sight problems, difficulty with reading or understanding English.

Social events

Many pre-schools organise social events and this again helps parents get to know the committee members. Social events may include outings and quizzes as well as events for children such as parties or magic shows. Some annual general meetings are combined with social events so that parents can attend the meeting and then socialise afterwards. It is important to recognise that social events should be inclusive of all the families who might wish to attend. For example, if a setting holds a social event in premises that serve alcohol, this could mean that some parents would not feel able to attend. Dietary considerations should also be taken into account, for example, some families might be vegetarians or vegans. When holding an event outside the normal premises of the pre-school, matters of accessibility need to be checked and reviewed, in the same way as they are for access to the pre-school property itself. Clear signage directing families to the event will also help them to feel welcome.

Activities for children

Many pre-school committees provide specific activities for children alongside the staff of the pre-school, such as Christmas parties, seasonal celebrations, magic shows or outings. Parents are invited to join in the fun and so again have an opportunity to learn about the role of the committee and about its work, especially if a committee member introduces him or herself during the event.

Thinking and research

Find out about events that your pre-school has held over the past three years. How have these contributed towards children's play and learning?

Collecting feedback from parents

It is important that committees are in tune with parents' needs and thoughts. Many committees therefore find it helpful to ask for feedback or information which will help the decision-making process; for example, they may wish to find out whether there would be demand for an outing, holiday club or changes to hours. Collecting feedback and information from parents can take place in a variety of ways but is useful because it helps parents to see how there are connections between themselves and the organisation.

Ensuring effective communication between the parent management committee and the staff of a pre-school setting

Why effective communication between the parent management committee and the staff of a pre-school setting is important

For the pre-school to function as a whole effectively, the links between the parent management committee and the staff need to be seamless. For this to be the case there needs to be good communication so that each can fulfil their tasks and responsibilities. Feedback and the sharing of information is also required so that decisions can be made with the maximum amount of information; for example, the committee will need to know about the condition of resources so that they can allocate sufficient monies for replacement. They will need early warning of the wear and tear on equipment so that planned replacement and budget allocation for this can take place. Good communication therefore means that the pre-school is able to run smoothly but also allows everyone within it to feel that they are pulling together as a team. This creates a pleasant and supportive atmosphere that benefits the adults as well as the children.

Ways through which staff can share operational and curriculum plans with the parent management committee of a pre-school setting

Whilst the parent management committee has overall responsibility for the running of the pre-school, the staff team take particular responsibility for the care and education of the children. This is their area of expertise and includes both operational planning such as staff deployment as well as curriculum planning. It is important that staff are able to share their operational and curriculum plans with the committee so that the committee can support them in their work. The committee may also be able to contribute to the plan by, for example, making resources available or using member's contacts to enhance the plans, e.g. a parent who works as an optician may bring in some spare spectacles and a sight chart. It is also useful for the committee to understand and be involved in the operational and curriculum planning so that members can share their knowledge with other parents. Finally, the committee also has to ensure that operational plans meet the registration and inspection standards.

Ways in which staff can share plans with the committee

There are many ways in which the staff may share plans with the committee; some of these are described below.

Attending meetings of the committee

Most pre-school leaders attend some or part of the committee meetings so that information can be shared about the operational and curriculum plans. As many committee members will be parents, they will be naturally interested in the care and education of the children.

Inviting members of the committee to planning meetings

Some pre-schools invite a member of the committee to planning meetings. This might be the Chair or another member of the committee who might have particular responsibility for supporting the pre-school staff. By being involved and seeing the planning process, a committee member can be knowledgeable when talking to other committee members and parents about the curriculum and activities within the pre-school.

Providing plans and minutes of staff meetings

Staff can also share information with the committee by providing them with the curriculum plans and also minutes of their own staff meetings. Some pre-school leaders will be invited to committee meetings to talk through the plans or to give a synopsis of the meeting.

Committee members visiting or volunteering in the pre-school

As the majority of committee members are parents, there is frequent contact between them and the staff. Many committee members come to the pre-school on an almost daily basis. They may drop off their own children or come into the pre-school as volunteers. This is another way in which information about the operational and curriculum plans can be shared.

Ways through which the parent management committee and staff can work together to review the effectiveness of operational and curriculum planning

The operational and curriculum plans have to be reviewed in terms of their effectiveness. This is becoming increasingly important as self-evaluation is recognised as an effective tool in helping to maintain and increase standards in the early years sectors. Self-evaluation is also required as part of the inspection process. By working together to look at effectiveness, the staff and committee members can support each other and also bring a range of information to support the evaluation process. For example, staff may be aware of the latest curriculum developments whilst committee members may, through their contact with other parents, bring information about aspects of the pre-school's operational plan. The case study below illustrates this quite well.

Case study

Working together to review effective practice

At a meeting between the pre-school leader and the committee, a member of the committee passed on some feedback about the key person system gained from a couple of the parents. Parents had wanted increased contact at the start of the session with their child's key person. The issue was discussed and various options were considered that would balance the organisational needs with the parents' wishes. As a result it was decided to trial a new system for a period of one month and then to consult further with parents before reviewing its success.

New information

Sometimes plans have to be reviewed as a result of new information such as changing requirements of the curriculum or the inspection process. By working together to look at what needs to be done, the load can be spread. A committee member may, for example, offer to produce a new format on the computer to assist with the planning whilst another member might take responsibility to review the health and safety policies alongside the latest regulations. By reviewing the effectiveness of the operational and curriculum planning together, the committee remains in contact with the day-to-day issues affecting the pre-school and so is able to offer support. Committee members are also in a better position to disseminate information to parents.

Ways through which the parent management committee and staff can share information about operational and curriculum plans with the pre-school's parents

As pre-schools are run to encourage parental involvement, it is important that parents are able to find out about the operational and curriculum plans. By both staff and committee working together and sharing information, this means that many people are able to explain to parents how the plans work and also to gain feedback. There are many ways of doing this which include putting copies of planning available for parents to see on the notice board, sending copies of plans home for parents or making them available on the website. As curriculum plans in themselves may not be meaningful, pre-schools might also encourage parents to come into the pre-school and see how the activities and sessions link to the plans. Committee members can 'walk and talk' parents through what they are seeing or may help out in the pre-school to make staff available to spend time with parents. Some pre-school committees also regularly hold coffee mornings in the pre-school. This is a good way of helping parents to see the pre-school in action, meeting members of the committee and also raising awareness of the operational and curriculum plans.

Involving parents in the review of planning

In addition, from time to time, the committee in association with the pre-school staff may decide to use information from parents which will help them shape future plans and activities. Committee members who have met with parents in the ways suggested above are able to share with the committee and the pre-school staff information and feedback that they have gained. Parents may, for example, have commented about aspects of the routine or organisation which can then lead to a review of that area, e.g. the ease with which parents of younger children can leave their pre-school children.

The responsibilities of the parent management committee and the staff of a pre-school setting for creating and implementing policies and procedures for the setting

In order for pre-schools to work effectively, but also to be registered, policies and procedures have to be in place. Policies give clear indications about what should happen in any given area, whilst procedures give instructions as to how the policies should be implemented.

The parent management committee's overall responsibility for the adoption, implementation and review of policies and procedures

The parent management committee has the overall responsibility for the running of the pre-school, and this includes its policies and the procedures that are put in place to make the policy work. Policies cover many aspects of the running of the pre-school and must comply with National Daycare Standards as well as legislation such as the Health and Safety at Work Act and the Disability Discrimination Act. The spider diagram below shows some of the key policies that are essential for pre-schools to have in place.

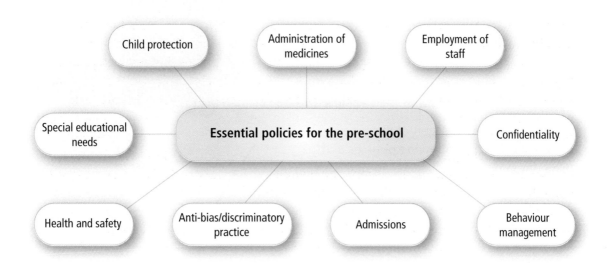

Written policies are looked at during the inspection process as well as whether the procedures laid down in those policies are being followed. As the committee has the overall responsibility for the policies and procedures, it is important that committee members are aware of them and review their effectiveness alongside the pre-school staff. By working jointly on the policies and procedures with the pre-school, the load can be shared and different expertise used, for example, a committee member may design, produce and laminate some 'reminder' signs for the pre-school.

The responsibilities of staff for supporting the parent management committee to adopt appropriate policies and procedures

Good communication between members of the committee and pre-school staff is essential in order for the pre-school to run smoothly. In terms of policies and procedures, it is especially important for the committee and the staff to work together. Policies can often become outdated as new guidelines for best practice are developed in the early years sector. It is vital that policies are kept in line with the law, and may need review when laws change.

Pre-school staff are often in a good position to find out about developments that may affect the policies and procedures of the pre-school. They may gain information via the Pre-school Learning Alliance and its development workers, the early years service in their area, and early years magazines. Pre-school staff may therefore need to support the parent management committee when it comes to understanding the role of the policies and the subsequent procedures that need to be developed. Pre-school staff can also help the committee by providing feedback about the feasibility when adopting new procedures as they have invaluable experience within the pre-school. In some pre-schools the Chair of the committee liaises with the pre-school leader and, at the beginning of his or her term of office, is shown and talked through the policies and the procedures for their implementation.

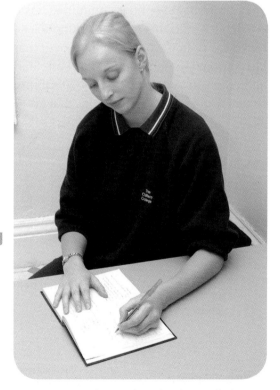

The responsibilities of staff for implementing policies and contributing to their review

As you have seen, the staff of the pre-school are responsible for following policies and using the procedures on a day-to-day basis. It is therefore important that staff themselves are familiar with the policies and the resulting procedures. New staff should have an induction period where the pre-school leader can go through the policies and the

It is important that staff are familiar with the pre-school's policies and procedures.

procedures one by one. It is also important for volunteers and helpers to learn about those procedures that directly affect their work with children, for example, what to do in the event of a fire. Signs and checklists that help adults in the pre-school to follow procedures can be extremely useful, e.g. a checklist to go through when organising an outing or when a child has an accident. Staff also have to know where policies are kept within the pre-school as the new inspection regime means that an inspector can visit without warning and as part of the visit needs to see the policies.

In order to implement the policies and to share the load, many pre-school staff take responsibility for different policies, for example, one member of staff may be responsible for special educational needs whilst another might be responsible for child protection. Staff may attend training related to their specific area and then relay this back to the rest of the staff and the committee.

Thinking and research

For each of the policies listed below, write down ways in which your pre-school implements them; an example is given to start you off.

Policy	Procedure
Child protection policy	*Volunteers are supervised when they are with children.* *Supervision at the end of the session to ensure that children leave with nominated adults.*
Anti-bias/discriminatory policy	
Health and safety policy	
Behaviour management policy	

Reviewing policies

You have seen that policies need to be kept up to date to reflect changes in legislation or good practice in educating and caring for children. This means that reviewing policies as well as procedures is essential. In addition, procedures might be shown to need reviewing as a result of a comment from a parent or a 'near miss', for example, a child nearly 'escaping' at the end of a session. Where there are any difficulties or suggestions, staff must report them to the pre-school leader who in turn needs to inform the committee. In some cases, this might result in the immediate review of a procedure and the need to establish a better procedure. It is important that policies or procedures are not changed without the consent of the committee as they have the ultimate responsibility for the pre-school.

The responsibilities of staff to work with the parent management committee to make the setting's policies and procedures known to all of its members

It is important for parents to understand the policies of the pre-school as many of the procedures that are used to implement the policies will directly affect parents and their children, for example, the procedure for leaving and collecting children or the procedure for administering medicines. Parents can therefore find it easier to understand the need for some of the procedures and may also be able to provide feedback about them after understanding their context. The pre-school staff and the parent management committee have an important role therefore in providing information for parents. Many pre-schools produce a handbook that the pre-school leader or a committee member takes time to go through with parents. In the handbook, key policies are often explained as well as some of the essential procedures. In addition, some procedures are explained to parents by using notice boards and new policies or procedures that are adopted might be outlined in a newsletter. Information can also be provided at relevant times, for example, when a letter about a proposed outing goes out, information about the procedures for outings might also be provided.

The role of the parent management committee and the staff of a pre-school setting in ensuring that the setting has the resources to implement the setting's plans, policies and procedures

The range of resources, including funding, which the pre-school setting might require in order to implement its plans, policies and procedures

For a pre-school to run smoothly and to work effectively, it has to be well resourced. Resources include premises and staffing as well as toys, equipment and furniture. The availability of resources can have knock-on effects in terms of the success and sustainability of a pre-school. A well resourced pre-school will have good staffing levels, a good range of equipment and so be in a better position to implement its policies; for example, a member of staff may be available to have free flow outdoor play or the equipment is available that meets the needs of a child with visual impairment. Resourcing a pre-school is closely linked to the finances of the pre-school and so it is essential that there is sufficient income and also that the finances of the group are closely monitored.

Sources of income

There are several potential sources of income that pre-schools may use. The spider diagram below shows some of the major sources of income.

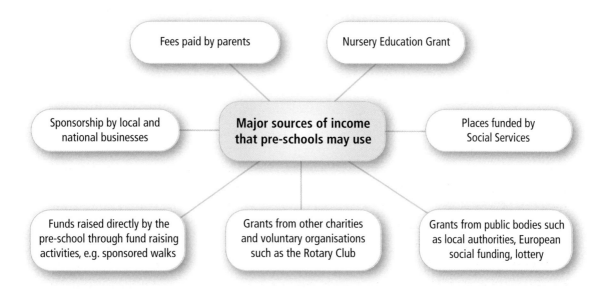

Book-keeping

Regular and accurate book-keeping is essential for any organisation in order to monitor the flow of money in and out. It is also a legal requirement as the accounts of a pre-school with charitable status have to be made available for the Charity Commission, and in the case of pre-schools that are companies they are needed for preparing the annual return for Companies House. This is because as a public organisation, the pre-school is accountable.

In its simplest form, all income has to be recorded and all expenditure must be noted along with receipts. For books to be kept properly, it is important that everyone involved in any way with either taking or spending money keeps records and passes them onto the Treasurer promptly. This allows the Treasurer to keep an overall view of the expenditure and to report back to the committee.

Where the pre-school's income is large and the burden of book-keeping and payroll duties is too great to be reasonable for a volunteer with other commitments to undertake, the pre-school could consider employing an administrator or book-keeper, who should be responsible to the committee and its officers (Chair, Secretary and Treasurer).

Ways through which staff can work with the parent management committee to check the availability and condition of resources

It is essential that staff and the parent management committee are able to communicate well together in terms of resources. This is to prevent situations where key equipment

⬦	A	B	C	D	E	F	G	H
				St George's Pre–school Accounts				
1	Profit and Loss accounts for year ending 31st March 2006							
2								
3		January	February	March	April	May	June	July
4	Income							
5	Fees	XXX.XX	XXX.XX	XXX.XX	XXX.XX	XXX.XX	XXX.XX	XXX.XX
6	Fundraising	XXX.XX	XXX.XX	XXX.XX	XXX.XX	XXX.XX	XXX.XX	XXX.XX
7	Donations	XXX.XX	XXX.XX	XXX.XX	XXX.XX	XXX.XX	XXX.XX	XXX.XX
8	Bank loan	XXX.XX	XXX.XX	XXX.XX	XXX.XX	XXX.XX	XXX.XX	XXX.XX
9								
10								
11	Expenditure							
12	Staff salaries	XXX.XX	XXX.XX	XXX.XX	XXX.XX	XXX.XX	XXX.XX	XXX.XX
13	Purchases	XXX.XX	XXX.XX	XXX.XX	XXX.XX	XXX.XX	XXX.XX	XXX.XX
14	Equipment	XXX.XX	XXX.XX	XXX.XX	XXX.XX	XXX.XX	XXX.XX	XXX.XX
15	Office stationery and postage	XXX.XX	XXX.XX	XXX.XX	XXX.XX	XXX.XX	XXX.XX	XXX.XX
16	General expenses	XXX.XX	XXX.XX	XXX.XX	XXX.XX	XXX.XX	XXX.XX	XXX.XX
17	Total Expenditure	XXX.XX	XXX.XX	XXX.XX	XXX.XX	XXX.XX	XXX.XX	XXX.XX
18								
19								
20	Opening balance	XXX.XX	XXX.XX	XXX.XX	XXX.XX	XXX.XX	XXX.XX	XXX.XX
21	Inflow/Outflow	XXX.XX	XXX.XX	XXX.XX	XXX.XX	XXX.XX	XXX.XX	XXX.XX
22	Closing balance	XXX.XX	XXX.XX	XXX.XX	XXX.XX	XXX.XX	XXX.XX	XXX.XX
23								
24								
25								
26								
27								
28								
29								
30								
31								

Sheet1   Sheet2   Sheet3

The Treasurer is responsible for an overview of expenditure.

or resources cannot be replaced or purchased because of a lack of funds. Managing the budget is, as you have seen, a key task in the smooth running of the pre-school and so staff need to work with committee members in helping them to set aside sufficient funds. Staff have an important role in this as they are working in the environment on a day-by-day basis and so can see at first hand the condition and availability of resources.

The role of pre-school staff in monitoring resources

Staff can also help the committee by providing information about the condition of resources promptly and predicting what is likely to be required in the future. This is important in terms of budget setting as a committee needs to be able to work out how much money is to be allocated to different areas. In addition, staff need to be aware of the physical environment and its condition as this can have cost implications, for example, that paintwork is looking shabby or that the hot water system is less effective. Below are some of the ways in which you might monitor the pre-school's resources.

Inventories

Inventories are detailed lists of resources. They are needed for insurance purposes but also as a stock-taking mechanism. Toys, kitchen utensils and large pieces of equipment such as furniture can all, over time, require replacing. Taking a regular inventory means that the committee are aware of what will need to be replaced. Inventories may also from time to time reveal that items have gone missing, especially in situations where premises are rented. Taking an inventory may also therefore reveal the need for better communication between the groups using the premises or ways of making equipment secure.

Passing on information

As well as wear and tear, sometimes equipment may need replacing or new equipment bought in order to comply with the latest good practice, curriculum requirement or legislation. Staff may learn about these developments via contact with the Pre-school Learning Alliance, local early years advisors and development workers, as well as from attending training.

Maintenance reports

Some pre-schools may have a log in which any requirement for minor repairs or replacements of the building are written. The committee can send this onto the landlord where the building is rented. Where the pre-school owns the building the maintenance reports may help the committee to know what needs to be done. They may then 'buy in' help or ask amongst the membership for volunteers.

Helping the committee

It is always easier for decisions to be made when the committee has good information. Passing on information in written format is helpful for the committee. The following structure can be used to ensure that the committee has a good range of information on which to base its decisions:

- requirement
- purpose
- cost
- other information.

Requirement

This is what needs to be done or purchased. This needs to be as detailed as possible, for example, if a new programmable toy is required, provide the catalogue details, price and a photo. Being detailed prevents any misunderstanding that may lead to the wrong equipment being bought.

Purpose

Budgets are often tight and so to help decision making it is helpful for the committee to understand the purpose of any new purchase and how it might add to existing provision. Sometimes equipment is needed in order to fulfil curriculum requirements, for example, programmable toys are required to deliver the ICT aspect of learning within the Foundation Stage.

Cost

It is also important to provide the price including VAT so that budgeting can be as accurate as possible.

Other information

In this section, any other information that might be useful for the committee may be given such as the urgency or suggestions for suppliers.

Activities which the pre-school setting might use to raise funds

One of the many advantages of a pre-school run by a parent management committee is that people are able to bring a variety of skills, contacts and knowledge to the pre-school. In terms of fundraising this can be invaluable and can lead to a wide range of activities that will raise funds. A good example of this is sponsorship. Through the network of parents, committee members and staff, a small business or company might be contacted to see if they would help in some way. This might be the provision of anything from stationery and photocopying through to a cash donation. Local businesses are often able to donate prizes for events such as summer fêtes and raffles. Many fundraising activities also provide an opportunity for a social event where parents, committee members and staff can come together. Below is a table showing some of the more common fundraising activities, although many pre-schools think of some wonderfully original ideas.

Common fundraising activities

Sponsored events	Sponsored events can involve the children of the pre-school, e.g. a sponsored walk, cake making or sing-a-long. Other sponsored events might include a parent taking part in a marathon, parachute jump or head shaving!
Social events such as quiz nights, bingo	Social events can be opportunities for fundraising. The type of event should reflect the tastes and interests of the pre-school members and thus be popular.
Jumble sales and boot sales	The traditional jumble and boot sale remains popular and is a good way for everyone to contribute.
Coffee mornings	These are ways for parents to meet together as well as fundraise.
Bring and buy sales	Bring and buy sales can involve children of the pre-school by, for example, making simple gifts and cakes or donating outgrown toys.
Summer fêtes and winter fairs	Fêtes and fairs are ways in which the local community can join in and are good fundraising events as they provide opportunities for everyone to contribute in some way.
Raffles	Some pre-schools use raffles as a way of fundraising, e.g. books of raffle tickets are sold by members to others in their family or community.
Book club and catalogues	Many pre-schools operate a book club or other type of catalogue. Parents can see the goods or take a catalogue and then place the order. Profits can be in the form of cash or goods, e.g. a book club provides the pre-school with a certain number of free books.
Professional photographs and videos	Some pre-schools invite professional photographers to photograph or video children. The photos or videos are then sold to parents. It is important, however, to ask for consent before children are photographed. Some of the proceeds are then donated to the pre-school.

How the parent management committee and staff can work together to raise funds

You have seen above that there are many ways of raising funds for the pre-school. Involving everyone in the pre-school community is the ideal way of fundraising. This means that the committee alongside staff can make sure that everyone can have the opportunity to help if they wish. By working together, staff and the committee are often able to maximise fundraising events. The staff, for example, may organise an event with children but members of the committee may organise the paperwork and press coverage. As staff may have more opportunities for direct contact with parents, they may be able to make sure that information is passed first-hand. Word of mouth, leaflets and information on the notice board can all be ways for parents to either find out about how they can help or participate at events. Staff may also pass on suggestions and feedback from parents about fundraising events. In addition, staff may be able to organise some events that involve children as part of their curriculum planning. They may, for example, organise a sponsored 'obstacle course' with the children or have a master baking class. In addition, staff might find out about possible sources of grants and income as a result of their training and contacts with other organisations such as the Pre-school Learning Alliance.

 Case study

Val is pre-school leader of Bankside Pre-school. She has been a leader for 20 years and has always had great support from the parent management committee. The Chair pops in twice a week and together they talk through anything that has cropped up. Val uses this time to pass on any information that she has gained as a result of any training that she or her staff has attended. Today she feeds back that on an ICT course she saw some programmable toys that would be perfect for some of the younger children. They agree that Val would provide further details for the committee along with costs and suppliers. Val said that she and her staff would be happy to do some of the fundraising with the children. A few months later as a result of a sponsored event, contacts with a local business and also an application for a grant, ten programmable toys are purchased. The committee members and other parents come to watch the children using them.

1 Why is it important for staff to work closely with committee members?

2 How can a joint approach to fundraising be of benefit?

3 Why is it important that information from training is passed on to the committee?

Test yourself

1. Outline the different ways in which a pre-school may be operated.

2. Why is it important that the constitution is adhered to?

3. Describe the roles and responsibilities of the parent management committee.

4. Explain why effective communication is essential between the staff team and the committee.

5. Explain why it is important for the staff team and the parent management committee to have clear roles and responsibilities.

6. Identify three benefits of a pre-school being run by parents.

7. List four ways in which the pre-school might raise funds.

8. Identify three ways in which the pre-school may help parents gain awareness of the role of the management committee.

9. Give two examples of how the staff team may help the parent management committee to meet their legal obligations.

10. Describe ways in which a parent-run pre-school may benefit local children and their families.

Further reading and references

Pre-school Learning Alliance publications:

- *Effective Marketing and PR for Early Years Settings* (A075)
- *Finance in Early Years Settings* (A078)
- *Policies for Early Years Settings* (A074)
- *Pre-schools as Employers* (A121)
- *Risk Management in Early Years Settings* (A079)
- *The Complete Guide to Incorporation for Pre-schools* (A124)

Glossary

Active learning: learning as a result of being engaged and involved rather than passive, e.g. playing rather than listening.

Allergen: a specific substance that triggers an allergic reaction.

Allergic: a physical reaction to a substance.

Anti-discriminatory: ways of working which include and value all children and their families regardless of their ethnic or cultural backgrounds.

Areas of learning: sections within the Foundation Stage curriculum containing learning outcomes.

Articles of association: regulations for the management of a registered company.

Attachment: a close and enduring bond that gives children emotional security.

Behaviour: responses and reactions to people and situations, in particular socially appropriate or inappropriate responses displayed by children.

Behaviourist: theories that suggest patterns of learning and behaviour are repeated because of associations with positive or negative experiences.

Bilingual: a person who speaks two languages.

Confidential: information that should not be passed on to others without consent.

Conserve: understanding that certain things do not change in quantity or quality, even though their appearance does change; one of Piaget's tests of children's logic.

Constitution: a set of rules and functions that, in the case of the pre-school, sets out how why and how it is to be run.

Constructivist: theories that suggest that children are active in their learning and draw conclusions based on what they have seen, done and heard.

Critical period: the theory that some aspects of child development are time sensitive and have to take place within given periods.

Curriculum: a programme of activities or learning intentions.

Developmental psychology: the study of the development of the brain, thinking and behaviour.

Discrimination: a term used to describe situations in which a person or group of people are not treated as fairly as others based on judgements of gender, sexual orientation, lifestyle, religion or culture.

Early Learning Goals: targets given in the Foundation Stage curriculum for children to reach by the end of their reception year.

Feedback: information gained from others which can be used to improve practices or performance.

Fine manipulative: hand movements that involve the thumb and fingers, e.g. drawing or picking up objects.

Fine motor: movements that involve the hand and wrist.

Formative assessment: assessments that are ongoing and focus on progress.

Gross motor: movements that involve the use of a whole limb, such as walking or throwing.

Hand–eye co-ordination: movements that involve using vision to direct the hands.

Heuristic play: play with everyday objects that allows toddlers to discover concepts.

Hidden curriculum: the way in which children pick up on the attitudes and underlying values of the culture of a setting.

Holophrases: (early language development) a word that is used by the child for a variety of purposes.

Holistic: relating to the whole person including mental and social factors.

Horizontal relationships: relationships that children have with other children of a similar age.

Inclusion: an approach to working which allows all children to participate in the activities of a setting regardless of disability, gender, religion or culture.

Individual Education Plan (IEP): a plan drawn up by a setting in conjunction with parents to target support for children who have some area of difficulty in learning.

Individual Learning Plan (ILP): a plan of activities tailored to help children's learning and development.

Key person: the named member of staff with whom a child has more contact than other adults. The staff member's role is to develop a strong relationship with the child.

Longitudinal: a term used in conjunction with assessment to suggest monitoring over a period of time.

Memorandum: a constitutional document of a legally registered company.

Metacognitive skills: the ability to retrieve and use existing memories and information in order to make sense of new information or situations.

Milestone: skills that are looked for as children develop, and which are usually linked to age.

Multilingual: a person who speaks more than one language.

National Standards: a set of standards against which early years settings are inspected.

Normative development: a term used to suggest which skills the majority of children will have at any given age.

Nativist: a biological approach to psychology which highlights the instinctive or inherited facets of behaviours and learning.

OFSTED: the Office for Standards in Education (England), the organisation which inspects early years settings and schools.

Object permanence: the realisation that objects and people, when out of sight, continue to exist.

Parent Management Committee: an elected committee, under the terms of the pre-school's constitution, that is legally responsible for the management of the pre-school.

Parent Support Group: a group of parents who advise and support the direction of the pre-school in situations where the pre-school is run as a limited company.

Personal Development Plan (PDP): plan to help professionals improve their practice and further their professional development.

Physical development: the gaining of control over bodily movements.

Play leader: job title for the staff member of a pre-school responsible for managing the day-to-day provision of care, usually employed by the parent management committee.

Pre-linguistic phase: the stage in language development that precedes a baby's first recognised spoken words. This phase includes babbling, gestures and understanding the meaning of a few key words.

Procedure: a set way of carrying out actions, e.g. fire drills or responding to an emergency.

Risk assessment: an assessment of the degree of risk associated with an activity, procedure and item, and ways of minimising the risk.

Reflective practice: a way of working whereby practitioners think about their own effectiveness in order to improve the quality of their work.

Role model: a person who a child watches and consequently learns behaviour and attitudes from.

Role-play: also known as pretend or imaginative play, in which children pretend to be something or someone other than themselves, e.g. the part of an animal, other children or an adult.

Routine: regular events and timings of a session or day.

SEN: acronym for Special Educational Needs.

SEN Code of Practice 2001: government guidelines on which early years settings and schools base their decisions and practice of Special Educational Needs.

SENCO: acronym for a Special Educational Needs Co-ordinator; the person in a setting who co-ordinates and oversees the setting's Special Educational Needs policy.

Scaffolding: a term used to describe how adults support children's learning by sensitively intervening, questioning or planning appropriate activities.

Separation anxiety: a child's fear of being separated from his or her main carer.

Settling in: the process by which early years practitioners help babies and children to be at ease in the pre-school or school setting.

Small-world play: pretend play in which children use figures of people or animals and create an environment for them.

Social learning theory: theory which suggests that children learn by watching the actions and reactions of others.

Social referencing: the way in which babies and young children look at the reactions of adults in new situations in order to understand how they should react.

Special Educational Needs (SEN): a generic term used to identify children who may need additional support in order to facilitate their learning.

Stakeholder: someone who has a vested interest in the pre-school; stakeholders are usually parents.

Statement: a term used for the process by which children with identified special educational needs received a statutory assessment of their needs.

Stepping Stones: a term used in the Foundation Stage curriculum indicating skills that children will master on the way to reach the Early Learning Goals.

Stereotype: generalised conception of a group of people which is not necessarily accurate and so can lead to prejudice.

Stranger danger: babies' and young children's reluctance to leave their parent or carer to stay with an unfamiliar person.

Summative assessment: an assessment, often in report format, that summarises a child's progress to date and may compare it to what children of a similar age are expected to achieve.

Vertical relationships: relationships that a child has with adults and older children.

Weaning: the process of encouraging a baby to take food in addition to milk feeds.

Zone of Proximal Development: a term used by Vygotsky to explain the relationship between a child's possible learning and his or her current abilities.

Index

abuse, child 268–85
    disclosure 278–9
    and human rights 268–9
    involvement of professionals 281–2
    legislation 276
    responding to parents 280–1
    signs of 270–5
    types and definitions 269–70
accessibility 203, 356
accident procedures 224–7
activities 150–1, 157, 162–79, 180, 203
    0–3 years 171–3
    3–5 years 173–5
    outdoor 89
    reflective questions 124
ADHD (Attention Deficit/Hyperactivity
    Disorder) 43
adult role 72, 80, 85–8, 150–1
    in activities 150, 171, 172–3
aggression 78
Ainsworth, Mary 59–60
allergies 233, 252–4
anti-discriminatory environment 196–208
    legislation 198–202
    role of policies 205–9
    see also discrimination
articles of association 370, 375, 376, 377
assessment of children 94, 107–9
    against milestones 108–9
    formative and summative 96, 107, 110
    using curriculum frameworks 108
associative play 39
Athey, Chris 71
attachment 37, 56–62
    Ainsworth 59–60
    Bowlby 58–9
    critical period 58
    and grief 61–2
    insecure and secure 60
attention 42–3

babies 2–10, 35, 115–16, 157
    activities for 171–3
    bottle-feeding 240–3
    needs of 3, 4, 5, 6–7, 8
    personal hygiene needs 256–9
balance 28
Bandura, Albert 77–8
bathing a baby 256–7

behaviour 54, 81–3, 123, 156
    learning socially acceptable 118–19
    responding to 117–18, 352–3
    and social learning theory 78–9
    and unmet needs 204
behaviourist approach 63, 79
bereavement and grief 61–2
bilingual children 51–2
Birth to Three Matters 138–9
    four aspects 138–9
    links to National Curriculum 141–2
    reflective practice 187–8
Bobo doll experiment 78
book-keeping 391
books for babies and toddlers 157
bottle-feeding 240–3
Bowlby, John 58–9
brain research 54–5, 69
breastfeeding 240
Brown, Roger 50
Bruner, Jerome 73–4, 80
    influence on practice 74

central nervous system 29–30
charitable status 370, 371, 376
child protection *see* abuse, child
child-rearing practices 132–3
Children Act (1989) 200, 213, 214, 217–18,
    227, 276, 277
Children Act (2004) 202, 276
choice, providing 111–13, 175
Chomsky, Noam 80
chromosomal disorders 91–2
cleaning 220–2
co-operative play 15, 39–40
co-ordination 27–8
cognitive development 7, 25, 41–5, 86–7
    and behaviour 82
    Bruner 73–4
    Piaget 68–71
    role of language 44–5, 71–2
    stages and sequences 45, 46
    supporting 350–2
    theoretical perspectives 68–78
    Vygotsky 71–2
collection procedures 235–6
communication 267–8, 346–50
    3–5 year-olds 116–17
    aids 51, 357

babies 3, 5, 7, 9–10, 115–16
   checklist 349–50
   development 45, 157–60
   with parents 287–9
   toddlers 116–17
   types of 288–9
   visual cues 346, 348
   see also language development
computers 166–7
concentration 42–3, 350–1
concepts, learning 45
conditioning 75–7
confidentiality 181, 287, 306
   and abuse 280, 281, 282
   and observations 104, 105
conservation 70–1
constitution for pre-school 376, 377
cooking 85
COSSH Regulations 217, 221
creative development 170–1
creative play 177
cultures and beliefs 89–90, 153, 168
curriculum frameworks 138–42
curriculum plans 143–54
   activities 147, 149–51
   identifying adult role 150–1
   implementing 149–53
   inclusive 152–3, 203
   long-term 143–4
   short-term 144–5

Data Protection Act (1988) 104
de Groot, W. 61–2
decision-making opportunities 111–13
depression 184
deprivation 57
development 26, 54–5, 94–107
   areas of 25
   assessment 94, 107–9
   babies 2–10
   and behaviour 81–3
   by age 10–24, 31–7
   economic factors 92–3
   effect of relationships 111–21
   environmental and social factors 88–91
   genetic influences 91–2
   holistic nature of 53
   intellectual 41–5
   and lifestyle 94
   role of play 84–8
   social and emotional 35–7

theoretical perspectives 55–83
developmental delay 54, 108, 110–11, 336
diabetes mellitus 254
diarrhoea 258
diet and nutrition 93, 240–3, 254–5
   nutrients 248–9
   sample weekly menu 249
   see also food
differentiated curriculum 180
disability 326, 327
   medical and social models 328–9
   see also special educational needs
Disability Discrimination Act 200, 330, 387
disclosure of abuse 278–9
discrimination 197, 202–5
   challenging 204–5
   legislation 198–202
disposition and attitude 155
Donaldson, Margaret 71
dysfluency 349

Early Years Action/Plus 332–3
Early Years Foundation Stage (EYFS) 138
emergency procedures 222–3
emotional abuse 269–70, 272–3
emotional development 18, 25, 35, 54
   see also social and emotional
emotional security 264–8
   coping with change 266–7
empowerment
   of children 111, 116, 283
   of parents 135, 182, 319
environment 210–13
   division of space 176–7
   hygienic 220–2
   inclusive 196–208
   legislative requirements 213–19
   outdoor 89, 176
   safe and secure 89, 175–8, 285–9
EPPE project 89
equal opportunities policy 206–7
Equal Pay Act (1986) 199–200
equipment 32–4, 85–8, 211
Erikson, Erik 63, 66–8
evacuation procedures 222, 223
event sampling 99, 100–1, 105
Every Child Matters 111, 202, 276
exploration and investigation 166, 177

families
   expectations 129–30, 138, 299–301

lifestyle variations 94
values and beliefs 90–1
family structures 130–2
feedback 119–20
from parents 134, 186, 323, 384
financial assistance 203
fine motor control 27, 32–4, 85–6
fire procedures 214, 216, 222
first aid procedures 224–7, 228
food 239
allergies 233, 252–4
attitudes towards 251–2
cultural and religious needs 252, 253
foods to avoid 251
safe preparation 246–7
snacks 250, 251
see also diet
formula feeding 240–3
Foundation Stage curriculum 139–41, 155–6
communication and literacy 158–60
creative development 170–1
Early Learning Goals 140–1, 142
knowledge and understanding of the
world 165–8
links to National Curriculum 141–2
mathematical development 160–2
physical development 168–70
reflective practice 188
Stepping Stones 140, 142, 155, 158,
166–8
free play 112
Freud, Sigmund 63–6
psychosexual stages 64–6
unconscious mind 64
friendships 18, 19, 21, 23, 30–1, 40
sociograms 98–9, 106
supporting 175
fundraising 394–5

gender roles 90
Gessell, Arnold 28–9
Goldschmied, Elinor 164
grammar 47, 49
grief 61–2
gross motor control 27, 32–4, 85–6
growth and development 26

hand washing 239, 262–3
hand–eye co-ordination 28
Harlow's attachment experiment 57
Hartup, Willard 38

Health and Safety at Work Act (1974) 214,
216–17, 387
health visitors 363–4
hearing impairment 336–7, 348–9
heuristic play 113, 165, 170
holophrases 49, 50
housing 88
Human Rights Act (1998) 201
hygienic environment 210, 220–2

illness 229–33
signs of 230
treating common 231–2
imaginative play 170, 176
impairment 326, 336–7
inclusive setting 325, 326–35
creating inclusive culture 329–30
legislation 330–3
income of pre-schools 391
independence 22, 28, 173
Individual Education Plans 332, 333, 334,
337–45
involving children 344–5
involving parents 344, 358
reviewing 341–2
Individual Learning Plans 110, 145–6
infection, avoiding spread of 230
injuries, minor 227, 228
intellectual development see cognitive
inventories of resources 392

key person 60, 110, 113–14, 145
emotional security 264–5, 266, 267, 268
role in physical care 239–40
knowledge and understanding of the world
163–8

language 44–5, 71–2
and learning 73, 74
partner 346, 349
and thinking 158, 351
Language Acquisition Device 80
language development 7, 10, 11, 25, 45,
47–52, 79–80, 116
and behaviour 82
behaviourist approach 79
constructivist approach 80
critical period 48, 80
delay 54
equipment/materials for 86–7
inability 50–1
language of setting 52

nativist approach 80
   promoting 157–60
   receptive language 48, 49, 52
   role of adult 80
   stages of 49
layout 177–8, 211
   creating safe 175–8
   different areas 176–7
learning community 182–93, 319
   training opportunities 182
   see also environment; parental
   involvement
learning difficulties of parents 297
learning theories 68–78
   behaviourist 75–7
   conditioning 75–7
   constructivist 68–74
   social learning 77–9
   see also cognitive development
listening skills 287
literacy area 177
literacy, numeracy and language needs of
   parents 296–324
   assessing support agencies 311–13
   building network of contacts 313–15
   enabling access to support 307–23
   encouraging first steps 320, 321
   identifying need for support 303–4
   national and local strategies 307–10
   opportunities within pre–school 315–18
   reasons for needs 296–8
   responding to parents 304–5
   reviewing support 319–23
   role of setting 301–3, 305–6
   signposting sources of support 307, 318
   using written information 322
   working with adults 311
literacy skills of children 18, 19, 157–60
longitudinal observations 100

Makaton 51, 357
mark making and painting 85, 158, 170
mathematical development 160–3
medicines, administering and storing 234
Memorandum 370, 375–6
memory 44, 74
modelling behaviour 352
modelling play 172, 175
multilingual children 51–2
Munchausen Syndrome by proxy 269
music 171

nappy changing 238–9, 257–8
   toddlers and older children 259
narrative or written records 97–8, 105
National Standards 197, 214, 215–16
nature–nurture debate 56, 91
neglect 270, 274–5
newborn babies 2, 31
non-verbal communication 267, 288
nose blowing 263
noticeboards 317, 382, 386, 390

obesity 93
object permanence 7
observations of children 94–107, 109–10
   analysing 108
   checklist and tick charts 102–3, 105
   comparison of methods 105–6
   consulting with children 103
   limitations 105–6
   methods 96–103
   naturalistic 96–8
   special educational needs 338
   validity and reliability 106–7
   voice recording and filming 101–2, 106
   working with parents 103–5
Oedipus complex 66
operant conditioning 76–7
outdoor environment 89, 176, 211
   cleaning 221
outings 236–7

parent management committee 133, 371–2
   benefits of 372–3, 374
   communication with staff 384–6
   information required 391–3
   resources for plans and policies 390–5
   responsibilities 377–80, 381, 387–90
   reviewing plans 385–6, 387
   sharing information 380, 381–4
   sharing plans 384–7
parent partnership services 363
parent-managed setting 370–95
   types of 370–1
   see also parent management committee
parental involvement in setting 128–38
   activities 178–9
   benefits of 134–8
   and curriculum plans 153–4
   factors affecting 183–5, 299–301
   and observations 103–5
   profiles 179–81

reasons for lack of 183–5
strategies to encourage 154, 185–7
parentese 116, 157
parenting styles 132
parents 128, 287–9
educational background 129–30
knowing 287
learning opportunities for 136
literacy, numeracy and language needs 296–324
partnerships with 286–8
see also literacy; parental
Parten, Mildred 39
Pavlov, Ivan 75
perception 41–2
personal hygiene needs 255–63
personality development 63–8
behaviourist theories 63
biological/trait theory 63
Erikson 63, 66–8
Freud 63–6
psychoanalytical theories 63–8
physical abuse 269, 270–2
physical care needs 238–40, 263
physical development 5–24, 25–34, 168–70
1–7 years 32–4
atypical 353–5
babies 31
and behaviour 81–2
co-ordination 27–8
equipment/materials for 85–6
principles of 28–9
Piaget, Jean 68–71, 80
place, sense of 167
play 84–8, 172, 176–7
social stages of 39–40
types of 39–40, 163–5
policies 387–8, 390
implementation and review 388–90
parent management responsibilities 387–8
resources for 390–5
staff responsibilities 388–9
pollution, effects of 89
Portage 364
poverty 92, 183–4
pre-linguistic stage 48
pre-school, benefits of 89
see also parent management; parental
Pre-school Learning Alliance 332, 335
and parent management 370, 375, 376
pretend play 12, 13, 14

problem solving 41, 161, 166
Professional Development Plans 191–3
profiles 95–6, 107, 145, 182
and differentiated curriculum 180
parental participation 179–80
psychoanalytical theories 63–8
puberty 22, 23
puppets 120, 348, 352

Race Relations Act (1976) 198
Ramsay, R. 61–2
reading 157, 158–9
records, children's 95–6
reflective practice 111, 121–4, 330
Birth to Three Matters 187–8
on learning communities 187–93
own effectiveness 289–93
professional development 191–3, 292–3
using profiles 182
reflexes 2–3, 30, 31
registration and collection 235–6
reinforcement 76–7
relationships, children's 37–8, 155–6
and development 111–21
horizontal and vertical 38
parent partnerships as model 120–1
role of key person 113–14
repetitive play 9
resources for policies and plans 390–5
role of staff 391–3
respect for individuals 289
rhymes 158–9
rights of child 196–7, 268–9
Rights of the Child, UN Convention 196–7, 201–2, 269, 326
risk assessment 219, 221, 236
Robertson, James and Joyce 59
role modelling 114, 119, 252

safe environment 89, 175–8, 210, 285–9
reflecting on practice 289–92
and staff teamwork 285–6
safeguarding boards and committees 276–7
safety equipment 213, 214
scaffolding learning 73
schema 68–9
second language users 331
parents 287–8, 297–8, 302
security 210, 235–6
self-confidence 155
self-direction 44

self-esteem 22, 23, 24, 111, 155
    and developmental delay 336
    and obesity 93
    and poverty 183
    role of adult 54
self-reliance 41, 111
SEN Code of Practice 110, 326, 327, 330,
    331–5, 336
    and IEPs 338, 340
    and parents 357–9
SENCO 54, 333–5, 338, 341
sensory impairment 353–5, 363
sensory play 163
separation anxiety 56, 58
settling-in 60, 113–14, 122, 203, 264–5
Sex Discrimination Acts 199
sexual abuse 270, 273–4
shadowing 191, 192
sign language 45, 357
Skinner, B.F. 76–7, 79
small-world play 13, 15, 177
SMART targets 192, 339–40
snapshot observations 98
social and emotional development 25, 35–7,
    352–3
    and behaviour 83
    equipment/materials promoting 87–8
    experiences to support 154–6
    psychological perspectives 56–62
    stages of 35–7
social interaction, stages of 40
social learning theory 77–9
social referencing 37, 120
Social Services and SEN 364
social skills 39
socialisation 37, 39, 71, 72
sociograms 98–9, 106
solitary play 39
speaking and listening 157
special educational needs 327, 335–57
    advisory teams 362
    ensuring participation 345–55
    importance of early recognition 336–7
    information sources 335–6, 364–5
    interaction cycle 347

local services 362–4
observation and assessment 337–45
parent partnerships 357–9, 361, 366
reactions of parents and family 360–1
required policy 332–3
role of SENCO 333–5
specialist equipment 355
staff responsibilities 365–6
working with agencies/professionals 361–
    4, 366
Special Educational Needs and Disability Act
    (2001) 200–1, 330–1
    see also SEN Code of Practice
Speech and Language Team 362
sponsorship 394
stakeholders, parents as 372
stranger danger instinct 59, 60

tactile defensive 353–4
target sampling 99
teamwork of staff 143, 285
teeth, care of 258–9
telegraphese 49, 50
thinking and language 158, 351
Thorndike, Edward 76
tidying up 120, 156, 211
time sampling 99–100, 105
time, sense of 167
toddlers 10–12, 36, 116–17
toilet training 13, 259–60
toileting 239, 260–1
    accidents 260–1
toys and materials 212, 221
treasure basket play 113, 164–5, 170
turn-taking 19, 20, 39, 114, 118, 180

visitors' book 236
vocabulary development 49, 50, 116–17, 158
Vygotsky, Lev 71–2, 80

water play 84, 163
weaning 243–6
Wood, David 73
working relationships 285–9
writing 159–60